THE MORE YOU WATCH,
THE LESS YOU KNOW

THE MORE YOU WATCH,
THE LESS YOU KNOW

NEWS WARS/(SUB)MERGED HOPES/MEDIA ADVENTURES

Danny Schechter

FOREWORDS BY JACKSON BROWNE AND ROBERT W. McCHESNEY

SEVEN STORIES PRESS / NEW YORK

Copyright © 1997, 1999 by Danny Schechter
Foreword © 1997 by Jackson Browne
Foreword © 1997 by Robert W. McChesney
Preface © 1999 by Danny Schechter

Originally published in hardcover October 1997.
First trade paperback edition February 1999.

Published by
Seven Stories Press
140 Watts Street
New York, NY 10013
www.sevenstories.com

In the U.K.:
Turnaround Publisher Services Ltd., Unit 3, Olympia Trading Estate, Coburg Road,
Wood Green, London N22 6TZ U.K.

In Canada:
Hushion House, 36 Northline Road, Toronto, Ontario M4B 3E2, Canada

Library of Congress Cataloging-in-Publication Data

Schechter, Danny.
    The more you watch the less you know: news wars/(sub)merged hopes/media
adventures / Danny Schechter; forewords by Robert W. McChesney and Jackson
Browne.
    p. cm.
    ISBN: 1-888363-40-1
    ISBN: 1-888363-80-0 (pbk.)
    1. Mass media. 2. Schechter, Danny. I. Title.
P90.S337 1997
302.23—dc21   97-502
                                     CIP

Book design by Cindy LaBreacht
Printed in the U.S.A.
10 9 8 7 6 5 4 3 2 1

For Sarah Debs, hoping her generation
will make the changes ours hasn't

TABLE OF CONTENTS

9 Acknowledgments

15 Preface to the Paperback Edition

29 Foreword by Jackson Browne

33 Foreword by Robert W. McChesney

39 Introduction: The Many Fronts of the Media War

PART ONE: A MOLE IN THE MACHINE

99 1. News Dissecting: Inside the Rock Radio Revolution

125 2. Elevating Journalism (through Harvard Yard)

135 3. Going Local: Breaking into the Business
and Being Broken by It

PART TWO: NETWORKING

155 4. CNN: The World's Most (Self) Important Network

177 5. *20/20*: We're in Touch So You Be in Touch

199 6. The Control Room

213 7. Defecting: Becoming a Network Refugee

231 8. Globalvision: Downwardly Mobile and Upwardly Global

PART THREE: COVERING SOUTH AFRICA

267 9. Passion and Discovery: That Was Then

321 10. On the Island

335 11. Contradictions, Contradictions: This Is Now

PART FOUR: REMOTE CONTROL

349 12. Media Worlds in Collision

369 13. I, Rupert

389 14. The Mergers of July and the End of Journalism

PART FIVE: TRANSFORMING MEDIA

461 15. What We Can Do

479 16. The Media Channel

485 Selected Media Reform Groups

487 Filmography

493 About the Author

497 Index

ACKNOWLEDGMENTS

*W*here should thanks begin and where can they end in a career that has been so collaborative, a life that has been so collegial? On every job, on every adventure, and on every detour, there were friends, partners, guides, instructors, colleagues, comrades, and enemies to sharpen my focus, deepen my commitment and challenge me to do a better job of living up to my values. Whatever insight is in these pages owes a lot to the communities, collectives, and collections of people I have plugged into over all these years, and to those I have had the good fortune to know well who deserve more than I can repay. I have always had a tendency to try to do too much too quickly, sometimes driven more by passion than prudence. "Your problem, Danny," my father, Jerry Schechter, once told me, "is that you want to dance at every wedding."

It always starts and ends with family: my parents, my brother Bill and his partner Sandy, my incredible daughter Sarah Debs, her loving mother Valerie, Denzel McKenzie and family, my Aunt Dana and Uncle George, and cousins Marc and David. And rippling out from that circle, there were neighborhood childhood cronies Stevie Kazan,

Robby Easton and Bernie Moss, DeWitt Clinton High School running buds Russell Smith and Paul Yergans, and *Clinton News* journalism guru Lou Simon. And then, at Cornell University, *Dialogue* magazine co-conspirators Ken Rubin, Fred Rosen, Judy Bourne and also Dan Cassidy, Paul Epstein, Eric Craven, Tom Hanna, Tim Hall, and Arlene Eisen. My many movement buddies in SDS, NSM and SNCC, especially Tom Hayden, Frank Joyce, Mike Ansara, Bill Strickland and the great ones whose lives I was blessed to personally intersect with and be enriched by, and who are gone now, including Jimmy Baldwin, Fannie Lou Hamer, Saul Alinksy, Fred Ross, Malcolm X, Betty Shabazz, Paul Goodman, Ricky Dutka, and Peter Countryman. My fellow cultural warriors Abbie Hoffman and Jerry Rubin awakened my Yippie instincts. My London School of Economics classmates and London mentors Ralph Miliband, Ruth First, Z. Pallo Jordan, Carolyn Roth, Joe Slovo, Gwigwi Mrwebi, Marshall Bloom, Laurie Flynn and, especially, Linda Gordon, all deepened my analysis. The debt grew in the Boston years thanks to the Africa Research Group, Old Molers, WBCN radiomates Andrew Kopkind, John Scagliotti, Sue Sprecher, Jamaica Plain Jane, and Charles Laquidara et al., as well as audio inspirations Wes "Scoop" Nisker, Larry Bensky, and Peter Bochan. There were also my fellow Nieman fellows, Somerville housemates, my favorite shutterbug Jerry Berndt, the incomparable Vicky Gordon, and, without fail and forever, Gerry and Hila Feil. It was in Beantown that I also met Rory O'Connor, who became my business partner and the indispensable roc(k) of our Globalvision enterprise, which has been aided and abetted by Cathe Ishino's personal support and graphic imagination, Jordan Silver, Lisa Williams, Kendra Lowery, and Sam Shinn, and the special smile and style of Anne Hemenway, among many others. I am indebted to all those who gave so much of themselves for so little on our underfunded projects, particularly *South Africa Now* and *Rights & Wrongs*. I am grateful for all my schmoozes in Boston's Shanghai Press Club and the New York Media Forum. And to Nelson Mandela and my many friends in South Africa, especially Z PeeJay and the Niddries, who allowed me to share the lessons of a struggle I had the privilege of studying up close. Righteous respect and gratitude too to Bill Adler, Nenad Bach, Sid Blumenthal, Jackson Browne, CharAce, Jeff Cohen, Carolyn Craven, David Fenton, Ham Fish, Danny Goldberg, Don Hazen, H. L. Fuller, Noah Kimerling, Barbara Kopple, P. C. Lavin, Marc Levin, Little Steven, Christopher Maji, Leonard Marks, Phil Martin, Marty and Miki, Robert W. McChesney, Rhonda Modansky, Louise and Sid Peck, Hart Perry, Rosko, Stuart Sender, David Silver, Anant Singh, Yvette and Phillip Tomlinson, Meryll Zegarek, and *por supesto*, Jack and Maria's dad, and so many more who know who they be and how they've helped. And to poet-inspiration-friend Allen Ginsberg, who died as this book was being born, for always reciting news that The News wouldn't. Special thanks to the friends and funders who supported the Global Center's Media Education Project, which is helping to bring my media adventures to the public, and for legal advice, to Mark Lafayette and Gold, Farrell and Marks.

If reading this book proves entertaining and, hopefully, a bit edifying, all praises are due to my editor Elinor Nauen and publisher Dan Simon, who forced me to struggle with this manuscript after I felt I had struggled enough. And gratitude, too, to the Seven Stories crew, especially Jon Gilbert and Greg Ruggiero.

Special thanks to musician Polar Levine, whose Polarity One created a hot and kicking original rap song inspired by this book: "News Goo—The More You Watch, The Less You Know."

My ambitions for the book resonate with the sentiments of the late journalist Martha Gellhorn, whose work I admire. "A writer publishes to be read," she writes in *The View from the Ground*, "then hopes the readers are affected by the words, hopes that their opinions are changed, or strengthened or enlarged." And in my case, there is also a faith that citizens will act—eventually—to promote a democratic renewal of a media system that I labor in, despite an oozing despair of the kind that led National Public Radio talk show host Ray Suarez to leave TV. "Every time those of us in the newsroom thought we'd hit another bottom," he says, "there was another lower bottom waiting down the road." I'm looking for the road in the other direction.

As I tell my story, I am also reminded of an aphorism shared with me by a Bosnian colleague, then living under siege in Sarajevo: "Only fiction has to be plausible. Real life has no such constraint."

And finally, a last word from the poet who gave me life, my late mother, Ruth Lisa Schechter, who knew me best and whom I miss most, from her verse, "The Journalist," in her ninth book of poems, *Chords,* dedicated "for my son, Danny," published in January 1986:

> Never one to go gently
> up or down a staircase, skipping
> a step or two
> you fly. Even the ceiling shifts
> I hold my breath
> as though you were a child
> I want to shout: *Careful, Hold On*
> *to the banister.*

—D. S.
July 1997
New York City

I really wish they would invent something else in addition to the radio.... Future generations would then have the opportunity to be astounded by the way broadcasting made it possible to say what it had to to the entire Planet Earth and at the same time enabled the Planet Earth to see that it had nothing to say.—Bertolt Brecht, 1927

I believe that television is going to be the test of the modern world.... In this opportunity to see beyond the range of our vision, we shall discover either a new and unbearable disturbance of the general peace, or a saving radiance of the sky. We shall stand or fall by television, of that I'm sure. —E. B. White, 1936

The strength of the American system is possible and can be nurtured only if there is lively and provocative dissent. In a healthy environment, dissent is encouraged and considered essential to feed a cross-fertilization of ideas and thwart the incestuous growth of stultifying uniformity.—Walter Cronkite, 1996

It's their hidden credo: "Let them eat television." —Youth Activist Robin Templeton, 1997

"This business of giving people what they want is the dope pusher's argument. News is something people don't know they are interested in until they hear about it. The job of a journalist is to take what's important and make it interesting." —Reuven Frank, 1998

THE MORE YOU READ,
THE MORE YOU'LL DO:
BOOK TOURS/ ON-AIR CHATTER / BEAT THE PRESS

*T*he hallowed halls of the stuffy University Club in New York would not exactly be my first choice for a *Columbia Journalism Review*-sponsored panel discussion on the "capital C" Crisis in journalism. But there I was, in exalted company, with sixty minute man Mike Wallace, an editor at the *Times*, and other big time media heavies, knowing that this crisis was as much in da house, as the rappers say, as outside of it—and so I figured that perhaps the only way I could reach the collective hearts of this news biz ensemble was to proclaim truths rather than descend into the details of the debate about the vanishing soul of journalism. So I began with a reference to an infamous Columbia grad who would have definitely been considered persona non-grata in these environs:

> "This is the year that we lost the reporter who called himself a poet—the Lower East Side's Allen Ginsberg. So in his honor, may I say that I see the best minds of my profession justifying the Cable Nanny Network, regurgitating legal minutia about back to back newsy soap opera-like trials as O.J.

begat JonBenet who gave way to the Tim Mcveigh show with a pause for a Monica moment as Terry Nichols fights the Unabomber for face time, and my, my, thank heaven for Princess Di..."

And to my surprise, after going on in that vein, chanting my complaints, I received an ovation. What a shock: it is rare to encounter any expressions of emotion in a media world known for jaded detachment. Yet today, those closest to the problem are upset, anguished, and not sure about what to do. They see the great media institutions they've worshipped and worked for marching in lock step in the wrong direction, virtually immune to criticism and self-correction.

Critics like myself have another challenge: to be taken seriously, to crack through a wall of arrogance and limited accountability. How does someone from outside the comforts of the mainstream cut through a fog machine fueled by vast marketing and PR budgets? What is it like to try to use the media to challenge the media, to go on TV shows with a no-holds-barred assault on TV news practices? How open is our nominally diverse media system to dissident voices and calls for far reaching reforms?

In the course of promoting *The More You Watch, The Less You Know*, I have been testing that openness. Labeled by some a manifesto, this book is really about a personal and serious quest, continuing with this updated paperback edition, to challenge a media world I am part of, to identify defects, shame unethical practices, and add one more voice to those hoping to stop its continuing slide into a "post-journalism era" of gossip mongering, sensationalism and slime.

The last time I looked, the Television Academy establishment was not giving out Emmys in the category of hardest hitting criticism of TV news. But before I take on the mantle of Media Martyr of the Western World, let me admit that the critique I initially thought might mark me as the ultimate TV turncoat actually turned out to be quickly assimilated into a growing chorus of media criticism. On the day this book was first published, Walter Cronkite gave a speech blasting his old haunt, CBS, in more strident terms than I use. Shortly afterwards, *60 Minutes'* Don Hewitt condemned the merger of show biz and news biz. Suddenly I wondered if I had become a moderate without knowing it?

Soon, newspapers were packed with op-eds on media industry malpractices. A group of news pros formed the Committee of Concerned Journalists to sound the alarm. Steve Brill, the founder of Court TV, launched a high-profile slick media review called *Brill's Content.* The once staid *Columbia Journalism Review* ran a cover story called "Money Lust: How Profit Pressures are Perverting Journalism." It had suddenly become fashionable to lambast media practices. Perhaps I was not as daring as I hoped or self-destructive as I feared. Then, the question became: how do I compete with big names big footing the issue, or with celebrities condemning celebrity journalism? Suddenly, media bashing was being co-opted by the very people who were once its targets.

There continues to be plenty to complain about. According to a 1998 survey, feature stories covering celebrities, scandal, and human interest increased from 15 percent to 43 percent of the total coverage provided by the three nightly network TV newscasts, major newspapers' front pages, and weekly newsmagazines from 1977 to 1997. Variety reports that network newsmagazines like ABC's *20/20*—where I was a producer—and NBC's *Dateline* say that "celebrity stuff" gets them better ratings than the "more newsy stuff." (Remember this phrase because it is indicative of how journalism itself is regarded: MNS, more newsy stuff. TV news, it is clear, is now about selling commodities [including itself], not raising consciousness.)

What is happening to radio, a subject I delve into through the prism of my own experience, is even more insidious but less visible, and is rarely reported on even though more than 4,000 radio stations changed hands after the passage of the 1996 Telecommunications Bill. "The corporatization of radio matters because it is destroying a uniquely intimate medium," reports Dan Kennedy in some detail in the *Boston Phoenix*, "replacing real community voices, people with a sense of place and purpose, with the same sound-alike shows in city after city, town after town." The obvious effect of all of this is to promote syndicated comedians like Rush Limbaugh and fellow conservative Dr. Laura, who laces her right-wing message with tough-love pop psychology. Less obvious, notes Kennedy, is the inundation of a sameness in the form of "bland accent-free disc jockeys (or hyper-energetic shock jocks selling the same brand of pseudo-wacky 'originality' in market after market).... It's highly profitable. And it sucks."

Amen. And this is happening by design.

In late May 1998, I was invited to Greece to keynote a conference on the dark days of the media. On the plane over, I met a young public relations woman from a high profile agency in Washington, DC. I told her about my book and its assault on the trivialization of news.

She laughed, quipping, "Its my job to keep it that way." Joking or not, there was candor in that confession, perhaps because PR people now outnumber journalists three to one.

Overseas, as I learned when I met colleagues and critics on other continents, the American way of de-newsifying the news was having an impact. An old friend of mine in England, Laurie Flynn, told me about an award-winning documentary about Colombian drug dealing that was later sold to *60 Minutes*. He and his mate had discovered through detailed checking in England and South America that it had been insidiously faked. He blames the infiltration of tabloid techniques into television and worries about the destruction of the English tradition of hard-hitting factual programming. (Here in the USA, reports of fake articles and columns rocked the *New Republic* and the *Boston Globe*, while CNN rather unbravely retracted a story about the use of nerve gas in the war in Laos while the *Cincinnati Inquirer* fired a reporter and apologized for carrying a corporate exposé because it was allegedly obtained in part through unauthorized voice-mail messages.)

I later spoke with Jonathan Dimbleby, a respected presenter (anchorman) of TV news in Britain. He confirmed a dramatic decline in factual programming that deals with important issues, revealing that apolitical wildlife films are now favored; critical documentaries that deal with political and economic issues are least desired. "The more channels that are on, the less coverage we get," he wrote in the *Guardian* citing, to my delight, this book. "And this shrinkage—the retreat from analysis and interpretation—coincides with the growing recognition that we now live in an age of globalization."

In America, meanwhile, the *Los Angeles Times* notes that there is now a new wave of documentaries on the air, but most of them are superficial, look-alike, cut and paste biography style shows with little critical insight. While PBS still airs some series with depth and dimension, the trend is in the other direction, towards cheaper-to-make *"Reader's Digest*–like" films. Increasingly these "docu-lites" imitate the narrative arc of fictionalized storytelling at the expense of information and analysis. Such emotion-driven story-telling has all but replaced whistle-blowing.

There are now 370 channels worldwide—and everywhere, the story is the same. More privatization means more commercial channels. More pay TV. More specialized thematic programming; movie and entertainment channels are in the lead, according to a survey prepared for Italy's public broadcaster RAI in November 1997. "Focused thematic" channels (e.g. sports-only channels, cooking channels, financial news channel, etc.) often prove to be less costly and more profitable.

And what is the social and political effect? More education for the illiterate? More information to encourage solutions for global problems? No, quite the opposite.

In India, Manik Mukherjee speaks of the replacement of culture "by sheer entertainment which is again watered down to avoid any depth or seriousness that might interfere with the primary commercial or corporate message."

In Egypt, the acclaimed feminist author Nawal El Saadawi, who was placed under house arrest for six years for challenging Islamic fundamentalists, writes that "never before in history has there been such a domination of people's minds by the mass media.... It gives you the impression that you are free to choose while it robs you of all means of free choice."

In Latin America, intellectuals and activists gathered to discuss the relationship between communication and citizenship. In the invitation, they speak of global media assuming the role of social control. "It is now commonplace," they write, "that the media determine what is socially relevant or not, who is worthy of being considered a social actor, etc., thus seriously distorting democratic processes."

These are concerns that do not reflect a hostility to core Western values so much as a criticism of the kind of consumer-driven TV that has become both a product of, and instrument for, the spread of the global market.

But why is this happening? What are the underlying dynamics? What accounts for media trends that seem to be in play everywhere, transcending borders and mere political ideology and transforming the global media system? This could be the subject for another book or another series of investigative documentaries unlikely to get on the air. The media historian Robert McChesney believes that a deeper look at the forces reshaping the media takes us into the muck of neo-liberal economic policy and theory.

"Society is being deliberately restructured to limit democratic participation.... Those in charge don't want a media that encourages active citizenship," he says. "They want passivity. They want a media subtext that tells ordinary people, over and over, 'shut up and shop.'" If this is the case—and there's lots of evidence to suggest it is—it is no wonder that serious journalism is on the wane. It is not dying. It is being killed off by market logic and economic policy.

In his new passionate and informative memoir and media critique *Hidden Agendas*, the Australian-born British-based journalist John Pilger savages media institutions for abandoning the cause of truth. He indicts what he calls "omission on a grand scale, the repetition of received truths, and the obfuscation of causes." I join Pilger in his call for a return to the "moral courage to clear away the ideological rubble that smothers the independence of the mind and leads to self-censorship."

Objective journalism, declared T. D. Allman in a tribute to the late Australian reporter Wilfred Burchett, is that which "not only gets the facts right, it gets the meaning of events right. Objective journalism is compelling not only today. It stands the test of time. It is validated not only by 'reliable sources' but by the unfolding of history. It is reporting which not only seems right the day it is published. It is journalism that ten, twenty, fifty years after the fact still holds up as a true and intelligent mirror of events."

Where, my fellow Americans, do you see that kind of journalism on TV today?

Touring to promote this book was an uphill battle. It is hard enough to get media coverage for any critical, non-mainstream perspectives. It's even harder when the media itself is your target. But once I got out there I discovered how many people seem to agree with me. Perhaps I am not as much of a rebel *enfant terrible* as I thought. When I am in a studio, invariably, before or after the show, the interviewer will add personal media-biz war stories to rival or one-up mine. It is hard to find anyone who really likes what's going on, who agrees with its trajectory, or who defends its content. Instead there's the heady whiff of resignation which quickly turns into rationalization.

In broadcast interview after interview, the host first tells me how much he or she agrees with me, but then immediately switches into "devil's advocate" mode once the little red light flashes on. An interviewer can't appear to be credible, it seems, if he or she doesn't immediately distance him or herself from my perspective. That is because American television is built around conflict and con-frontation. Some interviewers try to pick a fight. Heat sells. Light doesn't. Being contrary is the vogue. Again and again, I'm chal-lenged with the assertion that the TV business is only giving view-ers what they want. It's a mantra. A self-justifying article of faith.

Sure, I respond, that is the essence of market logic. But why, then, are so many viewers tuning out, why so much viewer "erosion" and low-rated network shows if people are getting what they want? Why are they watching quality reality-based drama programs like *ER* and *Homicide*, or newsmagazines like *60 Minutes* more than the tabloid trash that is shoveled at them constantly?

It is fascinating to note that at the very moment that media establishment is concentrating its power to achieve dominance, the internet, which is, as of now, still not controlled by gatekeepers, has emerged. The network powercrats hadn't banked on its growing appeal. In May 1998, internet advertising was growing at four times the rate of cable TV advertising and 10 times the rate of broadcast TV advertising. In five years the advertising on the internet is expected to hit $6.5 billion, a figure that it took cable 20 years to achieve; meanwhile, in 1998, network viewing was at all time low.

But the business of the media business receives little attention on TV. I would have loved to see how the networks would have han-dled that *New York Times* story revealing that most of the techno-predictions and prognostications of the overpaid geniuses who run the TV industry have been wrong over the years, way wide of the mark, at a cost of tens of billions.

If I was conspiracy-minded, I'd say there was a consciously class-based information system: Bloomberg financial news for the elite classes, Jerry Springer and dumbed-down local news for the masses.

A year after the Clinton Administration claimed credit for forc-ing the networks to add three more hours of children's TV weekly— a modest achievement hailed as a victory at the time—the Annenberg Public Policy Center released a report concluding that the quality of children's TV went down. Of a thousand programs rated only one third ranked "high quality"—a drop of three percent from the year before.

In late 1997, ABC's Ted Koppel criticized the "trivialization of our industry and the over-coverage" of the death of Princess Diana at the annual Committee to Protect Journalists dinner, but soon thereafter led the over-coverage of oral sex in the oval office. His more worthy programs continued to win awards, including coverage of the trial of the late Cambodian mass murderer, Pol Pot. The only problem was that, in that case, the journalist who actually reported the story, Nate Thayer, refused to accept the award, charging, "Ted Koppel and *Nightline* literally stole my work, took credit for it, refused to pay me, and then attempted to bully and extort me when I complained." Denouncing this as an "egregious violation of basic journalistic ethics and integrity," Thayer told the *New Yorker* he had become incredibly disillusioned because "the industry has taken control of journalists."

Koppel said he was sorry that Thayer wouldn't accept his award while ABC said blithely, "It might be that he had no idea that this is what happens when you deal with a large news organization." ABC, which later announced that it would be promoting its shows by affixing ads to bananas and other fruit, just accepts that the business routinely treats stringers this way.

Throughout the industry, as catalogued weekly in the pages of trade papers like *Variety* or *Electronic Media*, there is more of the same: deals, power plays, failed pilots, and more mergers, all amidst the continuing dumbing down of the "product."

For all of its arrogance and current wealth, there are trends towards a future that no one in the business really wants to face: the end of television as we have known it.

Consider:

+ Viewers are tuning out. In the 1980s the networks had a 90 percent audience share. In 1993, 35 shows rated a 20 share or better. A year ago, only 11. Ten years ago, 90 percent were watching networks. This year: 59 percent. Cable viewing has grown but the audience is fragmented. An MTV executive boasted to me that their ratings had risen from .05 to .06, not much to write home about.

+ Greed is pervasive. Shows cost more than ever to make and somehow are worse than ever. And why? Because the networks are now mostly airing shows they make and own, thanks to a rule change they won from the FCC. By 1998, out of 65 shows on the fall schedules, 25 were fully or partly network owned. The "science" of dealmaking now overshadows the art of program making. The networks retain more money but when only profits matter, quality is what goes.

+ More commercials aired than ever. An industry newsletter, the *Myers Report*, found that the top four networks ran 18 more hours of commericals than the year before. In this same period, the FCC bemoaned the shrinking number of public service announcements. In July 1998, the Clinton Administration announced that it would allocate a billion dollars for more anti-drug PSAs, paying for spots that many networks used to provide for free. This latest boondoggle was justified in the name of the failed War on Drugs. (Disney got $50 million; Murdoch $13 million.) So with ads and promos up, and watchable shows down, there are more look-alike newsmagazines—more *Datelines*, 20/20s, even a second *60 Minutes*. TV writer Verne Gay calls this the "McDonaldization of network news."

Ironically, as the V chip, designed to give parents the power to tune out objectionable shows, began to come on line, there was speculation that its "techno-fix" could be extended to commercials and actually allow viewers to block them. How bizarre, a "reform" agreed to by the industry that could be its own downfall. Contradictions like this never seem to amaze—or disappear.

These trends are rarely if ever discussed on the air. Also not covered were the many brushfires of opposition to this system—the Media and Democracy Congress of a thousand media workers; the nationwide forums of the 400-plus-strong Committee of Concerned Journalists; a march on "Mogul World" that brought hundreds of protesters outside the gates of the media conglomerates in midtown Manhattan; the growth of the micro-radio revolution that is creating scores of low-power neighborhood-based "pirate" radio stations; the struggle of my colleague Gary Webb, who broke the decade's big story of the Contras, the CIA, and cocaine only to be driven from his newspaper; and, once again, for one more year, the annual findings of Project Censored, detailing the news that is not in the news in America, the top 25 censored and self-censored stories.

So, increasingly, it becomes clear to me that to get closer to the truth, one needs to recognize the absurdity of media pretensions, and go beyond much of what passes for non-fiction, to seek truth in the insights and cultural probings of great writers, filmmakers, playwrights, and artists.

Perhaps that's why I found myself paying tribute to Allen Ginsberg, the beat who was never beaten. I did so for that *Columbia Journalism Review* panel but also in a more serious way, in Ginsbergian form, for the magazine of Harvard's Nieman Fellows in Journalism, which asked me to remember his talk years earlier to a group of unimpressed and skeptical media mavens. An excerpt follows:

> Wait
> Journalists wait
> Producers Wait
> Op-Ed columnists and
> J School teachers, Wait
> Editorial Writers and
> NPR Radio editors, wait
> Think Ginsberg anew
> for a qwik minute
> Think
> of what he had to
> say to us and for us
>
> Allen Ginsberg from lower east side ny
> hipster and hopester
> language provocateur

rock & roll with and without music
looking for detail in the details
looking for what's being left out
and finding it again and again
not in safe surfaces or
formula foolishness
not in official sources
or approved resources
rejecting all isms
not the least journal-ism
and yet when he checked out
his facts and life checked out

There are other Ginsbergs out there, friends,
critical voices clear as a bell
oozing truth power's way without a
lousy cable channel to call their own.
Allen Ginsberg was a cable channel on his own
was a million poems
was one of the best minds of his generation
was an investigative reporter without portfolio
was a guide into the American darkness
without a press card
without a regular outlet
without a Pulitzer prize
without a Sunday slot on beat the press
no network would have him
no magazine pension plan insured him
no schoolyard of fact checkers checked him
no control room of know it alls controlled him
Just him:
no media merger
no beeper
no cellphone

no nieman fellowship
He was never
acquired or downsized
Disneyed or Murdoched
In the age of 'branding,'
he branded himself
He felt the news
we rarely received
He was GNN—Ginsberg News Network
a poet ahead of The News
with The Times never quite able
to catch
up.

I read this praisepoem at a packed memorial tribute in New York's cavernous Cathedral of Saint John The Divine. Thousands showed up despite the *New York Times* reporting the wrong date. Just a block away, on the same night, at Tom's restaurant, the *Seinfeld* cast celebrated their last airing on NBC. The event commemorating the "show about nothing" was bathed in saturation coverage as TV trucks lined the streets, their microwave attennas ready to go live. The poet whose work was about everything was not covered at all.

There you have it.
Two Americas, and a one note media.
Yada Yada Yada or Howl?
One has been cancelled.
The other lives on.

D.S.
October 1998
New York City

*I*s the truth still the truth if nobody knows it? There were events in the struggle for democracy in South Africa that were largely unreported in the United States—but they still happened. And there have been other events, in other countries, including our own, the truths of which are unknown to us because for some reason they don't penetrate our culture. Why? Is it that these truths seem unimportant next to the truths we prefer? Aren't there many truths? Which is your truth? A truth that exists in itself—apart from a quest for profit and ratings—and which is the truth whether you know it or not? Or a truth that is researched and shaped and marketed for your consumption, and which must compete with entertainment news for your attention? Which is your truth?

Like Danny Schechter, when I heard the phrase "the more you watch, the less you know" it moved me to talk about the impact television has on our lives. Jeff Cohen and I wrote a song called "Information Wars," about the control of information, and in it we portrayed TV as a battleground.

I salute those people in the trenches of television who labor to bring us programming of depth and substance. Because that is work. And those who fight for programming and coverage that is inclusive and democratic, I salute them. Because democracy is work.

Who has the right to control what we know? Nobody. But let's not ask who has the right, but who has the power.

> "Give us twenty minutes and we'll give you the world"
> "We bring good things to life"
> "The news you need from people you can count on"
> "Doing what we do best"
> "The heartbeat of America"
> "Your true voice"
> "You're in good hands"
> "Now more than ever before"
>
> And in the flickering light and the comforting glow
> You get the world everynight as a TV show
> The latest spin on the shit we're in, blow by blow
> And the more you watch, the less you know
> Beyond the hundred million darkened living rooms
> Out where the human ocean roars
> Into the failing light the generations go
> Heading for the information wars
>
> Do people really spend millions upon millions
> To make us think we care about the planet—
> At the same time polluting and looting the only world
>   we've got
> So they can maximize their profit?
> People do.
>
> "The heartbeat of America"
> "Your true voice"

"For the life of your business"
"It's everywhere you want to be"

And there's a front row seat for the precious few
The latest war as a pay per view
Famine and disaster right in front of you
And the more you watch, the less you do
Beyond the hundred million darkened living rooms
Out where the human ocean roars
Into the failing light the generations go
Heading for the information wars

"Information Wars" © 1996 Swallow Turn Music

This is a war. It's the most important war. In an economic struggle, a human rights struggle, or an ecological struggle, you don't have a prayer of winning if the truth about what you're doing is controlled by somebody else. If you can't get your message out, if you can't get your information to people, you lose. That's the reality of any contest in the 20th century. Further, what is at stake is our ability to educate ourselves and form our own perceptions.

It's a war. It's the war for your mind. It's the only war. It's what will decide the outcome of every other struggle that is important to you.

FOREWORD BY ROBERT W. McCHESNEY

*W*hat is unusual about the following two sentences?

Danny Schechter is a highly acclaimed active working journalist who looks forward to many productive years in the media industry. This book, by Danny Schechter, is a thoughtful, sometimes hilarious, and always provocative critique of just how much damage the media industry is doing to journalism and democracy.

What is unusual—perhaps unprecedented—is for a working journalist to take on the industry in which he or she works. What Danny Schechter does in these pages is to apply the same criteria that the best journalists apply to powerful political and economic institutions to the industry journalists should know best of all, their own. He is breaking the implicit code of silence that compels journalists to look the other way when the issue turns to how corporate control and commercial pressures have distorted and degraded our communication system.

This is not to suggest that the many working journalists who may well sympathize with Danny Schechter are cowards because they refuse to speak up. One of the important functions of the profession of journalism is to make journalists and the public regard issues of ownership and control as unimportant to explaining how the media operate. It is worth noting that professional journalism was born almost a century ago precisely during the era that newspaper ownership was consolidating and advertising was becoming the primary means of support. Urged on by the largest publishers, professional journalism was supposed to assure readers that the news could not be influenced by owners or advertisers or the biases of the journalists themselves.

In fact, as Ben Bagdikian has pointed out, professional journalism internalized the overall political values of the owners and advertisers, and recognized a decontextualized "neutral" coverage based upon "official sources" as legitimate news. But journalism has also spawned many brilliant careers and much commendable work during the 20th century, not the least of which is Danny Schechter's own remarkable tour through contemporary history. And it has attracted some of the most principled and talented of our citizens as its practitioners.

But increasingly concentrated corporate ownership and hyper-commercialism, along with the complicity of a political establishment that benefits from a depoliticized citizenry, have effectively destroyed the autonomy and democratic capacity of journalism over the past 15 years. In 1982, Bagdikian calculated that fewer than 50 conglomerates dominated the U.S. media, and that figure seemed scandalous at the time. By 1997, he put the figure at around 10 enormous firms, after waves and waves of mergers and acquisitions. As recently as the 1950s, most journalism was produced by firms that devoted the lion's share of their resources to that enterprise; today the largest news gathering organizations are part of entertainment empires owned by firms like Disney and Time Warner. Journalism, like amusement parks, TV shows, action movies, and music CDs, exists to generate profit, pure and simple. And in this brave new world, a firm's journalism is required to support its other commercial activities, not to mention its political objectives.

Consequently, there has been a real crisis of confidence among journalists about the status of their field. When I left journalism in the early 1980s to become an academic, my old friends were dismissive when I argued with them about the effect of owners and commercialism over the news. "You don't understand how things work in the real world of the newsroom anymore," they'd assert. In the 1990s when I'd make the same critique—often to the same friends—the response was: "It's much worse than you can possibly understand."

Indeed, one of the growth industries of the 1990s is of journalists who have thrown in the towel on the profession and have moved into academia, retirement or some other field. Numerous memoirs and exposes of journalism have been published. Entire shelves at the library include books by people like ex-*Chicago Tribune* editor James Squires or former CBS legend Walter Cronkite bemoaning the death of journalism at the hands of Wall Street, Hollywood, and Madison Avenue. All of these studies link the decline in political understanding, debate, and participation, to the tabloidization and commercialization of journalism.

Even some prominent working journalists like Ted Koppel, Peter Jennings, and Dan Rather will give one or two talks each year where they express grave reservations about what corporate control and commercialism are doing to the media. But these celebrity journalists are careful to keep these views in check when they return to work. For less established or marketable reporters and editors, the pressure to conform is overwhelming as the corporate noose tightens. Internalized self-censorship is now the primary threat to free speech in U.S. journalism today. And the penalty for veering away from the corporate world view is the guillotine. Even mildly dissident voices like The *Washington Post*'s Colman McCarthy and *USA Today*'s Barbara Reynolds have been fired for apparently not fitting into the mindless and narrow political mainstream. When Gary Webb of the *San Jose Mercury News* opened the door to a long overdue examination of CIA activities, the response by the corporate media was a thinly disguised assault on his research, rather than a commitment to investigating what this enormous top secret agency has been up to all these years. That topic is apparently "off-limits" to our free press.

Nobody understands these issues quite like Danny Schechter. He combines a remarkable understanding of the best scholarship on the topic with the street smarts of a working journalist who knows how to cut through the bull and get to the point. He develops his critique while providing us with a lively tour through his remarkable career at Boston's WBCN, Harvard's Nieman Fellowship Program, CNN, ABC News, and as the producer of the brilliant public television programs *South Africa Now* and *Rights & Wrongs*.

The corporate media giants, advertisers, and other powerful forces that benefit by the status quo have no interest in encouraging the discussion. It is quite all right to bash the media for its alleged "liberal" bias; indeed, our airwaves are dominated by millionaire right-wingers who constantly assert such claims with no sense of irony. But it is strictly forbidden for there to be a candid analysis of the implications of corporate media control on our journalism, culture and democracy. It is not purely a coincidence, for example, that there was virtually no coverage of the crucial 1996 Telecommunications Act in the news media. This monumental law, which gave the green light to corporate media mergers and said to hell with notions of public service, was only covered in the business press, where it was presented as an issue of importance to investors, not the general public. Likewise, don't expect any time soon to see broadcast news covering the FCC's 1997 giveaway of the airwaves to the media giants for digital broadcasting.

Unlike most of the other critics, however, Danny Schechter hasn't thrown in the towel on journalism or the possibility of changing this nation for the better. That explains the irrepressible charm, energy and optimism of this book. If cynicism has become the occupational hazard of contemporary journalists, as so many now argue,

Danny Schechter provides the antidote. The solution is not for journalists or citizens to put their heads in the sand and pretend nothing is wrong; that option is no longer tenable. The solution is to tell the truth, actively discuss and debate the situation, and seek out workable solutions. And any solution will have to involve structural changes that reduce the amount of control corporate executives have over media content, and increase the diversity of viable noncommercial media.

Danny Schechter also rightly emphasizes our need to reform our media if we want to rejuvenate our democracy. Journalism has always been indelibly linked to democracy, from the passage of the First Amendment in 1791 to the dictum of "afflicting the comfortable and comforting the afflicted" in the late 19th century. Journalism should be feisty, controversial, engaging, and honest. Like politics, it should be fun, and it should always piss off those in power. Today's journalism has substituted celebrity lifestyle exposés, trivia, shopping tips, crime and violence, and subservience to business, for anything remotely democratic. Little wonder so few young people read or watch the news anymore, as it almost never addresses the basic political issues of who controls society, who doesn't control society, and in whose interests decisions are made. Journalism, like the mainstream political discourse it contributes to, is being forced to recognize something new—its own irrelevance.

When my students read this book, with its searing critique of the present U.S. media system, there will be a strong temptation for them to say, "Gosh, the system is screwed up, I better find a different field than journalism." That is exactly the wrong response. Today more than ever we need talented and principled people devoted to democratic values in journalism. True, the system is stacked against those people and will frustrate them at every turn, but that only makes the fight that much more important. Perhaps the next wave of great journalists will appear on the margins, much like I. F. Stone, Seymour Hersh, and George Seldes once did, providing an ever-present kick in the butt to the media and the political powers-that-be. We need 50, 100, 1,000 Danny Schechters. And we need everyone to take his words to heart and to begin to demand a media system that serves our democratic needs rather than the commercial imperatives of a handful of massive corporations.

THE MANY FRONTS OF THE MEDIA WAR

"I love television, but the majority of people who work in television hate television and hate the audience. I know what television means; I always have. It's our companion, it's our teacher, it's our everything."—Roseanne, from an interview in *Spin*, 1996

*C*an we begin by imagining how television could be different, how it could shape a meaningful culture instead of undermining one, how it might serve a broader public interest?

What if one of America's most celebrated working class performers relayed the news her way, informed by her values, world view and subjective notion of objectivity? In other words, what if Roseanne, now that her sitcom star is setting, took over from Brokaw, Jennings or Rather? Imagine RNN—the Roseanne News Network. It would definitely be more poignant and probably better produced than most of what we see. It might also be more honest. It would certainly connect more effectively with a vast audience that is part of that growing bloc of viewers deserting the TV news shows in droves.

I love the idea that Roseanne has been a big deal on television, like an erect middle finger permanently waved in the face of all those conservative media moguls who use the broadcast spectrum so effectively to sedate and stupefy millions. In so many ways, her presence reaffirms for me a faith that television can be saved. I can identify with what she said because I, like many, am part of that audience that feels TV treats us with contempt. In these pages, I'll be drawing on my experiences as an industry insider of sorts to talk about the great damage our media is doing to our culture, our common dreams and desperate needs, our everything.

I am also part of a smaller tribe—those who continue to work in television with the conviction that the medium is worth trying to improve. I don't hate the audience. If I hate anything, it is an industry that has swollen into an arrogant global power center, a force more powerful than many governments and more conformist than many corporations. It is that industry that is at war, within itself and with its own traditions, which it tends to glamorize and mythologize as the golden age. "Like the Republican Party," writes John Leonard in his compendium of TV criticism, *Smoke and Mirrors*, "it remembers, mourns and mimics a past when reporters were private eyes and cowboys, rather than blow-dried performing seals tethered to a Teleprompter."

❶ OPENING SALVO

We are living at the end of the first Media Century, an era in which the press, radio and television, and now computers, literally revolutionized our lives. In developed countries at least, but also in every capital of the world, few can imagine life without access to telephones, radio, television, beepers and cellphones, and for a growing number of the cyber savvy, the Internet and computer-based interactivity. The effect of these new media is total on social relations, on political culture and discourse, but also on entertainment and economics. Many of its implications are troubling for the intellectual, socio-cultural and economic life of our country and others, most profoundly for the future of democracy. The determinative role of modern commercial media is rarely examined by a media which has no interest in having attention focused on its own role.

Usually media issues are downplayed in the business or feature pages of the newspaper. This book wants to move them up on to page one as a war story—*the* war story of our times.

The media war is an undeclared war, one that is chronicled in gossip columns but rarely examined in depth. Yes, the war's battles are often reported—in a manner of speaking. If you want to find out which suit is now in charge or who's bought what, you can. But more often than not, this saga is covered only as a chronicle of business decisions, with the cultural and political implications rarely spelled out or followed up. I draw on some of that reportage in these pages, not as a clip and paste job, but with the intent of fusing my own experiences, specialized information, and the insights of other insiders to delve into the larger meaning of the changes taking place at such breathtaking speed.

"This is a war on several fronts," acknowledges England's *Guardian*, "in which timidity won't be the winner. The world's telephone, wireless, and cable companies are battling it out to become the dominant conveyors of information, while media giants such as Disney, Viacom, Microsoft, and Rupert Murdoch's empire are restructuring to become the dominant suppliers of entertainment and software." To compete effectively, these companies have opted to become colossal conglomerates through mergers and acquisitions, aided and abetted by government policies. These companies have become cartels, operating globally with little regulation or social responsibility.

Truth is as much a casualty in this media war as in any other. Intentional or not, one effect of what is called the information age is the continuing underinforming of the larger public, while an elite sector is inundated with more news and information than it can possibly absorb.

And it is not just the media corporations that have merged; there has been a merging of business and journalistic values as well, such that the different companies have become practically indistinguishable from one other. As the companies grow, often by taking on vast loads of debt, the inevitable downsizing and scaling back of news divisions has contributed to this sameness.

This media war is being fought not with guns but with marketing strategies and corporate logos that value entertainment more than information, diversion more than democracy. No wonder that Larry Gelbart, the screenwriter who created *M*A*S*H*, reached for a military metaphor as the title of his 1997 TV drama skewering media moguls, calling it *Weapons of Mass Distraction*. Those weapons, he told Howard Rosenberg of the *Los Angeles Times*, "take our eye off the ball. We're more concerned with who is sleeping with whom, and who is having a baby. The real problems in America and in the world go unnoticed while the prurient side of us is appealed to."

Media executives speak in the language of war—of *bombarding* audiences, *targeting* markets, *capturing* grosses, *killing* the competition, and *winning*, by which they mean making more money than the other guy. Some news organizations even refer to their employees as the *troops*. This high-tech war *deploys* technologies whose goal, in part, is to expand, domestically and globally, an entertainment-information economy now valued, in the United States alone, at $150 billion a year. Already, well over 50 percent of the revenues for America's cultural export industries are raised overseas. As the companies duel, countries and communities often find themselves in the crossfire.

Between April and October 1996 alone, by actual count, 56,949,501 commercials aired on American media nationwide. The TV industry made $34 billion in profits. One survey of local news shows found that 30 percent of their ads were for media and entertainment products. "Who knows better than the media that TV sells what it shows," commented researcher Paul Klite, who also quotes editor Harold Evans about what that means for the future of news. "The challenge of the media," Evans says, "is not to stay in business but to stay in journalism."

Media companies make no secret of their international ambitions. In March 1996 the *Wall Street Journal* quoted HBO's new

CEO, Jeffrey Bewkes, as calling overseas expansion his company's manifest destiny. Increasingly, the new class of media moguls has taken "We Are the World" as its own mantra.

Like all conflicts, the media war leaves a trail of victims and marginalized peoples. In the former Yugoslavia, it is widely recognized that propaganda posing as news, on both Serbian and Croatian television, fueled dormant hatreds and spurred on the right-wing nationalist movements that launched a genocidal conflict. Constantly replayed footage of World War II, in which both sides used the same footage to accuse each other of atrocities, brought on more atrocities. The nation went from watching war on TV to becoming caught up in a war that was shown on TV. It was a media war before it became a shooting war. The people were saturation bombed with hate messages before the first shot was fired. (This happened on radio in Rwanda and Burundi as well, but has gone largely unreported.) At the end of 1996, when Serbian pro-democracy protesters took to the streets challenging the Milosovic regime, they spoke out continuously against the state-owned media, brandishing slogans like "Turn Off Your TV. Turn On Your Brain."

In the West, there was a virtual media cleansing of the forces behind ethnic cleansing. It took years before the news networks shifted the way they framed the story of the former Yugoslavia from a case of ethnic and religious hatred in which all sides were equally to blame, to a story about premeditated Serbian and Croation nationalist aggression. By then it was too late. The horrific images of the war had already overwhelmed interpretive coverage. I am convinced that because so few viewers understood the conflict, few spoke out, including antiwar activists. You can determine if I am on target by asking yourself (and your friends) if you know, after all those years of watching news from Bosnia, how the war started and who was behind it.

As globalization restructures the world economy and uses the media as its global marketing arm, there is less, not more, coverage of global trends. As global news becomes more important, it is covered less. There is half as much international coverage on the broadcast networks as there was ten years ago. Stephen Hess, author of *International News and Foreign Correspondents*, surveying 404 foreign correspondents, concludes that coverage has declined in newspapers too, and that violent images characterize half of the stories, what is often called "bang bang" coverage. Why is there so much of it? Writer Neil Hickey in the *Columbia Journalism Review* recounts a conversation with one Gulf War journalist who spoke of getting a "rocket from New York"—a missive telling him what competing networks were airing—ordering him to file more on various firefights, regardless of their military significance. "New York wants John Wayne movies," he said. "not talking heads." Images, not explanation.

Two thirds of the largest 1900 newspapers have no foreign correspondents at all. Johanna Neuman of *USA Today*, in her book, *Lights, Camera, War*, quotes a comment from the *London Spectator* in 1889 on the impact of the telegraph: "The world is for purposes of intelligence reduced to a village. All men are to think of all things at the same time, on imperfect information and with too little interval for reflection." Sound familiar?

Subcommandante Marcos, the charismatic Zapatista rebel leader, taped a message in the mountains of Mexico's impoverished Chiapas region for screening at a January 1997 *Freeing the Media* teach-in in New York. No networks covered it. You will see why from the following excerpt: "The world of contemporary news is a world that exists for the VIPs—the very important people. Their everyday lives are what is important; if they get married, if they divorce, if they eat, what clothes they wear or what clothes they take off—these major movie stars and big politicians. But common people only appear for a moment—when they kill someone or when they die. For the communications giants, the others, the excluded, only exist when they are dead, when they are in jail or in court. This cannot go on."

It will lead, Marcos warns, to more confrontation. "Sooner or later this virtual world clashes with the real world." Significantly,

Marcos and his guerrillas use modern media to transmit their messages, which tend to get stripped of their substance on image-driven TV programs, but do, nevertheless, find a supportive global audience via lengthy communiqués relayed over the Internet.

Yesterday, great empires colonized countries. Today, great companies colonize markets, which they call territories. Centuries ago, slave traders turned people into property, physically branding the bodies they claimed ownership over. Today, transnational corporations invest in intellectual property and legally and artistically brand the programming they claim ownership over. Years ago, those brands were owner-specific, intended to last for a lifetime; today, copyrights and corporate logos are asserted in perpetuity and can impose a stranglehold over creators and the creative process.

This media war has yet to produce an effective opposition, an antiwar movement or cultural resistance that can challenge its trajectory and impact. Such a movement, however, is bubbling up from below, with parents calling for a more informative way of rating TV shows to safeguard their children, teachers promoting media literacy, activists asking for corporate accountability, consumers demanding enforcement of antitrust laws, media watchers critiquing news coverage, critics seeking more meaningful program content, producers creating alternative work and independent producers like me agitating for better and fairer journalism.

In other countries, media control is more obvious. North Korea is an extreme example, where every house is outfitted with a radio receiver bolted to the wall and locked on the government station. You can flip the TV dial but all the stations play the same programming, produced by the same state propagandists who operate on the not-always-incorrect assumption that whoever controls communication controls the nation.

Our techniques of media manipulation are less crude, hidden rather ingeniously, according to one scholar, by their own transparency. Our media is supposedly driven by market forces, but the media helps shape the market. TV's role in guiding our understanding of the world and serving as a weapon of control have been written about by critics but not always appreciated by the public at large.

Our media system influences us almost by osmosis. It is rarely obvious, rarely calls attention to its techniques. Its products are usually packaged to blend in with everything else on the tube and in the culture. It works on our collective consciousness to the degree that it is an almost undetectable part of the environment, like the air we breathe. We have air conditioners to keep out the heat. They've created a virtual "mind conditioner." That's why media activists today speak of the cultural environment as being as important as the physical environment.

There's a reason they call their products programming.

"It is so 'normal' that anyone with another view appears abnormal," writes Douglas Rushkoff in *Media Virus*. "By presenting news and media as a clean, uncomplicated, top-down, inaccessible, linear, soundbite continuum, public relations artists prevent individuals who have independent feelings from getting any positive feedback from the world around them. Dissidents must be made to feel that they are alone." That feeling neuters dissent and undercuts critical thinking. Television's negative impact on our culture is an issue seldom discussed on television.

The English writer Raymond Williams spoke of television in terms of its continual flow, which in its finished form appears to be "the result of natural rather than unnatural processes." It invites your belief "not only in what's being said, but that what is being said represents the only proper way of saying it." I have always been struck by the fact that almost every child is taught who invented the light bulb; few know who invented television or why he later admitted never watching it.

Marshall McLuhan had a similar view, calling television "a hidden environment, pervasively invisible." TV triumphs when we believe that it just *is*, like an old comfortable piece of furniture, squatting in our living rooms, not to be criticized or even taken seriously but just enjoyed as passively as possible. "TV or not TV" is not even supposed to be a question.

Partly that's because television tends to influence in a seamless way—it helps cultivate our world view by repetition of similar program forms and a limited universe of ideas as expressed across the dial in dramas, comedies, sitcoms and news. TV is an environment that sucks us into its own meta "reality" without our always knowing it, sometimes subverting our prejudices as well as reinforcing them. At the same time, as a window on the world it is narrower than we think.

This is especially true of news. "The immediacy of TV news coverage—the strong images and documentary feel—give people the impression they're better informed than ever before," note the editors of the international magazine *Colors*. "When you turn the TV off, the [people on the news] disappear...TV reduces us to spectators."

Jackson Browne writes about this in a song called "Information Wars" in which he sings the line that provided the title for this book: "The more you watch, the less you know." He adds another thought that speaks to the kind of desensitization and passivity excess TV watching can produce: "The more you watch, the less you do."

When it treats reality, television news wants to be believed, seen as conveying truth by upholding objectivity. Yet all too often it equates empty-mindedness with open-mindedness. Media gatekeepers in our commercial culture invariably screen out perspectives that challenge the conventional wisdom.

When we turn the TV on, many of us turn our critical faculties off. Rarely do we realize how many decisions have been made—in government, in studios and at networks—that have predetermined just what there is to watch. Government policy provides the framework; it permits and encourages a commercial TV environment dominated by a small number of companies. That regulatory framework interacts with the rules and prejudices of the marketplace, where layers of salespeople and development executives decide, on the basis of often flawed research, what people "want" to see. We don't see those executives, their meetings, their lunches or the creative compromises they extract from writers and directors along the way to keep the product recognizable, formularized, and marketable.

When we watch the programs, something else happens. Television's images, characters and scenarios become part of our own lives and imaginations. As Jerry Mander put it in his provocative *Four Arguments for the Elimination of Television,* "The more television people watched, the more their view of the world matched television reality." Plenty of evidence, research and studies back this up. Mander cites a National Institute for Mental Health report to the effect that we see television portrayals as realistic even when they are fictional. "These dramatic programs are most often seen as realistic.... Viewers evidently take fictionalized content of dramatic programs more seriously and literally" than most of the experts expected. If fiction is seen as reality, what about reality itself? Is news seen as fiction, perhaps as images that are so disconnected from most people's lives that they distance us, rather than engage us?

Journalism appears to be above the fray, "without fear or favor," in Harrison Salisbury's famous phrase. Yet in its mainstream milieu, critics and activists are invariably considered noisemakers, visually arresting but anonymous faces in colorful mobs, people to warn others against. Oppositional movements are often reduced to slogans and soundbites. Advocacy is a no-no, unless it's done on behalf of God, country or the charity of the company chairman's choice. The people behind the box swear they have no point of view or opinions. It's not true, of course, but many believe it.

The industry *has* staked out an arena for opinions where newsmakers and journalists can wrangle entertainingly over the meaning of the news, but the news itself is so rarely contextualized that the criticisms are often as superficial as the coverage. It is left to panel shows and commentators to decode the significance of current events and to supply the ways we should think about it.

But at the same time that we constantly hear about an information explosion, there is actually less new information being dug out. Despite more media outlets, there is less original reporting. The rationale is economic. *Time* magazine confirmed the trend, reporting that, "in fact, cost-cutting at the networks and major newspapers has reduced the number of correspondents digging up stories around the country and the world. What has exploded is not news but *talk* about news, commentary not information." Or as the English press puts it, "facts are expensive; opinions are cheap."

But not that cheap! Who sponsors the opinion shows? Two companies are the leaders—GE and Archer Daniels Midland, both active internationally, both beneficiaries of government favors, contracts, subsidies and tax concessions. In the 1950s, GE execs were convicted of price fixing; in the 1990s, GE's insistence that the PCBs it dumped into the Hudson River will clean themselves up, despite studies indicating the contrary, is a model of the opposite of corporate responsibility. And recently, charges of illegal practices were filed against the politically well-connected ADM.

What about the opinion makers and pundits subsidized by these companies—how qualified are they? Margaret Carlson commented to the *Washington Post* about her work on CNN's *Capital Gang* show. "The less you know about something, the better off you are." Producers and bookers, she says, are "looking for the person who can sound learned without confusing the matter with too much knowledge. I'm one of the people without too much knowledge. I'm perfect."

In these panel shows, the pithier your language, the more effective you appear. You are often cast to play a specific role, such as the cantankerous conservative or mushy-headed liberal, the tough interlocutor or whimsical philosopher. The panelists have their own goals: to have an impact, to be sure, but also to be invited back— TV visibility also drives a lucrative secondary career on the lecture circuit.

ABC's David Brinkley, whose last hurrah as a political commentator included denouncing President Clinton as boring when he thought his comments were not on air, told *TV Guide* that he felt the same way about his own weekly talk show's most frequent guests. "I hate to fill it up with a boring senator or a boring congressman who's telling the same story he's been telling for years, which we don't believe anyway." Then, why do it week after week, year after year? It is meaningful that many who live off the land of television are often the most hostile to it. Madonna, who owes her career in part to exposure on MTV, said she would not allow her daughter to even watch TV, because "it's poison."

TV is not just damaging because it's boring but because of the ideas it excludes. Commentator slots and opinion columns are dominated by voices on the right or center-right even while conservative groups insist that the media leans left. *Playboy* asked Walter Cronkite about this years ago. "I think newsmen are inclined to side with humanity rather than with authority and institutions," he responded. "And this sort of pushes them to the left. But I don't think there are many who are *far* left." Sadly, in our culture, few positions to the left of center are considered legitimate. They tend to be branded far left or just far out.

At CBS some years ago, Don Hewitt, the legendary producer who runs *60 Minutes*, put it this way: "If I detect a left-wing bent around here, that person's out the door...and I haven't detected it. I don't like left-wingers any more than I like right-wingers. I love the middle."

I am not a man of the middle, but I am also not an elitist. I watch TV. I even like lots of it and know that I am just as acculturated by its cultural smorgasbord as most other Americans. I also know that TV is more than just a tool of manipulation. It is more complicated than that.

Most people enjoy their cathode rays, and in fact believe they need them. Many can't imagine living without the "plug-in drug." Americans spend a huge amount on TV sets, satellite dishes and cable channels. No one forces them to do it. TV meets social and personal needs just as it creates them. Scholars disagree on the precise effects of so much TV watching. Some even feel it is the medium itself, not the message, that does the damage and that content doesn't matter.

I believe content matters.

② CONSCIOUSNESS AND CONSPIRACY

The media is not one big conspiracy. With thousands of component parts, its effects are much more subtle than that, operating as a complex interplay of consciousness, culture, class and contradictions. For one thing, many viewers are smart enough to see through attempts at manipulation. Not every attempted media sales pitch works; many backfire. For example, Vietnam battlefield footage that was first shown to ensure support for "our boys" actually ended up galvanizing antiwar activism and widening a credibility gap between what we could see and what they said.

While small groups of people do plot in their own interest and make decisions reflecting their own world views, they are also servants of an intrusive but almost invisible market system, which, as Rutgers professor Benjamin Barber points out, "runs on automatic pilot: that is the whole point of the market. The influences it brings to bear are not mandated by the imperative to control, only by the imperative to sell." He makes a convincing case that in our media-mediated world, we are no longer dominated by political dictators but by media-induced appetites and a consumer culture that gives us the feeling of having power even when we don't. In a sense, we have gone from the fear of Big Brother brainwashing to a do-it-yourself society in which we are washing our own brains often without even knowing it.

During a 1996 TV interview, America's most controversial media critic, MIT's Noam Chomsky, was asked about the media as conspiracy, the notion that it is run by a cabal that meets regularly, a view that is alive and well among paranoids on both the Right and the Left. His response: "No, of course not. They don't have to meet. Any more than corporations have to meet to decide to spend whatever it is—a trillion dollars a year—on marketing to try to stimulate artificial wants and control market share. They don't have to meet to do that, that's their nature. That's the institutional structure.... The media are huge corporations selling a product, namely audiences, to other businesses. It's a complicated system, not like a total monolith. Nothing works that way." That is what he said—word for word—yet speak to many mainstream journalists about him, and the first thing they'll say is that Chomsky spins wild conspiracy theories. But why?

Mark Crispin Miller, who teaches at New York University, identifies several defense mechanisms that seem embedded in journalistic discourse and that invariably tarnish all critics who focus on structures as conspiratorial, even paranoid, and hence dismissable. "It is a way of invalidating all discussion, of pretending there is diversity because of the number of channels or magazines on the newsstand but missing their essential uniformity of view." A recent example of this obfuscation appeared in a *Time* cover story that offered some solid analysis of how the news business is being changed by media mergers, but then asserted: "Though these corporate ownerships are becoming more apparent (*Good Morning America* travels to DisneyWorld more often), the homogenizing forces may be the result of profit pressures and competition rather than some sprawling conglomerate conspiracy." Yet who contends that such a conspiracy exists? Glib sentences like this are a straw man tossed out to obscure discussion not further it.

Chomsky believes that the media does have many journalists with integrity and that many of them consider his critique mild. "Many of them, in fact some of the best-known investigative reporters, would be much more critical of the media than I am. They don't say it publicly often, for obvious reasons."

When I discussed his critique with colleagues I found a tendency to minimize his credentials. "He doesn't watch TV," one said, "so how does he know?" Another, media writer J. Max Robins, a senior editor at *TV Guide*, said, "I think there is a lot more independence than Chomsky suggests. It isn't to say that there aren't real constraints that are going on in media, and I think they are basically bottom line ones. How much money are news organizations going to have to do comprehensive, international coverage? How much money to go into the long process of investigative journalism? But I don't think there is somebody picking up a phone and calling down to some line producer on ABC *World News Tonight* saying, Hey, I don't like the way you guys are covering the crisis in the Middle East; cut it out."

I know what Max means. He has a valid point. It's easy to assume premeditation by the media when you are on the outside, while on the inside you often experience chaos, confusion and even incompetence. The people in charge are more often than not operating on the run, guided by their gut and instinct, seemingly unconscious of the implications or impact of what they do. They often tell you they have little time to think because of all the deadlines. When they do, they often operate from a narrow or skewed knowledge base.

In a recent critical independent film about the news business, *Without Fear or Favor*, virtually all the journalists interviewed acknowledged that there were constant pressures towards self-censorship. Yet almost invariably they were described as subtle, never crude, rarely explicit. "Everyone plays by the rules of the game if they want to stay in the game," said ex-CBS producer Richard Cohen. Challenges to standard operating practices often result in reassignments, transfers, even dismissal. It is always easy for an executive to find a reason why some stories shouldn't be done or done in a certain way, why viewers won't watch it or why it is just "not for us." "People who are rebels or idiosyncratic are made to feel uncomfortable," confirms former NBC news president Larry Grossman. "And that's a big loss for journalism."

Most of the gatekeepers are there because they play by and enforce rules that share the world view and assumptions of the people who hired them for that very reason. Perhaps that is why so many seem so closed or even hostile to a critique that looks at the routines of news organizations and media business practices, not just individuals. Their rules are written and also unwritten, influenced by precedent and prejudice and forever shifting. "I don't want to see any more ugly people on this newscast," one producer tells me he was told. "Stay away from old people and blacks, they talk slow or funny," was a stricture at another program. A human rights organization official told me they had footage of a massacre in Zaire well before anyone else, but not one network would air it unless American troops were dispatched there. "I was told no one cares what happens to Africans."

Chomsky and his colleague Ed Herman believe in what they call a propaganda model, a somewhat rigid and deterministic concept that rests on an analysis of the filtering and repetition of certain kinds of information and perspectives amidst the systematic exclusion of others. It is a critique that pisses off segments of the media intelligentsia. Tom Wolfe calls it "the most absolute rubbish," while my childhood friend and former ABC colleague Jeff Greenfield says, "The stuff to me looks like it's from Neptune." In contrast, Chomsky devotees like David Edwards, writing in Z *Magazine* in September 1996, calls most journalists "intellectual herd animals who instinctively seek safety among the tired but rarely tested clichés of the mainstream."

Are journalists herd animals or is it that we work in institutions that subtly and not so subtly impose a kind of conformity and framing that discourages deeper probing? There tends to be a unified news culture and consciousness that is easier to see from afar because its products so often look and feel the same whatever channel you watch. No, rarely is someone picking up the phone and telling some producer to skew the news. The boardroom rarely faxes orders to the newsroom. But then again, they don't have to if they hire professionals who share the same world view and language, rely on the same sources, and tend to shape their reporting the same way.

What is needed are more world views, not the same old routines. And what is needed even more is an informed citizenry that pays more attention to what it reads and sees, a public that demands a different type of media.

In part, this book is aimed at those who would change America, arguing that unless and until their issues are on television, unless and until the companies that program television are forced to some higher standard of responsibility and diversity, meaningful change in our country will not occur. Unfortunately, most constituencies oriented toward progressive social change do not place media reform high on their agenda, when it is on it at all. In contrast, right-wing groups give media strategy top priority.

If politicians are held accountable for their actions, so should the media. Yet in a commercial culture, ensuring media responsibility is enormously difficult. The owners are well-insulated, wrapped in First Amendment constitutional privilege and surrounded by highly paid PR priests who are adept at deflecting any and all flak. Those who criticize this "free press" are often made out to be enemies of freedom itself. This media elite insists that it is, by its mere existence, serving the highest standards of social responsibility.

The corporate media also wants us to believe that it operates along rational lines, while critics are out of touch with reality, living in some idealistic bubble. All the big media companies claim they are simply serving the competing demands of the public and their shareholders, their bottom line needs and the marketplace, just giving the people what they want. Speak to any programmer about the show they are about to launch or movie they are about to make and they will tell you that's what the audience wants. Yet when the lousy ratings come in, or the grosses are pitiful, their conversation shifts to the search for scapegoats, for someone else to take the blame and a fall. It's the same in the news room where news managers and editors always rationalize their story selections as a concession to public taste and market needs. Sometimes they are right, but more often they're not. Yet their "logic" is rarely questioned. It just reasserts itself, season after season, year after year.

Nothing new here. Robert McChesney, who studied the battle for the control of U.S. broadcasting back to 1928, concludes that the "corporate media have actively and successfully cultivated the ideology that the status quo is the only rational media structure for a democratic and freedom-loving society. The corporate media have encouraged the belief that even the consideration of alternatives was tantamount to a call for totalitarianism."

❸ WHAT DO WE KNOW AND HOW DO WE KNOW IT?

We have all heard that more Americans get their news from television than any other source, but it is clear that many different media affect the ways we see the world, and that they interact and crosspollinate.

The notion of "the more we watch, the less we know" has been borrowed, with permission, from the findings of Professor Michael Morgan's University of Massachusetts study during the Gulf War, which found that people who relied the most on television coverage for their news knew the least about the war and its origins. Many of them also had the strongest opinions, which not coincidentally echoed precisely what they had been hearing and seeing. Like the media they depended on, they were virtually of one mind in uncritically embracing the U.S. government position. Most insisted that they arrived at their opinions independently. Who among us does not believe we think for ourselves?

Yet at the same time, when you talk to ordinary people about the way news is reported, most are unhappy. Many say there is something missing, that parts are left out, but also that there doesn't seem to be anything you can do about it. "That's the way it is," as America's kindly TV uncle, Walter Cronkite, used to say.

But even Walter no longer says that. Today, as news channels proliferate, actual news watching is falling off. Fifteen years ago, 41 percent of the American people watched one or more network newscasts. It is 16.1 percent today and shrinking fast. Increasingly, news is being delivered on a special-interest basis. Business news for one group, rock 'n' roll for another and celebrity coverage for everyone. In some cities, newspapers offer business news or world news in supplements that you have to special order and pay extra for. Fewer young people seem to be watching than other groups. Thirty-six percent watched the networks ten years ago. It is now, after years of inundation by an entertainment-oriented culture, down to 22 percent. "Faced with personalities they don't trust who interview people they don't know about stories that don't concern them," they are tuning out and turning off, explains the insightful writer and ABC newswoman Farei Chideya in *Time*.

Charges of media bias are more common than ever on all sides of the spectrum, especially when information is offered that contradicts or challenges partisan convictions. At the same time, within the industry there is an unease with the world of celebrity journalists and the slick packaging of the news. We are bombarded with information, although if you look closely, most of it has a similar grammar, a similar focus and similar sources, all revolving around institutions and topics that most viewers admit in survey after survey they don't really understand. Politicians speak politician-speak; and people who hold real power or who make critical investment decisions or formulate behind-the-scenes strategies rarely speak at all. The world of news and the world of truth are often worlds apart.

Often when you watch an item on the news, then flip the dial or hit the remote, you find the same item repeated in virtually the same way across the spectrum of all the channels. Unless one of them breaks an exclusive or enjoys unique access to a key source, which does occur from time to time, the lineup of stories and the language used to deliver them are virtually identical. So are the pictures and the punditry, when there is any commentary at all. Pack journalism prevails. Regular followup, nuanced explanation or context is mostly missing. No wonder it's hard to make sense of complicated stories.

One example: In September 1996, during the presidential campaign, Saddam Hussein's Iraq was bombed by the U.S. The stated reason was that Iraq had violated the terms of the Gulf War cease-fire agreement and sent its forces into the north of the country to dominate the Kurds. For good measure, the U.S. fired cruise missiles against Iraq's air defenses in the south, which were allegedly violating a no-fly zone. Washington announced that it was sending 5,000 ground troops to protect Kuwait, which had not asked for them and objected to their presence.

Soon reports that the CIA was mounting a not-so-covert campaign to topple Hussein, which he had infiltrated and stopped, began to dribble out. We learned that other UN members did not agree with the U.S. action; that some of the Kurds the U.S. had been supporting had actually invited Saddam to block advances by another faction backed by Iran. Who was backing whom? How did *we* screw it up? That was barely covered. And as the story became more complex, contradicting its first simplistic news frame, it moved off the front pages.

Rarely is this kind of information woven together in a way that would make sense of, or unravel, the nonsense of U.S. policies. "Facts we have in abundance," writes historian Bruce Cumings in his must-read *War and Television*, "but interpretations that put them together are rare.... Most of the time TV leaves the facts uninterpreted." The more you watched, the more confusing it became, and the less you learned. On the networks, crisis reporting reduced it to black and white: us, the good guys, versus them, the bad.

Scholars like Daya Kishan Thussu, author of *Contra-Flow in Global News*, see this as a pattern. "The coverage pattern is such that the immediate event highlighted by the media is partial and selective in its emphasis," he wrote in *Toward Freedom*, an informative small magazine published in Burlington, Vermont. "Significant facts are omitted that would throw a very different interpretation on the story. The language characterizes any actions of the U.S. and its friends as nonaggressive, reasonable and restrained.... The result justifies any action by the West, demonizes those who stand in the way and detracts from the real issues." Unfortunately, research like his is rarely given mainstream exposure.

Not surprisingly, confusing coverage produces viewers who have few if any coherent opinions, much less any grasp on what's happening in the world. It also produces a certain hopelessness, says Diana Griego Erwin of the *Sacramento Bee*: "What journalists tend to provide is a bevy of contradictory information and opinions on complex subjects that serve to further frustrate and confuse, leaving readers feeling more isolated and hopeless." How much people don't know about current events has become a big joke. Comic Jay Leno started showing photos of political leaders, celebrities and corporate logos to people on the street. They couldn't recognize Jimmy Carter but could easily identify Mr. Peanut. Two years after he left office, they were stumped by the image of former President Bush but readily named Madonna.

This lack of recall may have something to do with a media-fostered sense of amnesia, where nothing is particularly memorable except world historical moments like the John F. Kennedy assassination or the first moon walk. In part, it is a function of the fragmentation of the media itself, which was once a universal unifying experience. "That universality has been shattered, probably for good," writes former CBS producer Jon Katz in *Wired*. "Information now splits along demographic, political and cultural fault lines. We all look into our separate mirrors now and see only ourselves looking back." A *New York Times* sample found that although most Americans watch a lot of television, "a little more than half *could not think of a single good thing* to say about [it]." Not a single good thing!

The *Washington Post* surveyed 1,514 Americans in 1995; fewer than half could name either of their senators. More than two thirds didn't know that a balanced budget proposal had just been passed. Global awareness is even more pathetic. Eighty percent of highschool seniors couldn't find Japan on a map according to a *National Geographic* survey. Twenty percent couldn't find the United States.

Only 42 percent could understand a newspaper editorial. How many of us know that of the 158 countries in the United Nations, the U.S. ranks forty-ninth in literacy? An estimated 60 million Americans, a quarter of all adults, are considered functionally illiterate.

"Instead of the greening of America," critic Paul Fussell wrote some years back, "we can now speak of the dumbing of America," or, as Christopher Lasch has put it, "the spread of stupefaction."

In May 1996 I produced an episode for *Rights & Wrongs*, "Media and Human Rights," that reported on the decline of world coverage in the U.S. and overseas. We spoke with a leading French TV producer who told us that the BBC had cut back news and commentaries about the rest of the world by 40 percent, Channel 4 in London by 15 percent. "It's a global trend," he said. On local news, the situation is even worse, with many programs compressing world headlines into a minute of air time, when they cover the world at all. "The world in a minute" is how some actually package it.

The *Washington Post*'s former ombudsman Ben Bagdikian thinks journalism is failing humanity. In an interview with *War and Peace Digest* in May 1996, he said, "The record of the media reporting the most important issues facing America—and indeed the human race—is not encouraging. The major issues that face the average person have tended to be subdued compared to the interests raised by the media, which have a great deal to do with the stock market and with the top 20 or 30 percent of society. A very low priority is given to the issues which affect the rest of the world."

And even when there is coverage, it can get in the way of solutions because it is so transitory and episodic. In November 1996, I participated in a World Television Forum at the UN called to debate some of these issues, especially the survival of public service broadcasting. Outgoing Secretary General Boutros Boutros-Ghali noted that "decisions about which stories to cover and for how long have a real and lasting impact on the course of international events." He called CNN the sixteenth member of the Security Council. Others decried crisis coverage as promoting the culture of the moment, when cameras jump from bloody flashpoint to bloody flashpoint but rarely focus on what can or should be done about the problems. Kofi Anan, who would be named to replace Boutros-Ghali within a few weeks, called for preventive journalism in which networks might operate more responsibly to try to help head off genocidal conflicts. That idea was shot down by none other than Christiane Amanpour of CNN and CBS, who restated journalism's most basic shibboleth, that news is a "just the facts, ma'am business" and has no business doing anything more.

Have the media's technical advances outpaced the capacity of groups and individuals to understand the issues? Do all the images we are exposed to overwhelm the information and bring us a shallower understanding? Are large numbers of people excluded from the global media flow being stereotyped in the process? All these issues were raised. Few were or could be resolved.

One of the few mainstream journalists present doubted that anything could or would be done by commercial broadcasters to change the situation. Veteran TV reporter Garrick Utley, once a fixture at NBC News, then with ABC News, and now with CNN, said, "We may have to resign ourselves that certain issues will not be covered by commercial broadcasters. Commercial pressures will determine what news directors put on the air. If it doesn't meet commercial criteria, it doesn't get aired." Utley later spelled out his views in *Foreign Affairs*, warning that "the drive to penetrate new markets, and build media imperia raises serious concerns for international reporting and broadcasting.... When interests clash, as they inevitably do, good journalism is likely to be sacrificed."

Does this all add up to a blanket indictment of everything on TV and everyone associated with it? Of course not. Even commercial tastes change and space still exists for excellent programs to be produced and aired worldwide. And many are watched. *60 Minutes*, for all its faults, not only takes on tough subjects occasionally, but is consistently among the most-watched shows, year in and year out. Hard-hitting documentaries and diverse views do pop up from time to time. But the trends are not encouraging in what writer Susan Faludi calls the "unbrave new world" of media.

And this has very little to do with whether journalists are conservative or liberal. Old ideas about media bias are becoming obsolete as the media itself becomes biased against ideas themselves. Yet when ideas do get on the tube, they rarely have a progressive tilt. One conservative think tank, Brent Bozell's Media Research Center, has pledged to spend $2.8 million decrying leftward bias, while a 1996 Roper Poll reported in the *Wall Street Journal* in May 1996 that only 22 percent of the journalists surveyed said they considered themselves liberal. "I would challenge Brent Bozell to a media bias debate on any talk show in America," said T. J. Walker of a group called Progressive America. "But the reality is that most programs won't let liberals on."

What are the prospects for a more enlightened media in the United States, a country with the most sophisticated and most watched TV system in the world? Will this situation improve in an era of market-obsessed media monopolies? Do I even have to ask?

④ THE POLITICS OF TELEVISION AND TELEVISION AS POLITICS

Could we even have a political system in America without the media? Would elections even take place? Today, in many ways, all politics are media politics. In 1992, the slogan "It's the economy, stupid" drove Bill Clinton's campaign for the presidency. It was plastered all over his headquarters on the premise that the campaign needed a focused message and a central theme. I would have chosen "It's the media, stupid," to point out that the media now play the central role in framing political issues, and in the process, undermine our political culture and democracy. These days any strategy for political change that lacks a media strategy is bound to fail.

No sooner had Clinton entered the White House than he lost the media offensive. He seemed to forget that he was still campaigning—for legislation this time. His media operation fell apart. He was forced on the defensive on issue after issue. His health care reform was never packaged or explained successfully. He reached out to Republican David Gergen, who had advised Presidents Nixon, Reagan and Bush, for media guidance, then fired him amidst reports that his agenda was being sabotaged from within. A man who had used the media so well as a campaign tool was now being abused by it and didn't seem to know what to do.

What Clinton failed to understand was that the press had long since integrated itself into the dominant political culture and tends to close ranks against those who challenge the status quo in any serious way. The prominence it repeatedly gave to attacks from the Right reflected its own conservatism. It could be that media culture is more institutionally cynical and conservative than even political culture.

That cynicism is apparent at events organized by journalists. In March 1996, Washington's Radio and Television Correspondents Association chose shock jock Don Imus as the keynoter for its annual Washington dinner, where he savaged the president and embarrassed his media hosts. The choice of Imus, whose reputation for tastelessness is exceeded only by Howard Stern and Rush Limbaugh, says more about the world of big-time journalism than it does about off-color radio talk show hosts who specialize in crudity day after day. The Association apologized, when it should have reflected on what led them to make the invitation in the first place. Was it their own need to add celebrity and controversy to the drab routines of Beltway life? Why would they help debase the culture of debate by showering attention and status on the Don Imuses of the world? (It took Imus himself a year to realize how inane he— and, by extension, his many boosters in the journalistic establishment looked. At least he admitted it, telling *George* magazine, "Now that I've had time to think about it, [my material] was hideously inappropriate.")

Two months later, when it was the White House correspondents' turn to honor each other at a black tie dinner, also televised by C-

SPAN, they featured Al Franken, Imus's alter ego, a comedian from the other end of the spectrum. The author of *Rush Limbaugh Is a Big Fat Idiot* was as sharp-tongued against the Republicans as Imus had been against the Democrats.

What wasn't funny was what these events said about the deeply symbiotic relationship between reporters and those they report upon. I found myself agreeing with the conservative *New York Press*, which called "the mere thought of journalists and politicians putting aside their differences for a night of revelry, self-congratulation and mild barbs vomitous. The whole notion of an adversarial press in D.C., as it should be, is ridiculous; reporters and politicians know that they are of the same culture and that's what they want to preserve," the editor noted. I heard James Fallows, former editor of *U.S. News and World Report*, speak about this cultural symbiosis in more personal terms, remarking that the elite media and the politicians they report on often socialize with each other, live in the same upscale neighborhoods and send their kids to the same schools.

Mutual deference is at work. Years ago, journalist Mark Hertzgaard wrote about the subservience of the press corps to the politicians. He called his book *On Bended Knee.* Today, as the press gets more adversarial—usually on personal matters, not policy issues— the politicians work hard to seduce and use "friendlies" while denying access to "hostiles." They increasingly try to go around the press by taking their message directly to the public with staged events, photo-ops, satellite press tours, and similar maneuvers. This is one reason President Clinton's 1996 campaign invested so much time raising large sums of money from donors near and far. It was to buy time for political commercials—what political consultants call "the air war." The scandalous stories of soliciting funds and shaking down businessmen from all over Asia in exchange for visits to the White House and other high-level access speaks to more than the role that big money plays in politics. The media investigated where the money came from but not where it went—which was largely back to the media itself—to carry commercials.

A firm called Competitive Media Reporting found that the Democrats and Republicans together aired 1,397 hours of commercials in 75 major media markets during the period of April 1 to October 31, 1996. If they were run back to back, those ads would add up to 58 straight days of broadcast time. During this same period, a study by *Rocky Mountain Media Watch*, a citizens group that monitors local news in 41 cities, found that there were more election ads than news on local TV newscasts. Said the organization's director, Paul Klite, "If all we know about local issues and candidates comes from thirty-second TV ads, our precious right to vote is a sham."

If you track the campaign of 1996, you can see how the coverage fueled cynicism with its constant focus on polls and point spreads instead of policies. It started ominously with conventions designed for TV consumption.

While the political convention as an institution was marked for extinction years earlier when the networks abandoned gavel-to-gavel coverage, no party gatherings in recent political history were as sanitized and stage-managed as the spectacles in San Diego and Chicago. The political parties and TV news were effectively in collusion in presenting a pseudo-event as real, as the parties hired their own producers to turn them into TV shows. For once the *New York Times'* Walter Goodman had it right: "Television news met its enemy this week and it was television.... The networks were trapped by the tricks they had perfected and exploited over so many years."

The Republican convention resembled an infomercial that looked the way a convention should look, but with all the drama, conflict and debate carefully eliminated. The fierce battles between the party's religious right and its center were not allowed to surface. All speakers were preapproved and pretimed. The networks ran this made-for-TV movie with a minimum of comment or reporting. The *New York Times* noted that the networks "devoted most of their hour-long broadcasts to scenes that the Republicans had scripted."

Serious challenges to this carefully crafted charade were not permitted, or when permitted, were not shown. "Just how scripted was the GOP convention?" asked *Electronic Media*, a TV trade magazine, which noted that protesters were kept to a tight schedule as well. "To keep things moving at an orderly pace, a nearby traffic signal was put to use. If the light was green, speakers had plenty of time left to make their point. When the light turned yellow, it was time to wrap things up. If the light went to red, all power to the protest microphones were turned off." None of these protests were covered in any depth by network reporters.

When General Colin Powell spoke, the cameras focused on black faces in the crowd. Blacks were in a fifth of the shots but only made up 3 percent of the delegates. *Mother Jones* reported that one of the black faces that was shown repeatedly belonged to a female reporter who was covering the event. Two networks broadcast a Reagan tribute propaganda film unedited and unseen. This staged "no news except what we say is news" event reportedly so sickened Ted Koppel that he pulled his *Nightline* operation out of town, winning praise for what was pictured as a brave dissent. Critics, including Alexander Cockburn, later challenged Koppel, noting that there were many other stories in the greater San Diego area that merited coverage but might have embarrassed the Republicans or even the TV industry. "Why not cover the *maquiadoras* (small factories) in neighboring Mexico? We could show the anti-union policing and how 12,000 Mexicans in the Tijuana area are paid $35 a day to assemble TV sets—12 million a year—VCRs, tape cassettes..." To my knowledge, *Nightline* had no response.

When ABC reported that viewing levels for the first night of the convention were extremely low, correspondent Cokie Roberts asked the panel's moderator not to say that too loud because "we like covering these events." It was a revealing point—elections are news rituals that many journalists build their working lives around even when there is relatively little public interest. Republican spokesman Mark Merrit understood what most journalists didn't about how the media-fostered entertainment culture overshadowed politics, telling the *Wall Street Journal*, "Our difficulty is that we're competing with *Seinfeld*, not media ideology."

There followed a campaign that was barely covered. TV's political coverage was down almost 50 percent from four years earlier, reported the *Tyndall Report*, which monitors network coverage for high-paying clients. On the Sunday before the elections, the *New York Times* made the same discovery, when its reporters watched local news outlets in the country's largest media markets. "Ads are frequent, coverage isn't" was their subhead. Collectively, the TV ads cost some $800 million, contributing to the bottom line of TV stations but little to honest voter education. Columnist Norman Solomon suggested that a new criterion—"dollars per vote" or DPV—might put the situation in perspective. He calculated that Bill Clinton's campaign spent $61.8 million of taxpayer money to win 45.6 million votes so the cost per vote was $1.36. Overall, the presidential contest of 1996 was the most expensive in American history and probably the most superficial.

It was not surprising then that in places like New York, the campaign hardly stirred emotion. *Times* columnist Maureen Dowd reported that there was more popular debate about whether Madonna should breastfeed her baby than about what the candidates were doing or saying. "The Big Shrug" was what her column was titled. It was becoming hip not to care or even spend much time reporting on politics. Meanwhile, out of frustration, the Republican standard bearer Bob Dole spent more time denouncing the *New York Times* than Bill Clinton, in the false belief that the so-called liberal media was turning the election against him. His press secretary, Nelson Warfield, knew better, admitting to the *L.A. Times*, "Have they been fair to us? By and large, I think so. That the press is liberal doesn't mean they write liberal."

Writing in *Time*, Margaret Carlson revealed that journalists actually encouraged Dole to get tough with Clinton just to give themselves something new to write about. "Last week by some subtle communication about the new rules of engagement, the members of the press let Dole know they would not call him 'mean' or a 'hatchet man' if he would finally get tough." This subtle communication was not so subtle, taking the form of countless and seemingly repetitive articles and columns speculating about whether or not Dole would go after Clinton's character. The exercise seemed to offer more evidence of collusion than conspiracy. "The more you observe politics," the humorist Will Rogers once remarked, "the more you got to admit that each party is worse than the other." Can't the same be said of the media covering politics? (Today, the White House calls the news media "the beast.")

Most of the journalists were as bored by the vapid nature of orchestrated politics as the public. The Marist Institute, a polling organization, reported that 60 percent of the voters it surveyed claimed to be bored—in part no doubt by the coverage as well as the campaign, a point that conservative and liberal critics agreed upon.

The payoff came on election day. Voting levels plunged to 1924 levels, the lowest point in the century for a presidential election with only 23 percent of those eligible to vote actually supporting the winner. Voter turnout fell by at least 13 percent from the 1992 race. Was the media partially at fault? "Having decided early on that the contest was boring, journalists moped and groped and conveyed the unmistakable message that nothing very significant was going on," concluded then *Boston Globe* ombudsman, now media reporter, Mark Jurkowitz in a postelection *Nieman Reports* assessment, "Did the Media Kiss Off the Election?" "After a while, that became something of a self-fulfilling prophecy."

Media cynicism did not just impact on voting patterns; it also reported them badly. Green Party candidate Ralph Nader, who ended up winning more votes than Ross Perot in New York and San Francisco, was barely covered at all. Progressive candidates also did much better than you'd think if you'd relied on the media coverage. The Progressive Caucus in Congress has 52 members; it only had five in 1990. That caucus believes that "corporate control over media" makes it difficult for them to win support for their initiatives. "Americans just don't know that health care is free in places like Britain, that a college education is free or at least affordable, and that other industrial countries don't share out their wealth in this divisive way," says Congressman Bernie Sanders from Vermont. "The reason is pretty simple. Most Americans get their news from the big four networks.... You just don't see these corporations reporting on trade unions, on the wealth gap, on the fact that over 90 percent of the budget cuts the last Congress passed were taken from the poor." Not surprisingly, this complaint didn't even appear in the American press but in England's *Guardian*, in January 1997.

No wonder that there is so much passivity and turning away from politics altogether. A Harvard study has equated more TV watching with a drop in civic participation. One reason: Our powerful cultural industries shape the narratives by which ordinary Americans interpret their lives and outlooks. When those narratives never emphasize how ordinary people can change things, cynicism becomes rife in the public at large, where "people have lost all faith in the capacity or interest of institutions like unions, political parties or governments to fight for them," according to pollster Stan Greenberg as quoted in the *Left Business Observer*.

News programming reinforces this. A friend of mine reports for a Boston TV station that practices "user friendly news." She told me, "In almost every newscast we treat viewers as consumers, not citizens. For example, we give people tips on what to do if you have a cold, but no information about the crisis in health care. All problems are privatized and individualized; people are encouraged to think and act only for themselves or their family, not as members of a group, a class, or something called society. We want to help them improve their lives, not their communities. We cover elections like horse races, but never focus on the issues and real choices. Are you surprised that people don't know what's going on?"

In his post-victory press conference, President Clinton admitted that he didn't really understand why so few had voted. NBC's Tom Brokaw blamed it on a cultural blandness and pervasive escapism, in effect, blaming the people. Conservatives like ABC's George Will spun nonvoting positively, as a way "many contented people express passive consent to current conditions." But Curtis Gans, who has been studying nonvoters for years, went deeper, indicting a culture atomized by media that foster an entertainment culture that leaves individuals feeling isolated.

The future of a meaningful democracy is on the line. Rather than encouraging and inspiring citizen participation, the news media may actually be turning people off politics and the press itself. "For years, political journalists have been reporting primarily for themselves and their sources," writes Stan Cloud, who heads the Citizen Election Project, which encourages participation in the political process, "and have been doing so in a language ('spinmeisters,' 'soft money,' 'tracking polls') that a great many Americans find foreign and alienating." Citizens cannot make intelligent decisions without information—and yet they are expected to, and do so, every day on the basis of distorted and often incomprehensible reporting. When news becomes programming, its rejection barely becomes news.

"The presidential campaign and the electorate this year are strangely wan," reported the *New York Times* in a front page report on why the campaign failed to stir passions. *Strangely wan?* Huh? Or perhaps the electorate understood, even if the media didn't, how few differences separated the candidates, who were all beholden to big money and shared corporate agendas. "Where's the outrage?" Bob Dole kept shouting without seeing how he and President Clinton had both succeeded in dampening public enthusiasm.

I have been asked why, if the conservative media is so dominant, Dole didn't win. The question assumes that Clinton, the choice of many business leaders, is not conservative or virtually a Dole twin. Conservative media showed its primary influence at the state level, where Republicans won a majority of state houses, and in Congress.

"People ask me about the need for a third party," quipped radio talk show host Jim Hightower. "But I tell them that a second party might be a better idea."

In fact, as the Clinton Administration and his Republican opposition began to reach compromises on many policy issues, the Clinton Democrats and many Republicans became almost indistinguishable. As the president adopted and coopted conservative positions, the hard right shifted the drumbeat of its attacks from his politics to his character—an area of undeniable vulnerability. As a result we were treated to constant front page and TV news lead stories about Paula Jones case and then the Monica Lewinsky affair.

❺ *JUDGING JOURNALISM*

During the year I spent at Harvard as a Nieman fellow (see Chapter 2), I felt I had at last penetrated the inner sanctum of mainstream journalism. I spent hours in the foundation's small library reading volumes of books by journalists about journalism—critiques, memoirs, calls to reform and apologias for institutions that have long since failed or faded.

I was thrown into a group that worked for far bigger media companies and who certainly had less zeal about changing the world or even the places they toiled in. (Perhaps that's why the *Harvard Crimson* called me an Unlikely Nieman, or was it because I told the student newspaper that "I came to Harvard to lower my consciousness"?) Many felt they were lucky to make a living doing work they loved, could do well and be recognized for it. The tension between the mandate to keep one's distance from political engagement frequently clashed with the desire to do something meaningful and have an impact. "Scratch a reporter and you'll find a reformer," an unnamed editor told the *Washington Post's* Lou Cannon, who used the quote in his book on reporting. But what happens to that reformist impulse in this era of pro-corporate media?

I was always drawn to and inspired by journalists who not only reported or explained, but conveyed some understanding of the limits of conventional journalism. I grew up on writers such as Murray Kempton, George Seldes, Studs Terkel and I. F. Stone, who transcended those limits. In the '60s I worked for *Ramparts* and underground newspapers for whom press criticism was a staple. In the '70s I attended conferences and wrote for *MORE*, a magazine of media criticism written by working journalists. I adored the acid and often contentious criticism of Alexander Cockburn and had the privilege of working with Andrew Kopkind, the late *Nation* editor, whose style and insights were without parallel.

But those are my contemporaries. As you read the history of the profession, you'll find that media criticism is not new by a long shot. As long as we have had newspapers, radio or TV, we have had critics whose dissents have been noted or largely ignored, depending on the public mood. I am old enough to remember the writings of A. J. Liebling in the *New Yorker*, which skewered not only the content of many stories but a "monovocal, monopolistic, monocular press," words that sent me rushing to the dictionary. It was Liebling, of course, whose famous remark that "a free press belongs to those who can own one" reminds us that the exercise of journalism is always constrained by institutions and their owners.

In a footnote in his book *The Press*, Liebling recounts a proposal by the French writer Albert Camus to create what he called a "control newspaper," to be published each day shortly after the principal newspapers are on the stands, "with estimates of the percentage of truth in each of their stories, and with interpretations of how the stories were slanted."

Imagined Camus: "We'd have complete dossiers on the interests, policies and idiosyncrasies of the owners. Then we would have a dossier on every journalist in the world. The interests, prejudices and quirks of the owner would equal Z. The interests, prejudices and private interests of the journalist Y. Z times Y would give you X, the probable amount of truth in the story." With the power of the Internet and today's database software, his idea is probably feasible, although it is not clear if people want to know as much as he would like to tell them. Even Camus wasn't sure if his control paper would sell, assuming it could be produced. Can you imagine doing the same thing for TV news? Would a TV program that attempted that kind of monitoring be possible to produce, and if it could, would any station carry it?

In our culture, Xs and Ys, sources and journalists, newsmakers and news breakers tend to fuse into XYs, power brokers with overlapping identities. Increasingly, they look alike and often sound alike. Bias is a word that journalists use to describe others, never themselves. Many of us really believe that we are neutral, because we see ourselves as practicing fairness and balance. But do we?

Joan Didion tears this idea apart in an examination of the work of that doyen of Washington reporters, Bob Woodward, whom she skewers in the *New York Review of Books* as overly deferential to power. "The genuflection toward 'fairness' is a familiar newsroom piety, the excuse in practice for a good deal of autopilot reporting and lazy thinking." Didion notes that news is no longer just reported but *managed* in a way that sets its terms, dictates its pace, allocates time and space, and shapes its overall content. She reports that it takes 20 people to oversee important Washington stories in a process insiders call running a story. In this context, she writes, "what fairness has too often come to mean is a scrupulous passivity, an agreement to cover the story not as it is occurring but as it is presented, which is to say, as it is manufactured."

Today, many journalists have turned to fiction to tell the truth about themselves, their profession and how they look at the world. Joe Klein, who I first met as a writer for the alternative press in Boston and whose book on folk singer Woody Guthrie was praised by Bruce Springsteen, once profiled me when I was a radio newsman. He seems to have turned sharply to the right as he moved up the media hierarchy, sparking a scandal in 1996 with the political novel *Primary Colors*, which he published as Anonymous. The flap about his unwillingness to disclose his authorship of the best seller—which I saw as just a clever marketing ploy—was hypocritical and unfair, even though valid criticisms can be made of the editors who dissembled. More interesting to me that Joe felt he had to turn from traditional journalism to fiction in order to bring out what he thought was the deeper story of the Clinton years. While the book showed how profoundly political skepticism has corroded the process and exhibited certain narrow-minded beliefs, it also underscored the limits of mainstream journalism.

More recently, *New York Times* reporter Christopher Wren published a thinly disguised autobiographical novel called *Hacks*, about a foreign correspondent sent to a mythical place called Equatoria. There he breaks a big story only to find that a focus group of kids convened by his own newspaper to counteract its graying demographic (guess which paper he had in mind?) killed the story because they couldn't locate the country on a map. At least he acknowledges the way marketing strategies influence journalism and help shape what is and is not fit to print. Andy Kopkind understood that relationship years ago when he led a piece for the *New York Review of Books* about his years of writing cover stories for *Time* magazine with the words, "I used to work for *Time*, or was it sell?"

Increasingly, reporters themselves are grousing against the distorted priorities in American journalism which puts coverage of the world off the charts. "It's all stuck on page A 23, deep in the back of the paper," moans columnist Christopher Caldwell in the *New York Press*. "It's yet another thing that makes me miss the cold war. When we were locked in a global fight against the Evil Empire, every place in the world was important. Now, no place is." He goes on to decry editors who once sent him packing to overseas stories in a hot minute, but who now say "who the hell cares about _____? (Fill in the blank with the name of the country.) Clearly they don't."

The first generation of TV newsmen, the Murrow and Cronkite generation, came into a new medium with the tools and ethics of an old. They were print reporters, often wire service veterans, who lived on deadlines. They were not part of the generation that grew up on television, or learned its craft within just one medium where packaging takes precedence over substance.

Yet who am I to judge either my better-paid colleagues, or journalism itself? There is no question that excellent work appears regularly on the air and that many documentaries and programs deserve the recognition they receive, like the Emmy Awards or DuPonts, the Polk and the Peabody. Visit any television station in America and the first thing you see are all the well-polished plaques and statues. We have a wall of them ourselves at Globalvision. The news business knows how to honor and promote its achievements. Many stations use the recognition they garner to hype themselves to an embarrassing degree. You know what I mean—the constant promotion of the "Associated Press Station of the Year" and so forth. Today, *Variety* keeps a running "kudo-count."

These awards rituals go on despite the fact that the public seems to be tiring of them and even turning on the press. The Columbia Graduate School of Journalism even hosted a panel called "Why do they hate us?" at the 1997 DuPont awards, which tends to give out its awards year after to year to the same programs and networks. Outgoing Columbia Dean Joan Konner broke the bubble of self-congratulation to admit that many of the wounds journalism is suffering are self-inflicted because of arrogance, poor judgment, insensitivity, and a variety of excesses. Journalists also tend to be blamed for what their companies are doing or represent. ABC's John Martin called investigative journalists a "vanishing breed," noting that many TV companies are no longer willing to fund expensive team efforts that can result in even more expensive lawsuits. Brave reporters toil on, but they often must battle to get the resources they need—and many, unheralded and unrecognized, are losing that battle.

The distinctions between news organizations are vanishing as well, with the tabloid press winning new legitimacy. Consider the case of Richard Gooding, who broke the story of President Clinton's advisor Dick Morris' kinky affair with a $200-an-hour prostitute he let listen in on his confidential conversations with the White House. (Of course, the *real* Morris scandal—his role in White House money grubbing, was not even investigated. It was reported *after* the election, in the *New York Review of Books*.)

As it turns out, the *Star*'s star investigative reporter started his promising career as news assistant to A. M. Rosenthal, then the cantankerous editor of the *New York Times*. When the Vietnam War invaded his life with a draft notice, he became a resister and dropped out of the mainstream. He later attracted attention as a talented writer and ended up working for the pre-Murdoch *New York Post* and then the *Daily News*. He was known as someone who was contemptuous of supermarket sheets like the *Star*. After he lost his job at the *Daily News*, Gooding freelanced, then went with the *Star*, making more money and perhaps having more of an impact, however perverse. While Ted Koppel treated him sanctimoniously in a *Nightline* interview, many of his colleagues were impressed with his enterprising and aggressive, albeit purchased, scoop. What does the arc of Gooding's career say about the direction the news business is heading?

Even prominent mainstream journalists admit that tabloid stories drive the editorial direction of many media outlets. Michael Boylan, vice chairman of the company that publishes the *Star* and the *National Enquirer*, confirmed the trend. "When Zsa Zsa (Gabor) slapped that cop, in the old days, the only people who would have been at the courthouse would have been us and maybe the local Beverly Hills paper. The last time Zsa Zsa showed up, there were 400 reporters and television crews, including the *New York Times*."

Gooding left one job track for another. I did the same, but in another direction. When I was still at ABC News, clinging to the tenuous security of my job and my pension, I went back and forth about making a move into independent production as I became more outspoken about the often vacuous news culture of the networks. On some days, I felt like an alien from another planet. On others, I accommodated quite well, thankful for the resources and the chance to get my kind of stories on the air my way.

I was a social change-oriented journalist in a medium that is uncomfortable in raising unsettling questions or challenging established power. I began thinking of myself as a mole in the machine, an agent of another America—one forged in the counterculture, nurtured by civil rights activism and informed by critical journalism and dissident literature. Yet there I was, stuck—by choice—in a medium that I knew shored up the status quo. (I still think of myself as a mole, perhaps because I wrote for a newspaper once called *The Old Mole*. I may have Norman Mailer to blame. In college way back in 1962, I read his interview with the *Realist*'s Paul Krassner in which he counselled those who really wanted to make change "to join the mass media...to bore from within." "It is better to work alone," he advised, "trusting no one, just working, not to sabotage so much as to shift...always knowing that the work, no matter how well intended is likely to be subtly hideous work. The mass media does diabolically subtle things to the morale and life of the people who do their work; few of us are strong enough to live alone in enemy territory. But it's work which must be done.")

I may have considered myself an outsider or an infiltrator, but to my employers I was just one more worker with a photo ID and accounting code, expected to perform and conform like everyone else. And I did, but with a split identity. Part of me liked the headiness of being the hotshot network producer on a show that the kid behind the counter at Burger King knew and watched. Part of me detested that I liked feeling that way.

Was it snobbery or just paranoia left over from my days in the underground press where the big-time, capital-E Establishment media was considered the enemy? Was I selling out or buying in? Was I changing them or were they changing me? Would I be co-opted? In 1996, as I write my media-ography, Walter Cronkite's memoirs are already in the bookstores. And what is he doing? Why, savaging the news for carrying, well, little news. Cronkite a news god turned media critic! Maybe columnist Jon Katz is right to say that there is "nothing daring about attacking the media these days because journalism has become a cultural free-fire zone."

Everyone seems to be lambasting the media—and sometimes the attacks bounce off their targets or are skewered like marshmallows. In October 1996, Globalvision won an award from the UN Correspondents Association for a report we aired on UN complicity in the genocide of 10,000 people in Srbenica in Bosnia. I was pleased that colleagues who report on the UN honored it. But then, as I received the plaque, none other than the UN's own Secretary General Boutros Boutros-Ghali stepped alongside me for a picture-taking session. How absurd! He was running the very institution we had indicted and was ultimately responsible for the UN's role in what happened. No one commented on the irony, and I'm sure he never saw our report. I just hoped the Bosnians weren't watching.

❻ DOCUMENTARIES: AN ENDANGERED SPECIES

Documentaries offer the chance to fulfill the promise that network news so often shortchanges, the chance to tackle a subject in depth, tell a great story, probe, investigate, expose, contextualize, be comprehensive, teach. Everyone in the business admires serious documentaries; unfortunately, few are aired, or watched when they are.

I first thought about becoming a documentary filmmaker after I saw *Nanook of the North* in elementary school. Later I became a devotee of Edward R. Murrow's *See It Now* series, especially his classic *Harvest of Shame*, which exposed the plight of America's migrant workers. As a kid, I used to write to CBS for the mimeographed transcripts, which I stuffed away in my closet, convinced they would become valuable and useful.

I stumbled into doing my first film when I was a student at the London School of Economics and thought it would be great to document the student uprising that shook that fabled Fabian acade-

mic outpost in 1967-68. I knew nothing about filmmaking but figured doing is the best way of learning. I was chutzpah driven. I had
an idea but no script, treatment, or plan. If I knew what I was getting into, I would have dropped the project, and fast.

Fortunately, I had help from Norm Fruchter, who worked with
Newsreel, the '60s political film collective. Poof! We had cameras,
a crew, "liberated" film stock. After months of work in an unheated
room near Covent Garden, on a £500 grant from the British Film
Institute, Jane Grant, a skilled editor, helped me impose coherence
on *Student Power*, an agitprop manifesto that actually played in the
London Film Festival of 1968 alongside films by Godard and other
movie greats. It was met with thundering indifference, some pats
on the head and one polite, understated review.

A year later I played it before a New Left conference at the University of Wisconsin where my subjects, a group of intellectual English Marxists using phrases like "pedagogic gerontocracy" to describe
the school administration, were all but incomprehensible to American activists. The film that followed featured pitched battles at
Columbia University between police and militants and had the
audience on its feet chanting "off the pig." My film was a curiosity in that overheated environment. I never showed it again, and
somehow my one print disappeared. (The British Film Institute did
circulate *Student Power* to UK campuses on the twentieth anniversary of the LSE uprising.) The whole no-budget filmmaking exercise was so exhausting that it was 20 years before I tried it again.

England has always been considered the home of the TV documentary, where well-funded factual programming had a mission
to be challenging, critical and rigorous. Yet according to a 1996
report by communications analyst Williams Rossa Cole, the dissenting documentary in England is fading fast, thanks to the infiltration of an American-style market-oriented world that imposes
commercial criteria on TV documentaries. The number of serious
documentaries decreased while "there is plenty of room for cost-

effective, high-rating, fly-on-the-wall series that slavishly follow police cars and ambulances, or glitzy quasi-investigations into the surreal lives of Hollywood personalities."

This trend toward the replacement of investigative reports in the Ed Murrow mode with softer, risk-free programming is far advanced in the United States, where entertainment values and escapism have long displaced education and enlightenment as the primary motivation.

I know because I am still stuck in the old mode.

By 1997 I had produced and directed seven long-form documentaries, some shown on TV, others in universities, festivals, screening rooms and a couple of theaters. They have been written about in newspapers but, candidly, none have made money yet and probably never will. In 1995 only seven of the relatively few theatrically released documentaries earned over $150,000, and most cost far more to make, even if you value the labor of the filmmakers on the scale of the wages of coolies in Burma. But should you evaluate creative and important work by how much it costs or how much it makes? I don't think so, but the industry does, focusing attention on best sellers as if they are the best products. "After all, it's always been a business, show business, as the saying goes, not show art," laments director Ed Zwick. "Is it the legacy of the go-go eighties that everything, *everything*, must be defined in terms of price?"

"I realized early on that to work in the arts in America is considered un-American," filmmaker Michel Negroponte told an audience at the annual Independent Feature Film Market (IFFM). When the audience of documentary makers was asked how many of them can make a living doing what they love, only a handful of hands went up.

The documentary, especially those that deal with "controversial," which is to say relevant, subject matter, is an endangered species in America. The term is not even used in polite network company, where programmers speak instead of programming blocks, specials, or nonfiction films. D now stands for "dead." The nets run no regular documentary series anymore. Most of what there is airs on the cable channels, which together aired 2,000 hours of them in 1995, according to Pat Mitchell, an executive of Turner Broadcasting. But most dealt with soft and safe subjects—superstars, animals, nature, the Mafia, World War II, airplanes, pets and so on. (Several cable outlets have been ridiculed as the Hitler Channel because of all the films about the Nazis that they run.) Mitchell said her company asked her to try to come up with shows that didn't feel as if you were being forced to eat spinach. I thought, Maybe *that's* my problem—I like spinach.

One of the most successful cable series is *Biography*, a well-packaged but formulaic daily series that recycles archival footage with voice-overs and a few new interviews. Only the networks can afford to produce these docs in volume because they own archives, while independents would have to license footage at high rates. They are rarely films with depth or dimension or insights you haven't heard before. The Arts and Entertainment (A&E) channel, owned by Hearst and ABC, has been stockpiling the programs and plan to recycle them one more time by creating a twenty-four-hour biography channel. They have created a fully owned franchise by "repurposing" material, and adding spin-offs like *Biography for Kids*, a *Biography* Web site, *Biography* dramatizations and *Biography* audio and traditional books. Biography was once a category and a genre. Now the name itself has been appropriated as a private brand. CBS is doing something similar on its cable channel called Eye on People, mostly featuring repackaged material and updates of old CBS shows.

The commercial channels all say that PBS, the traditional outlet for docs, is too generous to filmmakers, paying too much. That's a joke. The situation with PBS is so confused that Jonathan Stack, a very successful filmmaker, rose at the IFFM panel to ask if anyone could tell who he could call at PBS. "There's no there there," he complained. "I don't even know how to get someone on the phone." This is not to say that some filmmakers with giant reputations do not attract large grants and blocks of public television airtime. They do, but perversely, the acquisitions and commissioning process is less accessible than it is in the private sector. Filmmakers like Ken Burns have practically taken over PBS with safe and sprawling, expensively produced multi-hour series like *The Civil War* and *The West*, subsidized to the hilt by General Motors, which has no problems underwriting hours on the escapades of Grant and Lee. (Burns says he doesn't tell GM how to make cars and they don't tell him how to make films, a comment that avoids the stickier questions of corporate intent and impact.) Yet PBS would not commission or back Michael Moore's successful *Roger and Me*, which exposed GM's assault on auto workers in Michigan. Corporate underwriting for that film was tough to find until Warner Brothers realized they could make money showing it in theaters and stepped in.

Hard-hitting documentaries are an endangered species even on public television. PBS's *Frontline* series began to transform itself in the mid-1990s, moving away from hard-edge investigative reporting to profiles and more sensational subjects. In 1993 *Frontline* won its highest ratings with a show revealing that FBI director J. Edgar Hoover wore dresses and was probably gay. The program was not based on their original reporting as many in the past had been but was adapted from a book. Optioning books was once just a movie tradition. It is now a practice in documentaries. *Frontline*'s work is usually of a high standard but it too has been cut back or moved rightward, as in a 1997 film defending nuclear power.

Presenting information and analysis used to be the documentary's raison d'être; now TV executives stress style and look. How the interview is shot—the lighting, camera angles, rich, textured background—is often more important than what is said. The rationale is always that higher-quality production values will draw a larger audience—often true—but viewers don't end up humming the scenery or the music. Besides, the television networks overflow with expensively produced fluff. In the end, it is content that counts.

It is an entertainment movie channel that has become known for harder hitting documentaries than PBS or any of the networks. Home Box Office has made some 200 non-fiction films, some quite brave and socially relevant, even controversial, from a report on the drug war to a film about death row prisoner Mumia Abu Jamal. Unfortunately, such shows tend to be denigrated as worthies—programs that win awards but are not really respected internally or representative of the dominant sensibility; those tend to be documentaries on sex or a series called *America Undercover*, which features tabloid tales of the mad, imprisoned, drugged out and victimized, of gang wars and dope fiends. They are stylishly produced, often intimate, in-your-face explorations of worlds that middle class people rarely experience. But there can also be a titillating pandering about them with a walk on the wild side appeal of the old freak shows at the circus. Many are verité without responsibility, like gawking at an accident on the side of the road before whizzing by in the safety of your own car. They feature strong storytelling without a social framework, more often producing pity, not outrage. These shows are very well made but the emphasis is on sizzle, not steak, driven by what one top gun in the industry told me every successful TV show needs: the three Ss—sex, sensationalism and salaciousness.

Most documentary filmmakers will tell you that most of their time is spent raising money, not making films. "We are stuck with an impossible problem," admits D. A. Pennebaker, one of the deans of the modern documentary. "It's a trap." He's right—it is harder and harder to find funding for independent films, partly because right-wing attacks on the National Endowment for the Arts and PBS have had a hugely chilling effect. But the intrusion of media monopolies and market values are making a more dramatic if less visible impact.

In the old days, many independent filmmakers were trust fund kids with access to family wealth to finance their "hobby" or fanatics determined to live for their art, willing to live in poverty as the price of creative freedom. Today, independent filmmaking is a small industry supporting hundreds of documentarians. We all have to struggle to finance the means of production. And if you want to preserve editorial control over your work, well, that's another story. My friend Barbara Kopple, a brilliant two-time Academy Award documentary winner, still goes from project to project, hustling support, taking as much as five years to finish great films. Fortunately, her talent has finally been recognized by the commercial channels and she is getting sporadic work, but not always the work she chooses.

Today, what most of us lack is the means of distribution. "It is very hard, Danny," one commercial distributor told me. "I like your work but five companies control most access to theaters and they reserve it for their own product." Henry Hampton, whose 30-year-old, Boston-based company, Blackside, is well-known for series like *Eyes on the Prize*, warns that the situation facing independent filmmakers is critical and that we must act or "settle for the back rooms and back alleys and live marginal existences." Speaking at the Independent Film Market, he described his problems raising money. A year earlier Bill Moyers, sitting in an office overflowing with Emmys and other statues, told me almost exactly the same thing. If such well-known producers as Moyers and Hampton are having problems, you can imagine how the rest of us are doing.

The commercial cable outlets do not seem too bothered by this. Their response has been to seize control of the process by forcing filmmakers who want to work for them to do so on their terms, as if it should be self-evident that exploitation can be the only logic of the marketplace. Speaking at another IFFM panel sponsored by her own company, Cheryll Miller Houser of NFF (Non Fiction Films) laid it out. Their budgets are low—$100,000 per hour and you must give up creative control and all rights. Michael Cascio of A&E offered a similar scenario, explaining that his network demands control of all rights, on even lower budgets. He shrugged, adding, "If you can't do it for that, then don't." He noted that PBS is emulating the approach of the cable outlets by airing similar formularized, down-market programming. To his credit, Cascio also opined, "Personally, I think they should be going in another direction."

These documentary companies don't position their efforts in the tradition of independent or political filmmaking. Market, not mission, defines them. In 1994, I was invited to speak at the Sundance Film Festival about the politics of independent filmmaking. Perhaps because the idea of politics has become so foreign, I ended up on a panel with producers and directors from around the world. The turnout was large, and many spoke about the lack of government support for American independents, noting that Canada and European countries spend so much more per capita to support film, and the arts generally. Robert Redford and Sundance were referred to as an oasis in the desert, where integrity was rewarded and dissenting voices could be heard. Three years later, Sundance, now the most influential festival in America, was being rapidly commercialized, turning into a market more than a showcase. Dissent was hard to find; deals were all anyone discussed. Part of the reason is economic. All the major studios have their own entities—New Line, owned by Turner; Miramax, owned by Disney; Polygram's Gramercy; and Fox's Searchlight—to exploit so-called smaller pictures. These companies, all with platoons of ski-toting, cell phone-carrying and cigar-smoking hip executives, have tremendous influence because of their control over distribution. Independents are dependent on them. So here too media mergers are having an impact—providing an outlet for the lucky few but further marginalizing those not well enough connected or not considered commercially viable.

Variety quoted one director as saying, "The experience of being an unknown filmmaker at Sundance is absolute isolation. If you arrive with an umbrella organization, with inside clout consisting of an agent, lawyer, publicist and distributor, you are coddled. To go there cold, with no power, no money, no influence behind you, you want to leave immediately."

The hype about the explosion of independent films may be just that—hype. Sundance, once a challenge to the commercial culture, has evolved into one of its centerpieces. Bold political films have given way to the style-over-substance work of a new class of film school grads—starlet-driven, edgy, dark and graphically violent, prompting one reviewer to quip: "Sometimes something not worth doing is not worth doing well."

In 1995, *Pulp Fiction* earned over $100 million in box office receipts. Yet according to a 1997 *Variety* survey, the independent sector only reaches 4 to 6 percent of the market. Because of the hegemony of the mall-centered theater chains, most of the old "art-houses are gone or going. Studio films still dominate with the highest percentage of returns. Captioned, non-English foreign films enjoyed 7 percent of the market fifteen years ago. Today they are down to .7 percent. Jan Sverak, the Czech director of *Kolya*, which won an Academy Award in 1997, partially blames the news media for encouraging isolation from the world. "Most Americans only knew about the fall of the Berlin Wall because it was in the papers during the week that Ivana and Donald Trump split up," he says. No wonder the market for documentaries has dried up.

In early February 1997, I ran into Al Maysles, one of America's legendary documentary makers, in many ways the father of the modern documentary. We had just seen Leon Gast and Taylor Hackfield's *When We Were Kings*, on Muhammad Ali's 1974 rumble in the jungle, a film that was done well and worth doing, taking over twenty years to complete. The film ends with Spike Lee complaining about how young people don't seem to know anything about the past or even remember what happened a year ago, much less the time when "The Greatest" ruled the ring.

Maysles told me he had become obsessed with why so much modern media seems to be lowering consciousness rather than raising it. "I'll give you the name of a book first, and then tell you what it is about," he said.

"Sure."

"*Driven to Distraction.*"

"Is that a book on the media?" I asked.

"No—it's on attention deficit disorder, ADD, but funny you should ask."

His point was that the trendy media techniques—dating back to *Sesame Street*'s quick-cutting and evolving into video games and MTV-style off-center camera moves—promote the condition.

Wow, I thought, could this disorder be a new cultural disease, a media-induced sickness of the TV age?

"Driven to distraction," he repeated with a smile. "Remember that." He added that he would like to work with me someday but wasn't sure if he could afford it.

7 DUMBING DOWN AND COVERING UP

The people who watch more and know less don't necessarily know they are being politically massaged or how media manipulation has become so invisibly institutionalized. They don't know that dumbing down is not just an incidental effect of the way many media outlets operate but a reflection of conscious and calculated policies of down-market targeting.

The talk shows plastered all over the dial have taken the trend in a deliberately sleazy direction. Guests are often referred to by producers as trailer trash and used to titillate and boost ratings. In some instances, the same guests appear on different shows, sometimes playing different roles.

In 1995, a backlash against these shows began to build. Even TV station managers who had been promoting and profiting from the trend started to speak out against it. According to one survey, 80 percent of the people who ran TV stations and carried the shows denounced them.

They hate it, but they show it. TV programming reflects trends and creates them. When tabloid talk shows generated ratings, more followed until the market was glutted. Competitors tried to outdo each other with shameless inanity. It became a question of "how low can you go."

Dumbing down has long been part of the news business too. *Forgetting the News*, an academic study by Barrie Gunter assessing what viewers retain from the way TV news is presented, found that journalists often package news to serve their own needs, not those of their audiences, relying on their own lingo, their "inside baseball." As a result, many viewers misunderstand or are confused about what they've just seen. In some cases they retain only the images, not the information. They are left with impressions, not ideas.

A friend of mine, anthropologist Robert Deutsch, who does focus group research, has made a study of U.S. coverage of Japan. "I asked Americans to name a single Japanese person," he told me. "They came up with three: Yoko Ono, Godzilla, and Bruce Lee, who was not Japanese. When I pointed that out, they said, 'It doesn't matter.'"

Deutsch's research found a huge gap between news reporting and audience comprehension. Audiences deal more in terms of metaphors than linear content, he claims. He also says that the American news coverage he watched distorted not only Japan, but America's relationship with Japan, often overemphasizing Japanese rates of productivity and falsely making American workers out to be inferior. We may have stereotyped them, he says, but we also stereotyped ourselves—a point that *Nightline* edited out when they interviewed Deutsch in 1996.

The definition of news is now in dispute. In 1996, when a new classification system for TV shows was under consideration, news was to be exempt because of First Amendment concerns. Fourteen members of Congress, led by Joe Kennedy of Massachusetts, called for distinguishing between "traditional legitimate news programs" and tabloid infotainment copycats, as well as those trashy talk shows.

The trade magazine *Electronic Media* sneered at Kennedy's concerns. Citing a dictionary definition of news as "new information about anything," the magazine—which often speaks for the industry—said that, by that definition, all talk *and* tabloid programs must be considered legitimate news programs and be exempted from the ratings system. Thus the *Jenny Jones Show* and *Tales of the Highway Patrol* would earn the imprimatur of news.

No wonder that even insiders tend to get disgusted. Here's Dan Rather in a candid moment: "Too often we start out as watchdogs of those in power and end up as lapdogs of the powerful. Not all. Not always. But all too often."

"When I was a young reporter the great weakness of journalists was whiskey," Paul Simon, a former reporter turned U.S. senator, told *U.S. News & World Report.* "Today the great weakness of journalists is cynicism." *Harper's* notes that 45 percent of the American people say that journalists are more cynical than other professionals; 54 percent of journalists say the same thing. Perhaps that's why surveys of journalists increasingly report mounting disaffection and frustration.

Many political reporters say that they owe this cynicism to the company they keep. When repeated in print or on air, politician-speak sounds like the "newspeak" Orwell warned against. Clearly, all of society's problems cannot be dumped at the media's doorstep. But the media's contribution needs to be admitted and confronted.

If journalism is a fourth branch of government, then it is no wonder that many political journalists take on the trappings of being officials of that government and increasingly report for the elite of which they are part. James Fallows, a former White House staffer under President Carter, has written about this phenomenon, especially in the case of Washington-based reporters, for the *Atlantic Monthly* and in his book *Breaking the News.* More recently, in the pages of the *Nation,* he took note of the structural pressures that make this worse: "The more basic concern is the conversion of the news business to just another corporate operation where whoever is in charge must be driven by the demands of the financial markets."

As the framework in which journalism operates changes, public attitudes toward journalists also change. In 1994, *U.S. News & World Report* reported that 71 percent of the American people believed that "the media gets in the way of society solving its problems." Another report that year, *Politicians and the News Media* by Beverly Kees and Bill Phillips, went further in documenting an erosion of public trust in the media. This survey, promoted by the Freedom Forum, highlighted a number of charges against journalists including:

+ they're more interested in sensationalism than issues;
+ they're political insiders who can't report fairly;
+ they don't understand the real issues facing the country;
+ they underestimate the public's taste;
+ they conspire to disgrace politicians.

The study found that the public thinks of politicians and the people who cover them in pretty much the same way: as using the claim of public service to disguise the pursuit of profit and power. Describing published stories that are based on a single source or questionable source, longtime *L.A. Times*man Jack Nelson says, "We jump to conclusions without evidence." Unfortunately, large segments of the public are taken in by this, often looking to the news to confirm their suspicions, not learn the truth.

The structure of news presentation contributes to the problem. An English report called *Television, Mythinformation and Social Control* makes this point: "We get delivered straight to our living rooms the newest news every day, now, this minute, as each news bulletin consumes the one before it. Images are no sooner presented than replaced by more infotainment in a void, having no connection to past or future, only an illusory present. Through immediacy, fragmentation of reality is guaranteed."

Sometimes journalists become more famous than the people they cover— famous, in some instances, for being famous. Fighting for face time on TV, politicians and pundits often compete for who can be the most clever. No wonder pose and showmanship is often more important than sincerity or integrity.

It is easy to forget that while it markets information, the media is always at the same time marketing itself. This is why media companies are concerned about promoting their identities, branding their products and selling their symbols. Most have insulated themselves from criticism but they do respond to competition. They can be challenged. They can be changed.

⑧ *FLASHBACK*

My first encounter with TV, after one brief visit to the Howdy Doody *peanut gallery as a six year old, was as a guest on a New York version of* American Bandstand. *Back in the seventh grade, I took part in a dance contest with a friend who had some serious modern dance training. Everyone in my neighborhood watched. We won a gold (painted!) Coke bottle and a pair of white bucks from Thom McCan shoes. I kept them clean for years. We were invited back for the contest of the week but lost embarrassingly to a more polished duo that seemed to have Olympic gymnastic training.*

Years later, in 1963, one of my first media protests brought me back to television, to another TV dance show, this time as part of a civil rights action that may have inspired a movie. In that year, I was a civil rights worker in East Baltimore, a ghetto that would still make any top ten list of America's worst neighborhoods. The teenagers there were upset that the local version of American Bandstand, *the daily afternoon* Buddy Dean *show, was segregated. Dancers on the shows were all white except for one day every other week when they were all black. To add insult to injury, the show packed in twice as many dancers on the black kids' day, so that no one could really show off their best moves.*

We came up with a plan to desegregate the show through what no doubt was the first and probably last civil rights "dance-in." Using our BAYOU (Baltimore Area Youth Opportunities Unlimited) group as a cover, the kids secured tickets to one of the black-only sessions presided over by Fat Daddy, a black radio DJ who co-hosted these

"Negro shows." With my encouragement, they invited a group of white college tutors from our Northern Student Movement (NSM) "each one teach one" tutorial project to come along. The black students went into the studio first while the whites waited in the parking lot until the last minute. With two minutes to air time, we rushed into the studio for the live show. The ticket taker was confused but let us in. The TV crew was equally perplexed. TV then was still black and white but those two colors weren't meant to be mixing in Bal'more, not then, not ever.

It was probably the first interracial dance party on TV. On Buddy's shows, the guest organization was invited to say a few words about who they were and what they did. One of the black teenagers and I were pushed forward. We made political speeches, speaking out against segregation on the show, looking right into the stupid grin plastered on Buddy Dean's face. He was beside himself. Seething. Fat Daddy chuckled.

A day later, I was summoned to a meeting called by the executives of WJZ, the Westinghouse-owned station, with then–Baltimore County executive Spiro T. Agnew (yes, the one and same!) who told me that our guerrilla TV demo had "set back race relations in Baltimore County by twenty years." They were upset not about racial segregation but because the station had received bomb threats.

The Baltimore African-American newspaper reported the story with glee. Years later, writer-producer John Waters, who grew up in Baltimore, dramatized the incident as one basis for his hysterical film Hairspray. The Buddy Dean Show was eventually desegregated but the incident dogged him and the station for years.

9 CHANGING MEDIA

Happily, it looks as if more and more Americans are becoming receptive to thinking about what they can do about the media's impact on their lives. A group called TV-Free America, which reported that American families collectively watch 250 *billion* hours of TV every year, also produced polls to show that 49 percent of people think they watch too much, while 79 percent believe that TV violence helps precipitate real-life mayhem. They want to get rid of TV altogether.

I don't. I do want to change it.

Quite a few of the sources for this book in the media world asked for anonymity. "You understand why, Danny?" Yes, I do.

My maxim has always been that you commit yourself and then see what happens. Does that cast me as a perpetual troublemaker? Well, yeah. But I would prefer to just do my work as a perpetual program maker.

I am just one journalist with testimony to offer on the demise and possible resurgence of truth-telling in our time. I hope this description will become grounds for a prescription for media reform and renewal, and that the public will speak out and act. I hope my colleagues who spend so much time bitching and moaning about their latest compromise and outrage will find the heart to put their careerist needs aside to speak out as well.

It doesn't have to be this way.

⑩ DISH*CLOSURE*

Before Seven Stories Press welcomed this book, earlier drafts made the rounds of some publishing houses that are owned by the very media conglomerates I've set out to critique. One editor denied vehemently that the fact that Rupert Murdoch owns his company has anything to do with what they publish, while another admitted that publishing my book could lead to problems with other potential TV clients. Veteran publisher Andre Schiffrin has criticized the integration of American publishing into the media industry, arguing that the colossal communications conglomerates impose a form of "market censorship." A friend, writer Meredith Tax, goes further, arguing that the result is a "global monoculture that has become a threat to cultural diversity," driving idiosyncratic and critical voices to the margins.

Some publishers told me that a book too critical of TV could never sell because an author must get on TV to promote it. That tautology makes some sense, although I'm not paranoid and can only hope the book will be judged on its merits. I was bemused when I read that some of the very executives who passed on my work were later shuttled out of, or jumped from, their senior perches in leading publishing houses precisely because, by comparison with their even more commercial colleagues, they were predisposed toward more serious books and fewer fluffy, big-name titles.

(*The Nation* devoted a memorable issue to exposing "the dark heart of the empire where conglomeratized publishers pay millions for books they'll synergize but never really sell [and their celebrity authors will never really read, much less write].")

As this manuscript was readied for publication, I read of mega book deals with the likes of ex-Clinton "family values" advisor Dick Morris, who was signed to write a tell-all based as much on his after-hours peccadilloes as his insider access. It came out that he had shopped the deal around on a confidential basis even while he was still serving as the president's close advisor.

I had a tell-all book too, I thought, but it seemed to be missing one key component. A conversation with a well-known publishing exec explained what that was: dish. This is as good a place to start as any:

"Dish," she said. "You need dish. Or no one will be interested."

"*Dish?*"

"You know, like some juicy disclosures about Barbara Walters?"

"*Barbara is in there. I worked alongside her.*"

"But is it dish?"

"*Dish?*"

"You know, will it titillate us? Will it make the columns?"

"*Well, I think it's embarrassing, but it's not, like, gossip.*"

"It's not? You've got to play the name game. If not, well, I don't—"

"*What about Geraldo?*"

"You got Geraldo?"

"Well, I have a critique of Geraldo."

"Everybody's got a critique of Geraldo."

"I go inside the news business, revealing why it's so screwed up."

"Business is boring. You need people."

"I've got people. Big people."

"Are they famous enough?"

"Oh, they're pretty famous, actually infamous."

"Infamous? Infamy is good."

"Well, it's actually about the media and me."

"Sorry, you're not infamous enough."

"Not yet, but maybe the book will help."

"If anyone reads it. You can't dish yourself."

"It's ironic and funny. It's a media adventure story."

"Adventure stories were last season."

"It offers a strong analysis."

"So what? Analysis leads to paralysis."

"But the media is everywhere."

"Yeah, they all watch it, but will they read about it?"

"You bet. I've got some revealing stories to tell."

"What about O. J.? Is he in there?"

"Yeah, O. J. is in it, well, kind of." (O. J., oy vey!)

"Well, maybe, in that case...."

PART ONE

A MOLE IN THE MACHINE

CHAPTER 1

NEWS DISSECTING:
INSIDE THE ROCK RADIO REVOLUTION

"There is no such thing as pure *objective* obser-
vation. Your observations, to be interesting, i.e.,
to be significant, must be *subjective*. The sum of
what the writer of whatever class has to report
is simply some human experience..."
—Henry David Thoreau

*I*n the fall of 1970, the two-year-old WBCN, Boston's top twenty-
four-hour rock 'n' roll station discovered that it was not providing the newscasts it had promised the FCC in their license
application.

Founded by T. Mitchell Hastings, an engineer and radio pioneer
whose claim to fame was the car stereo and other technology indispensable for the spread of the FM phenomenon, BCN had been a
classical station. Breakthroughs in technology had ushered in a new
radio age. Frequency Modulation, or FM, produced a superior
sound. As the technology's booster, Hastings built a classical music
radio empire up and down the East Coast, but initially his Concert Network only reached audiophiles who could afford the expensive receivers. As a result, his network became financially moribund.

In 1968, T. Mitch was struck down by a brain tumor requiring
immediate surgery. When he went into the hospital, his Boston station was playing symphonies and barely paying its bills. When he

came out, BCN was under new management that had rolled over
Beethoven and was rocking around the clock—and making money.
Handel was out; Hendrix was in. The convalescing owner may have
hated the music, but he liked the cash flow. "I was in the hands of
a higher power," explained Hastings about the format change. "I
know it was the hand of a higher power because I never would have
had the guts." WBCN's 1973 income quadrupled that of 1967.

FM made broadcasting in stereo possible, which in turn begat
album-oriented radio, known in the trade as AOR. FM DJs began
to challenge and compete with the hit parades and screaming disc
jockeys of AM, what the FM crew called ugly radio. BCN was a
leader in shaping a free-form, formatless format featuring hip personalities with a laid-back style playing longer sets of commercial-
free music. DJs were known by the music they chose and the mood
it created. Rock radio became the megaphone for sex, drugs and
rock 'n' roll, '60s-style. It was a generational thing, and it thundered
with a political edge. While AM stations played Army recruiting ads,
BCN offered information on draft resistance counseling.

Writing in the *Boston Phoenix* about WBCN's rebirth, the late
Dave O'Brian enthused: "It was a warm day in March 1968. Everyone knew that that evening this station was going to start playing
the music everyone at Brandeis was already listening to. And lo and
behold, at the proper moment, after a fair amount of dead silence,
this voice came on and said, professionally and youthfully: 'This is
WBCN, Boston' and then Cream started playing 'I Feel Free.' It was
sensational. The entire campus turned up their radios, and you
could hear Cream down every hall and out every window pulsing
through the spring air. It was a freeing moment in an otherwise
oppressive year. And we knew it was the start of something. We'd
even taken over the airwaves."

At first, BCN's news department consisted of one constantly
spewing wire service machine. To underscore the station's uniqueness and in part because it was cheaper, BCN used Reuters rather
than Associated Press. Back then news was an afterthought at a sta-

tion whose musical style was among the most innovative in the country. But then someone had an idea: If the music was going to be different, why not the news? Bo Burlingham, an up-and-coming writer for the *Boston Phoenix*, a weekly underground newspaper, was brought on board to create a news department and at the same time to protect the license, any radio company's most valuable asset.

Every radio station in those days was required by the FCC to provide a certain amount of news and public affairs programming. (Years later, in the Reagan era, when radio was deregulated and FCC news requirements dropped, many newscasts and independent news departments followed.) Stations that didn't comply could have their license renewals challenged, although that rarely occurred; station owners saw these requirements as a burden to be satisfied at the lowest possible cost. Most either aired network news feeds or offered local news, which usually consisted of rereading the wire, "ripping and reading," it was called. Sometimes, the news included rewriting local newspaper articles and very occasionally, sending a reporter to a local event. Only all-news radio and some AM talk-oriented stations had real news staffs, although even they usually devoted as much air time to the weather, traffic and sports as they did to current affairs. Radio news consisted of headlines and sound pops of five- to fifteen-second duration. Across the dial, news all sounded the same. It all *was* the same. National Public Radio was just getting going, aiming for the up-market mainstream.

Locally, radio news was seen as a loss leader and not yet a profit center or important service. Only the national radio networks offered more in-depth coverage of events outside the local broadcasting area. FM radio, which had higher sound quality, included entertainment features to supplement music programming, and was even less committed to news. "More music, less talk" became a popular slogan and selling point.

From the start, WBCN committed itself to providing independently produced news that spoke to the concerns and passions of its youthful audience. It was news that didn't stop at the borders of Boston. Draft-age listeners were interested in the war in Vietnam, so BCN reported it with some scope along with local and national news. Alternative news soon became a daily complement to alternative music. That commitment stood out in an industry faithful to the institutional proposition that the audience doesn't need to know anything, and doesn't much care anyway. (It's always been my experience that when managers say people don't care, it's because *they* don't care.) Fortunately for its listeners, to protect its license, WBCN took its FCC responsibilities seriously.

Soon Bo Burlingham was writing the newscasts. The DJs read them and, together with Bo, would from time to time add other voices, music, sound effects and prerecorded interviews. These features would be played while the news was being read live. At most stations, then as now, DJs stick to the music and do their shifts. But at BCN, there was a collective spirit that led to many collaborations across traditionally segmented lines. In many stations today, computers have replaced people altogether in programming music mixes. It is all run by the research and the numbers. In those days, individual creativity was encouraged.

After just a few weeks in the newsroom, Bo himself unexpectedly became news. While scouring the wire one afternoon, he found his own name prominently mentioned in a news flash. The FBI had just filed indictments against Bo and a group of his one-time political comrades in the Weather Underground Organization, a breakaway faction of Students for a Democratic Society (SDS) which advocated revolution in America through armed struggle. Bo had long since defected from the Weather ranks, but now stood accused of participating in an antiwar bomb conspiracy. With that bulletin he joined the FBI's most wanted list. He clipped the wire story, slipped it into his pocket, took the elevator down three flights and disappeared into the fugitive underground. Unlike many others, he soon surfaced, turned himself in and pleaded not guilty. (The charges were dismissed years later, recognized as one more abuse by Richard Nixon's Justice Department, which had concocted the phony case.) Bo's travails, though, became my opportunity. J. Edgar Hoover had inadvertently created a vacancy that BCN manager Ray Riepen agreed to let me fill even though I had no radio experience. It didn't matter. WBCN was in the business of reinventing radio, and he needed a journalist on board.

Like Bo, I set out to write the news. Unlike Bo, I had poor typing skills and worse handwriting. The DJs had trouble reading my sloppy copy. So one afternoon, when I handed a script to J. J. Jackson, the afternoon DJ, he took one look at my piles of papers, shrugged and said, "You read it!" He had to go to the bathroom. He told outgoing jock Jim Parry that I was about to make my on-air debut. (I never thought it would be possible to become a radio announcer because my Bronx twang stood out like a sore thumb in a town with that distinctive *Bah*-ston accent.) J. J., who became one of the first VJs on MTV, and the only black one, didn't think it would matter. Parry gave me a James Brown-like longwinded intro, with a bunch of phrases, invented on the spot, that rhymed with my last name. "Here he is, folks, the news detector, news reflector, news inspector and news dissector, Danny Schechter."

The radio gods were with me. My first newscast went off smoothly. "Hey, I can do it," I thought to myself. "Hey, you can do it," the two DJs said to me. I would have to read my own chicken scratch. And I did. I would remain on the air in my own voice for the rest of the decade. The news dissector tag stuck. Now I had to live up to it.

At BCN, DJs for the most part selected their own music and made occasional creative contributions to the news department. The sparkplugs at the station, Charles Laquidara, Maxanne Sartori, Al Perry, Sam Copper, Jim Parry, Tommy Hadges, and Norm Winer, were especially interested in involving the listeners. They provided information on activism, sometimes encouraging protests. Volunteers manned and womanned a hotline where callers could get concert info, hitch a ride, find a lost a cat or dog, request a song. The BCN listener line was always open and helped thousands deal with bad acid trips and even career tips. BCN became the community switchboard and in turn, a community of very loyal listeners formed around it.

It was druggy, sexy, and always rocking, countercultural and oppositional, amplifying our side of the generational wars. BCN played trippy music and rock anthems that became the soundtrack for movements for change. We were among the first stations to play reggae, to play Springsteen, to mix the energy of rock 'n' roll with the insurgency of the times. Abbie Hoffman was a frequent guest, along with a constant parade of activists and musicians. Boston bands like J. Geils, Aerosmith, and the Cars were always around. Just about every rocker who played Boston visited the station, recorded station promos and IDs, and hung out with the DJs. I met most of them and attended more shows than I ever had before or since, largely because I was comped along with the DJs. We covered all the big concerts, but if there was a demonstration underway in Boston, the DJs would announce it as well, and BCN news would be there.

At the same time, I knew I was not just working for people who already agreed with me. BCN was not an alternative station but a mainline commercial outlet. I was a journalist, not a propagandist, and so was bound by the rules of fairness and accuracy that the profession demands. I did the grunt work of checking facts and seeking other viewpoints. The most challenging work was not the coverage of spectacular events but the day-to-day news reporting. I am sure that my sense of humor, use of diverse sources, and experiments with audio collages made it difficult for those who held other views to simply be dismissive. I was very conscious of broadcasting to young people who often lacked background and needed stories to be put in context and followed up. I believed in explaining news, not just reciting it. That meant that sometimes my newscasting would resemble storytelling, with a beginning, middle and end. I tried to be satirical without being sarcastic, clever without being cute, and funny without being sophomoric. It didn't always work. Fortunately, I could come back the next day and try again.

I took a risk because I had a hunch. The risk was trying to crack into broadcasting by breaking most of the rules. The hunch was that people would be willing to listen to news and views that weren't necessarily popular or slanted in the traditional way. I intended to "dissect" news, that is, break it down into elements that explained what was going on, rather than just report the familiar surfaces. I wanted to present news that looked at the world from the point of view of people trying to change it, rather than just those who would keep it the way it is. No newscasters have all the answers but at BCN we had some questions, and if we could involve some of our listeners in the quest for truth, it was worthwhile.

BCN was also not a collective but a company, a business with advertisers, salesmen, and executives to please. Unlike some of my colleagues at nonprofit stations where political infighting drains a lot of energy, and hot rhetoric or identity issues polarize staffers along gender, racial, or political lines, our news team had to function alongside people with very different agendas. And that meant winning their respect with work that won recognition, occasional awards, and positive listener feedback. Music radio tends to tolerate news, not welcome it. Yet at BCN we sustained the backing and support of the powers that be. BCN news became an organic part of the station's national image and local identity. And we did it without sucking up or softening our product. We also did not alienate the listeners. All audience surveys showed enthusiasm for a strong independent news department, and I'm told, for my own role. In some ways that was our most enduring accomplishment— to be able to keep a unique news service going, day after day and year after year, even when we were alone in the market or even considered way out.

At its best, broadcasting can be a team enterprise where the strengths and talents of many people combine to create the product. This cooperative and collective accomplishment is getting rarer these days as broadcasting becomes more hierarchical and geared toward stars and individual ego trips. A spontaneous combustion made BCN special. Two forces—exploitation and liberation—co-existed, competed with, and contradicted each other.

The DJs could be more incendiary. On one occasion when the ratings results were disappointing, DJ Charles Laquidara, through his invented radio alter ego Duane Glasscock, told the audience to send "a bag of shit to the Arbitron research bureau." He didn't say caca or feces or number two, he said send a bag of shit. He also gave out Arbitron's address on the air every fifteen minutes. Duane, but not Charles, was fired for that stunt.

The impact of this type of bold, outspoken, in-your-face programming was not lost on Washington. In 1970, the late Vice President Spiro T. Agnew gave a speech criticizing certain unnamed radio stations for airing songs promoting "drug culture propaganda." In March of 1971, as BCN prepared to celebrate its third anniversary in its rock format, the FCC warned broadcasters that there would be penalties including a loss of license for playing songs that "promoted or glorified the use of illegal drugs." This did have a chilling effect at BCN, although in reality the only song we were not allowed to play was John Lennon's "Working Class Hero," because the word "fucking" was in the lyrics. A departing DJ made sure to play it as the last selection of his last show. At BCN, we were hostile toward any attempt at censorship, and mostly we got away with it. Who would have imagined then that in 1997 a network like NBC would air *Schindler's List* with the profanity intact?

After hearing my news reports about anti-personnel weapons manufactured by the Honeywell Company for use in Indochina, Charles added some unasked-for commentary to an ad for Honeywell cameras being sold at a store called Underground Camera in Harvard Square: "Go out and buy yourself two or three Honeywell cameras and help support one of the corporations responsible for all those dead Cambodian babies." Underground Camera charged he accused *them* of killing Cambodian babies and sued for $200,000. The case actually went to trial, in the very Dedham courtroom where Sacco and Vanzetti were convicted. BCN used a truth defense, proving that Honeywell—not the camera store—made the bombs. No big secret. We won.

In the late '60s and early '70s, the war in Vietnam and the protests against it were the major story of our generation. I wanted to offer coverage you couldn't hear elsewhere. I turned to the alternative media, as well as overseas outlets like Agence-France Press. I also sought out Vietnamese sources so that our coverage would be balanced, that is, not totally pro-Pentagon.

In those days, all the wire services routinely transmitted the Pentagon's self-serving worldview along with the weekly body count communiqués as released in Saigon at what reporters called the five o'clock follies. The other side was always referred to as the enemy, as in "Enemy sources claim." "Enemy sources" were always "claiming," while macho American or American-backed sources "charged" or "asserted."

As Arthur Ponsonby observed, truth is the first casualty in war. I decided to make a minor change in the wording we used—to call each side by the terms they used to call themselves, not each other. That meant dropping the word Vietcong from our newscasts. According to MIT's famous linguist, professor and media critic Noam Chomsky and others, Vietcong was a propaganda phrase that the Vietnamese resisting the U.S. intervention never used; it was like calling someone a nigger. It was also inaccurate because it branded all resistance fighters in the South as communists, neglecting the fact that many were nationalists, Buddhists and so on. In any event, the antiwar movement considered it offensive. I decided to lose Vietcong and henceforth call the guerrillas by their own name, the National Liberation Front. (Some news outlets followed. When our B-52s pounded the North Vietnamese capital during Christmas 1972, Ray Riepen's *Boston Phoenix* made a similar point with a headline that read: "Enemy Bombs Hanoi.")

I didn't think it was such a big deal. After all, neither was I using the terms the other side used to describe us—Saigon puppet regime or U.S. imperialists. No, I just wanted to call them by the names they wanted to be called by, a point diplomats always acknowledge as proper even when the media doesn't. When he participated in the Paris peace talks, Henry Kissinger referred to his adversaries correctly as the Democratic Republic of Vietnam (DRV) and the National Liberation Front (NLF), later the Provisional Revolutionary Government (PRG).

Fortunately, many in Boston tended to share, or at least tolerate, BCN's views. Antiwar sentiment was the majority view in Massachusetts in those days, and BCN was partly responsible. The Commonwealth was the only state to go for McGovern in the Nixon tidal wave of '72. BCN news commemorated the event with an award-winning documentary, "Nixon 49, America 1." While many, if not most, Americans *were* against the war by then, a large number believed Nixon had a secret plan to end it. The media in Massachusetts, led by the *Boston Globe*, didn't buy it.

Our Vietnam War language issue raised a minor but important distinction, but it was also one way of challenging the seamless propaganda that had infected coverage of the war. What's in a name? A lot.

My "minor" point gave our station manager a major headache. He threatened to fire me over it and probably would have, had the station not been experiencing major internal convulsions including Charles's dismissal (he was quickly reinstated). That, in turn, led to threats of strikes and even an employee takeover. The BCN staff resisted management attempts to impose discipline and introduce a mandatory play list. Management was even more irrational. It looked as if my job was about to disappear in a spasm of overheated rhetoric and spontaneous activism. Our long-haired engineer had just been caught bugging the station manager's office and was dismissed. A confrontation was brewing. And there I was, the station's number one political journalist, counseling restraint and negotiation.

To calm things down, I brought a union into BCN—not a traditional broadcast union, but an old-line progressive industrial union, the United Electrical Workers (UE), whose link to radio was rather tenuous but did exist. The UE had represented thousands of workers who manufactured radios in the days when radios were assembled in America. Those days were gone, and the UE was holding on, having survived McCarthyism, opportunism in the ranks of the AFL-CIO, jobs exported overseas, and the anti-union climate stoked by Nixonism. UE field organizer Bill Murdoch cooled the hotheads and signed us all up. I became shop steward, which made it harder for management to just dump me. The union's presence stabilized the station and my own position by introducing work rules and blocking arbitrary firings.

In his book on the music industry, *The Mansion on the Hill*, Fred Goodman calls the unionization of BCN the knockout blow to management's attempts to assert control and "professionalize" the station. It also stopped them from muzzling the creativity and free expression of the staff. What Goodman misses is how the union unified and empowered the staff, and fought for WBCN's integrity throughout the '70s. Without it, the station would not have survived the decade as such a special place. He gets some of the details and the spirit wrong, but he is right to have chosen WBCN as a nationally significant epicenter of the collision between rock and commerce.

With all this commotion going on, management lost interest in battling with me over what we should call a bunch of guerrillas half a world away.

I won that battle, and after that pretty much won editorial control over the news. I could do it my way. And every day. That daily radio presence helped build a large following of BCN news listeners. My way consisted of reaching out for voices that weren't heard in the mainstream—area scholars like Noam Chomsky and Howard Zinn, or any number of representatives of movements, activists, community groups and causes to offer their analyses as well as information not available elsewhere in the media. We covered the grass roots leadership as well as the big name pols—the culture as well as the government. Most broadcast news doesn't.

The late Andrew Kopkind, hailed as the leading radical journalist of his generation, worked with our small news team as BCN's news commentator. He played Eric Sevareid to my Walter Cronkite. His brilliance helped us win further recognition and listeners. Andy's life partner John Scagliotti eventually joined the news department too, later becoming my co-news director. When I first broached the idea of Andy coming into the news department, he was unsure because he had a really terrible speech defect. He stuttered and stammered uncontrollably. But I watched him work at it, slowly and methodically. Soon, through sheer willpower, he overcame it. My own Bronx accent didn't always go down well in Boston nor did my difficulty in enunciating the letter *l*. Andy discovered that as long as the audience was interested in what he was saying, they would put up with his stutter. I stopped worrying when I learned that NBC's Tom Brokaw has a problem pronouncing *l*s, not to mention ABC's Barbara Walters, who's been kidded for years for her speech idiosyncrasies.

In addition to three solid daily newscasts, our news department did a weekly four-hour radio talk show, the *Boston Sunday Review*, which I co-hosted, regular documentaries and, for a time, a women's show, a black newsmagazine show, and a program for prisoners called *Lock Up*. Sunday nights, every jail cell in Massachusetts tuned in. John and Andy produced an innovative gay cultural magazine called the *Lavender Hour* and also worked on periodic specials.

The station also helped finance several reporting trips overseas. I went to Cuba and Jamaica, covered the revolution in Portugal, interviewed certified terrorists in Beirut, and even made it to Vietnam. That trip came about at the invitation of Jane Fonda, who was asked to recommend three independent journalists to go to North Vietnam. It was November 1974 and the war was still dragging on.

While I was there "doing radio" I asked to interview Hanoi's most famous radio broadcaster, the woman branded Hanoi Hannah by the American troops, who compared her to WWII's Tokyo Rose. She and her assistant told me they were fans of Pete Seeger and "Nick" Jagger. After I interviewed her, she asked to interview me about my impressions of Vietnam. It was only right that I agree. What I didn't know was that the interview would be intercepted by the CIA, who saw to it that the *Boston Globe*—for whom I was also stringing—got a copy of the transcript. When I returned to Boston, I was the subject of a distorted and inflammatory op-ed page attack on my patriotism for "broadcasting" on Radio Hanoi (which I didn't do—an interview is not a broadcast). I was furious—in part because what I'd said there was mild compared to what I reported every day on BCN.

So much has changed since then that it is not easy today to convey the impact of that war and the coverage of it. I woke up with it every morning. It stared out at me from the newspapers and on TV. There was the body count, the five o'clock follies, the credibility gap, and the cold reality of thousands, and then tens of thousands, of American kids dying without knowing why. I knew people who went and never come back. It invaded my dreams, and radicalized my outlook. I spent years untangling the lies that justified it, and resisting the draft. I saw my resistance as an act of fidelity to our country's founding principles, which were in conflict with our government's pursuit of the war. Today, no one really tries to justify the Vietnam war (it has become an "era") what with trade normalized and our dead memorialized. The right wing has kept the POW flags flying, but most Americans have put the agony of that defeat behind them with acts of denial, avoidance, and in many cases, acceptance.

When I finally did get to go to Vietnam, to feel its suffocating heat and smell its smells, I felt like I was on familiar ground even though I had never been there before. I rode a Russian-made jeep across the DMZ between North and South Vietnam at five miles per hour, zig zagging around bomb craters and land mines. Peasants rebuilding their bombed out villages was a common sight in the countryside, and you could buy baskets made from the colored wires of a multi-million dollar hi-tech electronic barrier (supposely inpenetrable) that our military geniuses had installed to prevent infiltration. Hah! I tried not to be cheerleader for my point of view but to ask personal questions of our hosts; to learn about their families, and reasons for fighting. I was impressed when a Communist Party hardliner told me he felt uncomfortable when he heard about American activists applauding the shooting down of American planes, because they felt it was tragic when anyone died. To him, patriotism was the faith that sustained him. He struggled to understand the American New Left's brand of patriotism, noting nonetheless that in Vietnam it was an article of faith that there was a difference between the American government and the American people. In Saigon, I made a point of visiting the American Embassy and being briefed on the very "enemy" areas I had just visited. I realized how little our government knew about the people they were simultaneously trying to defend and destroy, as I wrote in *Ramparts*. I also learned about the tensions between the North and the South which would lead to so much misery when so many fled "liberation" as boat people seeking refuge in other lands.

In what's now Ho Chi Minh City, I hung out with members of the American press corps, meeting some talented reporters who hated the war, but many others who clung to deep-seated cold war shibboleths. My own journalistic output on the war was always opinionated and anti-war, but never contemptuous of American soldiers, except when they committed atrocities like the ones at My Lai. Sure, the Vietnamese used me; and I used them: to put a human face on the war, and to help me see it for myself. I was scared shitless in Cambodia, and terrified that the South Vietnamese would find out that I had been North. Years later, when I worked in network television, I returned to the subject with stories investigating a babylift flight that crashed, critiquing the movie *Rambo*, that deceived, and explaining Bruce Springsteen's song "Born in the USA," which championed the Vietnam Vet. I also helped the feisty Vietnamese-born but American-educated filmmaker Tiana with her moving film "From Hollywood to Hanoi." The daughter of a hard-line, anti-com-

munist ex-Saigon government propagandist, Tiana went back to
Vietnam to search for her roots and to promote reconciliation
between those who fled and those who stayed. Today, she organizes
cultural tours to a country which has set out on the very capitalist
road it once opposed to the death.

Thanks to Tiana, I returned to Hanoi in 1997 in time to commemorate the twenty-fifth anniversary of Nixon's 1972 Christmas
bombings. The old Vietnam was struggling with the new, with way
over half the population born after the "American War," as they call
it, ended. I watched as a group of Vietnam veterans from the U.S.
and an equal number of the veterans they fought against launched
a bicycle ride from Hanoi to Ho-Chi Minh City as an act of friendship. It was a corporate-sponsored event called the Vietnam Challenge. "We ride the same road" was their slogan. But while corporate
interests are recognizing Vietnam as a market, its people still remain
largely invisible in this country. The image of the Vietnamese people has changed—they are no longer seen as commies or gooks—
but because of virtually no media coverage, our ignorance of the
country remains.

By blending music, political issues, facts, and a justifiable sense of
paranoia into creative newscasts and public affairs shows, the news
department became one of the most respected radio information
sources in our "Woodstock" nation. In 1970 I never thought I'd last
twelve days at BCN, much less twelve years, because I thought of
myself as far too outspoken, far too much the participatory journalist.

This spirit of engagement didn't make for smooth sailing. My
work provoked angry phone calls, letters to the editor, even threats.
There were many skirmishes with authorities. One day, some revolutionary zealots blew up a courthouse in Boston. They sent our
station a copy of their communiqué, which we promptly read over
the air. Shortly after, the FBI dispatched a pair of agents to our
offices to demand the document. I protested to my boss: "Do I have
to hand it over? What about the First Amendment?"

"Fuck the First Amendment," he told me. "Don't you know we are licensed by the federal government? *They* are the Federal Bureau of Investigation. *Federal*, get it!" He ordered me to give them whatever they wanted, pronto, and then went out for a three martini lunch. I thought about it and realized this was not the issue that I wanted to make my last stand on. I wasn't into the politics of dynamite anyway. So I agreed to hand it over.

Two young, identically dressed agents came into my office, which was plastered with political posters, and read the small sign I was standing beside: "A neat desk is a sign of a sick mind." The desk the sign was making fun of was strewn with a small mountain of newspapers, magazines, wire stories, postcards from listeners, reels of tape, and at least one half-eaten tunafish sandwich.

"Honest," I said, "it's here someplace." I spent the next twenty minutes foraging through the mulch for the document. I know I put it there, but I couldn't find it. The communiqué was missing. Honest, it was. I looked and I looked, while they looked at me, shaking their heads, as I looked some more.

Finally one Feebee exclaimed with disgust, "Just send it over to us when you find it." He put his card in my hand and beat a hasty retreat.

I promised I would.

Damn it, somehow I lost the card too. The communiqué never materialized, but thankfully, the FBI had other sources and never came back.

A few years later, when the Freedom of Information Act was passed, I wrote away to the FBI and CIA and got hundreds of pages of heavily censored files chronicling some of my activities over the years. The FBI had been tracking me ever since I wrote a letter to the editor of my college newspaper in 1960 defending the civil rights movement. Throughout that file, the term "Negroes" appeared with a small n. I had fun reading excerpts from those files on the air.

When I first requested my CIA files, I wrote to then-Director William Colby at "The CIA, Langley, Virginia." That letter came back Addressee Unknown. I eventually got some CIA files, even interviewed Colby, whom the antiwar people called Piano Wire because of his leadership of the Phoenix counter-insurgency program in Vietnam that tortured and murdered many prisoners, often tying up prisoners with piano wire. In the spirit of a line from the song that John Lennon wrote for Paul McCartney, I asked him: "How do you sleep?" He was taken aback. He stared at me, then said coldly, "I sleep fine."

I met John Lennon when Yoko Ono played in Boston in 1973, when he was being harassed by the FBI, which was trying to deport him. I interviewed him for WBCN, and there's a funny picture of the two of us. I am laughing and John is pointing to the cord of my microphone, which he noticed I had not plugged into the tape recorder because I was so nervous. My flub endeared me to the two of them, and Yoko invited me to visit her in their apartment in New York's Dakota. Years later, after John's death, I worked with her and their son Sean on a video documentary of a remake of Lennon's anthem, "Give Peace a Chance." It was a musical attempt to stop the Gulf War. (It failed.)

My battles with the intelligence community escalated. I lost a federal lawsuit, brought by the Civil Liberties Union, demanding to see files that the even more secret National Security Agency said they had on me. A federal court in Boston initially ruled against the NSA, but the spooks won on appeal. I've never found out what they had. Bear in mind that in the years when all this surveillance was going on, I was an accredited journalist. In those years, we also learned from Congressional disclosures that the CIA liked certain journalists and had many on their covert payrolls. They got my information without my knowledge or a paycheck.

The most amusing CIA file I obtained was an unidentified informant's report produced when I was in England from 1966-68 as a student at the London School of Economics and a reporter for *Ramparts* magazine, then America's leading muckraking journal. In the following excerpt, [DELETION] refers to blacked-out portions of the document, which the CIA withheld on grounds of national security to protect their agents and sources.

"*Danny Shekter* [sic] [DELETION] about 25 [DELETION] believed to be U.S. citizen [DELETION]. Single. [DELETION]

"Appearance: funky. He is about 6 ft tall with a round face, a very white pimply skin. He wears his hair in a sort of bouffant hairdo more commonly seen in women. Appears to be in good health and to be an energetic person, with organizational skills. (He was able to fill the auditorium of the school.) [DELETION] He speaks rapidly with authority but does not give the impression of being bossy."

Several deletions follow.

"His appearance is strange, but once over the first surprise one can find him amusing, good-natured and happy."

Is that all the CIA thought of me? I thought of myself as a dangerous character. They saw me as a teddy bear. What kind of an *enfant terrible* is that? It was humiliating, until I realized that these are the people whose intelligence wrongly estimated Soviet military readiness for years, misjudged the strength of the Vietnamese communists and miscalculated the staying power of the Shah of Iran. And now they had minimized me as a threat. In many ways, they were the last people to get what was going on.

The document continues: "Around him, one is comfortable," but politically he is "far left, a Marxist." This document—only parts of which were released—concludes: "His main characteristic is that of an odd but friendly person who is strongly devoted to a cause." How embarrassing! Anyway, this is how America's tax money was spent spying on students to gather intelligence, circa 1967.

A few years later, in Boston, a young listener, Yule Mahoney, called with a story. His conscience was bothering him. He disclosed that he had been assigned to report on me to the Boston FBI office. Mahoney had dropped out of a Vermont military academy to dodge the draft. The FBI caught him and offered a choice—inform for us or go to jail. He became a paid confidential informant and I became one of his targets.

"What you were doing," he said. "That was hot stuff." He would listen to me on the air, attend some of the talks I gave in the community, then tell the FBI, who of course could have found this out for free by tuning into 104.1 FM. I did a debriefing with him on his favorite radio station as well as getting him to set up a meeting with his FBI handler in the back of a parking lot in Brookline. A local alternative weekly, the *Real Paper*, hired a photographer with a long lens. We spied on the FBI. The story was called "Meet My Agent."

On another occasion, I got the upper hand on FBI agents who surrounded my home one morning with a warrant for the arrest of one of my housemates, Bill Zimmerman. Bill was accused of masterminding an airlift of food and other supplies to protesting Indians who had occupied Wounded Knee, South Dakota, a memorial to the Lakota Indians who were slaughtered there in 1891 while resisting an American military attack. In the 1970s, the American Indian Movement was continuing that fight and was now besieged by a small army of FBI agents who had cut off their access to the outside. Bill, a licensed pilot, and some friends took their solidarity to the skies, staging a daring resupply effort—and got away with it.

The FBI had tracked him to our communal home of sorts at 38 Dartmouth Street in Somerville. My trusty retriever Sophie saw them coming first, and despite the weapons they displayed, was soon fetching the balls they threw to her as they encircled our house. They actually had sharpshooters at the ready during their early morning raid.

We let them in, not wanting our front door destroyed. I demanded to see a warrant. They didn't have one but claimed it had been issued. (The lack of a proper warrant—which had *not* been issued—subsequently got the case dismissed.) Bill was busted, but in a moment of quick thinking I turned on my BCN tape recorder and captured the whole confrontation on audio. The Boston College student newspaper published a transcript that gives the flavor of the times:

Bob Smith, FBI agent: We have a warrant for other people. Are you a resident of this dwelling?

Danny Schechter: You have a warrant for who? [Disruption] Can you tell me who you have a warrant for?

FBI: We don't have to tell you anything.

DS: You don't have to tell me anything? Can I see the warrant you have?

FBI: We don't have the warrant with us, but it's been issued.

DS: You have a warrant but you don't have a warrant. You are inside this house—

FBI: Now, listen, we're not gonna stand here and explain anything—

Then I was repeatedly accused of interfering with justice. I got great sound, which was soon being heard in the four states that received BCN's signal. I intercut a comedy recording that said "This is L. Patrick Gray of the FBI. I know I am in there and I am coming in after me."

Not all our stories were that dramatic, until Boston became embroiled in a busing crisis that felt like a scene out of Little Rock in the 1950s. The images of snarling mobs and rocks being tossed at black students stirred the world. In 1974, during my visit to Vietnam, I was, to my surprise, asked to explain South Boston's resistance by none other than Le Duc Tho, North Vietnam's Nobel Peace Prize-winning Paris peace talks negotiator. (He refused to accept the prize because he had to share it with Henry Kissinger, whose Vietnam policies over the years were anything but peaceful.)

BCN's support for racial tolerance was not appreciated by all our listeners. In fact, at one point I even received a death threat. Just for the heck of it, I reported it to my old friends at the Boston FBI office. They did nothing and I figured my letter merely enlarged my file.

BCN in those years was not always an oasis of enlightenment. Sexism was alive and well, so much so that women's groups invaded the station and released a box full of young chickens to protest against an announcer who repeatedly called women "chicks." The world of rock 'n' roll was rather retarded on these issues. "The place has become a haven for large-breasted nineteen-year-old girls who coo and murmur on demand," one of the women DJs who left BCN to pursue a successful TV and radio network career wrote to me. "The time I decided it was time for me to move on with my career and life was the day that the program director said to me, 'Make the little boys want to fuck you.' Unbelievable?" Sadly, it wasn't.

All of us on the BCN staff kept pushing the envelope to keep the spirit and style of the station alive even after more commercial competitors tried to sound like us without doing as much, especially in news. The management always kept pushing back, trying to steer us in a more mainstream and conservative direction. In 1977, when I took a leave for the Nieman Fellowship at Harvard, the then station manager Klee Dobra, who had a background in government intelligence work, saw an opportunity. He replaced me with a black woman out of Texas named Abby Kendrick. That looked like a progressive move until the audience realized that she was a pro-lifer and tilted towards right wing politics. A nice person, she soon realized she was in the wrong place, and didn't last long.

In 1979 a new media company, New York-based Infinity Broadcasting, bought BCN. They marched in one morning and fired nineteen staffers, including me. A few days later, those employees that remained straggled out, leaving the station to import out-of-town scabs and security guards. We launched a three-week strike that galvanized people throughout the area, dried up advertising, and became a big local story. The fact that we had a union forced them to negotiate.

The management, reported the *Real Paper*, "really had no choice. The rallies and benefits, the streams of strike endorsements from bands, other radio stations and unions, and the petitions coming in from towns everywhere around Boston had a major impact. But the real punch was advertisers. Virtually all the local advertisers and record companies pulled their commercials off the air."

The union brought me in to head up its negotiating team. In the end I helped convince the new management that it was in their interest to settle on our terms since the station's uniqueness was its biggest asset. They did. We won the strike. I wrote separate victory statements for both the union and management. Impressed, the company hired our strike leaders as their managers. It was the most successful broadcast strike I've ever heard of. "It was a famous victory, everyone agreed," reported the *New York Times* two hundred miles to the south on March 13, 1979, almost eleven years to the day that BCN first burst onto the airwaves. "Boston had its WBCN back, an event as important in some circles as if New York's WBAI or Channel 13 had escaped dismemberment and returned to the air."

We were back, but so were all the commercial pressures. We had, as my BCN colleague Andy Kopkind noted in a thoughtful assessment in *Working Papers*, "stretched industry mores and federal regulations about as far as any commercial broadcaster in the country. The line between selling out and cashing in is hard to draw, and more often than not, the effect deemed the most 'commercial' is merely the one you can get away with." He understood the limits of what we were doing and the larger forces at play, but also the joy of creating space for meaningful work. "A real radical culture will not be televised, taped, and rerun," he concluded. "It will be live, and the media it spawns will organize and inform the culture, not supplant it."

Over the years, WBCN changed along with the culture, although some of its style and spirit survived. Activism receded after Watergate and the war. Disco fractured the audience. Punk drove out the old rockers. Some BCN jocks left to join other radio stations that challenged us in the marketplace with a similar sound, no political edge and a slicker, more commercial format. An alternative music scene soon emerged with attitude replacing activism and pose substituting for politics.

BCN responded by becoming more mainstream, tightly formatted and much more commercial. The news, which had always made the station different, became disposable and was scaled way back. I'm told that in 1982, WBCN had a reporter or a stringer covering the Israeli invasion of Lebanon. The reporting offended a conservative pro-Israeli media watchdog group who considered it biased and protested to the FCC. Reportedly, in response to the complaint, Infinity decided to cut the news department altogether.

In 1993, the station celebrated its twenty-fifth anniversary as a cultural force and symbol of rock 'n' roll. I was not surprised to learn that Infinity, which had used the station to build its nationwide chain and reputation, wouldn't put up a penny to celebrate its survival. Fred Goodman, describing the party in *Mansion on the Hill*, puts the station down by quoting a reflective DJ who admits he sold out, took the money, and buried his conscience. I am sure some staffers felt that way. What impressed me about the event was how much the station and its political identity meant to all the fans and bands who came through, and how a spirit of family and community still flickered. Everyone knew that their era had gone, that the market was in command, but all spoke of their days at BCN as the best of their lives. To this day, I probably get more praise for my work on the radio in Boston than for the "big time" jobs that followed.

BCN is still there, somewhat of an anomaly, still special, but not what it used to be. (I guess I'm not what I used to be either.) Business thinking long ago took over and demographics dominate. "Rock 'n' roll is here to pay," as my friend Reebee Garafalo's book had it years earlier. BCN aimed for males ages eighteen to twenty-four as its prime audience, attracting many much younger. Sports and macho posturing became more overt. Howard Stern's sexist and sophomoric ravings were imported from New York by Infinity, which had turned Howard into a national celebrity. In 1996, after Infinity purchased its forty-sixth station, the company announced plans to launch the Howard Stern Radio Network, which promised twenty-four hours a day of talk and music from jocks picked by Stern. (Happily, the idea was dropped as Stern moved into the movies, and now into TV.)

Howardization had become the latest product of media concentration in the radio industry. Infinity settled an obscenity complaint against Stern by "voluntarily" giving the FCC $1.7 million in fines. You can imagine how much money Howard was bringing in if they would do that. "But Stern was worth the money to Infinity," writes Robin Wilonsky in a profile in L.A.'s *New Times* that portrays him as bundle of contradictions whose public persona is an act fueled by personal neurosis and careerist calculation. "It was a minute amount compared to how much it brings into the company and affiliates every year. Stern won't disclose how much he makes in each of his markets; after all, this is the man who claims to have dropped out of the New York gubernatorial race because he didn't want to disclose his financial records." For all his outrageousness, Stern knows how to please his corporate bosses. One of his former colleagues told me his show carries, on average, twenty-five commercials an hour, while the average program only runs twelve.

Thanks in part to Stern, Infinity's profits mushroomed, until Westinghouse Broadcasting shelled out $3.7 billion to acquire the company. As part of the deal, Infinity's president Mel Karmazin took over Westinghouse's eighty-three-station CBS radio division (in Los Angeles alone, the nation's largest radio market, CBS owns eight stations), later was named to take over all of the CBS television stations, and within a year of that took over the presidency of CBS. I think it is fair to say that it was the acquisition of WBCN that started Infinity's long march to monopoly. We at BCN had long fantasized about remaking the media. Who would have thought that BCN's bosses would end up going from the control room of a freak station to the board room of a once great network?

In 1995, WBCN slid further in a mainstream direction by becoming the radio home of the New England Patriots. By then the difference between FM and AM broadcasting had all but dissolved. BCN had, in large part, become the ugly radio it started out opposing, although its turn in the mid-'90s to alternative music and new bands projected an insurgent image.

Handling the tension between commercialism and conscious-ness was always BCN's central challenge. Scoop Nisker, who worked at our sound-alike sister station KSAN in San Francisco, wrote in his memoir *If You Don't Like the News, Go Out and Make Some of Your Own*, "KSAN couldn't escape the basic contradiction: we were attacking the establishment while being supported by it and worse, our rebel broadcasting was beginning to make big profits for a giant corporation." Soon most of the original rock stations tightened, then changed formats. KSAN was gone.

When I was on the air, DJs often played a preproduced musical insert to intro a golden oldie. It featured an AM announcer's voice, proclaiming "One step forward—into the past." WBCN took that step, the ultimate one, on April Fools Day 1996, when it announced that Howard Stern's show would be moving from his rebroadcast slot at night to a live simulcast in the morning. That meant the sta-tion's longtime soul and defining spirit, my former partner in crime, the "morning mishigas" man Charles Laquidara, who invented many of the on-air shticks that Stern, as a BU student and early BCN listener, appropriated, was ordered into exile at another Infin-ity-owned Boston station, the classic rocker WZLX. Charles was hurt but well-compensated. Many of his listeners traveled with him. He beat Stern in the first ratings book released after the move, and told me he finds his new station more like the old BCN.

Stern's ascendance, facilitated by the promotional push by Infin-ity on the radio side and Murdoch on the print side (through his ownership of the company that published, some say created, Howard's best-selling books) has to be viewed politically as well as culturally. "Howard is much more conservative than people think," his publisher Judith Regan told C-SPAN's Brian Lamb in April 1996. "He doesn't entertain in a conservative way, but that's how he thinks." Stern in fact makes no secret of his political attitudes and conservative libertarian leanings. Although most commentators rarely take his political messages seriously, his audience does. The voice of the angry white man, his tirades are rife with sexism, race-baiting and homophobia, which help reinforce prejudices and encourage races and communities to oppose each other. His fans think it's funny.

As the old wave of listeners moved on, a new wave of listeners took over. Our We generation gave way to the Me Generation, then Generation X. Meanwhile, MTV displaced rock radio on the cutting edge of youth-oriented broadcasting. At the same time, the Internet began emerging with realtime audio capability, offering diverse radio programming. If history is any guide, Infinity's (now Westinghouse's) monopoly will not last for infinity.

Whenever I think of BCN and the glory days of its radio revolution, I recall one of my pal Abbie Hoffman's comments about the '60s: "We were young, we were reckless, arrogant, silly, headstrong—and we were right. I regret nothing." And, at least at WBCN, we were on the air.

In 1997, I decided to try to get back on the radio, at least once a week. I did a demo for a show like the very successful *Boston Sunday Review* that ran for years. It was played for Lee Abrams, a high-priced, super-successful radio consultant partly responsible for the trend toward tightly formatted commercial radio. His comments were generous toward me personally but kind of sum up everything that I consider wrong with radio today: "The feel seems too organic. Kinda '60s hip, which isn't what radio is looking for.... Needs to move faster...too in-depth...think *USA Today*...I'd kill all references to NPR or even the line 'commercial'—that will scare radio guys...they'll think this is 'too liberal/Public Radio' when you need to push this as a ratings and revenue generator."

Thanks, Lee, for being candid, but it is this kind of conventional wisdom that makes radio today sound so soulless and so cleansed of sentiments to the left of Rush Limbaugh.

Stay tuned.

CHAPTER 2

ELEVATING JOURNALISM
(THROUGH HARVARD YARD)

*W*hen I fell into radio, I never thought of my work in career terms because I saw myself primarily as a megaphone for ideas. My journalism was a mix of explanatory features, social criticism, media analysis, pop culture agitprop, populist advocacy and hard-nosed investigative reporting. I had a point of view and didn't try to hide it. It was the dark days of Vietnam and like many in my generation, I was at war with the war.

After seven years of daily dissecting, the war ended, wallowing in Watergate was over and the counterculture was fading. Nixon was history and Carter was no Nixon. Punk was in and I felt on the way out at a rock 'n' roll radio station that was becoming uncomfortable with serious news.

Meanwhile, I was starting to think seriously about a real career. Spontaneity can only take you so far. In my personal life, a collective living arrangement had given way to marriage and the birth of my daughter, Sarah Debs. The generational divide I had always celebrated was catching up with me. As Abbie Hoffman put it: "We went from not trusting anyone over thirty to not trusting anyone under thirty." In 1977 I was thirty-four and decided it was time to get serious if I was to be taken seriously as a journalist.

But how to make the transition to another position in journalism? Other broadcasting outlets in Boston were not exactly knocking down my door. I was perceived as too hip and probably too radical for National Public Radio, which was still a startup, yearning for network legitimacy. I decided that if I was to stay in broadcasting, I'd have to try TV. As I was driving through Harvard Square one morning I realized the opportunity was staring me in the face.

Harvard is the symbol of mainstream respectability. And they have a home for burned-out reporters in midcareer. It is called the Nieman Fellowship, one of the most distinguished fraternities in journalism. But would they have me as a member? And even if they would, could I, after all those years of hurling invective at the Establishment, feel comfortable in their midst? That question again: Would I sell out or sell in? The thought preoccupied me for about a half a second before I applied.

The Nieman is like an Oscar, except without the statue. Over the years, the program has rewarded many of the biggest names in the media world with a paid sabbatical year in Cambridge. You study whatever you want and take part in an ongoing schmooze-athon in the form of thrice-weekly discussion groups and cocktail parties. The booze is free and flowing. Harvard calls it "elevating the standards of journalism."

Despite Groucho Marx's warning against any club that would have him as a member, I applied and was accepted. I was told that the Boston press was amazed that a maverick of my ilk would get the nod over distinguished *Globe* columnists or *Christian Science Monitor* correspondents who usually monopolized the local slots. The Nieman enabled me to take a leave from WBCN and also leave a countercultural community that was splintering into warring factions. What had once been a movement was dividing along gender and other lines into a smattering of subcultures.

I ended up loving Harvard as a vacation destination. It offered a chance to think, make friends and get paid for not working. At one lunch at the Institute of Politics, we introduced ourselves. There was

Harvard dean Jonathan Moore, who called himself a liberal Republican. There was Ray Price, Tricky Dick's speechwriter, who called himself a Nixon Republican. And then there was me. I introduced myself as a Marxist Republican. That comment made the papers.

During the Nieman year we discussed and debated issues of journalistic ethics and the future of the business. All the network presidents came to town and repeated old refrains about how they were just giving the people what they want. Working columnists like Jack Anderson chastised what he called cocktail journalists, reporters turning into publicists. Writer Nora Ephron said that in Washington "it is considered bad form to question the status quo too intently."

I spent the semester scribbling notes and quotes like "You can be out of touch with news because you are in touch with social reality." One such reality was race. The late Bob Maynard, who had a distinguished career in Washington before remaking the *Oakland Tribune*, told us that "the press is the single most segregated of our major institutions. Of forty thousand professionals, only eight hundred are not white." That was 1977. The newsroom is still one of the most segregated institutions in America.

I also met some of the journalists I admired. Watergate investigator Carl Bernstein dropped by to tell us about his investigation of the CIA's covert infiltrations into the media. Wilfred Burchett, the Australian who covered the Vietnam War from the Vietnamese side, told us he wasn't a Marxist: "You'd have to study Marx and I found it boring." He shared three lessons for good reporting from his long career: (1) Be there and check your facts; (2) have independence; and (3) don't do what they tell you.

Throughout the year on the Harvard dole, we also lunched with luminaries as diverse as Rupert Murdoch and I. F. Stone, traded questions with poet Allen Ginsberg, mumbled with *Rolling Stone's* Jann Wenner and took expenses-paid trips to Canada and Japan.

One incident during that trip to Japan underscored a pervasive journalistic anxiety among my colleagues toward even the appearance of political engagement. Our guides, conservative representatives of a most conservative government, took us to Hiroshima to see the town devastated by the first nuclear bomb ever used in warfare. For many years, the townspeople, who, we learned, actually generate 10 percent of their electricity from nuclear power, appealed to the world to banish nuclear weapons. Their slogan is No More Hiroshimas—a universal cry that avoids criticizing any country.

As we prepared to visit the Peace Park, at ground zero of the blast, we were advised that official visiting delegations are expected to bring an offering of flowers as a tribute to the ordinary people who were melted there into the next world. It is considered a sign of respect, a ritual in a ritual-conscious country that all political parties, right and left, adhere to. Sensing a reluctance among some of us to comply, our ever-polite hosts bought a bouquet for us to take as our pro forma peace offering.

A bitter debate about the gesture erupted in our ranks. Some of my classmates, led by Fred Barnes, a born-again conservative then with the *Baltimore Sun*, later the *New Republic*, and now a TV pundit and editor at Murdoch's *Weekly Standard*, absolutely refused. He argued that it was an inappropriate act for journalists who must be perceived as neutral. Besides, we were probably being used by the Japanese for some nefarious propaganda purpose. When I looked at Fred, I thought of a remark by a slightly more famous reporter also from Baltimore, H. L. Mencken, who said, "All journalists are ignoramuses and proud of it."

I couldn't believe it. Who in the world openly supports the use of nuclear weapons? We weren't being asked to protest the bomb, just express compassion for its civilian casualties. We were guests in another society for whom nuclear war was not an abstraction or even a political question, but a human and moral issue. Is it really inappropriate for journalists to express human emotions and a desire for peace?

Don't forget, we were on a study tour, not on assignment.

The Japanese representatives were amazed that intelligent people would even debate this. They looked at us like creatures from another planet, treating us with scorn without losing their manners. In the end, a few of us, including myself, brought the flowers to the eternal flame. The others maintained a suspicious vigil behind us. Their real fear: What if some photographer captured the moment and sent the photo to their editors? They might be branded as peaceniks or worse.

In the adjacent A-bomb museum, which scrupulously detailed the bomb's damage without even raising the debate over its use, there was a guestbook for visitors to sign their names and share their comments. I paged through it, noting remorseful and moving sentiments from visitors from all around the world. The only crude and dismissive comments were American. "You asked for it" was common, along with "Remember Pearl Harbor."

It is obvious that this insensitivity is not just an individual problem but an expression of cultural conditioning. In December 1994, the United States Postal Service planned to issue a stamp showing the mushroom cloud over Hiroshima to commemorate the end of World War II. Protests the world over led to its being withdrawn. Some newspaper columnists spoke of the Japanese as being touchy.

A month later, the Smithsonian Institution scaled back a planned exhibition on the *Enola Gay*, the airplane used to drop the bomb on Hiroshima, because of objections by right-wing and veterans groups to an accompanying text explaining the reasons so many historians now believe that the bomb was not necessary to end World War II. The secretary of the Smithsonian noted a desire not to offend, commenting that visitors "were not looking for analysis." Journalists who for years had failed to set the historical record straight—or even debate the issue—dutifully reported the decision.

In marked contrast, in Japan at the same time, a leading publisher shut down a magazine after it was criticized for carrying an article alleging that the Holocaust was propaganda. The company not only ceased publication but issued an apology asserting that the editors and workers at *Marco Polo* "accept the responsibility for publishing this biased article." I couldn't imagine such an action, much less an apology or any sign of collective responsibility, from an America media corporation.

Nineteen seventy-seven was the fortieth anniversary of the Nieman program. The year started with a gala banquet at Boston's Museum of Science, amidst the dinosaurs and exhibits on how the hipbone is connected to the kneebone. Henry Kissinger, who had just departed as President Ford's secretary of state thanks to Jimmy Carter's election, was the guest of honor in what was to be his Harvard homecoming after all those years playing America's Machiavelli. His talk was billed as off the record.

This pissed off Harvard's student journalists who considered him a war criminal and demanded entry. When denied the right to cover a Harvard event because it was being held off-campus, they threw up a picket line. It was quite a spectacle: journalists-in-training confronting journalists who had made it into the highest circles.

The editor of the Harvard *Crimson* recognized me as I tried to slip around the picket line with my new suit and new wife. "How can journalists have an off-the-record soirée with that pig?" she asked me. "How can you, of all people, cross our picket line?" In response I whimpered that as a new Nieman I was expected to be there; then, thinking quickly, I told her that if I could I'd ask Kissinger the question she wanted to ask. She scribbled something on the back of a business card and I put it in my pocket.

Kissinger's presence inflamed some of the folks on the inside too. Peppered among the gowns and well-tailored haberdashery draped over this media elite were a few malcontents. One brought a sign: "Cambodia was off the record too." It drew laughs and hisses—for rudeness. Most of the questioners were polite, though, even fraternal. Henry responded by calling them by their first names, remembering this one from the shuttle to Damascus, that one from long nights at the Paris peace talks. You definitely had a feeling that most of the people present were members of the same club. *New York Times* columnist Anthony Lewis tried a tough question on

Angola, but Kissinger parried and swept it away easily. He was a master of obfuscation. He was so damn charming.

I was beginning to steam and shot my hand up.

Jim Thomson, then Nieman director—known as the curator as if we were museum relics or part of some journo-zoo—saw my finger in the air, nodded with a knowing smile and saved me for last. When called on, I stood and explained the deal I'd made with the pickets outside, reaching into my suit jacket for their card with the question. I hadn't taken the time to read it. The room quieted down after my warm-up. Kissinger stared at me, as if trying to remember who I was. We had had a rather strange encounter once before when with a smile I asked him for WBCN if he was prepared to make a confession for his crimes and misdemeanors. The good doctor had smiled back, saw that I had a tape recorder concealed in my hand and said: "You are such a sveet boy. I am too culpable to make a confession." That was two years earlier. You can bet we played that tape over and over again.

"Dr. Kissinger, here is their question," I said, underscoring the word *their*. For some intuitive reason, I began to sweat.

I was standing. He was standing. Our eyes locked. The room hushed.

"Yes?"

Sitting at Henry's side was his teenage son David, who eventually became a journalist for *Variety* before moving up to becoming an executive at a Hollywood studio. The table was flanked by Secret Service men.

"Vell?" Henry was waiting.

I paused. My knees shook. I was about to eat shit. "How, these students want to know, can you justify yourself to your own children after your policies caused six million deaths in Indochina?"

There was a gasp in the room. David looked up at his dad.

A trickle—make that a *tiny* trickle—of applause was barely heard amidst the louder sneers and boos directed at me.

Now it was Kissinger's turn to steam.

"Meest-er...Schechter," he began, spitting out the words. Richard Nixon had kept Kissinger in the White House basement all during his first term because of that accent. Nixon thought he sounded like a Nazi. I came to think of him in those terms too, not because of what he sounds like but because of what he did. "It is easy to challenge people who must make tough decisions. I vill not stand here and be lectured by you or any-vun. I have no apologies to make."

On that huffy note and with an officious thank you, he turned and walked out, pissed. Almost before the applause receded, he was out the door. Plans for a post-dinner VIP reception had to be scratched. A number of Niemans were soon out of *their* seats and heading my way.

"How could you?"

"How ill-mannered!"

"That was a disgusting question!"

"Didn't you see his son there?"

I closed my eyes. Why couldn't I have just shut up? My career was finished, I told myself. I had blown it and blown it big, offending my colleagues and embarrassing myself in front of the most powerful group of journalists on the planet. Now I would never win their acceptance or future employment. A friend joked: "You will never work in this town again." The mainstream had for me become a mud stream.

Unknown to us, a *Crimson* reporter had snuck into the event with his dad. He wrote up the encounter the next day. The off-the record embargo broken, so did the *Boston Globe*. Embarrassment turned to notoriety.

Some months later, Marvin Kalb referred to the incident in a *New York Times Magazine* piece about how the ghosts of Vietnam continued to haunt Kissinger. My question gave me a new status.

That made me feel better. I hate to admit it but the positive attention led to my changing my tune. I was no longer remorseful.

Now I began to claim credit for giving the hated Henry a well-deserved moment of indigestion. Heartburn for the heartless!

Today I can joke about that incident, but despite it, that year at Harvard made the difference. It conferred credibility by association. I did shed some of my more mechanistic formulations about journalism and journalists. My confidence boosted after cavorting with the profession's elite; I was ready to take on the big time. I didn't change Harvard and it didn't change me, but the pedigree helped.

And soon, I did work again. I discovered the promised land of television news.

CHAPTER 3

GOING LOCAL:
BREAKING INTO THE BUSINESS
AND BEING BROKEN BY IT

*M*y first TV job, in 1978, was as a summer replacement on WGBH/Channel 2, the PBS station in Boston best known for Julia Child, *Masterpiece Theater* and an anglophilia that plays well on Brattle Street, Cambridge's most upscale neighborhood. A consortium of blueblood, Boston-area educational institutions, including Harvard, holds the license for a TV station that has come to symbolize both production quality and cultural elitism.

PBS in those years was often referred to as the Petroleum Broadcasting Service because of all the oil companies that underwrote BBC imports to sweeten their public images. Channel 2 had a ten o'clock news show, and my Nieman credential became my passport to an on-air reporting gig.

A Nieman alumnus, journalist Paul Solmon, the brilliant economics analyst for the *PBS News Hour with Jim Lehrer* (and for years with the *MacNeil-Lehrer News Hour*) had won an air slot on Channel 2's local news. A former editor of a Boston-area alternative newspaper, he was willing to help with my tryout and teach me a few of the basics.

My first taping was embarrassing. I thought for sure I could easily do on-camera standups like all those bubble-heads so pervasive on TV. But I quickly realized that it is tough to look natural and make it seem effortless. I froze. I stuttered. I lost eye contact with the camera. It took me at least thirty takes to recite just one paragraph of copy. Paul was patient until I finally produced a tape he could show the station.

I got the job, and lots of experience covering a wide range of stories for a program anchored by ex-*New York Times*man Christopher Lydon. It was an excellent show and viewers protested when Channel 2 cancelled it ten years later, citing its costs. Lydon now does radio, the medium I left to do TV.

As I was driving to work on my first day as a TV newsman, Boston's all-news radio was reporting a multiple murder in downtown Beantown. It seemed clear that this would be the big news of the day on the TV newscasts, because when a story bleeds, it usually leads. I wondered how public television would cover it.

So I asked the assignment editor.

His memorable response: "We don't do crime."

Neither had I for the most part when I was dissecting news daily, but this story was hard to ignore. It was a sensational mess. Five dead. Bodies splattered all over the place. And one of the deceased was a former local TV investigative reporter. He was supposedly writing a book on the mob and ended up in the wrong place at the wrong time.

The WGBH assignment editor was still uninterested. "Just hang out today and watch what we do," he advised.

In a few hours, his boss, Judy Stoia, the managing editor, decided to do what they "never do," and that I would become the one to do it. And do it as that night's lead story.

It was crime time in prime time, and the word Mafia helped inflate the story's importance. But I was skeptical. At first hearing, it didn't sound like a mob massacre to me because it was too bloody, too public. Most Mafia hits in New England involved floaters, single bodies with concrete shoes dumped into Boston Harbor or the quarry in suburban Quincy. The real wise guys rarely turned so many people into Swiss cheese in a public barroom. This case smelled more like a drug deal gone sour.

So I decided to call a local drug lawyer, Joe Oteri, a smooth, silver-haired defense attorney who had publicly called for the legalization of marijuana and was notorious locally for defending drug dealers. I knew Joe because his pro-pot politics were popular with the kids who listened to WBCN and I'd interviewed him. So I wasn't surprised when he took my call. I *was* surprised by his saying that he couldn't talk about the case on the phone. He was upset and asked if I'd meet him in person.

You bet. Hey, maybe I was on to something.

Oteri had learned from friends on the police force that it *was* a drug-related killing and not a mob war. Some jittery young coke-fiends sought to rip off a drug delivery. They were challenged. A gun battle ensued. The punks didn't want anyone to know who they were. Bang bang. No living witnesses. In the scheme of things, this was not exactly Pulitzer Prize material, except for two personal and unexpected developments:

First, I broke the real story on the air before anyone else. Second, it turned out that the ex-reporter turned victim was preparing to produce a TV talk show for Oteri on a local independent TV station. They had just received the go-ahead to do a pilot. It was to be Joe's big break—but now his TV guy was six feet under.

"Hey, Danny," Joe said, "you're in TV now. Why don't you produce the pilot? You know how, right?"

I had been in TV at that point for less than twenty-four hours. I said, "Sure, I know how. I'm in TV now."

Overnight, I was a producer, one step up the TV food chain, working for commercial TV, WLVI, Channel 56, while freelancing with the public station WGBH. I now had two TV jobs. In essence, I got my new job through a Magnum 357.

Having left a $300-a-week, on-air gig at PBS for twice as much money as a behind-the-scenes operative in commercial broadcasting, I had to learn how to make TV shows.

The *Joe Oteri Show* presented an opportunity, and I seized it. The series was soon picked up and ran for ninety minutes a week in five major markets. We interviewed a strange mix of guests, including Abbie Hoffman, who came on the air when he was on the run. He had had plastic surgery and kept scratching his nose. He was manic as hell but funny, talking about his environmental activism under another name (Barry Freed) that had won him letters of commendation from New York Senator Daniel Patrick Moynihan. When asked what he missed most in the underground, he responded quickly: a good corned beef sandwich on rye. That was Abbie.

My boss, Lucie Salhany, loved to pluck stories and guest prospects from the *National Enquirer*. She had a gut tabloid sensibility and in fact went on to become one of the creators of *Entertainment Tonight* and *Hard Copy*, then chair of the Fox Network, and finally headed up United Paramount Network, at which point she was probably the top woman program executive in all of television. (In May 1997, the pressures and backbiting of Hollywood caught up with Lucie. She announced that she was quitting her UPN post and was moving back to Boston to set up her own consulting firm.) She started her career as a secretary at a local station in the Midwest but her success in Boston became her ticket to Hollywood. Although a local station programmer, she became well-known as an industry dynamo and was soon president of NATPE, the National Association of Television Program Executives. She was and is a big deal in the business.

I didn't always love Lucie. She and I fought constantly over what subjects to treat and how. I'd come in with issues. She'd suggest individuals. I brought in experts from the *Nation* and the *New York Times* while she looked for victims in *People* and the supermarket tabs. I wanted to use the media to inform and enlighten. She wanted to entertain. I gravitated toward information. She cared about emotions. She was sure that personal stories and gossip is what grabs people, because they grabbed her. I had to concede that her points were not always wrong. She was also the boss. So we compromised. The show's segments soon included both points of view. I had my experts and advocates, and she had her clairvoyants, UFO abductees and hookers. I have to admit that she was right in many respects: the personal dimension did animate many of the issues we discussed.

Lucie understood television. I was learning.

The show ended up winning a New England Regional Emmy. Massachusetts Governor Michael Dukakis presented me with the gold-plated trophy after I nearly tripped while racing disbelievingly to the stage. I remember my speech because it got a big laugh: "Ladies and gentlemen, last week in my WBCN commentary, I denounced these awards as a ritual in which this industry honors itself in a self-indulgent and self-promotional manner." Deep breath. "Well, I'd like to take that back. This is the best process of program evaluation known to man."

Cheers.

Our joy was short-lived. The *Joe Oteri Show* was abruptly canceled because Lucie's bosses at Field Communications were under pressure to run more than Saturday morning cartoons for kids and couldn't afford both decent children's programming and Joe's show.

Joe didn't complain. His drug dealer defense business was booming. In those days Joe spent a lot of time battling with the Feds, who wanted to seize his sizable retainers, which he usually took in cash. They considered his fees evidence, money derived from criminal enterprises. Joe took his payments upfront because drug dealers tend not to pay if they've been convicted. He didn't like the drug warriors, but he did win over juries. He knew how to talk to ordinary people, which was what made him so effective both as a lawyer and as a television host.

No sooner was that series canceled than I received another call, this time from a program executive at WCVB, the ABC affiliate in

Boston. The station had won its license through a challenge filed against the Boston Herald Traveler company, which had parlayed ownership of the town's afternoon newspaper into the license for WHDH-TV, a local station that made lots of money and plowed very little of it back into local news. Its practices were often criticized and complained about to the FCC. Little was done until it came out that the owner of the Herald Traveler company had had lunch with a crony in Washington who happened to be on the FCC just when the commission was hearing a challenge to HDH's license. The man swore up and down that they never talked about the station or the challenge, but it didn't matter. The appearance of insider dealing did. WHDH lost its FCC license.

A book was written about the case called the *$100 Million Dollar Lunch*, because that's what that major market TV license was then worth. A group of well-connected, Boston-area Harvard types and technocrats challenged the license, pledging to air more local programming, and the FCC transferred the station to them. They changed the call letters to WCVB, moved their facility to the suburbs and turned Channel 5 into a nationally known broadcaster.

Within a few years, these owners—who had paid nothing for the right to broadcast—would become millionaires when they sold the station and sold out their faith in localism, to nonlocals. WCVB went for $110 million the first time around to Metromedia billionaire John Kluge, who kept it a few years then quadrupled his money by inducing the Hearst Corporation to shell out over $450 million for it. This's why they say that owning a TV license is a license to print money.

WCVB's reputation for local programming was what made it unique. That reputation was built on a combination of some innovative shows, smart management and excellent PR. Channel 5's moment of glory came when the *New York Times* Sunday Arts and Leisure section called it the "best local station in America." And what made it best? The fact that it did more local programming than any other station. That's where I came in.

To produce more local programming than anyone else meant opening up time periods generally devoted to syndicated shows to self-produced fare. One of those time periods was the late night block. This led to a brainstorm: Why not go live while competitors are running B movies and syndicated reruns?

Why not, indeed?

"How would you like to produce ten hours of live programming a week?" I was asked by Steve Schlow, a program executive.

I was startled. "Ten hours a week? That's like the *Today Show.* That's a big deal."

"Well," he replied, "it's not exactly the *Today Show.* Our plan is to utilize our existing studios that are now dark at that hour for a low-budget, live, late night show."

He wasn't kidding about late *or* low-budget.

The show was called *Five All Night, Live All Night* and would go on the air just after the ABC network ended its national feed. That meant a two A.M. start Tuesdays through Thursdays, 12:40 A.M. on Fridays and 1:30 A.M. on Saturdays. I'd have Sunday and Monday off. I was hired to produce an old colleague of mine, Matt Siegel, a popular, congenial but not particularly well-informed WBCN DJ. He didn't always have a lot to say but he could say it with style. Burning passions? Nah. He wanted to give late-night advice to lovers and kibitz with guests. He made a sweet and sometime comic interviewer. We balanced one another.

And worked well together. I would arrive at the station in the afternoon and stay until we went off the air, a twelve- to fourteen-hour shift. I'd write the show, book guests and brief Matt. We'd have our preshow meetings in the station cafeteria, reading over the copy I'd written and kicking the soda machines. Matt liked to prance around and yell a lot, to loosen up and lighten up. Sometimes he would yell at me, especially when I threw a heavy political subject into shows that were pretty light.

Once I brought on Howard Zinn, the Boston University historian who had rewritten the history of the U.S. from the people's point of view in A *People's History of the United States.* Matt told me he hadn't had a chance to read the 573-page volume, which we had only received that morning, and was never a good history student in the first place. I tried to fill him in on two hundred years of key points in twenty minutes. He thought I was nuts. He may have been right.

It didn't always work, but overall, critical and audience reaction was favorable. "FANLAN (the show's acronym) is not strong on production values," one viewer said, "but it's got spirit and warmth." Wrote *Panorama* magazine, "The show comes across as a combination of ragged but sincere film student movie, *Groove Tube*-type video improv, underground cabaret, off-Broadway experimental theater and radio talk show." "I'm addicted to the show's live-ness," enthused Angeleynn Grant of Providence's *New Paper*, "bad mikes, forgotten lines, no-show guests or half-awake illiterate callers and the immediacy and intimacy of it all." She referred to me as "a blur of motion."

The show also received national attention, something few local programs attract. *Broadcasting* magazine reported that "the blend of spider monkeys, gossip columnists and financial writers is working. It reports eight thousand phone-ins on a recent Sunday morning." At that time, thirty-second spots went for $50 each in late late night, so it was bringing in $3,750 a week or $192,400 a year. Station manager Bennet told *Broadcasting*, "And even if it brought in only a hundred thousand dollars a year, it would be worth it to say we're doing it." I was then making under $30,000 a year as a hotshot producer.

The show, in those days before Letterman and Leno, was unprecedented in commercial TV. We had a token $100-a-night budget, which is more suited to cable access than a showcase on a major market network affiliate. Dunkin' Donuts became our caterer, although we sometimes offered bagels instead of those sugary twisted things. Our guests would be picked up not by the limo that serviced the live morning show, but by an intern who volunteered his pickup truck. Our studio had bare walls and a few boxes for a set. This low-rent atmosphere became part of our appeal. There was no cable in Boston in those days, and no one had seen anything like this before.

My associate producer Vicki Gordon, the only other staffer, was a talented idea person and also a master booker, who convinced all manner of big names to show up in the middle of the night. She was smart and convincing, articulate and vivacious. As director of the Cambridge arts program Articulture, she gave exposure to all the best local talent. The then-unknown Jay Leno actually helped her move apartments. She knew how to beg, stroke and cajole. She also knew that some people will do anything to be on TV. What *they* didn't always know was that anything could happen once we were on the air. During our premiere, we constantly lost the video portion of the program and then, when that was restored, the audio portion went. Fortunately, we achieved the integration of audio and video, sound and picture, just as the innovative Dr. Heimlich was demonstrating his famous maneuver on Matt, nearly strangling him live on our first broadcast.

During the week, we did the show with one camera. Pan right. Pan left. Zoom in. Zoom out. At one point the show even went on— live!—without a director, switched by technicians in master control, where the least competent union guys were sentenced to monitor TV monitors until they died or retired, whichever came first.

On weekends, we actually had two cameras and a real director. We even had a wonderfully enthusiastic floor director named Keifo, the station's solo Rasta-man. Vicki booked everyone from Bob Marley and Frank Zappa to Harvard's Alan Dershowitz and hundreds of insomniac authors and artists. Every star doing a gig in Boston who wanted someplace to go when their adrenaline kept pumping after their show ended could come to us. We were open! Live all night!

One Saturday, going on as *Saturday Night Live* ended, we did a punk rock night. It sounded like a great idea. First there'd be a fashion show of the latest punk designs by two great couturiers who called themselves Kitty Litter and Nancy Pants, and then a band would play live. We accommodated live audiences on Saturdays, so the punkers could bring their fans. It would look fabulous. Bald heads, purple hair, lots of leather. After helping put this craziness together, Vicki announced she was exhausted and was taking the night off.

"Don't worry, you can handle it," she said. "No problem."

Network shows have small armies of people to handle complicated multisegment programs like the ones we did. They have ushers and production assistants and battalions of peons. They have armies of writers and production assistants. We had—me! And Russell. Russell was the intern with the old pickup and a constant, beatific smile that seemed to elevate him to another plane of existence.

The punk rock fashion show went off smoothly. The place was thick with attitude. While sitting in the control room, I suddenly noticed that two of the models had spray-painted their outfits on their bodies. That's right. They were naked! I told the cameramen to only shoot their heads. I prayed no one noticed. Of course, everyone noticed, including our other guests, a punk rock band called Human Sexual Response. Unknown to me, they had been snorting in the bathroom. Or so I was told. I suddenly panicked. The station could lose its license. I was losing control. Vicki, how could you?

The band had rehearsed four songs, including their underground hit "Jackie O," a risqué satirical tribute to Jacqueline Kennedy Onassis as well as an attack on celebrity fetishism. ("I want to be Jackie Onassis, oh yeah," went one chorus.) It was pretty avante garde stuff, especially in Boston where bands with less to say had been banned in years past. When I realized that we had a few minutes left at the end of the show, I suggested the band do one more song so we'd have something happening on stage to run our final credits over. By this time the band was stoned, the punkers were running wild in the halls and I was praying that three A.M. would come quickly, with no more surprises.

Situation gonzo!

Human Sexual Response was happy to respond. They reached into their repertoire for a cult classic, a song they hadn't rehearsed with us.

They weren't called Human Sexual Response for nothing. Their last song would become my swan song in late night entertainment. It was called "Butt Fuck." Sample lyric: "It really reeks when you spread those cheeks."

I was in the control room while they were playing. The sound man, a cranky and aging union lifer, considered all rock 'n' roll too loud. So he brought the monitor down. Way down. We couldn't hear or understand the words. I even went out on stage to dance along with the guests, unaware of what was being sung. I was having lots of fun until someone grabbed me and filled me in on the joke. "That's not 'but funk,' it's 'butt fuck'!"

Ha ha. I told the director to immediately fade to black. An old yippie had just been out-yippied. Abbie would have loved it.

I was furious.

We received six calls at three A.M. Three wanted more. "Great man, wow." But three callers vowed to stop at nothing until whoever was responsible for this outrage was hung like the Salem witches.

Afterward I screamed at the band. They told me to chill out and said they'd be happy to write a letter taking all responsibility. They were having fun. What was wrong with me? Nothing. I just saw my career in ashes, that's all.

They did get it together to write a semi-apology. "Dear Danny: In retrospect, we regret only, but sincerely, the possibility that serious repercussions may ever be felt by yourself.... However and again, with the benefit of hindsight we feel that our impulsive actions were somehow appropriate to the spirit and the context of the program, as rock 'n' roll has always had an irreverent and irresponsible side to its nature.... We owe you an apology. Let the show go on. [Signed] Human Sexual Response."

I was more worried about the letter I feared the station would be writing, the one on pink paper.

Bob Bennett reassured me. "We can handle the FCC problem," he said at first. But then he asked, "Is that really what they do in those clubs?" He seemed very understanding as I explained and explained that it was not my fault.

The bottom line: The show would go on all right, but without me.

As it turned out, Friday the thirteenth was my last day.

The station spoke of "irreversible philosophical differences." The show, they told reporters, "could not progress in our (WCVB's) direction with Danny as producer." The news made the Boston papers. "Goodbye Schechter," was the headline in the *Herald*. *Five All Night* was thereafter broadcast with a six-second delay. Two years later, management pulled the plug on our adventurous nocturnal emission.

Vicki would end up in charge of *Five All Night* until she collapsed from a lack of sleep. She was the little engine that could, ending up as a senior producer for CBS, with Connie Chung until Chung was axed. There was no "get," as power bookings are called, that she couldn't get. Skater Tonya Harding was one of her catches when every competitor hungered for her. She also nailed Woody Allen for *60 Minutes*. No one says no to Vicki, who is as savvy and success-ful at the networks as she was at three in the morning back in Boston. She is now in a senior executive post at CBS. Matt Siegel went back into commercial radio. And some say that FANLAN became a prototype for David Letterman's late night madness. It's funny what a difference a few million dollars can make in the pro-duction values and promotion department!

When I lost my show, I was bummed. Who would hire the man who brought "butt fuck" to TV? Once again, I was sure I'd never work again.

I toyed with the idea of trying to get back into local TV news in Boston. I wasn't bad on air even if I was forced to dye my beard and upgrade my wardrobe. I wasn't sure if I could make it because every third reporter, male and female, had the prettiest hair on the air while I had a, shall we say, more disheveled look. They were mostly, but not all, cookie-cutter types, many of the blond persuasion. In fact, one critic put down the local stations for carrying "Aryan News."

The content was a bigger problem for me and still is. A 1994 study by the Rocky Mountain Media Watch (RMMW) concluded that Boston, which has always had pretensions as an intellectual center, leads the nation in what it calls "no-news news shows." It's a familiar story. A new station group, Sunbeam Broadcasting, bought Channel 7, changed its call letters back to WHDH and introduced flashy tabloid-style journalism, news shows with high story counts, more consumer tips, and less traditional reporting. The station's award-winning investigative reporter, known for hard-hitting multipart reports, was soon doing "one-part series." As one reporter there told me, "News has been redefined as 'news you can use,' not 'news you need to know.' " The internal atmosphere was described as "very top down, very rushed and led with a remarkable thoughtlessness." RMMW gave WHDH (Channel 7) a 97.2 on its Pavlov Index for offering mayhem, fluff and sports: "These topics have a common focus on violent events that purvey fear and alienation to the audience," the study says. The station came in second nationally in the fluff category, which includes, soft news, anchor chatter, previews/promos and celebrity stories. In general, they concluded, there is 39 percent more fluff than news. The survey found that crime dominated half of the newscasts they watched on a single day, with thirty-seven of the hundred stations running crime as a lead. (Unbelievable as it may be, this situation grew *worse*. When the media monitors took another look in 1997, 72 out of 100 lead stories were about crime and violence.)

Unfortunately, in order to compete, the other stations in the market began to soften their own product. When I watched local news in Boston in December 1996, I found the stations following almost identical story rundowns in styles that were more alike than different. Local news tends to a similar uniformity nationwide—the same type of sets, anchors and story lineups—all based on the audience surveys and the advice of consultants like Frank N. Magid associates, which advises 130 stations in America's 210 local media markets. They are hired to train talent, improve writing, redo graphics—also called enhancement elements—in order to boost ratings and profitability. It is they who created the action news format, the fast-paced format that offers the news in breathy style, whipping from reporter to reporter, emphasizing hot footage and headline capsules. Eric Braun, a Frank Magid vice president, told *Signal to Noise*, an ITVS public television show, that he considers his firm's work "the dark side of the First Amendment. Without profit there is no free press."

Local news shows are now more widely watched throughout the country than network news, whose viewership is eroding. More than a quarter of all Americans say they rely on their local six P.M., ten P.M., or eleven P.M. news as their principal source of information. From coast to coast, reports of excesses and inaccuracies in local news coverage have critics pulling out their hair and TV companies heading to the bank. The critics say the mayhem, fluff and celebrity hype are watering down and displacing journalism, while news managers point to the ratings, insisting they just give the public what it wants. "If you don't like it, change the channel," they say. "We're not C-SPAN or PBS's *News Hour* and don't pretend to be." But what do they pretend to be? "It's all based on what I call the simpleton theory of broadcast economics," former CBS and ABC correspondent Jerry Landay told me. "The more primal hot buttons you push, the more money you'll make. It's that thinking that drives these formats and it is, unfortunately, very effective. It also reinforces our dumbo culture."

In 1996, *Electronic Media* surveyed local news directors at a convention of the Radio-Television News Directors Association. They summed up their report with a quote from an unnamed big-market news director. "Journalism has given way to beautiful brainless people—they're the ones hiring too."

Now, I don't look like Godzilla, but I began to feel unwanted. If I wanted to work in TV, I concluded, I'd have to leave town.

My next career stop took me from off-the-wall, late night local television to the world's first twenty-four-hour news network. The industry sneered at it back then as the Chicken Noodle Network. We know it as CNN.

PART TWO

NETWORKING

"The obscure we see eventually.
The completely apparent takes a little longer."
—Edward R. Murrow

THE NETWORKS' primary role is as a switching apparatus through which centralized programming is fed to receptor stations, which then retransmit it to their communities. It's a one-way system driven by advertisers who want to buy audiences for their products. Viewers are targeted as potential consumers, broken down by their demographics—age, location, and gender. They become the market to be sold to sellers who turn them into buyers. Advertisers have used television to build and organize a culture around commerce—a national marketplace shaped by corporations that target and tailor their brand-name messages with specificity and sophistication. "When the public turns on their TV sets they think program," explains Ken Auletta. "But a network thinks advertiser."

Auletta quotes Mark Mandala, an ABC executive, as saying, "The network is paying affiliates to carry network commercials, not programs. What we are is a distribution system for Proctor and Gamble and other advertisers." This is the core financing reality around which everything else revolves. Marketing is the mission. In the world of television, stations do not serve cities or communities but markets. New York is the number one media market. All TV stations are ranked by their market size.

I have communications scholar Herbert Schiller to thank for digging out an essay that shows just how advertising people explicitly shape the media system to their needs—which they then redefine as ours. Leo Bogart, a former executive with the Newspaper Advertising Bureau, is very clear on this point in *The American Media System and Its Commercial Culture*, writing that "contemporary American culture assigns no value or meaning to communications apart from their market value, that is, the price that someone is willing to pay for them.... [They are] produced for sale to meet marketing requirements."

"What this means," comments Schiller, "is that the great majority of the country's creative workers are forced into a commercial straitjacket. What they film, televise, write or compose must be shaped, first and foremost, to the specifications of advertisers and corporate sponsors. The fulfillment of their own creative imaginations, or the public's need for substantive cultural satisfaction has little priority."

"Sell-evision" has helped make the market for goods and services a national and global one. This has meant that regional and cultural diversity have been subordinated to a system designed to project authority at the center while soliciting consumers and creating spectators at the periphery. As an example, when you listen to network programming you tend to hear a uniform mid-American voice, an accentless accent, that seems to be from everywhere and nowhere at the same time.

And just as uniform style and format tend to render TV stations indistinguishable, so do employees tend to adopt the values of the networks as their own. This type of co-optation works subtly. A friend of mine, University of Wisconsin political science professor Michael

Barnett, spent some time at the State Department and describes what happened to him in a way that felt very familiar: "Slowly I acquired more than the skills of a political officer—I developed the mentality and the mind set. After several months I became more comfortable with my position, better able to understand and share in the symbols, gestures and utterances of my colleagues and generally able to fit in. Said otherwise, not only had I entered the bureaucratic world, but the bureaucratic world had entered me. If once I thought of me and them, I now began thinking in terms of us."

On one level that's what happened to me too. When I entered the network world, it also entered me. Fortunately, because of my history, I was conscious of the dangers of co-optation. Yet, I still wanted to "tell a vision."

Despite the proliferation of cable channels and specialized program services that call themselves networks—MTV Networks, the USA Network and others—there are still three dominant broadcasting companies: ABC, NBC and CBS, with a fourth, Fox, coming on strong. Together they command the most eyeballs at any one time. The big four have different names, logos and personnel, but are more alike than different. Years ago, an executive at NBC explained the style differences among the networks to me this way: "CBS, the self-styled Tiffany network, is the church—the standard setter for broadcasters everywhere. NBC is like a morgue—staid and Protestant. And ABC, well, ABC is more like an insane asylum, younger, feistier and more willing to break the mold."

Church, morgue and asylum. Of course I ended up at the asylum.

My run with ABC news followed an even more insane detour at a network that set out to challenge all three.

CHAPTER 4

CNN: THE WORLD'S MOST (SELF) IMPORTANT NETWORK

I was invited to come down to the new Cable News Network in Atlanta in June 1980, a few days after CNN's well-hyped launch and my inglorious end at WCVB. Jane Caper, a former Boston producer, had just been put in charge of features. And she had a problem.

Ted Turner wanted a daily prime-time program that would combine Oprah Winfrey's strengths with Ted Koppel's timeliness. He built a talk show studio in his Atlanta newsplex, with room for six cameras and enough seats for a large audience. The program—live for an hour a night at ten P.M.—would deal with issues from the day's headlines and be open to input from the studio and from viewers at home via phone.

Today that slot—aired an hour earlier—belongs to electronic war-horse Larry King. But at the network's inception, CNN hired Sandi Freeman, the co-host of *A.M. Chicago*, the Second City's version of *Good Morning America*, to take the prime-time slot. The woman's role in these pairings has historically been to look pretty and do the softer features and bimbo subjects considered too superficial for the male, i.e. the "real" anchor. This is changing, but women are still unfortunately stereotyped and slotted into subordinate on-air roles.

Sandi got the job and the highest salary of any on-air personality at CNN—which would years later dub itself "the world's most important network"—thanks to the negotiating clout of her agent Alfred Geller, who also represented Connie Chung and other top TV talent. (Sandi later married him.) Savvy agents like Geller have come to play a major role in the news business as they have in sports, helping turn journalists into high-paid celebrities, reinforcing the star system and judging journalists according to the compensation packages that establish their market value. Geller won Sandi the best deal at the network, a fact he advertised widely to bolster her status. That also immediately triggered resentment from many of her colleagues.

Few on-air personalities make it totally on their own. Good producing is usually essential. Producers in television are like directors in the movies—they shape a show's look, prepare the material and handle all the details that make the host look good. Good programming is supposed to look like it's effortless. That's why insiders call television a producer's medium. To produce Sandi, CNN initially hired a brilliant, India-born documentarian with lots of BBC experience, Cyrus Barucha. He had sensibility, but didn't seem comfortable in the world of TV talk shows or maybe he lacked the patience required to work with a novice in network TV. CNN didn't have the heart to tell him he was in the wrong job.

So Jane needed a producer for Sandi's show—immediately. That's why she flew me down to Atlanta for an interview. She wanted me to start right away, but neglected to tell me.

When I first met Cyrus, he didn't understand why I was there. Neither did I. He told me he couldn't believe they would hire someone who "couldn't find Israel on the map," bitterly referring to Sandi. But that wasn't my problem—yet. I was just there for an interview.

Around four P.M. a group of young staffers, an associate producer and a few VJs came up to me and asked, "What's going to be on your show tonight?" (One of those interns, I'm told, was named Katie Couric, who went on, of course, to co-host NBC's *Today* show.)

My show? Since when?

At that minute, Jane called to tell me she was sorry she'd been so busy. CNN was just days old and their procedures were not all in place yet. She pleaded with me to help her out, to do the show with her that night. She asked me what subject should be on it.

What about her producer?

"Well, he's not happy anyway. He sort of knows." Cyrus ended up hanging around for a few weeks, getting his checks and mail, and using the phone. He had bought a condo in Atlanta so he couldn't just pick up and leave. He ended up spending the summer playing golf while trying to recoup his real estate investment. He struck me as very sophisticated and smart, someone CNN could have put to good use. But he kept wondering how he could have been so stupid as to have taken the job. What did that say about me?

Jane asked me how much I would need to stay. I was flabbergasted. I had only come for an interview because they gave me a free plane ticket and put me up for the night. It was a break from Boston at a time when I had just lost a job and was convinced I would never find another. I was also feeling out of sync with what was soon to become the Reagan era.

Besides, I lived in Boston. I had a life and a house there. My daughter was there, and I was in the middle of a painful marital separation, negotiating joint custody. How could I move to Atlanta?

"How much?" asked Jane.

Just to be extravagant, I doubled the salary at my old job in Boston, figuring I was demanding too much. She said fine. She probably couldn't believe how uninformed about network salaries I was. I also told her I would need to fly to Boston every weekend, sure that would be the deal breaker. She said fine again. I told her I wasn't sure how long I could stay. She said fine, no contract was needed. Jane liked me and was sure Sandi would too.

What was I getting myself into? After twelve years in one town, I had just agreed to become a long-distance commuter. I hadn't been in the South since the glory days of the civil rights movement. Hot-lanta had mushroomed into a modern metropolis. Malls and corporate headquarters abounded. I felt like a fish out of water. It was also hotter than hell.

CNN was then based in Atlanta's former progressive Jewish country club next door to Georgia Tech, home of the rambling wrecks. Ted acquired the plantation-like structure for CNN's first home for a song after all the "progressive" Jews fled to the suburbs. This was before he bought Atlanta's failing Omni hotel complex to create the CNN Center, a self-contained TV bunker complete with office buildings, a hotel, tourist shops and a movie theater permanently playing *Gone with the Wind*, the story of his alter ego, Rhett Butler. Under Turner's leadership, the South would rise again, but this time as a communications power.

He gutted the country club and rebuilt it as his TV headquarters. CNN was stuck in the basement, organized around a unique open floor design with anchor desks part of a newsroom, lined with editing rooms and desks for news writers and editors. When I arrived, the Georgia state flag with its surviving Confederate symbols flew out front next to Old Glory and, for a global touch, the UN flag.

I learned that CNN was not actually Ted's idea. It was concocted by Reese Schonfeld, who had run UPITN, a news film company tied to a wire service, and ITNA, another news distributor. Reese saw an opportunity in cable, a chance to retool the news radio format, with its rigorously formatted schedules or news-wheel, and turn it into all-the-news-all-the-time television. He became CNN's first president.

CNN gave the fledging cable business a distinctive product, available only to cable subscribers. Remember, cable started as a way to improve reception, as community antenna systems. To expand and bring in paying customers, the industry needed unique programs. The industry used CNN to convince Americans that it was time to pay for the TV that had always been free (i.e. advertiser driven and supported). Cable aspired to become a utility on a par with electricity and gas, as indispensable to the home as the TV set itself. So cable became the only place to see CNN, and CNN in turn helped sell basic cable. Years later cable operators led by TCI's John Malone would buy into the network in a big way, making Turner as rich as he made them.

Turner knew that selling news to advertisers was only one way to make money, and a tough one when ratings are low. The beauty of cable is that there is another way—revenue from cable operators who kick back a monthly per viewer fee to programmers *along with* money from advertisers. These two streams guaranteed that CNN could make money even with a small audience, in effect just by being there. As cable's penetration grew, Turner's cash flow grew with it. By 1996 fewer than 600,000 TV sets on average were tuned to CNN, but the company made $280 million.

Turner made the Forbes 400 list of American billionaires with CNN driving the growth of a media empire he later merged with Time Warner. But in June 1980 CNN was an audacious startup, burning up money. No one was sure it had a prayer of surviving.

After a quick Southern-style lunch with Jane, drowned with endless pitchers of heavily sugared ice tea, I was given the full, dazzling tour. For someone who had just produced the lowest budget program in America, CNN was an electronic Disneyland. Money buys a lot of toys, although many of the people who buzzed around this news factory were low-wage workers. CNN was located in Atlanta not only because it's Ted Turner's hometown. Georgia is also a right to work state, which enabled CNN to keep the unions at bay and costs down. CNN even created a minimum wage job category—VJ or video journalist—staffed by kids fresh out of school who work long hours for the experience and their résumés, not for the money. There was even talk of turning this cheap labor pool into CNN University so the company could charge *them* as students for their on-the-job education. The idea was dropped when it was discovered that no accredited school would honor the credits and that there was something called federal wage and hour laws.

These people seemed so straight, so sweet, so earnest, so capital-P Polite. And yet their leader was this kick-ass, good ole boy Southern rebel. What kind of news culture would he build? A conventional commercial one as it turned out, for all the talk of his revolutionary vision. Turner, apparently under pressure from his newly hired management, had promised not to get involved with the content of the news. Many thought he was a nut and would compromise their credibility. Unfortunately, Turner capitulated to the "we take ourselves very seriously" news professionals, ensuring that the content of CNN news would not be as adventurous as his hopes for it. Not a few critics pointed to the wide gap between what Ted said about revolutionizing television and what he was actually doing. The reality was never as much fun or earth-shaking as the sermonizing of the "mouth from the South." If CNN was Elvis, he was its Colonel Parker. From the start, CNN had a radical image but conservative content. The other networks laughed at its pretensions of competing against them on a fraction of their budget. They branded CNN "the chicken noodle network." It was true that CNN looked more like a local news operation with a national transmitter than a global news-gathering organization. But the critics wouldn't laugh long.

CNN then shared a facility with a local UHF station, Channel 17, which Turner had picked up for cheap. He renamed it TBS for Turner Broadcasting System and put it up on the satellite for cable operators anxious to provide programming that the networks didn't. For many years that programming was not much to talk about: a mix of family fare, reruns of syndicated glop, schlocky movies and hokey wrestling, which was staged live on the floor above CNN. Occasionally we would hear the thud of bodies slamming into the mat during one more phony bout.

The news guys often snickered behind Ted's back about one or another outrageous comment he made. Perhaps the one that stunned them most was his declaration of CNN's mission on Day One. Proclaimed Ted to his assembled staffers: "We're gonna go on the air June 1, and we're gonna stay on until the end of the world. When that time comes, we'll cover it, play 'Nearer My God to Thee' and sign off."

What kind of newsman talks like that?

Now, in the startup month, I was in the house or rather the basement that Ted built, with a show to produce, at least for one night. I hustled over to the news wires to read the latest bulletins. But there *were* no wires, no clacking machines spitting out acres of paper like I was used to. That information was now on computers tied to high-speed printers. Technology was transforming the business, as was evident by all the state-of-the-art gizmos and adjacent farm of satellite dishes. You can go anywhere live and offer stories as they happen.

That afternoon the Supreme Court had announced a ruling on abortion. I called Jane. "What about abortion? An important decision just came down."

"Sounds great," she said. She had to run to another meeting.

That night at ten, I produced my first *Freeman Reports*. We had pro- and anti-abortion people, experts I had interviewed before, sitting in CNN bureaus in New York and Washington, with one guest in Atlanta. There wasn't much of a live studio audience for two reasons: Not enough people at that time yet knew what CNN was or where it was based, and very few Atlantans wanted to come to see a TV show in the inner city at ten at night.

While there were a few technical hitches, my first show went well. I wrote Sandi's intros, helped book the guests and outlined the questions. The experts said their bit, but because we had an hour, there was time for some light as well as heat. Sandi challenged both sides. The technical problems occurred because no one told me a guest in Washington couldn't talk directly to New York but had to talk to Atlanta first because we were all linked, not by satellite but by one ground line. I feared I had blown it, although Sandi was pleased. When her agent called after the show, as he did most nights to critique her performance, he too was pleased. She told him she had a new producer, some guy from Boston.

Up until that point CNN had received a lot of press. And not all the notices were great. "CNN can be inadequate, frustrating and just plain dull," wrote Richard Zoglin in the *Atlanta Constitution* in the period I worked there. "The twenty-four-hour news channel has not really made good on Ted Turner's promise to provide news in-depth."

Turner was not known as a news lover. Back in 1976, four years before the advent of CNN, he once actually replaced a news anchor on the local TV station he owned with a dog, a German shepherd. "I hate the news," he said back then. "News is evil." Years later he reportedly put a *Playboy* model he was having an affair with on the air as an anchor. Ted's reasons for launching CNN had little to do with elevating public discourse, promoting journalism, or informing the citizenry. "I just wanted to see if we could do it—like Christopher Columbus," he said. "When you do something that's never been done before, sail on uncharted waters and don't know where you're going, you're not sure what you're gonna find when you get there, but at least you're going somewhere."

Turner's ego was as large as his ambitions. His "explorer syndrome" also convinced him that an investment in news could pay. To be taken seriously as a broadcaster, he knew you also needed to do news. The networks initially offered news as a loss leader, to earn influence, not money. In the early days, TV news was just radio news with pictures. It took decades for broadcast news to go from information center to profit center, but that is what happened in the 1960s, when local stations realized how profitable local news could be, and the networks expanded to half hour newscasts.

Plenty of advertisers buy time on TV news because they want to add credibility to their products, if only by association. (It also seems that the people who watch news regularly are more anxiety-prone; stomachache and headache remedies are frequent advertisers on newscasts.) Some advertisers buy news because it is a way to reach selected viewers, the so-called influentials, including opin-ion-makers, politicians, business leaders and journalists.

The next morning at three A.M., when *Freeman Reports* was rebroadcast, the TV critic of the *Christian Science Monitor* tuned in. He found the conversation intelligent and was impressed with Sandi's straight-ahead and engaging style. Until that point CNN had received coverage for what it hoped to become; the *Monitor* man filed one of the first reviews of what it actually did. The review was a rave. Ted Turner and Reese called to congratulate Sandi. I became a golden boy, at least for the day. A week later, I snagged my old runningmate Abbie Hoffman, who had just turned himself in to the authorities and was out on bail, to go on for an hour live with Sandi. Fortunately for me, the *New York Post* was watching and wrote that our interview was much better than the one Barbara Wal-ters had conducted for *20/20*. "Far less revealing" were the words they used to describe *20/20*'s far more ballyhooed "exclusive." All the brass liked that comparison. In TV, as I've learned, your worth is tied to how your bosses see you, which in turn is tied to how oth-ers see you—as well as ratings or what the critics say. If your story is well-received by the press, your boss will probably pat you on the head. External validation always reinforces internal approval.

We soon discovered that Reese and Ted had overestimated the willingness of key newsmakers to drop everything and hop a plane to Atlanta to be on our show. We could get the guests but we could-n't get them to Atlanta. So we had to go to them. *Freeman Reports* quickly became a frequent flyer program. In some weeks, we would be in five cities in as many nights, chasing the top stories and the people who made them. Reese wanted the show to feature the most up-to-the-minute stories. That meant we usually couldn't decide on the subject of the day until late in the day. We'd then scramble for guests and airline reservations, and race to the airport so we could originate live from CNN bureaus in New York, Washington or Los Angeles. Sandi felt she could get more out of guests if she could stare them down in person, using her charm to create personal chemistry. Let cool Koppel interact via satellites. We wanted to be hotter, be there in person, make eye contact. And she was great at it.

Our bookers were on constant burnout, working for a network with bigger aspirations than audiences, competing for big-name interviews with the big boys. Up in New York, we were not yet taken seriously by the serious. Down in Atlanta, we were the little engine that could even though many on the news desk were dismissive of our efforts because getting the story always had priority over interpreting or analyzing it.

The small staff at *Freeman Reports* worked its asses off, racing through Rolodexes, confirming guests, canceling them and then rebooking. I oversaw the research, wrote the intros and questions, and prepped Sandi. It was a constant whirl.

It may have been frenetic, but CNN was out to make a name for itself and Sandi was their new star. We interviewed members of Congress, authors and movie stars. We visited the White House, often beating *Nightline* to the top guests. We were scrappy, determined and on a mission from Captain Outrageous, a nickname Ted Turner was given during one of his many successful sailing competitions.

One day Sandi decided she wanted to interview Turner. He had by then spoken about CNN in every possible forum. He'd been on the cover of newsmagazines and trade publications. *60 Minutes* had done him as had every other news program. But he had never been on CNN. He had never spoken to his viewers, the folks he'd promised to serve until the end of the world.

Sandi and I were soon pitching Ted to be on our show. We told him it would be a chance to take calls from the people whose lives he changed. We told him he had a duty to do it. He sat there grinning, telling jokes about his other TV appearances. He showed us video clips on a big screen on his office, including a sequence, shown on *60 Minutes*, in which he collapses, dead drunk, under the table during a press conference after winning the 1977 America's Cup.

I wasn't sure if he was flirting with Sandi or just trying to charm her into being nice to him on the air. Perhaps he had heard that Sandi wanted to get him to talk about his father, who had committed suicide. He knew Sandi wanted emotion, to bring out the real Ted. I thought I established a bit of a rapport with him as well. I suspect everyone who meets him feels the same way. His breezy informality and first-name familiarity reinforces a sense of intimacy. After an hour of high schmooze and salty anecdotes, he agreed to do the program and we set a date.

On the appointed day, I put extra effort into shaping questions that wouldn't be considered softballs by the audience or offensive by Turner. Sandi was feeding her kids at home. It was about six P.M. when the phone rang.

"Is this Danny Schechter, the *Freeman* producer?"

"You bet. How can I help you?"

"You are doing Ted tonight, right?"

"Who's this? We don't usually reveal our guests until the first promo hits air."

"Dan, my name is Bill Bevins. I'm the financial vice president of CNN. I kind of run the company and I need to see you right away."

"With all respect, Mr. Bevins, I'm real busy." Just being in Atlanta had me unconsciously slipping into a Southern speech pattern, but everyone there knew I was a Yankee. By then, after years in New England my real accent was no longer hard-core Bronx but a cross between Yankee Stadium and Fenway Park, with some Dixie inflections beginning to creep in. I noticed that many of my fellow carpetbaggers from the "Nawth" were catching a similar regional bug. "Can't I come see you after the show? We all still have a lot of work to do."

"No, I need to see you right now," he said. "It's about your interview tonight. I'm on the third floor to the left of the elevator. Just ask for me. And please come right now. It's important."

Who the hell was Bevins and why was he demanding to see me? When I checked I learned Mr. Bevins was indeed Mr. Big, Ted's key money man, and not someone whose summonses could be delayed. I headed upstairs.

Bevins first asked that our conversation be kept between us, and then if I knew what the term *registration* meant.

"You mean like the selective service, the draft?"

"No," he said with a smile signaling that we inhabited different worlds, "like the SEC, the Securities and Exchange Commission. Please follow me."

He led me across the hall into a conference room with a massive circular wooden table. Seated around it were white men in suits. Lots of them. Bevins introduced them as members of a leading Atlanta investment bank that was working on bringing CNN public. They had compiled the volumes of data the SEC requires from companies that want to sell their stock to investors and were about to go into the period of registration, during which the government would scrutinize their submission. And they were worried about the man whose interests they were serving.

Bevins explained, "You see, Dan, under SEC rules, when a company goes into registration, the executives of that company have to be very careful not to plug the company publicly. It is considered a way of hyping the stock or trying to drive up its value. If you do that, your application can be held up or turned down."

I still didn't get exactly what he was driving at.

He got to the point with a question. "What do you think Ted will do if Sandi asks him about CNN?"

"What do I think? I think he'll do what he always does—rave about it, call CNN the greatest invention since white bread. That's what Ted does."

"Exactly," interjected one of the suits. "And that's why he must not go on your show tonight."

I looked at him. I looked at the room. It was seven P.M., three hours to show time. I didn't have any other guest lined up.

If they felt so strongly about this, why didn't they tell Ted not to do it? I asked Bevins, "Doesn't Ted know this? He agreed to go on. I'm not forcing him. Why don't you talk to him?"

"That's the problem, Dan, we *have* spoken with Ted. He insists he's going on the show because he promised you he would. He won't listen to us. Will you try to convince him?"

"You want *me* to talk to him? Are you kidding? I *want* him to be on. He's our only guest."

"Dan, you don't understand," Bevins said patiently. "If Ted goes on that show and says what we think he will say, the SEC could hold up their review, and then this company will not get the financing it urgently needs. That means you and everyone who works here may not get paid next week. In some ways the future of CNN is in your hands. You are the only one he will listen to."

Me? My hands? C'mon! I was speechless. There was a long silence. At that point, Sandi called wondering where I was, and I briefed her. She said she was on the way.

A few minutes later, the door to the room burst open and Ted himself walked in, yelling, "I'm doing that show! I promised Sandi and Danny, and I'm gonna do it. Did anyone in this room ever hear of the First Amendment? That's freedom of speech. I'm not giving that up. This is my company and nobody is telling me what I can and can't say. Danny, would you step into my office for a minute?"

Leaving the suits and Bevins, I follow Ted. I don't know what else to do. I sure don't want CNN to fail on my account. My hands, the hands that hold the future of CNN, are now in my hair, tugging ever so slightly.

Ted's office is dark except for a light on his desk that shines on a little sign: Lead, follow or get out of the way. He starts talking before I can. "These guys want to censor me. I promised to go on the show, and I'm going to do it. If I'd listened to my financial advisors, I would never have started CNN [putting in a reported $35 million of his own money]. I'm not to going to let them dictate to me now. No, sir."

Ted's insistence was just what I wanted to hear, because we really didn't have another guest, and it was kind of late to find one. And I had to respect his determination to stand up for himself and to take the risks he did on behalf of a speculative venture.

But I was also beginning to think about the registration mess. What if those guys were right? Was tonight's show or any one show worth the collapse of CNN?

"Look, Ted, I don't want to pressure you," I said. "Maybe you should just postpone your appearance. Maybe Mr. Bevins is right."

Ted would have none of my conciliatory jive. He went on about his experiences with various business advisors. It was clear that something else was going on and this wasn't just one of Ted's legendary manic moments. Sandi soon joined us and began playing the responsible mediator role. Ted, however, was adamant. He'd promised us he would do the show, and that was that.

We took our leave to go back to his antagonists and tell them that we tried but failed to persuade him. They were not happy campers. We then returned to our cubicles in the cellar to get the show ready. By now it was almost eight P.M. Sandi and I didn't even try to speculate on what was really behind this. We figured Ted was just being Ted.

At 9:30, there was an electrical storm in Atlanta. CNN actually went off the air, a most unusual occurrence. At 9:45, fifteen minutes to air, Ted passed by our office. He said he wasn't feeling well and promised he would do the show another night. I scrambled to find an evergreen interview I had pretaped, just in case some guest crapped out at the last minute. The show went on—but Ted Turner didn't. At least not that night.

What *had* really been going on? I pieced the story together later. Ted, it seems, was under pressure to bring CNN public but thought it was too soon and didn't want to dilute his control. I speculated that the brokerage house had been hired on a contingency basis and would only recoup their hefty investment when the stock was sold.

Turner may have decided to torpedo the deal. Our show was likely a maneuver in this battle.

A few weeks later, reportedly without telling anyone in Atlanta, Ted turned up on the *Phil Donahue* show in Chicago. He raved about CNN. The Atlanta firm was pissed. They withdrew their application for registration and sued Turner Broadcasting for millions. A small item appeared in the *New York Times*: "Ted Turner received a setback last week. His Turner Broadcasting System announced the withdrawal of a proposal to publicly offer a million common shares. The company declined to say why it was withdrawing the offer, which would have gone toward retiring company debt. One reason might have been a recent appearance on the *Phil Donahue* show in which he talked about the company—an action that could be construed by the Securities and Exchange Commission as promoting the offering."

This was no setback. There was a method to his madness. And I suspect that someone at CNN actually pulled the network off the air that night in a maneuver to convince Ted not to do our show. On the night they almost drove the new Dixie down, I had briefly believed that CNN's future *was* in my hands. It never was, of course.

I later learned that besides doing *Donahue*, Ted did some other talking in Chicago. He talked to people at the Continental Bank and came home with a $100 million line of credit. It's hard to resist the Mouth from the South. He now had the money to keep CNN afloat without having to prematurely sell more shares in his company. Ted was set.

But I wasn't. The constant traveling was proving too much for me. And who had time to use the free airline mileage? Producing a daily talk show was a grind, but beyond that was increasing pressure to keep the show safe by staying with the issues that the major media defined as news, then inviting the same guests the other media featured. It is this pressure, subtle and often unexpressed, that makes for the sameness across the spectrum of talk programming. If *Nightline* has a senator on, why not us? If CBS uses so-and-so as its terrorism expert, why not invite the same expert? Guests were soon being chosen for their name value and audience familiarity more than what they had to say. That's why this talk show business is called a circuit, with guests increasingly pushed by PR people, who often hire media trainers to prepare their clients for on-air appearances. For harried producers, this simplifies the booking process. One call gets it all.

I wanted us to be more original and provocative. When Jimmy Carter was running for reelection, many right-wing Republicans were baiting him for his membership in the Trilateral Commission, an elite group of power brokers from business, finance and government. They saw the Commission, which had been set up with Rockefeller money, as a stalking horse for some kind of a communist, one-world conspiracy. At the same time, the Trilateralists were characterized by the Left as the ultimate capitalist conspiracy. Both used the same evidence to reach diametrically opposed conclusions.

I decided to get the conspiracy theorists of the Left and the Right together on the same show. The program turned into a hot debate and was very popular with viewers, who flooded the phones with questions. CNN's chief executive Reese Schonfeld hated it, however, and told me not to rerun it as we did with some of our shows on weekends. By mistake it was left on a list of shows to be re-aired, and, when it was, Reese had a meltdown. I had actually told my production assistant not to schedule the show, but he thought I was kidding because it drew such a strong viewer response. I assumed my instructions would be followed but didn't double-check, thereby violating a well-known rule of TV production I had posted in my office: Assumption Is the Mother of Fuck-Up.

CNN's "revolution" turned out to be fusing the most innovative technology with the most conventional programming. For many years its reach mesmerized millions. But critics have emerged. "It hasn't done much to improve the way we get our news," Tom Rosensteil wrote in the *New Republic.* "In certain ways, the network has even had a pernicious effect on the rest of journalism; it has accelerated the loss of control news organizations have over content, which in turn has bred a rush to sensationalism and an emphasis on punditry and interpretation at the expense of old-fashioned reporting.... The constant clatter of its twenty-four-hour programming is more flattening than deepening."

After six months, I had ODed on iced tea and barbecue sauce. I felt like I was getting a reputation as a troublemaker and misfit. It was time to move on. Ironically, the network that Reese in effect squeezed me out of for being too independent did the same thing to him and for the same reason. It happened after Reese fired Sandi, who Turner reinstated despite a promise to let him run CNN. His power compromised, Reese was the next to go—with Sandi ultimately not far behind. That created the opening for Larry King to bring his radio show to CNN and become a TV star.

As I was leaving, I made one more little contribution to promoting CNN's global reach. I mentioned to Ted Turner that when I was in Japan as a Nieman fellow, I had noticed that the hotels carried a really piss-poor English-language TV news service. Within months CNN was available in hotels worldwide, beginning in Tokyo. Was it at my suggestion? Who knows?

As CNN started to go global, people all over the world began to think of CNN as the voice of America, the biggest network we had. Wolf Blitzer, the CNN correspondent, once revealed that the Pentagon had leaked a story to him rather than hold a press conference, because they knew that when people saw him standing in a suit and tie in front of an American flag they assumed he was a spokesman for government policy.

Over the years CNN has strengthened its reporting considerably. They now produce special reports, documentaries, investigative features, and significant environmental reporting with more coverage of the world than all the other American networks combined. Journalists like Christiane Amanpour have distinguished themselves on many battlefields, especially Bosnia. (Her work there won her an unusual deal from *60 Minutes*, who gave her nearly $2 million to also report for them.)

Turner has also used CNN to boost the United Nations, which has honored him repeatedly for providing the only sustained exposure of UN events and conferences, such as the Earth Summit in Rio in 1992 or Habitat 2 in Istanbul four years later. In the latter case, UN agencies helped fund some of Turner's coverage on one of his other networks, not CNN—a subsidy that other networks would never permit because of the conflict inherent in a subject of news coverage funding the coverage. Ted's association with the United Nations has won him more than awards and visibility. It was a great marketing ploy and opened doors to many countries that then imported CNN.

Turner was a featured guest at a 1995 New York conference decrying the lack of coverage of the UN. In a Ted Turner kind of way, he promised to do better: "I am one of those do-gooders and I am going to keep on doing. If the people don't watch the UN [coverage] this year, I am going to keep on running it. I am going to do the right thing. That's right. Shove it down their throats. I am going to keep on running it. Here's how we do it. We show a little bit of the UN and then we go right back to the O. J. Simpson trial. You know, like a little pill, put it with some orange juice."

Ted's words to the UN were considered credible because his company maintained its own virtual ambassador in the person of CNN environmental editor Barbara Pyle, a sincere and talented environmentalist and activist who attended all major UN events and lobbied internally to increase the network's coverage of them. As she was the first to admit, however, often very candidly and publicly, she had an uphill battle getting air time or resources even with Ted's ear and backing. She admits CNN is only making a token commitment to covering global issues in any depth. Notwithstanding Ted's heartfelt preaching, not to mention his subsequent pledge of $1 billion to the UN, CNN's principal UN discussion show, *Diplomatic License*, airs at four A.M. in New York—not exactly prime time.

The news world today, with its own lingo and frames of reference, is a world of its own. Perhaps that is why TV news reporting is often more distancing than involving. The classic journalist—someone with ideas, values and interpretative skills—has been replaced by the "post journalist" packager who imposes a standardized format on news programming. David Altheide and Robert Snow call this "information mechanics" in their book *Media Worlds in the Post Journalism Era.* "We are post journalism and very much in the age of media talent, performers and actors," they write, perhaps aware that the contracts that most on-air correspondents sign even label them performers. "With some exceptions it is no longer the individual creative work of journalists that gives us news of the world, but rather standard templates, routines and typical courses of action. No wonder so much news looks the same, no matter where it comes from." CNN is CNN, instantly recognizable and often instantly forgettable. Its sameness can deaden as often as enlighten. It became successful by imitating the formats and logic of its network competitors. Today, CNN is on constantly in every newsroom in the world, spawning its own imitators and often setting a world news agenda. News is increasingly what CNN says is news.

And now the networks are imitating CNN. In 1995, NBC, ABC and CBS all unveiled plans to launch their own twenty-four-hour news networks. Rupert Murdoch proclaimed that a Fox news channel was needed because CNN was "too liberal." NBC teamed up with Microsoft to launch MSNBC, although a top Microsoft executive was quoted to the effect that their first choice had been to partner with the *New York Times*, which turned them down. Earlier, ABC, flush with Disney dollars, proclaimed that their proposed channel would be best—until their financial projections led them to withdraw from the race. CBS created its own semi-news outlet, *Eye on People*, an exercise in recycling—or to use the new buzzword, *repurposing*—old CBS-owned programming and archival footage into new shows so as to profit from them again. In 1996, CBS bought a Spanish-language news network.

Many analysts doubt that there is a big enough market for so much news. Many professionals fear that more will, in the end, mean less. Tom Brokaw, for example, worries, "My concern is that an all-news channel will become an excuse not to do things at the network in news. Instead, we'll move very hard into entertainment and infotainment, more and more magazines and less and less attention to hard news." Marvin Kalb, who spent years at NBC with Brokaw before moving on to Harvard, adds: "As the quantity of TV news expands, the quality goes down. What we are dealing with here is a flattening out of journalism in America. This has been going on for ten years and is just getting worse. I don't see any trend at all the other way. I wish I did." Even if you make allowances for Kalb taking a rosy view of his years in the business, this is still a damning indictment.

I passed through CNN on many occasions in the years that followed my departure. What I found is that the bigger companies get, the less gutsy they become. CNN started out challenging the TV news business. Now that it is an established fixture, even top news executives recognize that there is little passion left. In 1996, I received a warm letter from Ed Turner (no relation to Ted), who ran CNN's news operations, pining for the days when they could be more adventurous. "Somehow crusading in journalism or in print (not being terribly sure what journalism is anymore) and on tape and film lost its cachet years back and I am not sure why; probably because it quit being a profitable vehicle for the owners."

Over the years, CNN has added many network veterans to its correspondent pool and does offer high-quality reporting and information on a consistent basis even if viewing levels do not yet rival that of the networks. (CNN finished tenth in the prime-time cable ratings in 1996 with an average of only 582,000 households tuned in. By February 1997, they had dropped to 371,000 households every 24 hours. CNN's competitors fared worse—MSNBC had a mere 30,000 homes while the Fox News Channel logged only 12,000. Those are 0.52, 0.125, and 0.07 ratings respectively. And as of July 1997, these numbers continue to shrink.)

The network produces even-handed documentary news-magazines and says it is broadening its range of non-news shows, its pundit forums are largely tilted toward conservatives. Pat Buchanan, who built a national following on the strength of his CNN exposure, ran for president in 1996 on a hard right-wing agenda. While appearing on *Larry King* during the election year, the president of CNN, Tom Johnson, called in to offer him his old job back. Despite its roster of conservative commentators, tepid reporters and mainstream Beltway pundits, CNN somehow has a liberal image. A CNN executive in 1996 told me pointblank that calling CNN liberal robs that word of any meaning it once may have had. "You know who runs the news on CNN, Danny! Most of them are Republicans and many of the others might as well be."

But even their ideology is not in command; corporate-style news packaging is. CNN imported former ABC news producer Rick Kaplan to bring slicker production techniques into the operation along with more newsmagazine programming, and by June 1998, introduced a daily prime-time newsmagazine, *Newsstand*, to ape NBC's *Dateline* and its many clones. The show consummated a fusion between CNN and *Time* magazine. (One of its first stories, which charged that the U.S. used sarin nerve gas in Laos, touched off an intense controversy and led to a network apology, the resignation of CNN's military affairs advisor, and the dismissal of two journalists who charged that CNN capitulated to military pressure by disavowing the story.) Time-Warner is encouraging more synergistic pertnerships between its TV properties and its magazines, e.g. CNN and *Time*, CNN and *Fortune*, etc. Perhaps all of this was more evidence of Ted Turner's own candid assessment as quoted in John Pilger's *Hidden Agendas*: "We are a lot like the modern chicken farmer. They grind up the feet to make fertilizer, they grind up the intestines to make dog food, the feathers go into the pillows.... They use every bit of the chicken. Well, that's what we try to do with the television product."

In 1990, my Globalvision partner, Rory O'Connor, and I went to Atlanta to take part in an annual conference of *World Report* contributors. We asked Ted for a meeting. We wanted to see if Globalvision could work with CNN, whose ideals at least we shared. With that good old Southern hospitality and a toothy smile, he agreed to huddle with us. He remembered me, of course, and asked Rory and me to follow him. Enthusiastically, we did.

We took an escalator downstairs in the Omni hotel, walking two steps behind him and wondering where he was going. We found out soon enough. He led us into the men's room. And there by the urinals, while taking care of other business, we had our meeting. He expressed interest in hearing more about Globalvision. That was it. Our conversation lasted as long as it took us to purge our bladders. We followed up but only to learn that CNN is open to raw material from stringers but not finished product from independents.

Upstairs, we were chagrined that CNN's choice of keynote speaker was William Colby, the late director of the CIA, who had ruthlessly run covert operations but later cultivated a liberal image by disclosing some of the agency's dirty tricks. Was this the image CNN wanted to project? A number of foreign journalists in the room wondered with us. The correspondent from Vietnam Television was especially uncomfortable. He asked me if I knew about Colby's leadership role in the CIA's *Operation Phoenix* counterinsurgency programs, which boasted of having liquidated forty thousand Vietnamese guerrillas and citizen sympathizers. Of course I did. When I told Jane Fonda, who Ted was then courting and later married, about the Vietnamese journalist's comments, she too was upset. She spoke with Ted, but to no avail. From the floor, Rory questioned Colby's presence. The ex-spook responded that today intelligence work and journalism have a lot in common. Sadly, he was right.

I don't think CNN liked Rory's question.

We haven't been invited back.

CHAPTER 5

20/20:
WE'RE IN TOUCH SO YOU BE IN TOUCH

When I was plotting my escape from CNN, I started thinking about a network job in New York. ABC News seemed initially interested in me on the principle that if you can't beat 'em, hire 'em. While in Atlanta I beat *Nightline* on occasion to some guests, and that got me in the door. Frankly, the "know who" factor also entered into the picture: Dick Wald, an ABC news vice president, was a fellow Nieman fellow.

When Wald received me at ABC's old fourth floor offices on West 66th Street, he told me that there were no longer any jobs open at *Nightline*. That was the bad news. The good news was that Av Westin, executive producer at *20/20*, did have a small budget allocated for freelancers who pitched him stories he liked.

Network newsmagazines had become the most watched news programming in America, the only news shows to crash the top ten most watched programs. CBS's *60 Minutes* begat ABC's *20/20*, which begat CBS's *West 57th*, which led to CBS's *48 Hours*, then ABC's *Prime Time Live* and *Turning Point*, which led to *Day One*, which inspired NBC's eighteenth newsmagazine attempt *Dateline*, and on and on, not to mention a host of syndicated, more down-market tabloid clones that succeeded while many more did not. In the 1980s and '90s, the TV newsmagazine became what *Life* and *Look* were in the 1940s and 1950s—mass circulation vehicles driven by visual content, a newsy feel and splashy features. All had similar formulas and formats, and were built around highly polished storytelling and star reporters.

My problem was that I had no experience producing newsmagazine stories. Most of my TV work had been as a live or talk producer with a short stint as an on-air reporter. I watched *20/20* closely, paying attention to the subjects that seemed to interest them. As a result, I dismissed all overseas stories, brainstorming instead about a domestic crime-related segment they might go for. One night, on the subway, it came to me—literally. It stared me in the face as a safety patrol of red-bereted Guardian Angels swept into the car, a menacing and at the same time welcome underground presence. Why not, I thought? A young Puerto Rican teenager wearing a Davy Crockett-style raccoon tail, the official t-shirt and fatigue pants told me that the Angels were about to expand to other cities. Here it was in front of me—an emerging national tale with strong characters, a citizens-fight-back-against-crime subtext and a swirl of controversy. The Angels and their charismatic leader Curtis Sliwa were big in New York but the rest of the country was not yet clued in. They soon would be.

When Av Westin told me he was interested, I panicked. I wasn't sure I could deliver the first time out, so I came up with a gambit: Rather than ask to produce the story, I'd request to work with or for *20/20*'s most experienced and perhaps least ambitious producer. I'd do the work and he could have the credit. In that way I'd learn the ropes, and I'd also position myself for a permanent post if I could cut it, and if one became available. If the story was a complete failure, he'd take the fall with me. *20/20* bought the pitch.

That's how I met Bernie Cohen, then one of the oldest and most experienced hands on deck. He was happy to have me run my ass off, set up the story and then take all the glory himself. He was a legendary operator and, lucky me, a great teacher to whom I feel indebted even if our points of view were often diametrically opposed. He knew what they wanted and how to give it to them.

Our story went well. I followed Curtis Sliwa and his band of red berets around the country. He told us dramatic stories of his fights with criminals, detailing one especially violent encounter at a subway station in East New York where he was shot and left for dead. It made for great TV. Unfortunately, it wasn't true. Years later, after Curtis was shot for real in a still shadowy incident, he confessed that he had made that and other stories up to promote the mystique of the Angels. To my knowledge, 20/20 never ran an update even though I called it to their attention because I felt our show had been used.

Usually, when it comes to using, it's the other way around. One minor but typical example. When we were producing that story on the Guardian Angels, Bernie decided that we needed an expert to legitimize Sliwa's argument that citizens have to become involved in crime fighting. He wanted to turn our profile into a broader trend story in order to give it more of a national dimension. I tracked down a professor in the Midwest who had written the definitive book about citizen crime control programs, neighborhood watch groups and the like.

He flew to New York at our expense. Bernie whipped into our makeshift studio in a corner of our conference room, shook his hand and asked one question: "Are ordinary people becoming involved in the fight against crime?" The expert said yes and offered a sharp ten-second soundbite. As he wound up to continue, Bernie abruptly stopped the interview, thanked him for coming and left the room. I didn't get it, until Bernie told me later that he had what he wanted. Why go on? Less tape. Less to edit.

The professor was stunned. Had he come all that way for a ten-second interview? I was embarrassed and felt compelled, out of courtesy, to tape a twenty-minute conversation with him. In the end, the professor and his ten seconds were edited out. The trend that had seemed so essential at story meetings ended up on the editing room floor.

Curtis Sliwa understood what the television cameras needed. He always tried to ensure that we'd have something to look at. In that respect he was in the tradition of Abbie Hoffman, an earlier generation's master media manipulator, who, with his publicist David Fenton, had used 20/20 as a way to publicize his decision to leave the underground and turn himself in. Abbie resented that phrase, saying, "How can they call me a manipulator? What media do I own or control?" In fact, Curtis told me he used to listen to Abbie on the radio before I brought them together for an uncomfortable dinner. They were both organizers but Abbie leaned left and Curtis was moving right. They had little to talk about.

As media manipulators, both Curtis and Abbie were novices compared to our media institutions, where a growing partnership between public relations specialists, political leaders and corporate interests routinely screens out unwanted perspectives. All successful politicians have to become media manipulators, routinely controlling access to information. Most of the money they raise while campaigning goes into hiring media-savvy consultants, making broadcast commercials and buying airtime. The government and military demonstrated their prowess at media marketing during the Gulf War. The White House attempts to control the news agenda every day. And corporate America sets its agenda by buying it— through advertising, sponsorship of TV shows, political action committees that finance campaigns, lobbyists, paid advertising and behind-the-scenes wheeling and dealing. Programs like 20/20 ultimately serve their agenda even if from time to time they expose a product defect here or a corporate scam there. The business of the mass media is first and foremost business.

20/20 was conceived as ABC's version of 60 Minutes, the super successful CBS newsmagazine. 60 Minutes was nearly canceled when it was first created because it was performing poorly (i.e., bad ratings) on a weekday night. The network bosses believed it was not what people wanted. Producer Don Hewitt begged them to give it a reprise. So it was decided to move its slot to Sundays at six and then seven P.M., a nonprime-time period considered more appropriate for family viewing. Over the years, in part because it had professional football games as its all important lead-in, the show became a TV institution, a ratings getter and moneymaker. *60 Minutes* went from being the profit center of the news division to the profit pump of the whole network. This lesson was not lost on others.

Roone Arledge, the sports impresario turned news czar at ABC, understood that a well-produced newsmagazine could compete with entertainment programming and might even become more profitable: It would be cheaper to produce than its competitors, and at the same time attract a higher income viewer, a prized demographic that certain advertisers would pay more to reach. What *kind* of people were watching had become as important as how many were watching. Programs like *20/20* were produced for and designed to attract a certain audience: "white women in the Midwest who like white bread," as one exec described them. At the time I joined the program, *20/20* was bringing in a reported $20 million a year in profits.

At first *20/20* had been pronounced a disaster. The premiere was a mess. The critics turned thumbs down, and Arledge, who was intimately involved with its design, disclaimed responsibility. "I hated the program," the *New York Times* quoted him as saying. He later revealed that he went to the theater the night it aired and only saw a cassette afterward. He decided to fire the anchors and some of the staffers. New executives were brought in to tinker with the original format that starred Geraldo Rivera, a cast of reporters and a mix of fast-cut stories that zoomed from place to place. The program was different every week. Too different. It had an identity crisis.

Hugh Downs, a broadcasting veteran and distinguished-looking uncle-type was brought in as anchor after Roone did a talent search that consisted of turning on *Good Morning America* and seeing Hugh doing a guest spot. By then, the onetime *Today* sidekick had been reduced to anchoring *Over Easy*, a talk show for seniors on PBS. ABC brought him back to the majors because his calming and reassuring presence could draw attention away from the hyperactive editing and add a credible and familiar personality to the mix.

I came to admire Hugh, although his job usually came down to reading lines he didn't write. He also fronted/reported some segments including some I produced, always displaying a broad intelligence and an earnest desire to get it right. He was one of the best-known personas in TV. His book *On Camera* was subtitled *My 10,000 Hours on Television*, and he is one of the few TV personalities to have had that much face time on the tube. He is also a licensed airplane pilot and once recorded an album of folk songs. As the American head of a committee that supports UNICEF, he held strong international interests, was very absorbed in science and aerospace, and wasn't shy about expressing independent opinions such as speaking out for marijuana decriminalization or even criticizing self-censorship in television. "The reason for a growing concern about censorship is because it does exist, in both subtle and unsubtle forms," Downs wrote in one of the annual reports of Project Censored, which covers suppressed stories in America. As he admitted, censorship occurred regularly at *20/20* too. Only it was called the editorial process.

Barbara Walters was imposed on *20/20* after her stint as an ABC news anchor imploded. In the early days of his teaming with Barbara, there was continuing tension about who would open the show, who would close and who would get to say the closing line that had until that point been his alone: "We're in touch so you be in touch." At first only he could recite the signature slogan, but slowly they began to alternate the copy line. To her credit, Barbara was sensitive to working with an older male anchor, perhaps because of her explosive experience as a co-anchor with the late CBS newsman and ABC anchor Harry Reasoner.

Av Westin, who had run ABC's evening news and was a veteran of CBS in its glory days, was *20/20*'s executive producer. Av had a reputation as a producer's producer, skillful in the edit room where he could, with a snap of his finger, shorten stories or give them more bounce. He laughed about being an editorial surgeon and mimicked putting gloves on before entering the operating, oops, edit room. He was a tough teacher, but essentially a fair and open person, attracting a diverse mix of producers of differing temperaments and attitudes. Many were traditional, but he did hire me, and I think came to respect me, although I never felt our relationship was all that comfortable..

His editing decisions were final and too often reflected cold war-era political biases. On occasion, that led to pointed exchanges, although I decided early on that there was no percentage or future in having political debates with the man in charge. Once a story I did exposing nuclear weapons storage facilities was cut when he felt I went too far in questioning Pentagon policies. Another time we quarreled over a story about a 1975 plane crash during the Vietnam baby lift, which left some of the surviving children brain-damaged. One of the key issues was the culpability of Lockheed, the folks who built the giant C-5 plane that crashed and who resisted for a decade claims by the children for medical redress. We looked into the corporation's coverup of problems with the plane, but most of that material was dropped. Examples of corporate irresponsibility often took a back seat to the emphasis on emotional storytelling, although *20/20* did do some strong reports on unsafe practices by car companies and consumer product manufacturers. (My complaint over shortening the baby-lift story was forgotten when the story won an National News Emmy.)

I remember another piece in which Av's editorial intervention spun a story on its head. It involved workers fighting to save their jobs and factory in the small town of Taunton, Massachusetts. I started shooting it but then had to turn it over to another producer when some other, more pressing assignment arose. In the original cut, the story closed with workers vowing to fight on, calling on others to join them. Too incendiary, Av decided. When that soundbite bit the dust, the segment ended on a note of despair with the union condemned to defeat. Either ending might have been valid, but the decision on what to cut and what to broadcast reflected the show's editorial orientation. The first showed sympathy for workers whose jobs were disappearing. The one that aired concluded that nothing could be done. Like most news programs, 20/20 offered viewers few stories on working people and fewer showing how ordinary people could change things.

All the segment producers knew that their stories could and probably would be trimmed to fit the format. One colleague confided to me that even after her segments were locked (i.e. approved for air), she physically guarded the tape to ensure against further cuts. I joked that there was a machine called the homogenizer somewhere in the basement of ABC that transformed diverse segments into a seamless brew of reports that looked and felt pretty much the same.

Av was a showman, not given to spontaneity and surprise. "Westin's push for control and efficiency," noted Marc Gunther in his book on ABC, *The House That Roone Built*, meant that stories had to be "plotted in advance, presold and market-tested before they were finally commissioned." He had a contradictory mix of neo-conservative ideological prejudices and neo-liberal enthusiasms for investigative breakthroughs. He was always willing to listen to a pitch, because he knew viewers often respond to segments that evoke a "Gee, I didn't know that" reaction. At the same time, he could be hostile to stories that were *too* new—news that had not yet been certified as important by appearing in the press. A colleague of mine says that most of what passes for news is old—"the olds," he calls it.

ABC is sometimes called the America First network; some say ABC stands for Always Be Conservative. It helped bring Jimmy Carter down with its *America Held Hostage* series that evolved into *Nightline*. Gore Vidal calls Ted Koppel "the most dangerous man in America for the ease and authority with which he bolsters a conservative world view in the trappings of journalistic balance." ABC's devotion to George Will as its principal news analyst is further evidence of this tilt. In addition, ABC radio was home to Rush Limbaugh and, in New York, to a slew of hate radio hosts like Bob Grant, who eventually was canned for making racist remarks. In 1997, under Disney control, New York's WABC toned down its angry white man routine adding popular right-wing psychologist Dr. Laura to its lineup and pairing Curtis Sliwa with radical lawyer Ron Kuby.

ABC is not unique in this respect. The former *Washington Post* editor and ombudsman Ben Bagdikian surveyed eighty-four studies of media content and concluded that they demonstrate that all the networks are overwhelmingly pro-corporate and conservative on foreign policy questions, although there is a tendency toward more liberalish coverage of domestic social issues.

A story on the first anniversary of the revolution in Nicaragua reveals *20/20*'s tone in dealing with stories outside our borders: "Up front tonight: What happens after a revolution?" But the story was not about the revolution, as the next line made clear: "What is the U.S. doing to ensure that the new Nicaragua turns out to be democratic instead of totalitarian?" The focus: Washington, not Managua. To my recollection *20/20* did not investigate the covert funding of the Contras until disclosure about Oliver North and Iran-Contra forced the issue onto the agenda. Recall that that scandal was not broken by investigators for any news organization; instead, it was revealed by the attorney general to preempt just such an exposé.

Unlike many producers who usually focused on the same type of story, I ranged among investigative reports, social issues, popular culture and breaking news. I produced stories on Tina Turner and nuclear war, on Bruce Springsteen and VCRs, on Bob Dylan and America's toughest prison. I had support to explore issues and was able to add a deeper spin from time to time, especially on cultural stories.

Despite the fact that few of my colleagues seemed to read the papers every day or talk about current affairs or politics, there were a number of journalists at 20/20 who took issues seriously, knew their stuff, had good ideas and were willing to stand up for them. My colleague Joe Lovett produced stories on AIDS that were way ahead of their time. Judith Moses blew the whistle on human rights issues overseas. Alice Peifer, Kate Wenner, Joe Fiferling, and Nola Safro, among others, all did stories with substance and style. Correspondents like Tom Jarriel, Bob Brown, Stone Phillips and Lynn Scher were strong and friendly, as were many talented editors like the now-heralded filmmaker Alan Berliner.

At 20/20 you learned, almost by osmosis, where the limits were—what you could and could not get on the air, what you could get away with, what tone was right, what soundbites would play. You were soon in that gray area where self-awareness and self-censorship meet and merge.

But sometimes, every so often, when 20/20 did something that I thought was embarrassing, the show would follow it up with stories with another spin, sometimes with real merit and impact. One example involved Geraldo Rivera.

Herrendo, as some critics call him, as a comment on the quality of his work, is a complicated figure, personally engaging and often brave, even brilliant. Roone Arledge had discovered him while watching him being interviewed on the air when he was a legal aid lawyer in the 1970s, still known by his childhood name Jerry Rivers. Geraldo soon took on the ethnic identity of his Puerto Rican father (rather than his Jewish mother) and displayed real promise in a medium that loves larger than life personalities. I liked Geraldo's flair because he had guts and passion, the very qualities that most correspondents lack, and in turn hated him for. Their condescension gave him a bit of an inferiority complex. Yet he knew he was undervalued by people whose hypocrisy he questioned. Many TV reporters are bland: Geraldo was anything but. But his boldness usually had a self-serving character. He was often spoken of as a champion, but for what? His rebel image was too often a pose.

Geraldo lost his job at ABC for publicly questioning Roone Arledge's judgment in killing a 20/20 investigative report on Marilyn Monroe's alleged affairs with John and Robert Kennedy. The piece implicated Bobby Kennedy and when word of it pissed off the Kennedy family, it was killed. Roone's number two, David Burke, later president of CBS news, was considered close to the family, having worked for Senator Ted Kennedy. He supposedly discussed the matter with Bobby's widow, Ethel Kennedy, before pulling the plug. The network cited journalistic problems with the segment, but never detailed them.

It wasn't even Geraldo's piece, but as a standup guy, he took on the brass. He defended the story's journalistic credibility and questioned management's decision. So did Hugh Downs and the other correspondents. Unfortunately for Geraldo, he questioned Arledge's judgment in *People* magazine. That's a no-no. Grumbling is acceptable, but pissing where you eat or in public is considered bad form.

Geraldo would soon learn that no one is indispensable. He had become too cocky, too independent. ABC honored his years of service but ultimately demanded its due: his servitude. Geraldo reached a financial settlement with a severance package and reportedly a clause stipulating that he couldn't publicly disclose its terms or criticize ABC. (He was later publicly attacked by Bette Midler, who claimed, also in *People*, to have been seduced into committing a sexual act with Rivera on ABC news property. Geraldo, a master of self-promotion, learned the old lesson that the media that builds you up will also tear you down.)

Geraldo was shell shocked the way the mighty are after a fall. He agonized publicly in the pages of *Esquire*, but was soon laughing all the way to the bank. He decided to drop out of news and cash in on his television celebrity. Since he was always accused of being more of a showman than a newsman, why not go all the way? He made it official, turning his visibility and cachet into a small media industry. He soon had his own syndicated talk show where he made headlines with a provoked slugfest with some Nazi guest.

He became a hit in the big time of talk show syndication, the network be damned. He also ran his own investigative tabloid program for a while and launched a TV talk show for CNBC, then being run by onetime Reagan advisor Roger Ailes. At the outset he borrowed a lesson from Ted Koppel's yearlong focus on the Iran hostage crisis and sought to "own" the O. J. trial—to be the show of record. He alienated many black viewers by turning his program into a bully pulpit, an electronic outpost of the L.A. prosecutor's office. He has since parlayed that role into a top position with NBC News itself—the number two man behind Tom Brokaw.

Geraldo is a TV natural. His smooth patter and Latino looks charm the housewives; his macho style impresses the guys. He parlayed that formula into a small fortune. In 1994, he became a partner in a consortium that bought several TV stations. By 1995, facing competition from talk show hosts who made his antics look respectable, he toyed with leaving the yak circuit, then decided he would clean up the business with a new code of conduct. His ratings reportedly plummeted.

TV is by and large a cool medium, which Geraldo often overwhelmed. While I never heard him talk about himself in the third person—a sure sign of an ego disease—he definitely put himself in the center of the action and was both loved and hated for it. I liked Geraldo against my better judgment even though he distrusted my political leanings. I even encouraged his former production assistant C. C. Dyer to marry him when she was wavering and sought my advice. I appreciated the brazen way he did things, even if I didn't like much of what he did. I especially appreciated the way his non-stuffy, in-your-face persona ruffled the stuck-up guardians of news protocol, who usually put him down for the wrong reasons. Like many, I felt he was wasting his journalistic talent by chasing celebrityhood. But I gradually learned that his principles were elastic, and that like many big names, his head often swelled. Some said he had become a caricature, even a cartoon—but then again, cartoons sell well.

Back in 1982, Rivera had a lucrative deal with ABC giving him a considerable amount of editorial control and autonomy. He talked *20/20* into doing an hour special on Palestinian terrorism. He promised amazing access to the terrorist underworld. Working with the active cooperation of the Mossad, the Israeli secret service, Geraldo was allowed to film their counterinsurgency forces in action and get exclusive and dramatic in-prison interviews with captured PLO terrorists. (I later learned that the father of one of Geraldo's assistants had been a top Mossad official, although I don't know if he was the key to his access, or if his producer's rumored and not that discreet, very personal friendship with a certain Israeli general won the entrée.) The Israelis and Geraldo had a mutual love affair. Perhaps it was because he was raised in a Jewish home on Long Island, and in his youth tattooed the Star of David on his arm.

The Israelis introduced him to one of their covert intelligence assets, allegedly also one of the producer's close friends, the late, swashbuckling, Lebanese Christian-Falangist Bashir Geymayel, who was viewed as an Israeli surrogate terrorist by Palestinians in Beirut. (Lebanon's Falangists admired and carried on in the tradition of Mussolini's Italian fascists.) The two of them bonded. Rivera did several war-zone standups in shirt sleeves with this Lebanese Rambo. His cheerleading coverage presented Geymayel as a heroic Che Guevara-like great white hope for the good guys—Western civilization in general and Israel in particular. Bashir, accused of personally massacring Palestinians, was killed by a bomb planted at his headquarters—part of a war fired by cycles of bloody reprisals.

After the program aired, a group of Palestinian scholars protested to ABC. They detailed numerous alleged errors, biases and distortions. They demanded that ABC show the other side, their people's side. In response, ABC commissioned a *20/20* story on Arab stereotypes in America, a strong story exposing intolerance and prejudice. The story was actually seen among Arab leaders as patronizing because it was totally unresponsive to the substance of their complaints. They were furious and came back to ABC asking if they had the guts to show what life is really like for Palestinians living under occupation on the West Bank. "Don't take our word for it," they said. "Go and see for yourself."

ABC doesn't take kindly to people accusing them of cowardice. 20/20 took up the challenge. Veteran producer Stanhope Gould and correspondent Tom Jarriel were sent to the West Bank. They decided to take a close look at a few key issues like water, shelter and hospital care. They met with ordinary Palestinians, then asked to interview the Israeli official in charge in the specific areas they were investigating. They met with General Ariel Sharon, then running the occupation. They briefed him on the specific subjects they wanted to discuss. He listened attentively but then categorically refused to go on camera. The Israeli government suggested they interview a university expert instead. They declined because they wanted answers from the man in charge. The government stood fast. It was a standoff.

Back in New York, a high-level Israeli official came to see Westin and urged him to drop the story because, he said, it was blatantly one-sided. The Israelis believed that if they refused to cooperate, ABC couldn't possibly air the story because it would lack balance. In essence, their nonparticipation was a calculated ploy to kill negative coverage. To his credit, Westin refused to be intimidated. 20/20 aired the story, called "Under Israel's Thumb." Anchor Hugh Downs reported for the record that Israel refused to provide an official to be interviewed. That disclaimer was unusual and was provided twice, at the beginning and at the end, in case anyone missed it.

It was a strong story, and there weren't many like it in the years that followed. What's significant was that it was outsiders who pressed for it by challenging the network. In the first instance, they criticized Geraldo's anti-PLO rant. They stayed on ABC's case when 20/20 offered up its story on Arab stereotyping. And they kept pushing until ABC sent a team from its offices on the west side of Manhattan to the olive orchards on the west bank of the Jordan. It was this informed and persistent media activism that pushed the network further than anyone ever thought it would go. They deserve credit for being pushy. ABC deserves credit, at least in this instance, for not being dismissive of their pushiness. There is a broader lesson here.

I was in the office the night the story ran. Hundreds of telegrams arrived attacking 20/20 for broadcasting the segment. They all said the same thing—that the report was one-sided and that the government of Israel was not represented. What struck me as funny was that many of the telegrams arrived an hour before the show even aired. You could see that this "protest" was totally orchestrated. Afterward, hundreds of phonecalls with the same message flooded the switchboard, and later, the Israeli government tried to discredit this powerful report by nitpicking a few details. Roone Arledge disclaimed all knowledge of the particulars, but ABC stood firm. I was proud of being part of 20/20 that night.

20/20 did do some international stories, usually with a star-spangled twist. Barbara Walters occasionally globe-trotted for breathy moments with the rich and the royal. As a power in the business, Barbara is on a first-name basis with high society around the world, so much so that her social activities get almost as much ink as her interview exclusives. But we didn't completely ignore the poor. We covered the Ethiopian famine through the efforts of American kids raising money for its victims and blindness in the Amazon via American doctors volunteering time there. To go overseas, you needed an American in danger, an American dispensing charity, or an American on an adventure. In other words, an American angle. We rarely heard from the people who lived in crisis zones. They were objects of our attention, not subjects with perspectives worth hearing.

In 1984, I was sent to El Salvador to investigate charges that forced sterilization was being paid for by U.S. dollars while the Reagan administration was suspending federal funds for abortions at home. Years earlier, 20/20 had aired a story on American nuns murdered in El Salvador. Now I was looking into what pro-lifers might consider another form of murder. In the end I couldn't quite prove coercion but I did find considerable steering of women toward sterilization in our foreign aid program that was heavily invested in a much bigger death (and death squad) business through a counterinsurgency war.

I managed to find a local doctor who had pioneered a quickie sterilization procedure then widely in use, who gave us an interview after letting me film an operation. He indicted the U.S. AID population control program, calling for broader reproductive rights for women in that very Catholic and patriarchal country. He agonized about talking with us on camera, then finally did the interview, a brave and important act. But his interview never made air. When I came back to New York with lots of powerful footage, the story itself was sterilized because 20/20 had recently run a totally different story about Salvadoran refugees seeking asylum in the Southwest. The story was dumped before it was even edited. We had "done" El Salvador.

Since Africa has always been one of my interests, I was eager to find a way to get a story about apartheid onto 20/20. The program had only done one piece before I got there, in the early '80s, focusing on South Africa's richest man, Harry Oppenheimer, and his diamond and gold empire, in which he spoke out unchallenged against economic sanctions.

None of my pitches on the subject were successful until I received a message in 1986 to call Jesse Jackson. Jackson was planning to visit the frontline states, the countries bordering South Africa, to investigate and document the destabilization caused by South African military and economic pressures aimed at cutting off support for Nelson Mandela's African National Congress (ANC).

I knew I didn't have the clout to get past 20/20's lack of interest, but I did have a brainstorm. Maybe Jesse could convince them if he would personally pitch Av Westin. Jackson said he'd give it a shot. Av agreed to see him when told Jesse requested a meeting.

At the appointed hour, the Reverend swept into our offices, shaking hands with all and signing autographs for the handful of black employees, who were thrilled to see him in person. In the meeting, Jackson detailed the plight of the frontline states, explained the economic significance of Mozambique's Beira corridor (which no one but me had heard of), and invited *20/20* to document this historic visit by a black leader to black Africa.

The room was silent. Westin thanked him for coming but said that a detailed story on Africa was not what he had in mind. He said he was more interested in Jackson's anti-drug work in inner city high schools. Keeping his eyes on the prize, Jackson noted that that story had been done many times, but no one had investigated South Africa's secret war. Jesse wasn't precisely correct, but close. According to *Africa's Media Image*, a book on U.S. coverage of Africa, only 117 stories on the frontline states aired on all of U.S. television in the 1980s. That added up to less than 0.1 percent of network foreign coverage. A region of a hundred million people got ".0009 of America's collective attention."

The encounter ended in a standoff. I knew that sending a correspondent to southern Africa for three weeks in mid-August would wreak havoc with the show's schedule and could be expensive. After Jesse left the room, I piped up: "What if we do this story in a different way, as a video diary, in Jackson's own voice? That would make it more of a personality piece about Jackson's trip, not analysis of some obscure Beira corridor."

I thought Av would shoot me down but he didn't. My suggestion would make the trip a lot cheaper to cover too. He thought for a minute, then asked, "But will Jackson do it?" I said I would ask.

I chased Jackson down the street. At first he was skeptical. He had never reported his own story before. I pointed out that if he was his own correspondent, he would have more control over the spin of the segment. He liked that part and agreed to do it.

I was soon off with him on a magical mystery tour of Africa, nine countries in three weeks, from the war zones of Angola to the ravaged countryside of Mozambique. It was an amazing and exhausting experience and one that deserved air time. When I came back, I found that the show had been preempted for two weeks for sports and that if our piece was to air, it would have to be edited over the course of a weekend. I had brought back thirty hours of material.

With two editors working around the clock, we made it. It aired and the ratings were strong.

The segment was attacked by a right-wing media monitoring group as one-sided. They missed the point—it was *supposed* to be one-sided. Jesse's side. That's what made it interesting. Unfortunately, although the video diary approach worked well, it was rarely repeated. 20/20, like all the magazine shows, is correspondent-centered, the same format week after week. TV news has its own unmistakable DNA, which needs no lab to identify it.

The real ideological bent of TV news and 20/20-like stories reveals itself most when confronted directly. Since I began this chapter with a story about one Bernie at 20/20 I will end it with another. Bernie Stone is his name, an editor who many of the producers wanted to work with because of his skill and sense of imagery. Opinionated and experienced, he was a graduate of the old school of the film industry that preceded the electronic age of digital videotape editing, a razor blade wizard who could cut and splice with the best of them. In addition to a good eye, he had the good fortune of having worked for years in England where television documentary was and still is an art form.

In October 1995, he told me that he was suing ABC news because of a work saga that featured three of America's top media personalities, Barbara Walters, Rupert Murdoch, and O. J. Simpson.

A year earlier, after a long stint at 20/20, Bernie had been assigned to ABC's docu-magazine *Turning Point*, working for an exec there known as a look man, one of those artsy senior producers who won't let too much information get in the way of a stunning visual. The two of them battled over content, and Bernie was told he knew nothing about editing, despite his four decades in the business and many awards. He was soon shuttled off that series and exiled into an editor's pool with many a frustrated but well-paid button-pusher.

Despite Bernie's demotion, many at ABC still held him in high regard. His next assignment was considered even more prestigious:

to edit part of a Barbara Walters special featuring her profiles of the year's top ten personalities. Although Barbara works for ABC news, she also has an exclusive production deal to supply her interview programs to ABC's entertainment division through her own company, Bar-Wal Productions. This side deal enables ABC's best-known personality to profit twice, once as the entertainment talent and again as the owner of a production company that hires her own services for a nice bundle.

Ever since her early days on the *Today* show, when she reportedly invested half of her researcher's salary in a press agent who got her more column ink than the program's host, Dave Garroway, she has known how to work the system. And she has had more staying power than most of the celebrities she brings into her spotlight.

Although nominally autonomous, her company's annual prime-time special for ABC was to be edited at ABC News as a reworked compilation of her 20/20 stories. Bernie, who had worked with 20/20 for years, would be working for Barbara directly. The story he was chosen to reedit was billed as a major encounter between media titans: the Walters profile of Rupert Murdoch.

As chance would have it, a week or two earlier Bernie had watched a PBS replay of a BBC interview with the dying English TV writer Dennis Potter, whose impressive body of work includes the inventive *Singing Detective* and *Pennies From Heaven*. It was Potter's last interview, and he meditated eloquently on the declining state of television worldwide while sipping morphine on camera. He would be dead within ten days.

His only regret, he said, was not killing the man he felt had destroyed the medium he (Potter) had served so loyally and creatively. The target in his imaginary crosshairs: Rupert Murdoch. "I call my cancer Rupert so I can get close to it," he quipped darkly. "I would shoot the bugger if I could. There is no one person more responsible for the pollution of what was already a very polluted press. And the pollution of the British press is a very important part of the pollution of British political life. It is an important part of the cynicism and the misperception of our own realities that is destroying so much of our political discourse."

These comments made headlines in England. Bernie saw Potter as an inspiration and Murdoch as the enemy. He told me he couldn't stand Rupert because of his role in breaking the newspaper unions in London and, closer to home, debasing the daily newspaper Bernie grew up on, the once liberalish *New York Post.*

Yet here Bernie was, waiting in his empty edit room as ABC wheeled in fifty video cassettes featuring Barbara's respectful, even loving encounter with Murdoch. "It made me sick," he told me. "She was fawning and sucking up to him. There was no balance, no perspective, nothing of substance, nothing critical. It was a puff piece." (In 1997, Roone Arledge served on the committee hosting a fundraising tribute to Murdoch.)

A former ABC producer confirmed to me that Barbara wanted it that way, nixing several strong interviews with Murdoch critics. A compromise, calculated to give the segment the appearance of credibility, was achieved with one cynical soundbite to the effect that Murdoch probably granted the interview as a calculated image exercise, to foster an impression of being open and reasonable. As he probably did. To be fair, the Walters profile was *not* an investigative story, focusing more on Murdoch's personality than on his power and impact.

As Bernie watched the Murdoch tapes, something in him snapped. He decided he had had enough, that he just wouldn't edit a smarmy salute to Rupert's genius. He told his supervisor that he was rejecting the job, that ABC should be ashamed of running it, it was a disgrace to journalism, and it made him want to throw up.

The Barbara Walters Company was shocked and furious, according to Bernie. "I thought they would just get another editor," he told me, "but they were so mad that they wheeled all fifty cassettes out, took the whole job away from ABC news and finished it outside."

It was ABC's turn to react. The phone rang in his newly reemptied edit room. It was the executive who ran ABC's editing operations. "Bernie, I understand that you refused to edit the Barbara Walters show. How come? What are you doing?"

At that point, Bernie cranked up both barrels once again and began denouncing Murdoch, telling him what Dennis Potter said on his deathbed and condemning the Walters-Murdoch interview as unworthy of ABC, "disgusting."

There was a pause. This type of exchange is a rarity within the network world.

According to Bernie, "I think he didn't want any trouble, any union problems, so he said to me, 'Oh, so you had *religious* objections?' Religious objections? I thought he was nuts, so I told him again what I thought of Murdoch. This time I was even *more* outspoken."

Another pause, Bernie says, whereupon the executive calmly told him that he personally liked Rupert Murdoch, but that Stone's reasons still sounded to him like religious objections.

It was then that Bernie got it: Religious objections are covered in the union contract as grounds for refusing work assignments; political objections are not.

So Bernie said, "Religious objections? Yeah, well, something like that."

Two days later, Bernie, now marked as a dissident, was reassigned once again, moved deeper into the bowels of ABC to a small room in the basement, where he was sentenced to record the incoming satellite feeds of the O. J. Simpson trial. "Every hour and a half, for seven months, from morning to night, I put four big beta videotapes in the machine and pushed the record button. That was it. A one-finger job! No editing. No sweat. I just had to push a button. That was my punishment."

When the trial ended, Bernie was reassigned once again, this time to the Siberia of the graveyard shift, midnight to eight A.M. He was often alone in the wee hours with his "religious objections" but little work to do. Bored and bitter, he had enough, and is bringing a case against ABC for age discrimination and not permitting him to work as an editor, which was what he was hired to do and had done all his life. His suit was not given much of a chance of succeeding.

Bernie was clearly out of sync with the times and had violated one of the network's prime requirements: get along by going along. He has since joined the growing ranks of network refugees.

CHAPTER 6

THE CONTROL ROOM

After the Gulf War, ABC lined up its news stars for a photo spread. Koppel, Walters, Sawyer, Jennings, Donaldson, Downs and Brinkley all posed in a straight line, staring outward, at attention—a strikingly composed advertisement that seemed inspired by a World War II recruiting poster. Air Power was the tagline. ABC called them the Magnificent Seven.

"There's a maw," one executive once told me, pointing to a giant calendar that listed tentative programs and segments. "My job is to feed it." Feeding the maw is what media workers do. Only a very few influence content, and even fewer find the opportunity or institutional support to consider other ways of doing or thinking.

At ABC news each morning, a desk assistant, the lowliest of novices, updates a computer list of where all the company's crews, correspondents and "corres-pundits" are worldwide, complete with their phone, fax and beeper numbers. That list is known as the troops. A friend of mine who has worked for years in television says, "If you've been in the media, you've been in the military." The command gives the orders, and the troops carry them out.

When you look like a soldier, you sometimes act like one, marching to the same drumbeat and waving the same flag. It's no wonder that the media is often in lockstep with the government, especially on foreign policy issues. Media critics Martin Lee and Norman Solomon call it the "we-we" phenomenon, in which on-air anchors speak of the government as if the separation between the state and the fourth estate did not exist. A we-we example from ABC's Sam Donaldson: "*We* have completed our tests to modernize our weapons, and if *we* were to stop testing now, *we* would be at a distinct disadvantage." Reporter Sam becomes General Sam fronting for Uncle Sam. That's a we-we. Watch for it.

Internally, this news army is mobilized by orders handed down by executives who frequently operate from a place appropriately called the control room. It is from there that TV directors decide what to show and how. Once the decisions are made, control passes down the line. The actual TV signal leaves the building on its way to the transmitter and our homes through another room called master control. At ABC news, every control room had a red phone in it, the so-called Roone phone, a dedicated line for then ABC news president Roone Arledge. I once watched an executive producer almost knock someone down as he reached over to snatch it on the first ring. Roone would be barking orders about the look of a shot or a question to be asked of a guest.

Control is always the operative word. News programming is no longer just about picking stories or programs but in effect programming viewers. News managers don't just manage news organizations. They manage how the news will be presented. The key task is referred to straightforwardly as packaging—compressing information and visuals into prescribed formats, usually short and tightly edited, to fit into designated time-slots between commercials. In the old days, journalism was about "all the news that's fit to print." Today, it's "all the news that fits." An acquaintance at NBC local news speaks of his newsroom as the "can factory."

Still, working in the 20/20 environment was heady. It was exciting to be part of a powerful news organization with large budgets and small armies of personnel. It was exciting to travel, to feel important, to work around skilled professionals. When ABC News called, people called back. And yet, being there often felt unfulfilling. The various shows at ABC probably spent as much time and effort in competing against each other as against the other networks. 20/20's offices could have been occupied by an insurance company. The work spaces felt like boxes. The edit rooms were built in the basement in windowless rooms with little ventilation. The halls were often lined with boxes of tape or films and were probably a fire hazard. Needless to say, there was a lot of grumbling. I thought of it as the mines.

Upstairs, producers each had small offices, while senior producers were given slightly larger ones. Barbara and Hugh each had corner offices. Barbara had hers redone with lots of mirrors, and room for her two secretaries who constantly sent personal notes as she cultivated her Rolodex of celebrities. ABC, like many companies, had whole directories of approved furnishings organized on a class system. There were A offices, B offices, and C offices. Mine was definitely a C—made smaller by the clutter of books, tapes, and documents I forever seem to collect. When 20/20 did a story on the crews that clean office buildings late at night, my office was chosen as an exhibit of the horrors they face.

In the days before voice mail, secretaries answered the phones. Back then, producers kept clippings, files, reports and story ideas. There were researchers who took pride in digging out forgotten facts. Today the researchers are gone and there is Nexis, an expensive online service that is accessed for background info. In my experience, Nexis just spewed out acres of paper summarizing the same Associated Press or *New York Times* story and its reprints in papers throughout the country. So much for original research. Today, it's mostly recycling within networks and between them—it's not surprising to see the same story redone by competing programs.

Insecurity is legion. You soon learned that the networks considered all employees disposable. "No one is indispensable," I was told again and again. When I started in network television, it was common to operate with a two-person crew, adding a lighting man when needed. Today, the trend in local news is toward the one man band, a camera jockey who does everything—sound, picture, standups, and what passes for reporting. Some cable stations, like Time Warner's News 1 in New York City, utilize correspondents who shoot and report their own stories with Hi-8 cameras. Some of their work is excellent, but when reporters are sent out by themselves, the producer-correspondent collaboration that once strengthened broadcast journalism is all but gone. Quality suffers.

I often felt like an outsider, albeit one who had somehow found a way to fit in. Although I was accepted among the rank and file, I felt compelled to push the predictable envelope of story ideas, and pushed myself as well to prove how productive I could be. In addition, I always found myself with projects on the side, which often seemed more interesting and relevant than the main work I was doing. Taking outside jobs, however, was frowned upon. ABC news did not want their employees doing or saying anything that might puncture the perception they promoted constantly of journalism as objective, above the fray. In short, don't embarrass us.

Questioning network priorities was not encouraged. In 1988, the year I left ABC, there was a controversy over how the networks were covering South Africa, an area that had been a major interest of mine for over twenty years. Richard Cohen, then Dan Rather's producer at CBS, wrote an op-ed piece in the *New York Times* accusing the networks of moral appeasement by not challenging the media restrictions Pretoria had imposed to limit coverage of the abuses of apartheid. CNN covered the controversy and interviewed me about it. I publicly supported Cohen's criticisms after I heard that more stories about South Africa were ending up on the shelf (shot but not run) than on the air. ABC had also cut back on coverage.

A day or two later, I received a memo from Robert Siegenthaler, the head of news practices (or VP of COA, vice president for covering our ass). It was not exactly supportive, noting that "our people who cover South Africa were in London and saw your on-camera interview this week on CNN." The memo continued: "Since they risk arrest each day when doing their jobs in South Africa, they were naturally nervous when someone labeled as being from ABC news 'rocks their boat.' Naturally you are free to hold your own opinions. Expressing them while being identified with ABC news is not free." The letter went on to require me to "pre-clear all media appearances and pre-submit any writings." Their goal, he assured me, was not to "hobble me," but to "protect our colleagues who are in the field." Talk about chilling free speech.

The ABC policy manual specifically overrules the First Amendment. Do not participate in politics or protests or even serve on a local school board. Keep a low profile. In March 1997, the highest court in the state of Washington upheld the right of a newspaper to bar a journalist's political activism in a case of a reporter's support of a gay rights initiative on personal time. "Under the Washington court's ruling," explained Jim Ledbetter in the *Village Voice*, "Rupert Murdoch would be free to give hundreds of thousands of dollars to a state political party advocating one side of a political initiative—that's free speech. But a reporter working for a paper [Murdoch] owned" could legally be prohibited from demonstrating for the other side—that's advocacy.

On a number of occasions I walked that thin line, refusing to muzzle my beliefs or my right to free association but careful not to drag my personal projects into my job. I mostly managed not to get called on the carpet, although there were some close calls. When I was helping produce the Sun City anti-apartheid record and video in 1985, I was told that 20/20 might want to do the story and I was being considered to produce it. Fortunately for me, the idea was dropped. It would have been a conflict.

On another occasion, Jackson Browne, one of the Sun City artists, called me about the possibility of helping produce a nonpartisan peace concert in Central America. He invited me to join him for a meeting with Nicaragua's then-president Daniel Ortega. Jackson went to the wrong Helmsley Hotel, however, so he arrived just as Ortega's motorcade was about to leave for a luncheon in the South Bronx. He was to have briefed me about the project before our meeting but didn't have the chance, and now he had to split. Ortega invited him to ride with him in a limo surrounded by the Secret Service. Jackson begged off but introduced me to Ortega and suggested that I hop in and tell him about our plans. The only problem: I hadn't been told what those plans were.

Motorcycles roared into position. I told Ortega that my name was Daniel too. I jokingly called myself *el otro Daniel*, the other Daniel. He laughed, opened the door and motioned for me to sit beside him as we took off, sirens blasting. This was at the height of the U.S.-funded Contra war, which years later would be blamed for shipping cocaine into Los Angeles. Ortega was not exactly President Reagan's favorite, and he had received threats from Contra types during his visit to the UN. The tabloid press mostly ignored his criticisms of U.S. policy and instead focussed on some expensive prescription eyeglasses he bought while in town.

We raced up Third Avenue, with me trying to sound knowledgeable about Jackson's plans, which were not simply pro-Sandinista. When we passed Yankee Stadium, I told him not to knock Yankee imperialism in that neighborhood. I think he got the joke. When we arrived at the destination, a Catholic church center that served the poor, I knew I was in a world of trouble. TV cameras were on the scene. If I jumped out with Ortega, I was sure my picture would show up everywhere, including on the monitors back in the 20/20 control room. So I just sat there after Ortega and the security men left the car. Two other Secret Service men noticed that I was in the car with no identifying pin, which would have marked me as part of the entourage. They had no idea who I was or how I got there.

Just as they jumped into the car to check me out, Ortega noticed I was missing and yelled in Spanish, motioning for me to follow him. I did—until I saw every local news photographer lined up in front of the walkway. I started walking in slow motion, then turned around with my back to the cameras. An ABC cameraman spotted me and waved. I didn't wave back. I raced back to work knowing that no one would believe where I had been. Later that afternoon, I was in the *20/20* studio when footage of the Sandinista commandante's visit to the Bronx flashed on one screen. For a split second, I saw my own head, moving backward. I was relieved no one else saw it.

20/20 staffers were constantly reminded that our programs were there to get the ratings, which are there to get the advertising dollars, which are there to please the stockholders, who in turn reward management, and on and on. The bottom line for media corporations is both money and power. U.S. companies know this well: They spend an estimated $120 billion a year on advertising, a good chunk of it on TV.

Noam Chomsky has detailed how the elite media set the agenda for the rest of the media, while promoting a distinct set of values and interests, usually reflecting those of its owners, whose experience of the world is far different from that of the audience. The owners then rent that audience's attention span to advertisers on a moment by moment basis.

News is a major profit center, but more importantly, news is an image center, a values center and an ideology center. It is part of a media system that plays a powerful role in all advanced industrial societies. Herb Granath of ABC put it this way in a trade magazine: "He who controls product, controls the world." A century ago, Thomas Edison saw this too: "Whoever controls the film industry," he said, "will control the most powerful influence over people."

The news world has its own logic, structured within a set of common beliefs and practices. "The journalistic enterprise, especially TV news, essentially is reporting on itself," argue David Altheide and Robert Snow in *Media Worlds in the Post Journalism Era*. "It addresses events that are cast in its own formats and frames of reference, rather than attempting to understand the events in their own terms, and then trying to communicate the complexities and ambiguities of real-world conditions." Some folks in the business call this processed news.

The news coverage that flows from this asserts its claim to a higher ground because of devotion to the biggest mythology of them all—conceits like objectivity and balance. I have to concede: We journalists are supersensitive and defensive when it comes to challenges to our craft. "Journalism doesn't admit that criticism is legitimate," acknowledges New York University journalism professor Jay Rosen. "One of the most powerful things about the declaration 'I'm objective' is the hidden corollary: You're not." In a conversation with the *New York Times*, Rosen named the you he was talking about: "Everybody but the journalist. So everybody who comes at the press with a dissatisfaction, with a complaint or even an idea is seen by journalists as subjective." Sometimes so-called objectivity is used as a cloak to hide behind. It also reinforces the sense that journalists have no accountability to any values other than their own professional (read: personal) needs and/or institutional prejudices. As journalist George Seldes, who died in 1995 at age 104 after a lifetime of criticizing the media, put it, "The biggest sacred cow of the press is the press itself."

On the inside of the news machine, it is difficult to deviate from formula, because programs are so tightly formatted as well as closely monitored by senior producers and lawyers. Promotions within the controlling echelons tend to go to people with the same mentality, and when people think alike, they act alike—and in many cases, produce alike.

Attitudes trickle down. Media corporations expect loyalty from employees, and in turn overlay an identity on them. Corporate logos become employee logos. Employees wear them on their jackets and t-shirts. They may not start the work day by singing company songs like some of their counterparts in Japan, but they might as well.

There, the process of corporate absorption is explicit. Here, it is implicit, working more invisibly, but working just the same. Unfortunately, insider status comes often at the expense of critical and independent thinking. Many journalists have a problem distinguishing complaints about what they do (or to be more honest, are required to do) from who they are.

Our media companies are better these days at admitting errors and even carrying occasional self-criticism, but it doesn't affect the thrust of their work. They may want to project different identities, but at bottom they tend to be the same. Key positions at one network are often held by exiles from another. NBC news is headed by a former CBS producer, while NBC's *Dateline* is executive produced by a former ABC *Prime Time Live* executive. *Nightline* is run by Dan Rather's ex-producer, while a former NBC producer is a key ABC executive. TV shows in our culture are like gasoline at the pump, sold by brand name. But is there really much of a difference? The octane and lead levels are preset. It gets you where you want to go. Three hundred miles later, you're empty again. Fill 'er up.

What's most distressing is how hard it is to get a critique like mine acknowledged, much less discussed, inside media companies. Known for their cynicism and hip detachment, media workers don't often think they have any right to have input into the directions their institutions take, even though journalists are infamous for bitching about how their stories are spiked, their assignments brainless, their ideas constantly shot down. Within the networks, there are few opportunities for critical debates about these concerns. Fear and insecurity are pervasive. For employees, the only certainty is uncertainty. Shows are constantly canceled, and cutbacks and downsizing pose a constant threat. It comes as little surprise that an Indiana University survey of American journalists, which in 1971 reported that 49 percent expressed high job satisfaction, had dropped by 1992 to 29 percent. One reason for the dissatisfaction is the sense that you can't really do anything about practices you dislike. There are no channels for dissent and most outside critics are not taken seriously.

This is especially true when news organizations are confronted with national security and censorship issues, as was the case during the Gulf War. As John R. MacArthur documented in his book *Second Front*, few journalists formally protested what was widely called suck-up coverage. CBS anchor Dan Rather was one of the few to admit it (at a media conference, not on CBS): "There was a lack of will, a lack of guts to speak our minds or for that matter to speak our hearts.... It's still not the role of the press to be an attack dog, but it's damn well not being a lapdog. These days, the lapdog is in."

The psychiatrist and writer Robert J. Lifton has described America's reaction to the nuclear bombs dropped in World War II as "psychic numbing." He believes that when an event is so horrific, it prompts psychological resistance, denial and defensiveness, a turning away because it is so hard to take in. Numbing also feeds the inability to express empathy or compassion, much less solidarity. Lifton thus explains why so many people tune out and are rarely motivated to question, express outrage or protest.

As I heard him discuss this, I thought it might also apply to news professionals who cope with the horrors they report by disassociating them from their own lives. I asked him about this and Lifton readily agreed, acknowledging that he hadn't paid enough attention to the media. One occupational hazard of media work is a psychological hardening or deadening, where everything becomes as important (or unimportant) as everything else. It is easy to become smug, blasé, a know-it-all. And when journalists are desensitized, audiences are quick to follow.

We journalists have a responsibility to care more deeply than we do. We also need to find ways of using our whiz-bang technology, craft and smarts to dig out important information and present it in ways that reveal, explain and inform. In the last few years, even the number of public service announcements on the air has shrunk.

Nietzsche once said that there are no facts, only perspectives on the facts. The problem is that our media embraces factoids while rejecting context and analysis. Hence, all the trivialization. Marketing concepts like the demographic targeting of viewers and readers have overshadowed notions of public service.

Even as the trend toward concentration in media ownership increases, people's ability to concentrate on what the media is reporting decreases. As media time speeds up, with more compressed and packaged news, so do our attention spans. It is as if we are being conditioned to be bored if the story slows down or too many points requiring thought are introduced. A study by the Pew Research Center for the People and the Press reported in May 1996 that younger people are turning away from TV news in greater numbers than older people. At the same time, they spend more time watching MTV or playing video games than reading or studying.

Why are young people not watching the news? asked the editors of the *Nation*: "Suppose they skip the nightly news not because it's boring or too complicated but because they don't trust its homogenized premise of objectivity, especially when Disneyized, Murdochized, Oprahized and Hard Copyized." I only wish that young people were that politically conscious and media literate. In fact, media literacy is barely taught in America's schools. If anything, what we have is a mood of anti-politics—all politics—fed by all the corporate propaganda and logos that have worked their way into instructional material though such TV outlets as Channel One, which brings sanitized news and commercials into American classrooms.

Selling Free Enterprise, by Elizabeth Fones Wolf, tells this sordid story in some detail. One of its effects, she says, is to encourage young people to tune out information for the excitement and stimulation of a 100 percent entertainment-sports culture organized around celebrity and celebrity icons. That is no doubt one reason why politicians seek to become celebrities and surround themselves with celebrities.

It would be unfair to deny that big broadcasting does from time to time go after big business—and sometimes that leads to lawsuits like the one involving the Food Lion food chain, where *Prime Time*

Live exposed sloppy food handling practices. In the aftermath of that case and other legal challenges to TV investigative journalism, the networks faced a serious public relations problem. Had ordinary people turned on them and their techniques? ABC news commissioned a poll that just happened to show that 84 percent of the public found TV newsmagazines credible and was cited repeatedly by network executives. Eighty-three percent of the respondents said the same thing about network news *and* local news—as if there were no distinction between the two. I was dubious about local news receiving such a high approval rating, because it conflicts with so many widely reported surveys saying the opposite. Ninety percent of people believe in UFOs too. It reminded me of that old axiom: Figures lie and liars figure.

After twenty years of exposure to TV newsmagazines, it's not clear if the public can tell the difference between the shows, as they all seem to blend together. When you only serve one type of meal, it's not surprising that people think it's the only type there is.

In February 1997, ABC devoted ninety minutes to a *Hidden Camera/Hard Choices* program that aired some of this debate. It gave the network a chance to answer Food Lion on its own turf. What became clear was that it was not the hidden cameras per se that were the problem, but the violation of corporate rights, i.e., allegedly fraudulent practices by ABC employees posing as Food Lion employees. What the hidden cameras saw hadn't been under consideration by the jury at all. Clearly, they were following the judge's instructions to only consider a narrow range of issues and weren't even shown the *Prime Time* report in question. *60 Minutes'* Don Hewitt announced somewhat self-righteously that his program had discontinued its use of hidden cameras so as "not to be tarred by someone else's brush." There was an aroma of self-consciousness and defensiveness on ABC's part, posing as openness and the willingness to be self-critical. Months earlier, an ABC News vice president had said that ABC apologizes more than any other network because it boosts its credibility. I was struck by the final comment of a Food Lion PR flack to the effect that if the story had been so essential for safeguarding the public and their whistle blowing motives so pure, as ABC claimed, why did the network wait six months before airing the report?

The fact is that ABC has no problem going after meat markets— but what about money markets? Corporate practices with far greater impact tend to get downplayed in favor of small but visible abuses that can be easily documented. And, as Susan Douglas reminds us, in the *Progressive*, "For every episode of dangerous business practices in the TV newsmagazines, there are five soft features on celebrity lifestyles, health and beauty, and Dennis Rodman's newest outfit."

While the media drifts away from innovative news presentations and an entertainment culture discourages reflection, millions of viewers do remain interested. It is no wonder that news organizations debate how to keep those viewers and readers in what is called a niched media environment. The Annenberg Washington program assessed the argument that "substance doesn't sell." What they found is that the impression that audiences only want entertainment and tabloid news is promoted and encouraged by the people who provide entertainment and tabloid journalism. "Even though our best journalism is flawed by strategy frames, cynicism and other bad habits, the audience for serious public issues is impressive," writes the report's author, Ellen Hume, who went on to PBS. "My initial hunch was that customers would be more interested in entertainment than information. In the long run, in spite of temporary ratings boosts, tabloid style newscasts don't generate the kind of customer loyalty that matters in the niched media marketplace."

People inside the media who live by the secondhand can become casualties of frenetic thinking. I have been in many meetings with executives who tell me to get to the bottom line before I can even sketch out the contours of an interesting, if complex, story. All they want is the ten-second conclusion or a simple headline. This attitude helps shape the public's response. CNN's Ted Turner believes that "the more complex and forward-looking the story, the smaller the ratings." No wonder the conventional wisdom, KISS—which used to stand for Keep It Short and Sweet—now commonly means Keep It Simple and Stupid.

This is why some of the people with the most glamorous seeming jobs become privately discouraged and disaffected. I was not alone. Steve Zousmer, with whom I worked briefly at ABC news, wrote about why he left the business at age thirty-seven in a book called *TV News Off Camera*: "The flaw with a career in daily journalism turns out to be the same quality that made it so attractive at the start: It is promiscuous. It shares many of the drawbacks of sexual promiscuity, notably the elusiveness of depth." After describing in some detail how the novelty faded, he notes, "The TV newspeople I worked with are not, I think, as keenly stirred as their predecessors by a dramatic sense of committment to great social purpose. Their purpose is more professional than social; their work is more likely to be good, less likely to be great." But why is that? What has happened to what he calls the "energizing sense of mission" that once motivated TV journalists? The fault, dear Brutus, is not in the stars or in the people whose idealism quickly dissipates, but in the mindlessness of corporate culture and its bottom-line mentality.

CHAPTER 7

DEFECTING:
BECOMING A NETWORK REFUGEE

*A*t *20/20* I sensed a kind of sameness and predictability to the story selections week after week. We did genres as much as stories—the limited exposé, the disease of the week, the relationship problem, new technology, child raising, consumer ripoffs, celebrity or newsmaker interviews. Week after week, we cut and trimmed, sliced and diced to ensure that the segments fit the time allotted. The content was finessed, fine tuned, even manufactured, to fill out the format.

TV magazine stories usually follow a formula. *20/20* stories are built along a narrative line driven by an articulate cast of characters, tearful and sympathetic victims or ordinary people who do extraordinary things. In his book *Newswatch*, former executive producer Av Westin admitted that these magazine stories are *constructed* to attract an audience that is assumed to have zero knowledge and zero interest: "The twelve-minute length provides some area for maneuver," he wrote. "Stories can be constructed. They are similar to the single segments or acts of a documentary. They should contain dramatic elements, have a story flow, demonstrate some surprises, pay off with a smile or a tear or a star singing a musical signature. Each piece is like a mini-play."

Av believed that 20/20 was like a circus tent and that people would stick around for the serious journalism only if there was a barker to bring them in using a lot of glitz—celebrity interviews, entertainment profiles and the like. "More than likely," he wrote, "many people who tune into 20/20 do not want to work to understand what we are talking about. They prefer to have things explicitly presented." That attitude ensures that the show will be constructed around its promotability and mass appeal, not content.

Thus, most "reality" journalism is designed with a promo in mind. These promos are like bumper stickers, ten-second ads used to tease viewer tune-in. These promos are clever but often misleading, making the reports sound much more exciting or weighty than they are. Such promos have become a high art, with whole departments assigned to do nothing else. Some local news departments spend more on promos than they do on stories. Some story producers find they can make more money making promos than making stories. My old friend Frank Radice went from *Nightline* to produce NBC's on-air news promo effort.

Increasingly, TV form is its content. Media formats often bias information in and of themselves by not building in time for a range of views or adequate explanations. Formats have logic to them, specific time allocations, organizational grammars, pacing, and structures. They influence and limit coverage. This is especially true of television newsmagazines and their audiences. In the first instance, these programs structure the way we see and understand information. In the second, they program the audience to become comfortable with the format so that—as with watching a sports event—they understand the rules of the game. "People draw on various forms to make sense of various phenomena," write David Altheide and Robert Snow. "People interpret or make sense of phenomena through familiar forms." That is partly why they say journalism is dead, because more energy is geared to serving media formats than elucidating topics. In fact, often the topics that get on the air are products of the media itself—shaped by its packaging needs, formats and practices.

At first glance, analysis like this may sound abstract or farfetched, but actually it helps explain why it is that the more we watch, the less we know.

After a few years on the air, the ABC audience research department began to convene focus groups, to probe what viewers liked about 20/20, what they would like to see on the air. We were, we were told, there to give them what they want, what they would watch. One year the notion of adventure stories was floated. The panel said they sounded great, so 20/20 committed a small fortune to sending Hugh Downs and Geraldo Rivera all over the world to swim with the sharks one week, whales the next. They raced yachts, went treasure hunting, visited the Great Barrier Reef in Australia. The stories were entertaining and visually stunning, although the journalism was often contrived. Hugh and Geraldo had great vacations but the ratings were only so-so. Future focus groups didn't mention them among the stories they cared about, and so the trips were quietly dropped. So much for scientific market research.

The importance of this type of research seems to have increased. The people who do it see themselves simply as relaying viewer desires and reactions. In 1997, I met a very bright woman who plays that role at one of the networks. She meets regularly with the executive producers who draw on her findings to shape their story selections and "news product." She suggested that ABC News' fall in the ratings could be blamed on its unwillingness to really listen to the research and devote as much airtime to the O. J. Simpson trial as its competitors. When I questioned the methodology and impact research like hers has, she paused reflectively, admitting that I was not totally wrong. "I am always struggling with a conflict," she acknowledged. "I keep telling them to 'dumb it down,' but then I ask myself: what am I saying?"

I worked at ABC in the glory days of Roone Arledge, who may be singularly responsible for creating modern TV news. Famous for never returning calls and second-guessing his line executives, it was Arledge who brought his signature whiz-bang sports-style coverage and the show business ethic to the news division. He was hands-on even as he liked to work from the shadows. His mystique helped deflect critical scrutiny of what ABC news was and was not covering. Even tough critics seemed to be mesmerized by the special effects he introduced into *Wide World of Sports* and the celebrity news stars he launched, including Howard Cosell, Geraldo Rivera, Ted Koppel, Barbara Walters, and Peter Jennings.

When *Detroit Free Press* critic Mark Gunther began writing a book on Roone's role, he sought me out, intimating that he had in mind a tough exposé. At first, Arledge wouldn't see him, but after winning unusual access, including more than eight interviews and a chance to hang out with his powerful subject, Gunther's *House that Roone Built* became a love letter with only occasional critical glimpses of a man he describes as "complex...whose inner self remained hidden from his close associates." Gunther does say that Arledge's "selfishness left him oblivious to the needs of others, and as a result he built few strong bonds with those around him." I never got that close. Most of my encounters with Roone took place in elevators where he would joke about my being the news dissector. He rarely got it right anyway, usually calling me the inspector or connector. What's in a name?

(In early March 1997, Disney dumped Arledge in true corporate style by bumping him upstairs to the newly created role of chairman of the news division. He was replaced by David Westin [no relation to Av], head of the ABC television network, a lawyer by training with no journalism experience, whose work as ABC/Cap Cities' general counsel put him on the fast track up the corporate ladder. Under Westin the network's ratings had slipped, yet he was the one called upon to fix them. That kind of reward for failure happens all the time in the networks. A shrewd corporate in-fighter,

Arledge let it be known that he will continue to play a major role at ABC. In May 1998, with news ratings down, Arledge ostensibly "retired," but shortly thereafter it was announced that while the corporate lawyer Westin would now run the show, Arledge would continue to play a vague guiding role to, in Westin's words, "keep the family intact." By 1998, Westin was in charge. At a meeting of producers, he announced that henceforth ABC would expect that all stories include the "three Cs—celebrity, calamity, and [sic] sensation.")

Like many critics who tend to become promoters of the industry they cover, Gunther, now a media writer for *Fortune*, pinpoints ABC's problems, then explains them away. "The defects of ABC were evident—the journalism was sometimes shallow, pictures overshadowed words, the range of ideas expressed were narrow and drama more than enlightenment shaped some stories—*but* [emphasis mine] these flaws were common to all television news, given the *limits of the medium* [emphasis mine] and its unceasing commercial pressures. ABC news was a class act." Unexamined in his book is just how those commercial pressures influence the news agenda. Many corporations are not as shy in talking about self-interest. As one GE communications manager put it: "We insist on a broadcast environment that reinforces our corporate message."

Writing critically about ABC news is even tougher when you have been part of it and still respect many of your colleagues as talented and hard-working. No one wants to come off as a self-righteous know-it-all or pompous scold, yet there are reasons why deeply flawed institutions happen to good people, why people become trapped in their own institutional realities and come to believe there are no other ways of seeing or doing. The limits of the medium are often created and then rationalized to justify business as usual.

When Cap Cities acquired ABC, it was not to add class but to add profits. They promoted their own honchos to oversee the news and entertainment divisions. They began another round of layoffs and cutbacks. For a time it looked like it was all over for 20/20. The new owners were convinced that the real money was in entertainment, not news, and so gave new entertainment programming chief Brandon Stoddard virtual carte blanche. It was Hollywood versus New York, and Hollywood was winning.

The entertainment division was not exactly brimming with new ideas. Their main plan was to resurrect an updated version of the old CBS *Talk of the Town* show, starring Dolly Parton as a latterday Ed Sullivan. (If I were Ed, I would have fantasized about coming back as Parton.) Dolly's talent was obvious but she was unproven as a host. Her variety show was scheduled to air in the old Sullivan slot on Sunday evenings. Doing so required a major shuffle in the week's schedule.

Now, time period is critical in network thinking, and all programming aims at capturing a particular night. (The best example being *60 Minutes*, which was on the verge of cancellation until it was moved from Tuesday night to Sunday; *Seinfeld* was the "anchor" of NBC's Thursday night, etc.) So if one night changes, others follow. Then *20/20* would have to move as well. As is often the case, these programming geniuses proved to be not so smart. Dolly took a dive after one soppy season. *20/20* is still there.

Before the Dolly dilemma was resolved, Av Westin became a casualty of Roone's paranoia and his own ambitions. Seeking to ingratiate himself with the Cap Cities brass he'd worked with years earlier, Av naively circulated an article in the executive suites suggesting ways that the news division might become more effective and cost-efficient. Roone took this as a bid for his job. He promptly suspended Westin and, after letting him twist in the wind for a few months, accepted his resignation. I felt that Av was treated unfairly and said so at a meeting with Arledge. A colleague told me that it was not smart to speak out if I ever wanted to be promoted.

With Westin weakened, Victor Neufeld, Av's assistant, began gunning for his job. Executives playing musical job chairs at the networks is an old story, but it is also common for media corporations to shower more money on outsiders—people they don't know but who look promising—than proven insiders. In this forest, trees that are too tall tend to get pruned first. Victor, however, kept his head down and stayed the course. With Barbara and Hugh's backing, he was soon given a chance to prove himself. He lucked out, and was well-rewarded as the ratings climbed.

As Av's alter ego, Victor had been even more into lowest common denominator journalism. He has an uncanny sense of what stories would build ratings, perhaps because his roots in middle-class Jersey City made him more savvy about how to reach *20/20*'s viewers than his colleagues, many of whom had come of age on Manhattan's Upper East Side. Neufeld made no pretensions at intellectualism or advocacy, vowing to keep the show on a middle-of-the-road trajectory. He is good at it. FAIR, the media monitoring group, attacked him for not airing more stories on nuclear power issues, charging that he suppressed them because his wife Lois was a paid flack for the nuclear industry. I thought the exposé was right about the show's priorities but wrong on Victor's modus operandi. He was never interested in those stories to begin with. He has always been a straight shooter with me, even if we do see the world through different lenses.

The correspondent who *should* have cared about those stories was the consumer reporter John Stossel. A libertarian and conservative, Stossel avoided Ralph Nader-like institutional critiques and instead went after small fish with blatant ripoffs, con men who could be caught in the act, for example, a group of peddlers selling counterfeit designer jeans at a flea market. One of his biggest stories was an exposé of professional wrestling that proved what all Americans already knew, that it's staged entertainment. Years later he would antagonize the environmental movement with a number of revisionist editorials posing as stories, which ridiculed claims that the earth is endangered.

Stossel once told me about a tactic that he liked to use in confrontation interviews to disorient the person he wanted to expose. He would start off, polite and smiling to make them feel comfortable. And then when the lights went on, he would stare at them, suddenly cursing, saying something like, "You better not fucking lie to me." Caught off guard by his unexpected venom, the subject would be thrown off balance, confused, and therefore easier prey— a calculated good cop-bad cop shtick performed by one person.

In 1981, I was tipped about a building scandal in the nuclear power program in the state of Washington that later led to the largest single financial collapse in the country's history, and a *Time* cover story. I brought it to Stossel because he was the consumer reporter and so much tax money was at stake. His response? "I hope it's not true. I have stock in that company." *20/20* never covered the story.

In 1996, Stossel became the target of the kind of undercover sting he often practiced. Independent journalist Mark Shapiro reported in the Internet 'zine *Salon* that Stossel, working on a special he dubbed *Junk Science*, had been planning to debunk the work of Dr. Grace Ziem, who specializes in treating medical ailments resulting from exposure to environmental toxins. Instead, Ziem, tipped off to the Stossel sting, invited two reporters from the *Baltimore Sun* and the *Washington Post* to a Baltimore hotel, to be present when Stossel arrived and then accused him and two associates of illegally taping her medical consultations. She accused him of producing junk journalism and sued, but lost in court. Media watchdogs like FAIR have criticized John repeatedly for "championing the overdog," while environmental groups have produced tons of documents and reports contradicting his dismissive attitude and "evidence," especially on such issues as dioxin and breast implants. Stossel seems to thrive on the controversy and as a result became a much sought after, highly paid speaker on the industry circuit. That is, until ABC regulated the practice of correspondents taking money from groups they cover. His commonsense-sounding reports scored well in the ratings and have been praised effusively in the business press. In January 1997, the *Wall Street Journal* published a self-justifying Stossel op-ed timed to promote *Junk Science.*

Stossel's polemical anti-environmentalist stance seems to reflect the network's attitude. A 1994 study of 250 newscasts by University of Arizona researchers Michael Nitz and Sharon Jarvis concluded that "the environment is not a priority for TV news." Reporting on fifty-four ABC stories, the study found that nearly a quarter focused on animals; 42 percent of the sources were laypeople not experts; and more than half were episodic and event-oriented, lacking in background. Technical or scientific evidence was found in only 22 percent; and only three of those were lead stories, aired before the first commercial break.

Victor Neufeld took over *20/20* when it moved from Thursday to Friday. As luck would have it, the competition was floundering. CBS's prime-time soap opera, *Falcon Crest*, which had in years past been getting great numbers, had run out of gas, and its older female viewers were getting bored.

20/20 moved into its new time slot with stories targeted at these older viewers. Barbara Walters's first, heavily hyped *exclusive* interview was with Katharine Hepburn. The story scored, establishing a beachhead on Friday nights. *20/20* became an even bigger hit as the story mix got softer and more infotainment oriented. It wasn't such an exclusive either. My friend Vicky Gordon had produced an almost identical interview with Hepburn for CBS months earlier.

20/20's practice of demographic targeting would be denied by most news executives but it does take place. Stories are not always selected because of their inherent value but because they might play well with a real or imagined audience segment. For example, when a show skews older, it presents more pieces on social security, recreational vehicles and stars of an earlier generation like Katharine Hepburn.

When *20/20* was competing against *Hill Street Blues*, which had a lot of urban appeal, *20/20* suddenly started counter-programming by profiling country music stars—almost one a week—to attract an audience in the suburbs and the South. There's another payoff besides audience share. While *Hill Street* was advertising Chevrolets, *20/20* was carrying ads for BMWs. Advertisers believe that a magazine show appeals to a more thoughtful and affluent audience. Those BMW advertisers paid a premium for their upscale spots. *20/20* could actually generate more revenue with lower ratings. Again, *who* is watching is more important than *how many* are watching. In 1995, *20/20* had a 7.73 cpm (cost per thousand viewers), the figure on which ad rates are based. In contrast, ABC News had a 5.38, while *60 Minutes* scored 7.40. The top entertainment show, *Seinfeld*, scored 15.51. No wonder NBC was willing to pay almost $5 million per episode!

Some critics of infotainment favor bland voice-overs or long, PBS-style interviews that rarely involve the viewer. Fast-paced, well-produced stories do grab viewers who are not necessarily drawn to slower formats. I don't think that news has to be presented in a boring way—after all, you do want viewers. But this notion has been taken too far, driving out more in-depth reporting.

Don Hewitt of *60 Minutes* speaks of a line that separates show biz from news biz. "The trick is to walk up to it, touch it with your toe, but don't cross it." But that assumes that the line is clear and visible. What if you no longer recognize its existence?

After Robert Redford's film on the TV quiz show scandals of the 1950s was released, a group of TV executives assembled to watch and discuss its relevance. Redford told them that "the danger is that the truth gets futzed around so much that people will accept fiction as fact."

Could it happen again? they were asked. No one was prepared to say no, although several executives spoke of ethical dilemmas and nuances and how issues today are more subtle. In writing about the conversation for the *New Yorker*, Ken Auletta catalogued deeply institutionalized practices of dramatization, sensationalism, coaching interview subjects, paying for interviews, and narrowing the framework of discussion on serious talk programs. "We remain married to the TV set," he concluded, "but we seem to expect and tolerate cheating."

The turn toward entertainment-oriented tabloid television drove out most documentary programming. The format that forged the credibility of TV news from the days of Edward R. Murrow to *The Selling of the Pentagon* became programma non grata. Stories became shorter and shorter. Soundbites that ran on average twenty-seven seconds in 1964 consumed but seven seconds of news time by the late 1980s. The shows looked spiffier but was the audience comprehending the information any better? I doubt it.

By the '90s, there were *no* in-depth, regularly scheduled documentary series left on the networks. ABC's *Close-up*, NBC's *White Paper*, and *CBS Reports* were long gone. What was left were episodic specials, usually ego vehicles for anchors. *Peter Jennings Reports* on ABC delivered excellent programs on Bosnia and Hiroshima, but shows like that are still few and far between. Tom Brokaw had a similar series on NBC but it was later folded into *Dateline*.

To pitch shows these days, journalists have to stress their entertainment (i.e. commercial) value. The graphics, music and pacing of a show are as important as its journalism, or more so. At *20/20* we used to call gratuitous post-production effects caca, a phrase any two year old will decode if you are not sure of its meaning.

Av Westin frequently repeated the three questions he used to determine what would go into a broadcast and what would be left out, the questions that guided America's expectations for TV news:

1. Is my world safe?
2. Are my city and home safe?
3. If my spouse, children and loved ones are safe, what happened in the past twenty-four hours to shock them, amuse them or make them better off?

These questions frame their own responses and produce television that is titillating but ultimately pacifying, even numbing. TV news encourages passivity by offering few reports on what people can do about what they're seeing and few profiles on people who are trying to change the system. There are fewer follow-ups or explanatory pieces. In all my years at the networks, I never heard executives debate the best way to really explain the issues. That may be why after four years of intensive coverage of Bosnia, most people said they didn't understand what the war was all about or who was fighting whom. Ken Auletta believes that "television has succeeded by degrees in numbing our sensation of outrage." I agree.

Perhaps that's because many journalists have become numb themselves, integrated into work routines that seem more and more like factory work—so repetitive are the stories—where a larger system of values doesn't seem to exist. Some years ago, Barbara Phillips spent thirteen months closely observing seventy-five TV radio and print journalists. She concluded that "daily news work itself *prevents* the development of cognitive processes which lead to theoretical or philosophical insight." In essence, the way news organizations work "inhibits broader insight."

When I was at *20/20*, many producers did struggle week after week to find meaty and important stories and try to get them on the air. Many of their ideas never survived the first pitch—they were denied, deflected or denuded of content. My own disaffection mounted, although I am still proud of most of the stories I did. Let me talk about two of them—one that I was assigned to produce against my will and one I helped uncover.

The first started with a request by a self-described "embarrassed" senior producer who asked that I help out on a story that "no one really wants to do because it's so disgusting." That's a real attractive way of enticing someone, isn't it? It seems that a friend of Roone Arledge's secretary had a problem that required a *20/20* story. (Executives often order up stories based on whim, personal curiosity, and cocktail party gossip.) The problem was an eating disorder called bulimia. It had to do with throwing up. Yuck! "I don't know how you're going to illustrate it," he said. "We can't really put a hidden camera in someone's toilet." A few weeks later *Saturday Night Live* did a sketch set in a Roman vomitorium, so at least the phenomenon was resonating in the popular culture.

At first I was insulted to be asked. I thought I had tons of more important issues pending about politics and world affairs. Also, 20/20 seemed to be doing a disease a week, alerting and alarming the audience about every possible malady. They covered so many that they actually hired a doctor to do regular stories on medical issues.

But after I examined it, the problem of bulimia proved deadly serious. It raises issues about our culture and affects millions of people (mostly women). It is a social disease of consumer capitalism. You don't read about bulimia in Somalia—it's only found in affluent societies. The story took me into a world of obsessive personal rituals I was amazed to learn about. It showed me the pressures our culture puts on women to be thin and how it erodes their self-esteem. As I delved, I found that many famous people were affected. 20/20 was pleased when I got Jane Fonda to talk with Hugh about her bout with bulimia, which gave the story legitimacy and star power. Producing it became a real education, and judging by the mail, it educated many of our viewers. It was only my ignorance that led me to snicker in the first place.

The next 20/20 story is about a scandal that led to my departure. The story was about America's real first lady—the Statue of Liberty. In 1986, the monument was being renovated through a national fund-raising drive headed up by Mr. Chrysler, Lee Iacocca. Begging letters flooded America warning that this national treasure was in danger of crumbling into New York harbor. Giant corporations rushed to her defense.

Through a friend, I met an architect for the National Park Service, which oversees the Statue. He was enraged by the campaign, which he saw as totally inaccurate and a case of private interests using and abusing public property. He was alarmed by what Iacocca and his crew were doing, not only to the Lady but to Ellis Island as well, where Iacocca's planners spoke of creating a museum focused on European immigration, "a white people's museum," as well as an exhibit to honor great American industrialists. Guess which American automaker would probably be among those so honored?

My bosses at *20/20* loved this and gave me the green light to investigate further. Tom Jarriel, Mike Smith, and I began to dig into a maze of interlocking directorates, high-salaried fund-raisers, mismanagement, and lack of public accountability. We found out that the companies were not really donating to the restoration effort, but buying the right to use the statue as a logo in their advertising campaigns. This is called cause-related marketing.

We interviewed a whistle blower from the Interior Department who was fired for challenging Iacocca and located documents that showed that more money was being raised than was needed to fix the statue. Iacocca had announced that it would cost $230 million— a figure that we were told by one of his fundraisers came out of his head and didn't reflect any professional estimate. He figured that there were 230 million Americans, and if each gave a dollar...presto!

I also found an engineer who claimed that the whole project was a scam, because the statue only needed minor repairs, not a complete makeover. There *was* corrosion, but it was only partial and didn't require such an expensive total restoration. Unfortunately, he spoke English with such a heavy accent that you could barely understand what he was saying. I could never fully corroborate his claims, because they turned on various judgment and technical issues, but I believed them.

The selling of the Statue of Liberty was a big story, and *20/20* agreed that it warranted not one but two segments. Our investigation, meanwhile, was coming up with even more outrageous twists and turns. Then Iacocca began stonewalling, refusing to talk to us. He later agreed to be interviewed by the *New York Times*; that reporter told me that his piece was the most heavily edited of any he had ever written for the paper, and that its investigative focus had been blunted. The *Times* ran it as a front page feature, with its disclosures buried on the jump page, in the middle of the paper. One reason may have been because of a conflict of interest: The

Times company was one of the corporate sponsors of the renovation campaign. Other media organizations, with the exception of the *Nation*, which did its own hard-hitting investigative report, were promoting this patriotic campaign—and self-promoting through it.

While we were preparing our report—which included the thrilling experience of shooting a standup on the giant scaffolding right below the Lady's nose—we learned from a newspaper column that ABC news was negotiating with Lee Iacocca for the exclusive rights to cover a giant extravaganza planned for the statue's July Fourth unveiling, complete with fireworks, tall ships, President Reagan and a live audience in the millions.

When we heard that Roone Arledge and Lee Iacocca had had a high-profile lunch, we feared our story would be killed. Inside *20/20*, the buzz was that the story was unlikely to get spiked because of all the bad press that had just subsided in the aftermath of Roone's decision to kill a story about a Marilyn Monroe murder investigation. "They won't make the mistake again of being so public and so blatant, at least not this soon," a wise head counseled. He was right. The story was not cut completely—it was just cut in half. Two segments were collapsed into one, so many of our findings had to be dropped or compressed.

Iacocca was not pleased with the story. Although he had refused to cooperate, after it aired his PR department sent a thirty-seven-page letter to Roone challenging my reporting. I spent nearly a week responding in detail. Iacocca's flacks corrected us on two relatively minor points, but I was able to verify all our major allegations. In the end ABC stood by the story and I kept my job.

But ABC also stood by what had become a multimillion dollar deal with the man we were exposing. ABC news became the official sponsor of a day-long extravaganza on the reopening of the Statue, to be hosted live by Barbara Walters and Peter Jennings. In effect, a simple ceremony was turned into a TV spectacular. Naturally, none of our investigative findings were reported during the coverage.

Other networks were muscled out of getting good camera positions because ABC "owned" the event. An event celebrating a *publicly owned* monument, a national treasure, was now privately controlled and exploited. My own network, *through its news division*, was not just covering this manufactured news extravaganza, but staging it. A tuxedoed Ted Koppel played emcee at the VIP ceremony on Liberty Island, introducing the President of the United States as if he were an entertainer on a variety show. Frank Sinatra and other celebrities followed. Did Reagan demand scale for his role? He would be entitled to it under his Screen Actor's Guild contract.

All I could see was a Nuremberg-style patriotic rally. I knew it was time to leave. ABC hadn't just crossed the line between journalism and entertainment, it had created a whole new line. Hadn't anyone at ABC news watched their own network's report on the sordid and seamy underside of the selling of Ms. Liberty? Incidentally, Iacocca was eventually pushed out of the Statue of Liberty-Ellis Island restoration business, not by news disclosures but by the federal agencies themselves, who got sick of his bullying and conflicts of interest.

The Statue of Liberty story, with all its symbolism and powerful aroma of collaboration with corruption, finally pushed me over the edge, maybe because of my own family's immigrant history. It took me two years to summon up the courage finally to walk away despite the financial risk.

After whining and complaining for years, it was time to put my own ideas and values to the test. I left to find answers to real questions. Is there another way? Is there still space for other approaches? The short answer: you bet. I remain an optimist. There *are* opportunities to create more meaningful programming. It is what I am still doing after eight years at the networks and another ten as an independent. I know that I, and others with similar beliefs, are definitely going against the current, now a tidal wave, of the corporate media culture, like salmon swimming upstream. The salmon do it in order to find a place to spawn and reproduce. We in the independent media still nurture our sense of purpose but need to find calmer and more economically secure waters in which to work.

My hope is that insurgent media work—other ways of thinking and doing—can also be spawned and reproduced in a world that clearly needs a media that does more than distort and distract.

I would soon get a chance to see what I could do. There was no turning back. In 1988, I defected. I left *20/20* for what at first was *0/0*—zero/zero.

CHAPTER 8

GLOBALVISION: DOWNWARDLY MOBILE AND UPWARDLY GLOBAL

*G*lobalvision, Inc. began in late 1987, although the idea had been years in the thinking. My old Boston media crony Rory O'Connor and I set out to try our hand at making TV. We wanted to work for ourselves not the corporate media. Rory's stint as a producer at CBS and mine at ABC convinced us that in our industry, independents working out of their living rooms simply substituted freelance hell for wage slavery. If you want to make money and/or a difference, you need a company behind you. So we decided to create one.

I admired Rory's writing, and we shared a critique of mainstream media. He is an excellent producer and far more businesslike than I. He has a scrappy, street-fighting Irish spirit, coupled with deep convictions about the need for change.

Rory and I began with a cultural bias. He was a rock critic and I had worked at a rock 'n' roll station. We both saw music as a universal language and a means of international cultural cross-pollination and communication. We were interested in music from many cultures, music with a message. We thought of it as the soundtrack of a changing world. Originally we started out writing about the globalization of music for a publication called *Rock Around the World.* That led to an idea for a book, then a TV show and, ultimately, a company to promote and practice the globalization of television as one way to bring the world together.

He became president and business maven. I became vice president and executive producer. We were ready to compete in the free marketplace of ideas.

We quickly learned that nothing was free.

We put our leaky rowboat into a turbulent media ocean hoping it would get us to the other side, wherever that was. We wanted to do good—and do well. We wanted to do it better than it was being done, to compete by creating our own programming, not just criticize.

Our vision has always been much bigger than we were: as big as the world! Friends thought we were nuts. We had no backers, no office, no equipment, no nothing, yet we were willing to leave high-paying jobs to chase a dream. Our idea: the world's first globally distributed magazine program designed to bring the best of the world to the rest of the world. The logic behind this was that the world was changing, social, economic and environmental problems becoming increasingly planetary in scope. Billions of people tune in to global events like the Olympics and the World Cup, or concerts like Live Aid. Why not, we thought, aim regular cross-cultural programming at this huge audience? Of course, there are obvious problems—language, cultural differences and the like—but we felt they could be overcome if the programming projected an inclusive spirit and allowed local broadcasters and producers to add their own input.

We were not interested in some homogenized, Americanized world-travel cavalcade, yet another nature series or a parade of soft features. We wanted to cover issues along with entertainment, politics as well as culture, journalism and jam sessions. We wanted to be provocative and relevant. We thought of ourselves as cutting edge, although we didn't want the show to be *too* different, for fear that would alienate buyers.

It costs money to fund a company and major series. Raising it took an inordinate amount of our energy and time. Several prospective big-money investments fell through for various reasons, including—twice!—the untimely demise of a principal, and once because our "big" Wall Street meeting took place on the day of the '87 crash.

We considered trying the National Endowments for the Arts and the Humanities for our non-profit projects. They finance public television projects, but preparing the application is akin to writing a dissertation and can take almost as long. The Endowments also require that you have advisors, usually academics who lend their names to these projects for prestige—and extra cash. So these endowments become, in effect, welfare projects for overeducated and underpaid professors. In recent years, the Endowments have come under attack from the right, making it even tougher to get money for independent work that leans liberal or left.

OK, if you scratch investors and the endowments, what's next? Private philanthropic foundations! They give billions of dollars away each year, but their priorities are usually hospitals or universities, places that honor them with plaques and buildings. Only 1.4 percent of all their money goes to media projects. We had to find the right handful of potential supporters, pitch them and then wait for what seemed like an eternity to learn that we'd met their rejection criteria. Needles in haystacks are statistically easier to find.

At the beginning we assumed that the people who supported our values would be most willing to back us. Wrong! Even though conservative foundations and companies pump millions into right-wing causes, most of the radical funders prefer to divide their money into micro-grants for grassroots groups. Their criteria often seem to have less to do with political impact than ideology or politically correct identity politics. So much for gays, blacks, women and so forth. Most wished us well but wouldn't fund media because they didn't watch it or didn't understand its impact.

To sell our global show, we produced a video presentation for the equivalent of $1.99 in TV terms, by reediting existing footage from network TV shows. We wanted to prove that there was a market for our ideas. We got a promising initial response. Most important, no one in the know told us we were nuts. Many were intrigued, but as we started making the rounds we realized that the idea of global any-thing was still a new one. Entertainment companies had overseas sales forces who rarely spoke with their domestic colleagues. They all knew that entertainment was one of our most lucrative national exports—the biggest dollar earner next to airplanes and arms—but most only saw it as a one-way street: "We make it and they take it." There was little interest in what other nations or producers were doing or say-ing, much less working with them in a cooperative manner.

Perhaps that is why there is so much fear and loathing overseas about American cultural imperialism, and why some Europeans try to keep the Americans out. The government of France challenged the GATT trade agreement over the issue of culture and the spread of U.S.-controlled global TV networks, which tend to promote a uni-formity of content. Washington responded fiercely to this and other attempts to limit Hollywood's dominance, which already assures that 90 percent of the films shown worldwide are made in the USA. When any foreign country becomes culturally protectionist, high-powered lobbyists for the studios, like Jack Valenti, become pro-tective of "our" economic interests and bring every pressure and hardball tactic to bear. Regis Debray, best known for his friendship with Che Guevara, has become a leading commentator in France on the conflict between commercial entertainment and cultural art-work. He calls them two competing world views in which "com-mercial entertainment products meet consumer needs whereas cultural objects create their own audiences, often against the grain of current taste."

"Political dominance always means that you kill off other ways of seeing things," Debray told an interviewer in *Wired*, the cyber-media magazine. "By transforming three quarters of the world into a cultural proletariat, you will make people of this class into more determined rebels in the twenty-first century." Maybe, maybe not— but at the end of the twentieth century, the imbalance between the information haves and have-nots is growing.

For all the talk of free and fair trade reciprocity, American TV programmers have monopolized international television. American-made TV shows, from religious broadcasters to wrestlers, are shown all over the globe, but foreign-made programming rarely penetrates U.S. living rooms. A few years ago, only .7 percent of the programs shown in prime time came from abroad, and that figure includes all those British imports on PBS.

This situation is not just unfair to foreigners, it deprives U.S. viewers of a window on the world. Our ability to relate to and empathize with other peoples will increase to the extent that we get a feel for their point of view and sensibility, their passions, cultural idiosyncrasies and heroes. A few foreign ambassadors every so often on *Nightline* is not adequate.

This American parochialism also masks greed. Time and again, we met TV executives who were out for the quick buck. Their only question was: "Whatcha got and how can we exploit it?" They had no convictions, just a hunger for cash and commissions. Social responsibility? Forget it.

In January 1991, as the debate over whether to go to war with Iraq consumed the country, Globalvision became involved in documenting a remake of John Lennon's classic song: "Give Peace a Chance." The project, initiated by John's son Sean and pop star Lenny Kravitz, involved thirty-nine prominent musicians from the worlds of rock, soul and rap, counseling sanctions, not bombing. We completed the project on the day that the NATPE television programmers' convention got underway in New Orleans, and we overnighted copies there in hopes of getting it out. How naive!

The giant hall was mesmerized by the countdown to the conflict being reported on CNN. Patriotic fervor swelled. The partying spirit of past conventions was dulled. No one seemed interested in a call for restraint. *Variety* did a front page story about our attempt to sell peace in a time of war. We had the stars. We were timely. We just had the "wrong message" at the right time. Or was it the right message at the wrong time? There were no buyers.

We still haven't capitalized Globalvision, despite having been courted by the world's twelfth-largest bank and sniffed around by other company-collectors. Ten years on, though, we have survived and are debt-free. No mean feat considering that at least half the companies we worked with when we started are now out of business.

We did it by financing the company out of the revenues we earned or solicited. We decided early on that we couldn't wait for angels to come flying or dollars to come dropping. We had to create programming we could sell.

We had to put the global show on hold for a number of reasons. We couldn't afford to launch it on spec. We didn't have the bucks or the backing. Also, the global market was not expanding as fast as we'd hoped. Competition within and between countries and companies was more of an imperative than cooperation. Globalization was too often equated with Americanization. Many international co-productions flounder because all the parties want to control their own product, with little spirit of compromise. What works in one country wouldn't necessarily play in another. Nationalism and protectionism challenge internationalism. The millions of people we were sure would watch global programming were not being given that chance by media gatekeepers who insisted that they knew best—and who also just happen to control the means of distribution.

As we began to create our own programming, we came to realize how important access to distribution was. Today, the struggle is for the means of distribution in an environment where there are more channels than choices. (Hence Bruce Springsteen's song, "57 Channels/Nothing On.")

It was one of our colleagues and my friend filmmaker Hart Perry who helped us get underway by inviting us to share his office at 361 West Broadway in Soho, now one of the trendiest restaurant rows in New York. Then, it was in the first stages of yuppification, still somewhat of an artist's neighborhood. We were based over a bar that served burgers that always seemed to be burning. The aroma of charcoal wafted into our two-room global headquarters where the floor creaked and the windows leaked. Our office was cold in the winter, suffocating in summer. To tell the truth, it was a slum. Our inadvertent retaliation came from our unfixable toilet that was forever flooding the patrons in the dining room below. Our production space down the street in John Gotti country, on Mulberry Street in Little Italy, was even worse. Journalist J. Max Robins, who praised what we did there, called it a "loft hovel." Jack Newfield, a genius of the coined phrase, went further in the *New York Daily News*, terming us "heroes of downward mobility." We may have been downwardly mobile but we aspired to be upwardly global.

Over the years, Globalvision produced many programs including documentaries, TV magazine segments, and stories for cable outlets including MTV. Rory did three investigative specials for *Frontline*. One exposed the Reverend Moon, another dissected the BCCI bank scam, and the third showed how Washington armed Saudi Arabia in the biggest weapons deal and Pentagon boondoggle in the world.

With two-time Academy Award winner Barbara Kopple and at Oliver Stone's invitation, I produced the documentary *Beyond JFK* on the issues of the Kennedy assassination, based on Oliver's controversial movie *JFK*. I also worked with multi-ethnic Bosnian filmmakers to make *Sarajevo Ground Zero*, a chilling chronicle of siege and destruction. But we developed our reputation in another part of the world even farther away and less welcoming: South Africa.

ENTER SOUTH AFRICA NOW

My South African connections plunged us into our first major project. I had first gone to the land of apartheid in 1967, and became somewhat of an Africanist after that, writing about and protesting against the situation there. In 1985, I came up with the idea of the Sun City project, a book, record and video featuring top musicians from the worlds of rock, R&B, rap and world music singing against apartheid. When journalism about South Africa was not getting on the air in America, I shifted my focus away from supporting a cultural boycott to challenging a news boycott. A Pretoria-imposed press ban had driven images of resistance off the air. Rory and I decided to try to do something about it.

It needed doing, and we needed some programming to show that Globalvision could take on issues others weren't taking on. Most of our friends doubted we could do it. The networks had a billion dollars to spend on news coverage and didn't seem to be able to get the story. What made us think that we could? We replied that they weren't doing it because they didn't want to. Surely if they could get pictures from Saturn, they could get them from Soweto.

We also thought we could get what they couldn't because we were determined to work with the people closest to the story—producers and crews in South Africa made up of South Africans who knew their own story best. Most of our anchors and stringers were black South Africans. A Namibian covered Namibia, while our multi-cultural staff ranged over a host of other stories. That inside-out coverage became our distinction.

We started out to prove that it could be done with specials produced by South African filmmaker Kevin Harris. Soon we developed our own approach. Each show included a report of the uncensored news, an investigation, profile or backgrounder, and a cultural segment. We looked carefully at U.S. policy toward South Africa and the role of multinational corporations. We covered the frontline states. We never ran out of material. With Hart Perry's initial production involvement and active support, we ended up producing 156 weeks of *South Africa Now*, a series that became almost as much about TV news and what it doesn't cover as the struggle for freedom in South Africa. It was widely considered an impressive achievement, but it was the moral support and encouragement from black South Africans and American viewers that kept us going.

South Africa Now put us on the map, all right. We won awards and press attention, but we also attracted attacks from the right and snipers in the mainstream. We were smeared as advocates, partisans, ANC propagandists. Magnus Malan, the defense minister of South Africa, denounced us, revealing on the floor of the Parliament that his intelligence apparatus had discovered that the show was hatched by Communists in Zimbabwe! In Los Angeles, leftist turned rightist David Horowitz targeted our show. He was almost successful in getting it dropped by LA's public television station KCET, but activists in the black community and a revolt among the staff forced executives to reverse themselves. We were being accused of airing Marxist, pro-ANC propaganda about the involvement of security forces in violence. All of our reports were later confirmed by South African officials and mainstream media outlets, and these crimes have since been admitted to before South Africa's Truth and Reconciliation Commission. Some critics challenged us because we admitted openly that we opposed apartheid, as if that stand was somehow incompatible with responsible reporting. Maybe we were naive, but hadn't the United Nations declared apartheid a crime against humanity on a par with genocide? No one but the white minority in South Africa, and only then the hard-line Afrikaners among them, even defended apartheid anymore. We didn't see it as a particularly controversial issue, much less a courageous stand.

It soon became clear that *South Africa Now* was not commercially viable. Back in the 1970s I was among a group in Boston who disrupted a public hearing of the National Association of Broadcasters to question why TV stations were carrying ads for Kruggerrands, a gold coin minted in apartheid South Africa and sold by the all-white government to generate money abroad. Those commercials were dropped because of national protests, but other South African enterprises were never curtailed. Soon, *Nightline* started running ads for diamonds, "a girl's best friend," placed by the DeBeers mining cartel of South Africa. I was startled to see them on a program Ted Koppel did on apartheid. No one mentioned that it was brought to you by the people who financed apartheid. With so many contradictions and lack of awareness in the media, it is not surprising that a show focusing on the liberation struggle in South Africa, reporting news that was being censored in America, would seem out of sync.

That meant that our company had to produce the series on a nonprofit basis, working with The Africa Fund, a tax-exempt foundation. That also meant it would be hard to fund it at a decent level. Our first *South Africa Now* programs were produced for $200 a week, on a grant from the UN's Special Committee on Apartheid. That's roughly the cost of one of Peter Jennings' better lunches.

On one occasion we asked a major foundation for $25,000. They turned us down, pointing out that our budget vastly underestimated real costs. They were right, but we didn't know it at the time. They gave us $100,000 instead. That was the exception. Most foundations didn't even respond to our requests. Sometimes there were problems even *after* we received grants. One foundation, which issued a check to us on a snowy Christmas eve, insisted that we get certain signatures to them by five P.M. or they would have to take the money back as their books were closing. We scurried in panic through a storm to complete the paperwork or say goodbye to Santa. We made it.

In another case, the Carnegie Corporation mistakenly sent their check to 361 Broadway, not West Broadway. We kept calling them, and they kept insisting they sent it. Finally, an assistant sheepishly admitted she'd never heard of West Broadway and so assumed our address was wrong. She also told us it would take at least a month to reissue the check. We didn't have a month. So we raced like desperadoes down to the huge office building at 361 Broadway. We knocked on doors, explaining that a $50,000 check may have been sent there in error. You can imagine what scam-conscious New York-ers thought of *that* inquiry.

Finally, we went looking for the building's superintendent. Maybe he knew something. He was an intimidating-looking black man, who clearly didn't want to be bothered. We tried our story out on him. To our amazement, a big smile swept across his face. "*South Africa Now*? I love that show," he told us. Unbelievable! "God exists," we yelled.

He took us by the hand and led us from floor to floor to every tenant in the building. We lucked out. One company with a G in its name remembered getting an envelope from uptown. It looked like a check, but since it wasn't for them, they sent it back to the post office. Rory shot out of the building. Two hours later, he came back to our office. He said he drove the postal clerks crazy until they found it in the dead letter office. If he hadn't retrieved it, our series would have been dead too. That check kept us alive for another two months

One more foundation story is worth recounting. In 1990, soon after his release from prison, Nelson Mandela invited us to docu-ment his historic trip through America. We approached the MacArthur Foundation to help us fund the video. Bill Kirby, a street-smart Chicago lawyer then in his 70s, had set up the billion-dollar foundation for his client, the late insurance magnate John D. MacArthur. It was Kirby who came up with the idea of finding and funding America's geniuses. He had turned us down once before, but since I was in Chicago, I called him and he offered to take me to lunch at the posh Union Club.

Kirby was the patron saint of American independent film-makers. Over many years he had dispensed millions to underwrite some of their best work. He was interested in what Globalvision was doing but more interested in telling me about his life and his many real or imagined love affairs. Kirby was a Chicago street fighter and alleycat, a lively raconteur. He could be as smooth as velvet one minute and a barroom brawler the next. When I met him, a triple bypass operation had slowed his body down, but not his banter. By meal's end he offered to give us $100,000. Not bad, *and* he paid the tab.

A week later, I was reading the *New York Times* and there he was, on the obituary page, William Kirby, dead. Another heart attack. The man really had moved me by his humanity and compassion. But had he done the paperwork on our grant? I waited a week before calling. I reached his secretary, a woman who had been with him for many years. Yes, he had mentioned something about the grant to her. No, she didn't have the paperwork. Mr. Kirby's office, she told me, was a mess, and no one was sure when they would be able to straighten it all out. Papers were strewn all over. She promised to call me.

Not again! Not another casualty in the Globalvision funding war. We waited. A week later, the secretary called. Yes, she had the grant papers. He had signed it. It was the last thing he'd done. She'd send the check.

Hallelujah! *Mandela in America* could get made.

By spending so much time on nonprofit work, we took on the aura of a charity, not a business. Although it gave us a moral edge, it didn't make us more attractive to financiers or the big TV companies. For them, we were the "South Africa guys," a peculiar tribe of single-issue crusaders. We were patted on the head regularly but that didn't put videotape on the table.

South Africa Now was seen on PBS stations nationwide but the national programming service refused to distribute the series, season after season. They took a bureaucratic, business-as-usual approach in the face of a global moral crisis. At one point, they told us they preferred specials to series. But when we proposed specials, they didn't remember asking for them. At another point, when they did like an idea of ours for a documentary on South Africa, they told us to send them a rough cut. How nice—but who was supposed to finance it? That's why we pitched them in the first place. We couldn't win for losing. They wanted us to stop bothering them and just go away. They wanted apartheid to end, I'm sure, but they could wait. In all those years, African animals had no problems getting on the air, but African people? Forget about it!

THE RIGHTS AND WRONGS OF PUBLIC TELEVISION

PBS never did distribute *South Africa Now*, but we did get the show on the air on public television stations and cable outlets in the U.S. and worldwide. PBS also hated our next series on human rights, *Rights & Wrongs*, prompting TV critic Marvin Kitman to ask, "What is it about a show on human rights that curdles the milk of human kindness in public TV?"

He asked that question when for the twelfth time in five years, the national programmers at PBS rejected a request that the program be considered for national broadcast. Kitman added that "not being associated with *Rights & Wrongs* is a tradition already. Every season, for a variety of reasons, the public TV establishment finds an excuse to turn them down." Earlier he had praised the show for "shaking the cobwebs" in his brain.

The story of the fight to produce a credible human rights show that can be seen on American television illustrates the media's resistance to independently produced programming that offers a diverse window on a changing world. On one level, it underscores the importance and limits of public television. On another, it offers another case of a noncommercial system that has betrayed its mission and broken its promise to TV viewers.

We created *Rights & Wrongs* because we believed that human rights was *the* post-cold war challenge, and that neither network news nor public television were paying enough attention to it. The networks were shutting down overseas bureaus and moving down-market with tabloid-style journalism. PBS was not rising to the challenge either, pumping out shows that were predictable and bland.

But what about the rest of the world? Where was the coverage of global heroes and people's movements? A network of diligent human rights advocates in groups like Amnesty International,

Human Rights Watch and the Lawyer's Committee for Human Rights were issuing carefully documented reports week after week about human rights abuses worldwide and the need for an international order built on justice and accountability. Yet their findings and recommendations were rarely considered newsworthy, much less spotlighted on TV.

For the most part, television's reporting on the world, including PBS coverage, remained shallow, superficial and one-sided, often just reflecting the views of the State Department or its detractors on the right. There was little balance and even less diversity. A presidential statement was unlikely to be challenged, especially on complex issues like Bosnia or China.

We felt there was a need for a regular series that would look at the world through a human rights prism, a program that would give TV viewers a chance to hear directly from people who are making history and fighting for their rights. That was the idea behind *Rights & Wrongs*.

We knew there was a small army of independent journalists and filmmakers, stringers and correspondents ready to support such an effort. It would not be a problem to tap their expertise or acquire footage. The camcorder had made many remote regions accessible. By employing our inside-out approach rather than rely on a network bureau model with high overhead, we could find journalists and visuals to offer reports from Boston to Bosnia, from South Central L.A. to Soweto.

We also knew how to produce such a show on the cheap, from our network experience and the years of producing *South Africa Now* on a shoestring. "They drive on vapors, not gas," said one critic. We also had a willing anchor: Charlayne Hunter-Gault, who brought sixteen years of an on-air track record on PBS's own daily news show, once the *MacNeil-Lehrer News Hour*, now *The News Hour with Jim Lehrer*. She was also a leader and a role model in the world of human rights, a civil rights pioneer who desegregated the University of Georgia in the '60s, and a high-profile, award-winning broadcast journalist.

We hoped the combination of Charlayne's visibility, hot footage with a unique spin, emotion, and nuanced storytelling would give the series commercial appeal, maybe even make it a hit.

First, we approached the networks. I queried Roone Arledge at ABC, even though we knew that the networks mostly insist on producing their own news and public affairs shows in-house. They occasionally will hire independents but rarely buy outside programming. We got no reply from Roone.

Next, we turned to syndicators, where we thought we had a nibble. A prominent Hollywood company told us our idea "sounded neat." Our pilot had been hosted by Jane Wallace, a former network anchorwoman, and segmented into features and analytical stories drawn from all over the world. Much of the footage had never before been seen on television. Some was shot with home video cameras. In part, it was a global showcase of Rodney King-type videos and solid human rights features. We probably overloaded the show with too much in an industry where less is usually considered more. We felt we had acquired so much great material and wanted to demonstrate the range of what was possible.

But the response from this well-known program distributor was telling. He liked the project but "had to pass." "We only do reality-based television," were his exact words.

Reality?

Even George Orwell, who wrote years ago about the perversion of language, might have been shocked by this twisted use of terminology.

Ian Mitroff and Warren Bennio dissect television as the "unreality industry," explaining that "with very few exceptions, most issues on television news are presented in a completely ahistoric context or no context whatsoever...the overall context is one of dazzling confusion. Little or no attempt is made to present a larger view in which the issues could be located in some coherent framework."

Despite the realities we were covering, we had to conclude that *Rights & Wrongs* was not a reality show, at least not in the way that term has been debased on television.

Next we reached out to the world of cable, which has continually promised viewers a cornucopia of programming choices. We approached Discovery, Lifetime, MTV, A&E, USA, and Turner Broadcasting. All the programmers were respectful of our concept and impressed by the treatment, but all turned us down, with the exception of Faith and Values, a channel reflecting the concerns of the mainstream religious denominations; they did carry the series but reached only a small percentage of cable viewers.

Executives of these channels constantly talk about content as king and yet a lesson I learned almost every day is that only a certain type of content is acceptable. Here's what one cable exec turned sales agent told me. "The business has changed in two ways. First, programmers look for programs of a genre they've run before and can order in bulk—nature shows, wildlife, history, biographies etc. They want a sameness in style and approach, not something that is different or crosses genres. Secondly, they want shows that can travel—overseas. Again, that means uniformity and no controversy. You have to structure your programs to meet their needs. Avoid philosophy—just show it. All the execs I know are terrified of taking a stand—whether of the conservative or liberal variety. They want you to keep it entertaining and energetic." Those are today's buzz words.

That left PBS. Our last choice became our only choice. We did find people at the PBS stations who were receptive even when the national programming bureaucracy slammed its doors. In theory, this shouldn't be the case. Public television was created in 1967 to offer an alternative to commercial broadcasting. A study undertaken by the Carnegie Commission, which led Congress to create PBS, explicitly called for programs that "can help us see America whole, in all its diversity," to be a "forum for controversy and debate."

I was struck by the values and hopes the Commission articulated: "If we were to sum up our proposal with all the brevity at our command, we would say that what we recommend is freedom.... We seek freedom from the constraints...of commercial television. We seek...freedom from the pressures of inadequate funds. We seek for the artist, the technician, the journalist, the scholar and the public servant, freedom to create, freedom to innovate, freedom to be heard in the most far-reaching medium. We seek for the citizen, freedom to view, to see programs that the present system, by its incompleteness, denies."

PBS's first president, John Macy, made it clear that "public television was intended to be a supplementary or alternate service that did not duplicate commercial offerings." *Public Radio and Television in America*, by Long Island University professor Ralph Engelman, documents what happened then: "The founders wanted public broadcasting to serve as a public sphere separate from both government and the marketplace. But it has been compromised into being quasi-governmental, quasi-commercial and quasi-public." Another study, *Public Television for Sale*, by William Hoynes, goes even deeper, detailing the betrayal of its mission, its conservative content and subservience to corporate interests and corporate values.

It was this reality that Globalvision came up against time and again when we sought to put human rights programming on the national schedule.

In first offering *Rights & Wrongs* to PBS, we turned to one of its more respected mainstream producers, Alvin Perlmutter. We asked if he would co-produce with us, because we feared residues of bureaucratic hostility to *South Africa Now* would bleed over into consideration of our human rights series. Al, whose series *Adam Smith's Money World* was a weekly paean to capitalism, liked the idea of our show and agreed to work with us. Although he was more middle-of-the-road than us, we were willing to share editorial control and give up half of any revenues if that would help us get our work shown.

We also knew that our chance to get the show on the air would be enhanced if we could fund it, so that the financially strapped stations would not have to pay for it. We estimated that we would need to find at least $1 million. It was difficult: 145 companies who support some public television programming were approached on our behalf by a firm with a great track record of attracting corporate underwriters. Every single company turned us down, many because they feared that an association with a human rights show might jeopardize their overseas business interests in places like China.

Al wrote to the top program executives at PBS and the Corporation for Public Broadcasting and told them what we were up to and sought their support.

We were startled by their response. We had assumed they might want to see a pilot or at least hear more about our plans. They wrote back dismissing the idea with a phrase that has since been ridiculed everywhere. They told us that they considered human rights "an insufficient organizing principle for a TV series." In other words, they were rejecting *Rights & Wrongs* not because of its treatment or quality, but because of its subject. Human rights had become a no-no on public TV. This response ruled out PBS funding or support, making it impossible for us to move forward with Perlmutter. He dropped out.

Many critics have had fun slamming the PBS rationale. Bob Herbert in the *New York Times* said he couldn't believe it when he read it, but confirmed that it was true. John Leonard was even more biting on CBS *Sunday Morning*, repeating the "organizing principle" phrase and adding "unlike, say, baseball or money or food.... Who wants to hear about Soweto or Rwanda, or child labor in China and India, or skinheads in Eastern Europe, or female genital mutilation in Africa when you can keep more comfortable company on PBS with odd scientists, spoon-fed bee eaters, and adhesive padded geckos?"

Executives at PBS tried to distance themselves from the embarrassing phrase. PBS president Ervin Duggan even told Congress that we took the phrase out of context, if it was even said at all. Unfortunately for him, we'd kept the letter.

We were outraged and so were members of Congress when they were informed about PBS's stance toward *Rights & Wrongs*. On August 11, 1994, ten members of Congress, including three committee chairmen, protested to Duggan. Initiated by Representative Bob Filner of San Diego, a letter of concern was endorsed by Armed Services Committee Chairman Ron Dellums, Human Rights Subcommittee Chairman Tom Lantos and Henry Waxman, the influential Los Angeles Democrat. "Human rights is a concern of many members of Congress," the letter read. "The American people cherish human rights as the bedrock of our democracy cherished in our constitution. Human rights issues both in the United States and abroad deserve the broadcast time that this widely admired program offers."

Many members of Congress were unaware of *Rights & Wrongs* at all because WETA, the principal PBS outlet in the nation's capital, wouldn't carry it. It's hard to stick up for what you've never seen. An executive at the station told Charlayne that they were carrying instead Tony Brown's *Black Journal*, a weekly show hosted by a black Republican and sponsored by PepsiCo—indicating that they saw our show as ethnic, probably because of the color of our host.

When the *Washington Post* and other national newspapers started carrying reports of an *L.A. Times* interview with Charlayne in which she blasted the glass ceiling at PBS for women and minorities and decried the treatment received by *Rights & Wrongs*, more leaders took notice. On August 17, 1995, thirty-two members of the Congressional Black Caucus challenged PBS to carry the series, writing: "We are at a loss to understand your rejection of a balanced and responsible program that not only analyzes current challenges to human rights but also provides a catalyst for improving global communications." Those letters were soon followed by calls for reconsideration signed by prominent Americans including Norman Lear, Oliver Stone, and Jesse Jackson.

PBS then fired back—using three new arguments and rationalizations.

First, they impugned the integrity of the petitioners. Duggan insinuated that we, as the producers and on-air talent (a reference to Charlayne Hunter-Gault), were only using the press to reverse legitimate decisions, advance our careers, and undermine the First Amendment by seeking government interference in internal editorial matters. This argument avoided the substance of our claims by mischaracterizing our motives in speaking out. Duggan compared us to porkbarrel politicians seeking special favors, labeling *Rights & Wrongs* as just one more parochial group serving a narrow advocacy agenda. He spoke of PBS's right to program without mentioning that that "right" had been bestowed by an act of Congress and was subject to serving the public interest.

Second, PBS argued that they were already covering human rights. PBS's then-program chief Jennifer Lawson pointed to a handful of programs as evidence of PBS's concern, implying that *Rights & Wrongs* was not needed. The fact that PBS documentary series like *Frontline* or *POV* include programs on human rights themes only speaks to the public interest in and the newsworthiness of the issues and not that they have been exhaustively covered. Neither *Frontline* or *POV* claims to do what we do. Henry Hampton, the producer of such series as *Eyes on the Prize* offered to write to PBS on our behalf. Letters like that only matter when someone is willing to listen.

Third, PBS turned the dispute into a left-right fight. In a widely reported speech, Duggan portrayed PBS as caught between two extremes, the "resolute Right that wants to censor and suppress programs" and the "coercive Left"—presumably our supporters. He positioned PBS as representing the "reasonable center." Congresswoman Eleanor Holmes Norton characterized Duggan's response as "screechingly defensive," but just at that moment, Congressional momentum was short-circuited when Newt Gingrich's Republican landslide rolled over Capitol Hill. Our issue died as the Republicans took cover. They didn't go after us, but PBS itself, which they branded falsely as too radical, confusing its warm and mushy programming with a leftist agenda. Their demagoguery silenced all debate.

When they did comment on the content of our work, PBS executives raised vague questions about a lack of balance, as if no program is valid unless there is a mechanical allotment of time to both sides, and as if there are only two sides on an issue. "Does that mean if it was balanced—for torture as well as against torture—they would carry it?" Marvin Kitman asked. "In Norway, Sweden and on the BBC they think the show is apolitical. Here it is considered ultra-left."

Fortunately for us, the rationalizations at the top of the PBS hierarchy were rejected at the bottom, and more than 140 stations carried *Rights & Wrongs*, a growing number of them in prime time. WNET in New York, PBS's flagship station, has partnered with us from the show's inception and is actively involved in our editorial process, while the American Program Service has distributed our shows. In 1996, we commissioned a survey of the stations, thinking they might prefer to carry a few specials rather than a weekly series. We were wrong. Most of the stations said they would run the show every week of the year. We, of course, can't raise that kind of money. But it was reassuring that many public television producers and staffers, especially at the local level, are still attracted by the ideals of public broadcasting and believe in the importance of noncommercial programming.

Even with friends in the system, and even after four seasons, sixty-three weeks on the air, we still have to fight for better air times and visibility. Perhaps that's why critic John Leonard branded us the "bad news stepchild of public broadcasting—overworked, underfunded, hidden away like some shameful secret in the closets of the schedule, or not aired at all." As I write in 1997, funding is harder than ever to find and the series may be silenced not by political censors but by economic censorship. By 1998, the weekly series was kaput when our funding went away just as we found more prime time air slots and legitimation. Instead, working with Charlayne, who had left TV and moved to South Africa as an NPR correspondent, we produced an hour-long special report on globalization and human rights. PBS ultimately agreed to distribute it.

Our problems with PBS did not turn on personal differences or politics, which are rarely discussed openly anyway. It was much deeper, a system thing. PBS had long ago watered down its commitment to its alternative mission. Timidity became institutionalized. In 1990, while the Gulf War was underway, we started work on *Eyes of the Storm*, a real-time look at how the media had embraced the military mission. PBS, which invested so much time and money on a series about the Civil War, was not interested in the Gulf War in the same way. It is far safer to treat issues from the distance of history. This is true in England as well. According to filmmaker Ken Loach, there is a reluctance to transmit events in which people can actually intervene. "As long as miners are not on strike, there are lots of programs that back them up. But if there is a struggle, one that shakes things up, it is more difficult to get programs shown...[until] after the strike—[when] it is no longer going to have the same impact." Well, after the war was over, reports of a variety of deceptions of the public by the government, with the full collusion of the press—known but suppressed at the time—were widely reported.

At many PBS stations, the most popular syndicated series (which reveals something about the age group PBS stations appeal to) are reruns of the *Lawrence Welk Show*. PBS stations try to play the ratings game too, targeting desirable demographics just like their commercial counterparts. Many programs are targeted at potential donors, often viewers who live in select zip codes, usually upper class suburbs or upscale urban neighborhoods. These stations often find that the programming that raises the most money for them are concerts by liberal performers like Bob Dylan or Peter, Paul and Mary. Progressive performers are used to raise money while progressive programming remains suspect. Most of the performers don't know this.

Many PBS stations have been open to more diverse and relevant fare. In 1997, we worked with New York's Channel 13 on a special with Nobel Laureate Elie Wiesel. We have been supported by ITVS, the Independent Television Service, which funds an excellent mix of shows. Although funded by Congress to promote more diversity on the airwaves, they have to fight with PBS for distribution, too.

At the same time, the right continues to bash away at what they say is public television's liberal bias. Lawrence Jarvik, a protégé of our *South Africa Now* nemesis David Horowitz (my onetime editor at *Ramparts*), has massaged that critique (with lots of right-wing foundation money and hamburger helper) into a book-length screed called *PBS: Behind the Screen*, which attacks me as a left-winger but has little to say about the well-documented right-wing bias of so many PBS shows. When Jarvik did a story about *Rights & Wrongs* for one of Horowitz's heavily subsidized polemical publications, my partner Rory challenged a string of errors and misquotations. "Oh, you know David," Jarvik replied. "He's gonna do what he's gonna do." In other words, why let the facts get in the way of a prefabricated putdown?

Writing in the *Nation* in February 1997, Eric Alterman cited a number of studies showing how few citizen activists or leftists actually turn up on PBS stations. "In partisan terms," he writes, "Republicans outnumbered Democrats, 53 to 47 percent. On PBS documentaries, the right's favorite target, Republicans outweighed Democrats 63 to 37 percent calculated by airtime, and 59 to 41 percent by [number of] appearances." A 1990 study by the City University of New York on programming devoted to the lives and concerns of working people found that the business and social elite get on average ten times more coverage. The report concludes, "Programming about workers makes up less than 1/2 of 1 percent of PBS prime-time programming offerings, and much of that minuscule amount is about British rather than American workers."

These national trends are mirrored on the local level, although some stations take their public affairs responsibilities more seriously.

"Public TV rarely risks anything innovative in news and public affairs," writes media columnist Dan Kennedy in the *Boston Phoenix*. He characterizes many of these shows as "tired, inside-the-Beltway smorgasbords of talking heads. This caution and unwillingness and inability to spend money extends to local stations across the country."

For the most part, executives on public television do not rise and fall with ratings. Playing it safe is a prudent way of guaranteeing personal sinecures and not alienating local business leaders who sit on station boards. Bigger program budgets often translate into more prestige, and increasingly, those budgets come from corporate underwriting. In October 1995, for example, Duggan announced a $75 million co-production deal with *Reader's Digest*, which is known for its cultural and political conservatism. (The deal went south when *Reader's Digest* itself began to fall apart.) Many big companies like to be associated with public television, which they consider a cheap media buy and good PR. Unfortunately, the shows we've produced—on apartheid and human rights—are not considered corporate friendly, a term actually used by a PBS station executive.

The business of public television has gravitated increasingly toward business. In 1996, PBS did a $20 million deal with the Williams Companies, a natural gas pipeline outfit, to provide business education on its Business Channel, a specialized service that PBS set up in 1989 to provide continuing education for corporate America. If you are looking for balance in the form of a labor channel, don't look too hard.

A year earlier, PBS announced rules to liberalize prohibitions against stretching underwriting credits into mini-commercials. Increasingly, the system and the stations use their funding as leverage to guarantee that they will get back part of any back-end royalties from home video sales or ancillaries like merchandising. Forget about human rights—the rights they care about are licensing rights, marketing rights, and residual rights. They are as into branding as Rupert Murdoch.

This entrepreneurial culture is continually bumping up against the noncommercial public service tradition. It has led to much competition and backbiting among the stations, and between the stations and the central offices. A prominent PBS personality told me: "If you think the war in the Balkans is bad, think what would happen if we armed the PBS stations."

Our long-running battle with PBS has had some benefits, especially in terms of visibility. Because many TV writers thrive on controversy, they wouldn't write about *Rights & Wrongs* unless we were being attacked or rejected. This has often meant that the *content* of our work is ignored in the stories about us. Many critics did comment on the substance of our work, of course. *Variety* praised us for keeping the focus "on the issues that have taken a back seat to O. J. on the networks." Mark Sommer in the Topeka *Capitol Journal* called the series fresh and hard-hitting. Marvin Kitman noted that "story after story, *Rights & Wrongs* was there when nobody else was or before the rest of the media."

We came to see that it is the gatekeepers who are ultimately responsible for sanitizing the airwaves, for echoing the choices of an audience they have helped condition. Increasingly, in our multichannel world with its confusing array of programming, viewers tend to cling to the familiar, and people on both the right and left gravitate toward shows that confirm their world views rather than challenge them. Conservatives tune in to the pundit shows dominated by conservatives spawning legions of Rush Heads or Ditto Heads. Unfortunately, too many progressives prefer to tune out, and place bumper stickers on their Volvos reading "Kill Your Television."

RUNNING OUR OWN COMPANY

Between hustling work and producing stories, we had to teach ourselves how to run and manage a company. That included managing people we couldn't always afford to pay properly or provide with adequate benefits. In some cases, they were kids just out of school, totally inexperienced—the only ones who could afford to work with us. They required training and micro-management.

We are also two men, who, while supportive of feminist values, don't always practice them perfectly. That's made for tension from time to time. Also, as white guys doing a series about black people, you can imagine the suspicion and testing *that* triggered, especially at a time when very few media projects were as interracial. I'm proud that our work has been honored by many leading black organizations and publications.

Progressive groups and companies are notorious for allowing political divisions, male-female tensions and racial undercurrents to tear them apart. Globalvision has stayed together for eleven years in part because the discipline and work involved in getting out a program every week doesn't allow much time for sectarianism, intellectual masturbation, or power trips. Rory and I and senior staffers run the company, and refuse to allow it to degenerate into a factionalized collective or debating society, perhaps because we've had all too many negative experiences with divisiveness in the name of political correctness.

We have pursued many socially conscious projects for a very unbusinesslike reason: We believe in them. Unfortunately, that choice has also sometimes isolated us. Some TV channels seem wary of working with us; others say no because they are perhaps uncomfortable with people who have a public profile that includes challenging the industry or questioning its priorities. While we may appear to be outsiders, we really want to be insiders. We've spent a lot of time battling with PBS when we would prefer to be producing for CBS. Yup, we want to be commercial, to make money, to be economically strong. We need to pay our bills and finance our lives and modest lifestyles. We want to be independent, not dependent on the largesse of others. We won't sell out but we do want to sell in. Also, we want our work seen. Besides, we know how to turn out network-quality work.

Do business and politics mix? A small number of companies say yes, but most of them won't support a television series either. Eng-

Editors Promoted To Key Positions On Clinton News

Mid-year promotions have produced a number of changes on the Clinton News Managing and Associate Boards for the spring term.

Daniel Schechter, former news editor, has taken over as editor-in-chief. He replaces Bob Schwieger, who has returned to the sports page. Emile Rosenberg starts his second term as managing editor of the newspaper.

Schechter

Both Schechter and Rosenberg are journalism class graduates and were on last term's Managing Board.

Completing the Managing Board are Edwin Weiss, Robert Wilkov, Steven Barth, and Ed Menkin. They head the first, fourth, features, and sports pages respectively.

Composing the Associate Board are Steven Banilower, Ed Bomsey, and Mark Haber, news; David Seplow, features; and Ted Ackerman, sports.

The promotions were decided upon by the members of last term's Managing Board at their final meeting, January 12.

My first foray into journalism—editing the DeWitt Clinton High School newspaper.

Voter registration in East Baltimore ghetto, 1963. The Civil Rights Movement brought me face to face with "the other America."

With Danny Cohn-Bendit (second from right), the force behind the Paris revolt of 1968, and other student activists from Yugoslavia and France.

Soweto Day Care Center. On a government-sponsored tour to show off how much the apartheid government was doing for "the blacks," 1967.

Dar Es Salaam, Tanzania, with South Africans in exile, 1967.

SLEGS VIR NIE BLANKES
NON-EUROPEANS ONLY

Apartheid, 1967. I chased the bus, thinking that since I wasn't European I could board. But in Johannesburg back then, "European" meant "white," and I was not allowed on.

The American Dream Machine at work in Soweto, 1967.

The ANC's Pallo Jordan,
London, 1968.

Johannesburg Stock
Exchange, 1967. Whites only.

The Student Revolt at the
London School of Economics,
1967.

Riding a "Tank" (before
Dukakis), Guerilla Theater,
London, 1968.

DON'T STEAL THIS PAPER

Buy it — if you want to know what Abbie Hoffman's been up to for the last six years.

Next week in The Real Paper, WBCN's News Dissector Danny Schechter interviews America's funniest fugitive, Abbie Hoffman. Find out why the famous Yippie leader, who's been underground since 1973, has resurfaced to appear on the Joe Oteri Show and grant a special interview to Schechter.

Everyone's favorite radical reveals his thoughts on everything from what went wrong in the Seventies to what's right about dealing cocaine. Is he still crazy after all these years? Why is he risking his anonymity now? The Abbie Hoffman saga continues.

IN NEXT WEEK'S ISSUE OF

The Real Paper

WE'RE GETTING NEWER EVERY WEEK

Above: News Dissecting with Andy Kopkind, WBCN, 1972.

Left: Abbie Hoffman, as he looked after altering his appearance—a photo taken on the *Joe Oteri Show*, 1979.

Below: John Lennon suggests that I plug in my mike during a 1971 interview for BCN.
(PHOTO BY STEVEN GOLDSTEIN)

Vietnam, North of the DMZ, 1974.
PHOTO BY STEVE KAGEN

A "Viet-Cong"
press conference, Camp
Davis, Saigon, 1974.
PHOTO BY JOHN SPRAGENS

Interviewing a North Vietnamese official for
WBCN, Hanoi, 1974. PHOTO BY STEVE KAGEN

Covering the Guardian Angels for
20/20, 1981.

With ABC's Av Westin, 1984.

20/20's tenth anniversary,
1988.

Covering Jesse Jackson at
the Mandela statue, London,
1986.

Interviewing Zimbabwe's
President Robert Mugabe,
Harare, 1986.

Opposite: A view of the Statue
of Liberty few get to see—with
Tom Jarriel and a 20/20 crew,
1986.

Sandi Freeman of
CNN, 1980.

On the set after the last taping
of *South Africa Now*, 1991.
Anchor Fana D. Kekana is in
front. L to R: (front) Mweli
Mzizi, Eric Nadler, Phillip
Tomlinson, Tandeka Gqubule,
(back) Rapitse Monsho, myself,
Joe Diescho, Rory O'Connor.

...he Zelig? Part of my "Wall of Fame"—

...e: (from top, left to right) The Dalai Lama, Peter Gabriel, Oprah Winfrey,
...Rivera, Muhammad Ali, Don King, Tom Hayden and Jane Fonda, Tina Turner.
...g page: Allen Ginsberg, Archbishop Desmond Tutu, Mozambique's late
...Samora Machel, Jesse Jackson, Johnnie Cochran, Former UN Secretary
...Boutros Boutros-Ghali, Hart Perry and Daniel Ortega, Elie Wiesel.

African National Congress

51 Plein Street
Johannesburg 2001
P O Box 61884
Marshalltown 2107

Tel: (011) 330-7273
(011) 330-7052
Fax: (011) 333-7739
Telex: 421252

OFFICE OF THE PRESIDENT

21st February 1994.

Messrs Rory O' Connor and Danny Schechter
Globalvision Inc.
1600 Broadway
New York 10019

Dear Rory and Danny:

The forthcoming South African elections are a historic turning point in our country's transition from apartheid to democracy. While the events will be covered in the mass media, we believe that the inside story itself deserves coverage by independent journalists for the public worldwide and for future generations. Daily news reporting is invariably superficial, often focusing only on the statements of leaders. An in-depth documentary film can bring out the story of how the people themselves, white and black, are participating in the larger process of democratization.

Out of respect for your work, we are inviting Globalvision to produce an independent film about this key moment in world history. The ANC is committed to providing you unique access, exclusive interviews, and will facilitate your entree into our campaign at the national and local level. You will be able to stay in the homes of our organizers, travel with me and our motorcades, and shoot various internal strategy meetings. We will provide as much support as we can without interfering with your editorial process. We understand the importance of your autonomy and credibility.

I understand that President Clinton had a similar arrangement with an independent film maker during the American elections that resulted in a useful "insider" film about the workings of his campaign. We are prepared to do the same, and are pleased that Globalvision has expressed interest in involving South Africans as professional participants and trainees in the production process.

The election is just 2 months away. We know that you will have to move quickly. We hope that this pledge of cooperation will help you find adequate funding and a television outlet. We certainly urge prospective funders or broadcasters to consider becoming involved because this a story of universal interest.

I have asked Z. Pallo Jordan, the Director of our Department of Information and Publicity to be your liaison and to confirm our intentions to prospective funders or television companies. He will report back to me on your decision and any other assistance we may be asked to provide

We hope you will be able to undertake this project and look forward to working with you.

Yours sincerely,

Nelson R. Mandela.
President.

Danny: Sorry not to have written in a while. I was waiting for an article I wrote on Pentagon to appear in the Realist. I send you it when it comes out Krassner is taking his merry ass time. He + I are off to the Florida Keys for a month, he's doing a movie + I'll write the book. —— Read Antonin Artaud "The Theater + its Double"... See the "King of Hearts" movie —— Ellen was really excited about her trip. You should come back here soon Danny + get your teeth into something. We have an excellent nucleus of artists, architects poets + politicos. like Tuli Kupferberg, Jerry Rubin, Krassner, etc., etc. + are developing a strategy of mobile tactics + mind trips The Free Store is being redesigned in Royal Blue, Stars, moons, planets, "free" blinking signs it will be called HEAVEN. Cardinal Spellman died + we are going to St. Patricks Cathedral three days later to wait for him to come back. War is Over Celebration was fantastic. We are now planning a huge spectacular for Democratic National Convention in Chicago next August. You must come back to work on this. We also formed a mythical conspiracy for the media. called Protesters, Terrorists + Anarchists their motto is "The PTA stands for Violence" Worse than the mafia. Total secrecy, leaflets claim credit for all violence at demonstrations. SMOKE BOMBS,,,,, Plastic Bags of BLOOD* "Birth of a Digger" Public birth of a free spirit. Doctor + father arrested. —— ZIP —— I'm really going away to Skin Dive —— besides I've had 4 arrests in past 8 weeks + I'm marked in N.Y. It's awkward throwing a bag of blood + the cop says "Hi Abbie." If it gets worse I'll cut my hair.

    Peace Peace Noel Blink Blink

        Abbie

A couple of letters from the files—

Nelson Mandela's invite to South Africa to chronicle his campaign.
Abbie Hoffman's invite to Chicago for the demonstrations outside the 1968 Democratic National Convention.

Singing "Sun City" in Tokyo, 1986. Little Steven, Peter Gabriel, Nona Hendrix, and Jackson Browne are among the artists.

Older and grayer but still rebels. Students for a Democratic Society (SDS) reunion, 1996.

In Memoriam, SDS reunion, 1996.

With Sidney Blumenthal (now a member of President Clinton's media staff) covering a speech by former CIA Director William Colby at Suffolk University, Boston, 1975. I asked Colby how he slept. He said, "fine."

The Stetsasonic rap band and the late Rick Dutka (bottom middle), New York, 1987.

Charlayne Hunter-Gault greets former President Jimmy Carter for a *Rights & Wrongs* interview at the UN, 1993.

The *Rights & Wrongs* producing team, 1993: Steve Anderson, Charlayne, and Rory O'Connor. PHOTO BY JERRY BERNDT

With Nelson Mandela in a township outside of Capetown, 1990.

Exhausted from trying to keep up with Mandela during South Africa's first democratic elections, 1994.

With Rory O'Connor at Globalvision, 1990.

With Sarah Debs Schechter, 1977.
PHOTO BY GERRY FEIL

land's Body Shop did help us launch the first season of *Rights &*
Wrongs. We met and were charmed by Anita Roddick, the
dynamic, driving force behind its success.

We first encountered this English "Shampoo Queen" at a meeting of the Social Venture Network in a ski resort in the Poconos.
When everyone else was huddled in some New Age self-realization
session, she was in the bar, nursing a glass of wine and talking ani-
matedly (the only way she talks) about the Body Shop's plans to
bring their stores and social message to America. We didn't know
much about her then, but pitched our global TV concept to her anyway. She seemed mesmerized. At last! A corporate visionary! A
potential sponsor! She agreed to bring our proposals to her board
and to her husband, Gordon, who ran the company. She told us she
had one more project to discuss and would be heading home after
the weekend.

We couldn't stick around. We had to speed home that afternoon
to oversee the completion of the first national edition of *South
Africa Now*. What we didn't know was that Anita's next meeting
was with a slick and articulate Canadian producer who didn't have
to rush anywhere. He had created a rather apolitical series about
indigenous peoples worldwide, with images that were striking and
beautiful, idealizing people living on the margins. She liked his proposal too. The price tag was $3 million, and when Anita told him
she had to go back to England, he wisely asked if he could go with
her, at his own expense, of course. Ever friendly, she said "be my
guest." And he was. He now had time to turn his pitch into a week-
long dog and pony show.

Guess who got the deal?

His show came and went without much impact, along with several million dollars of the Body's Shop's dinero. The reviewers
yawned and the company was "disappointed." Their enthusiasm
for television tempered by an expensive failure, we ended up with
nothing. Our lesson: Be ready to drop everything and take that
flight.

A few years later, we got the chance and we jumped at it. We went along with Anita to visit Body Shops throughout England, right up to Glasgow where the Body Shop manufactured soap in one of the most depressed areas of the city. We watched as she launched an adventure playground for the kids of Easterhouse, one of the city's roughest housing projects. The kids loved the playground and just about tore it apart after a few hours of play. We were impressed with the Body Shop's good works.

From Glasgow, it was on to Aberdeen and the Roddick estate in the highlands not far from where the Royal Family keeps some of its castles. Gordon, we learned, played polo with Prince Charles and had grown up in the upper classes; he is a very thoughtful and socially conscious businessman. Anita had working class origins. Their "castle," more like a renovated, twenty-bedroom manor house, was comfortable and beautifully furnished, right down to an American jukebox in the kitchen. The Roddicks frequently invited would-be investors and franchisees over. The message was seductive and often subliminal: Be part of the Body Shop; do well and live like us.

We bought the dream. Anita led Rory and me on a long walk in a chilly drizzle though the farmlands and thickets of a pristine countryside. To me, all that slogging through the mud felt like Mao's long march, and I struggled to keep up. Anita's energy was unflagging. Thank heavens, she had agreed not to force us to climb a nearby mountain with her to see the very tip, what she called the nipple.

Rory prodded me to keep up the pace. "We're being tested," he said, as I fought for breath, picking myself up from a fall from a wooden fence into a pile of hay. "Keep focused or we will never close."

I was focused all right—at keeping the brambles out of my hair. I plodded on but not without a lot of kidding. We must have passed Anita's endurance test because when we came home, we did a deal. Globalvision became the Body Shop's video production arm in the USA.

The Body Shop loved us. And we loved them, probably too much. They loved us until they didn't love us anymore. Their priorities shifted with the seasons. At first, they hired us to produce a twice-monthly video newsmagazine for distribution to their growing network of franchised and company-owned shops. Producing Body Shop TV enabled our company for the first time to retain and reinvest some profits. Not familiar with American slang, they called their show BSTV.

The Body Shop also provided a major grant for *Rights & Wrongs*. But they dropped their support in the second season and also decided to produce their internal videos inhouse—"to save money"—despite the awards that honored our version of BSTV. A year later they learned, as we predicted, that their cost-efficiency move actually cost them more and produced less. They also lost their PR touch. In 1994, their socially responsible reputation came under assault. When asked if she could find any silver lining in the controversy that followed a blistering exposé, Anita, in top form, responded: "That's like asking Mrs. Lincoln after her husband was assassinated at Ford Theater, 'Besides that, how did you like the play?'" By 1998, faced with copycat competition and management problems, Anita stepped down as Body Shop CEO and brought in a more conventional business manager. She remained a company chairperson, but the company was having hard times.

To support ourselves, Globalvision has branched out in five directions—producing our own programming, work for hire for other companies, promotional videos, corporate videos and some consulting. In December 1994, to cite just one month, these were some of our projects: videos of award winners for the annual National Urban League and Reebok Human Rights awards, two videos for UNICEF, one for use in Haiti that we produced in Creole, English and French and one about the needs of children in the Americas in Spanish and English that was introduced by Hillary Rodham Clinton at the Hemispheric Summit in Miami. We also shot the Playboy Foundation's First Amendment awards and a "birthday party" for the late Abbie Hoffman. We sold my South Africa film to Cinemax/HBO, researched footage on Nelson Mandela for a Jonathan Demme film and pitched programs on the Nazi war criminals of World War II, Serbian war criminals of the Balkan War and a bizarre show about bizarre families of the world. I went to California to discuss consulting for a new cable channel and to Morningside Heights to discuss producing an interfaith service for the fiftieth anniversary of the UN. Rory went to Florida to produce a segment for a syndicated special on conspiracies, investigating crazies who were killing abortion doctors for Christ. Plus we sent out fund-raising proposals, negotiated a contract and picked up a $250,000 check from a foundation for the next season of *Rights & Wrongs*. We didn't do as many of the big projects as we wanted, but we did make it through another year.

During this one month, we remained visible in the outside world. Globalvision programs were plugged or attacked in five different newspapers and magazines. The Rockefeller Foundation turned us down because of "limited funds," and we lost a shot at the Sundance Film festival because their director never got around to seeing our film. "I'm sorry," he told us, "I can't see them all." In the meantime our receptionist got sick, our editing machine broke, postage went up, the Christmas cards barely went out, and a syndicated show we did some work for went under. And for the umpteenth time, HBO told us to forget it. Still not enough sizzle! But despite it all, we survived. We more than broke even. A small but real victory!

We can also boast that we haven't done much work we are ashamed of. And that is an unusual claim in our business. To us, making a film on Nelson Mandela's victory is more thrilling than chasing O. J. Simpson.

When I was a college student at Cornell, I interviewed author James Baldwin, then at the height of his popularity and influence. While digging through old files for this book, I stumbled on his remarks in the pages of *Dialogue*, the student magazine I edited back in the early '60s, the days when television was still in its infancy and certainly not yet my idea of a vocation. At that time, there weren't more than a few sets on the whole campus. Yet for some reason, TV seemed to be on my mind even then, and I asked Baldwin for insight. His response thirty-four years ago anticipated many of the contradictions we still face today:

"Let's say I write a centennial TV spectacular to celebrate the hundredth birthday of Negro freedom. I write it and the sponsors say: 'Well, I think you ought to write cooler here and softer there. I want you to take that out.' And you can do it and justify yourself by saying 'Well, half a loaf is better than none. At least they're showing a TV spectacular.' But what you've done has wrecked the show, half a loaf is not better than none; half a loaf is like poison. It's like half a truth. And once you have done it, once you have persuaded yourself that you should do it, you begin tampering with something inside yourself, which is a very dangerous thing to do. You have attacked the very basis of your self-respect. What everyone has to understand, which is very hard to understand: The world says it is offering a choice between life and death; this is a lie. The world offers you the way you die; you die on your terms, or you die on their terms."

PART THREE

COVERING SOUTH AFRICA

FOR YEARS South Africa was one of the most compelling media stories in the world, and for good reason. It had drama, confrontation and clearly defined sides. The system of apartheid was an anomaly in the modern world and a fascinating topic to report on. Many careers were made by journalists witnessing the front lines of the struggle.

Like a lot of Americans, I first encountered South Africa in the media. But over the years, the more I learned, the more I realized that the press was, on the whole, a poor guide to understanding the real dynamics of the story.

I soon took on the role of covering the coverage. For me, the South African story is not only important in itself, but for what it says about the media. This is not a blanket indictment, because some terrific reportage was produced. But the hoopla has obscured deeper problems.

The newspaper and TV accounts about South Africa, which I have followed closely for nearly forty years, have tended to distort and simplify events in South Africa. Despite all the media attention, much was missed. The fuller story was rarely told or properly contextualized—but why? Reporters certainly considered themselves sympathetic to those fighting for freedom, but somehow that sympathy reduced its subjects to stereotypes. This engaged viewers and readers, but what did it explain? And what was its impact? After all, if words were weapons, apartheid would have toppled decades earlier than it did, under the weight of all the reports, studies, polemics, pamphlets, UN resolutions and denunciations. Maybe I expect too much from journalism. Perhaps I have a misplaced faith in the power of information.

The South Africa story teaches us how even good reporters can gloss over crucial aspects of stories because of cultural and political orientation. The heroes of the struggle, operating aboveground in South Africa, or from prison, or from exile, were rarely quoted, interviewed or profiled until the system was about to collapse. And it was not just the reporters who blew it—the organizations they represent almost require them to, by their biases, and by the structural limitations of the way overseas stories are covered.

The story was presented in stark black and white terms only as a racial confrontation: the economic rationale for and impact of apartheid were rarely discussed. Apartheid was also rarely presented as a system that was financed and supported in large part from abroad, through investment and trade in minerals, gold and diamonds. Cold war framing was pervasive. The ANC was always identified as Moscow-backed, never Stockholm-supported, yet the movement received as much or more help from the Swedes as the Russians.

The historic context was usually left out as well. The Afrikaners may have introduced the apartheid system, but its foundation was anchored in racist colonial policies originating in London, not Pretoria. How many Americans know that a delegation from South Africa visited America in the latter part of the nineteenth century to learn how we treated the "Indian problem"? Our Native American reservations inspired the South African system of native reserves.

This may seem unfair, since so many news media outlets point with pride to their South African coverage and the professional prizes it brought them. South Africa, they would argue, is an example of the one story that was handled right.

Wrong.

I believe that the victims of a racist system were victimized once again by a media that marched in lockstep with the system that profited from their misery. In many cases that media itself practiced apartheid—it certainly did in South Africa. Although, even so, for many years there were more blacks working in key media jobs in Johannesburg than in Jackson, Mississippi, or for that matter, in Washington, D.C.

The issues I've identified do not belong to the past. Now that apartheid has ended and the more visible struggle receded, inadequate reporting has given way to almost no reporting from South Africa, unless there is an eruption of violence, a natural disaster or some juicy tidbit involving Winnie Mandela. Some newspapers, like the *New York Times*, do continue to follow events there, but many news organizations have long since closed their bureaus. Barely three years after Nelson Mandela was elected president, South Africa barely exists in the world media, and most Americans have no idea what's happening there or what it may mean to them.

As I write, Howard Wolpe, a former congressman and chair of the Africa subcommittee of the House of Representatives, is completing a study showing how uninformed many U.S. journalists in South Africa are and how poor the coverage remains. Looking at the coverage of South Africa over the course of decades reveals the persistence of the problem—one that is not likely to be addressed unless and until there are more fundamental changes in how our global media addresses global stories.

CHAPTER 9

PASSION AND DISCOVERY: THAT WAS THEN

*M*any journalists have special stories or subjects that become consuming passions and define their careers. For Edward R. Murrow and his generation, it was World War II. For Av Westin, my old boss at 20/20, and many others in modern network news, it was the cold war. For most of my compatriots of the '60s, it was Vietnam. A few years later, for Woodward and Bernstein and their investigative protégés, it was Watergate.

But for me, across nearly four decades, it has been a cause and a country much farther away—South Africa.

After all these years, I am still not sure if I chose it or it chose me. I developed a passion for the country's people and their struggle that wouldn't let me go. I realize now that the relationship has been unequal: I have received far more than I have given. And it has influenced how I feel about the world and the press.

When people asked me when I was last there, I would often say "this morning," because for so many years I was nearly always reading about, researching, reporting on and in effect living South Africa. It has been as if some South African gene got mixed up in my DNA. Some South Africans were sure I grew up there, perhaps because one of their most famous race car drivers is named Jodie Sheckter. But I didn't. He is not related. I am from the Bronx, not Bloemfontein.

In fact, it was as a kid that the media first brought South Africa into my bedroom in the housing project I grew up in. I remember *Life* magazine's photo spread about apartheid in the late '50s with its striking pictures of defiant whites and downtrodden blacks, of the bus boycotts and passive resistance campaigns that foreshadowed similar events in our country. It featured images that didn't change for years—black men sweating in the gold mines, black women crying for their children, vacant stares from inside jail cells, striking contrasts between the lives of privileged whites and dispossessed natives. These images imprinted themselves in my mind and remain there still. Back then I treated them as a curiosity from another world, a world I never thought would touch my life.

Like so many other Americans, Hollywood films of Tarzan flying on jungle vines introduced and reinforced racist stereotypes that influenced our entire culture, black and white. (Years later, while profiling Tina Turner's comeback for *20/20*, I learned that her ex-partner Ike had been so influenced by a Tarzan-like movie serial called *Nyoka, the Jungle Girl* that he made his wife, Annie Mae Bullock, over in Nyoka's image. "She was wild," Ike told me. "Tina became my Nyoka.") Africa always seemed to be pictured as wild, primitive or exotic, a throwback to premodern times.

It was music that first challenged my own caricatures: upbeat folk songs like "Wimoweh" by the Weavers (repackaged as the hit "The Lion Sleeps Tonight"), "Zulu Warrior" by Marais and Miranda, and the resistence hymn "Senzenina," as sung by Pete Seeger. In my high school days, the energy of African people also came alive for me through the sounds of Hugh Masekela, the songs of Letta Mbulu, and the distinctive clicks of Miriam Makeba. I was introduced to the infectious rhythms of African music by Olatunji's hit "Drums of Passion," in my Cornell dormitory where freshmen blasted it on their phonographs out the window. "Acky wah wah," he wailed in Yoruba, not suspecting, I'm sure, that his Nigerian chants would turn on a bunch of crewcut adolescents in Ithaca, New York.

So I guess I felt Africa in my feet before learning about it in my head.

If I had to name a point of origin for my obsession, I'd go to my college years, starting in 1961, when some African students asked the late Ken Rubin and myself to help them organize a march to mourn the murder of the Congo's independence warrior Patrice Lumumba, who had died as a result of CIA complicity. Ken was my best friend and together we edited *Dialogue*, a campus political journal that began as a mimeographed pamphlet. We wrote a letter to the Cornell *Daily Sun* calling for a solemn protest on campus. The African students feared political retaliation by immigration authorities were they to write the letter themselves. The dignified march went well, with the Africans in native dress. Yet it was greeted with a counter-protest by campus conservatives who carried signs supporting Belgian colonialism and joked about cooking people in a pot.

As I write now, in 1997, the world is still living with the legacy of Lumumba's death as the Congo deals with the aftermath of the overthrow of President Mobutu Sese Seko, who was installed in power and kept there for a quarter of a century with CIA help, running a brutal dictatorship justly called a kleptocracy. The 1997 Academy Award-winning documentary on Muhammad Ali's famous "rumble in the jungle" against George Foreman in Zaire reports that people were tortured in those years in cells under the stands of the stadium.

Dialogue started carrying articles about southern Africa in 1961, in the aftermath of the Sharpeville massacre. After all, the world was changing. There had been a revolution in Cuba. The Third World was emerging as a battleground in the cold war, but also a collective force on the world stage, defining itself, challenging colonialism and its remnants. Young people were at the forefront of change, leading movements and taking over countries. Most American commentators today see the history of the '60s only as an American happening, but it was truly a worldwide phenomenon. Student movements in South Korea, Japan and Latin America inspired their American counterparts just as the protests in Paris and Berlin appropriated American tactics. I began to see our battles through a global lens.

The "winds of change" were sweeping through Africa. Many experts believed it was just a matter of time before the black majority would overthrow white minority rule. They did the math—so many blacks, so many whites—and took refuge in slogans like Change Is Inevitable. In theory yes, but in practice, many—including the leaders of the African National Congress—underestimated apartheid's staying power. There's a famous story of a talk that Joe Slovo, the white South African Communist Party leader who also commanded the ANC's military wing for many years, reportedly gave to the Central Committee of the East German Communist Party in 1960.

He was pressed to predict how long it would take to free South Africa. After citing many factors and trends, he guesstimated, "Five years, comrades, five years."

Twenty-nine years later, in 1989, he returned to the same Central Committee, then in its very last days, just before the fall of the Berlin Wall. The same man who asked that question, now in his 80s, rose, introduced himself and repeated his question: "Mr. Slovo, when you were here last, you told us it would take five years to topple apartheid. Now what do you say?"

Looking around, Joe smiled as he remembered the questioner and his response. "Well, comrade, I'll have to say that nothing has led me to change that original estimate."

Slovo—finally—was not off by a lot. South Africa would hold its first free elections five years later although Joe, tragically, would be dead of cancer in year six, 1995.

In the 1960s, we fought in the U.S. for civil rights and freedom struggles worldwide, and against the war in Vietnam. Like many of my movement colleagues, I romanticized guerrilla war and the Third

World, cheering on the heroism and sacrifice of soldiers who were fighting to free their countries from colonialism and oppression. I saw their battles as contributing to our own, to stopping the spread of a Pax Americana.

I may not have adequately foreseen the human rights abuses some revolutionary regimes would inflict on their own people, but that was a period when we often too simplistically divided people into those who were part of the problem and those who aspired to be the solution. We were probably not hard enough on the former, but too soft on the latter.

I remember a cover of *Ramparts*, a muckraking magazine I began writing for in that period, featuring a young American waving a Vietcong flag under a heading that summed up the feelings of many antiwar militants: "Alienation is when your country is at war and you are rooting for the other side." We *were* angry and alienated, and our understanding of the Vietnam War led many of us into solidarity with the Vietnamese resistance to the Pentagon's aggression.

So it shouldn't be surprising that I first thought of the African National Congress as South Africa's version of South Vietnam's National Liberation Front. They both were fighting liberation wars with armed contingents. They both were led by nationalists with communist backing. Their rhetoric was similar. And while there were also important differences between the two movements and the two societies, they were both revolutionary movements in a revolutionary time.

Throughout the '60s, I devoured all I could read about South Africa, but my primary focus was as a civil rights organizer and journalist in America. Some of us began to see apartheid as an expression of the internationalization of racism. When I took part in a Students for a Democratic Society (SDS) protest at the Chase Manhattan Bank in downtown Manhattan, we had no idea that it would take twenty-five more years before economic sanctions would squeeze out Pretoria's white rulers. Ironically, it would be David Rockefeller of Chase Manhattan, our target then, whose refusal to roll over South African loans would be a crucial step in a chain of influences that forced the Afrikaners to negotiate.

There were other early protests in America, including a march at the UN led by the Nigerian drummer Olatunji. I started meeting a few South Africans in exile, who told me more about protests like Sharpeville and places like the political prison on Robben Island. One of them was Pallo Jordan, then a University of Wisconsin student who was kicked out of the United States for his role in antiwar protests. He is now a minister in Nelson Mandela's government, a brilliant strategist and an unreconstructed independent thinker.

In 1966, I moved to London to pursue graduate studies at the London School of Economics (LSE). Admission there got me a draft deferral, and swinging London was a great place to be for someone drawn to pop music and activist political culture. Before I went over, I was told that the LSE was a radical institution because of its association years earlier with Fabian socialists such as Harold Laski and George Bernard Shaw. I was more impressed by the fact that Mick Jagger had gone there. But up close, the LSE was a suffocating citadel of British tradition and pretension, ruled over by stuffy administrators and a conservative curriculum. I was part of a group of American activists who would shake things up with our British counterparts and help lead student strikes a year later. I was called a "Bar-clay" agitator, although I had at that point never been to California. One newspaper tagged me Danny the Yank, a silly attempt to label me as the London counterpart of Danny Cohn-Bendit, the French student leader known as Danny the Red, whom I befriended. In those years, we Americans in Britain had a group opposing the Vietnam War. One of its supporters was a kid from Arkansas, also avoiding military service, studying at Oxford, Bill Clinton. (He's the one who didn't inhale.)

Not all the LSE faculty were part of the stiff-upper-lip professorial aristocracy. One of the most popular and political was Ralph Miliband, a democratic Marxist, whose book on the relationship of the state to society was a New Left classic and whose lectures were among the most intellectually challenging I ever attended. It was in Miliband's class that I connected with South Africa again, after meeting a fellow graduate student, an older woman who was far more polished and sophisticated than I.

Her name was Ruth First, a white South African and an exile. It took me a while to discover how famous she was (or infamous, depending on which side of the apartheid divide you were on). Ruth had been the editor of several militant anti-apartheid newspapers. She had been banned and jailed. She had written several books, including *117 Days*, a passionate account of her detention for anti-apartheid dissidence. She returned to school, she told me, because she needed to get the credentials to teach since it would be hard for her as a foreigner to get a newspaper job in England. It was Ruth and her family's story that was dramatized in the 1988 film *A World Apart*, based on a screenplay written by her talented daughter Shawn.

Ruth became my mentor for all things South African. She took pity on me as a poor student and invited me on many occasions to her home in London's Camden Town. It was there that I met her husband, Joe Slovo, a man dubbed by the South African police state as Public Enemy Number One. Pretoria's propagandists had denounced him as a KGB colonel. Joe and Ruth had been co-defendants along with Nelson Mandela and 153 others in South Africa's four-year Treason Trial in the '50s.

I was not particularly enamored of their Communist Party affiliation. Most of us New Leftists were anti-Stalinist, anti-Leninist and suspicious of the hierarchic structures of the old Left. (Rightists never got these distinctions, reminding me of the old joke about the guy who said he was an "anti-communist," only to be told by a cop, "I don't care what kind of communist you are.") I hated the rigidity, stale slogans, pro-Soviet apologetics and ineffective practice of most CP apparatchiks. I was more of an anarchist and cultural activist then, leaning to the Cuban approach to internationalism, but even there I wasn't thrilled by the cult of personality that surrounded Fidel Castro. I was fascinated when Ruth told me that she agreed with many of my criticisms, although she explained that the South African Communist Party was aligned with the ANC, and that in that alliance, contrary to most media accounts, the ANC set the tone, not the Party. This perspective directly contradicted all those cold war columnists who claimed that the ANC was manipulated by diabolical Reds. For years, the South African state premised its whole national security strategy on the false notion that it was the target of a total assault conspiracy plotted in Moscow. (Years later, the Russians sidestepped sanctions to trade with South Africa.)

At many a Sunday brunch, which Joe often cooked, I watched them go at each other on all sorts of issues, with Joe defending the more orthodox line. They were both stunningly articulate and equally adamant. It was a tough time for Ruth because her husband was frequently ducking out of the country on sub rosa political missions, while she stayed home, working on her degree and raising three daughters. The demands of full-time political work caused serious tensions in the family. Some of these are descibed in *Every Secret Thing*, a moving memoir by another of their daughters, the accomplished writer Gillian Slovo. She tells of Nelson Mandela's ruminations on the day her father died, saying that one of his biggest regrets was his forced neglect of his childen. He said one of his daughters told him angrily, "You are the father of the nation but you weren't a father to me." It was a common problem in their movement and in ours as well.

Ruth took an interest in me because I was a new kind of American for her, a part of the student insurgency of the times. I turned her on to many publications from America, while she exposed me to many books about South Africa, introducing me as well to her fellow countrymen, including Ronald Segal and Barney Simon. She embodied my image of a revolutionary, and we embarked on a genuine and deep friendship that lasted until her death. Pretoria hated her. I idolized her. Her mind was as quick as her tongue was sharp.

She had no patience with fools or fanatics, yet she could be warm and patient with my often uninformed questions.

She was often on edge, pressured on all sides. She never knew how long her exile would last. Should her kids be raised as part of English society or as South Africans? I soon understood why such questions troubled her so. She couldn't go home again. Her movement had been crushed, many of her friends and colleagues driven into exile, underground or imprisoned. She confided to me that the Communist Party had been sloppy, arrogant perhaps, to have underestimated the shrewdness and brutality of the security police. She reminded me that the top leadership had been busted almost en masse at a farm in Rivonia in 1963. She and Joe had managed to escape, but many of their comrades were behind bars or scattered around the world. Thinking about it now, with the ANC in power, it is hard to imagine what a protracted struggle it took to regroup, rebuild and fight back. There was plenty of legitimate paranoia too. Ruth knew her family was under surveillance. Later, the ANC office in London was bombed. She lived with constant threats.

And there were perennial strategic debates. What was the best way forward? Could an armed struggle be effective? At first, Joe was critical of Che Guevara's strategy of a revolution within a revolution led by a small group, or "foco," of armed combatants. Joe attacked it publicly in print as doomed to fail. But then he seemed to reverse himself as ANC soldiers went into their first, disastrous armed confrontation in the Wankie forest of Rhodesia in 1968, taking on one of the most powerful armies in Africa.

Unlike many of her comrades, Ruth scratched deeper, examining the behavior of Africa's coup makers and talking about Africa's struggle in world terms. She worked with the late Oginga Odinga in Kenya and knew many opposition political players all over the continent. As an academic, she did her own research, always asking tough questions and seeking original data. She wrote about the conditions of miners and migrant workers, and pioneered feminist ideas in a book (with Ann Scott) about the first great South African novelist, the early feminist Olive Schreiner, author of *The Story of an African Farm*. In fact, Ruth was always one step ahead, open to new ideas and looking for alternatives to party dogma and movement-speak without sacrificing her revolutionary ideals. Years later, on the eve of South Africa's first democratic elections, Joe Slovo told me that it was Ruth who had forced him to rethink his politics and champion compromises and negotiation. Ruth is clearly one of the heros of the new South Africa, and is recognized as such by Nelson Mandela and the ANC's old guard.

To be closer to the struggle, Ruth left England and went to teach in Mozambique at the Center for African Studies. We stayed in touch, and I've kept her cards and letters. One day in August 1982 while driving in New York, I heard the bulletin: Ruth had been assassinated by a letter bomb, no doubt because her writing and then her teaching had been so far-reaching while she lived. ("Ruth brought to her post a razor-sharp intellect, a flow of language that enabled her to communicate complex ideas simply, a deft organizational talent and an approach to teaching that firmly situated the student in society," wrote Joe of his wife.) Slovo also blamed the "Reagans of the world" for their complicity with Pretoria's many assassinations in that period. In 1986, I visited her grave in Maputo where she is buried along with other ANC fighters who were ambushed in Pretoria's many cross-border raids.

What a loss that was—to her family, her country and the intellectual wealth of the Left. A few years later, while with *South Africa Now* in Lusaka, I had the eerie experience of interviewing Dirk Coetzee, an Afrikaner former captain of the security police, who led one of the covert hit squads that targeted Ruth and many of her comrades, perhaps the one that had killed her. Though he had blood on his hands, he actually defected to and was embraced for some time by the ANC.

Joe Slovo died in 1995, after negotiating the deal that made democratic elections possible. He was minister of housing in Nelson Mandela's government and although he was white, he consistently ranked second behind Mandela as the person black South Africans respected the most. In the townships and military camps, militant youth sang his name and told tales of the heroism of a Jewish lawyer known for wearing red socks. He was buried with full honors before thousands of blacks in Soweto, with Mandela leading the tributes. "He can be credited with playing a seminal role in the transition that South Africa has undergone and is experiencing," the president said on September 15, 1995.

While F. W. DeKlerk acknowledged the positive role Joe played, at the same time, ANC militants questioned the compromises Joe backed, arguing that to allow the Afrikaners to retain control of the civil service would subvert the process of change. Fearful of a murderous, Pinochet-style counterrevolution in which the ANC could be destroyed, Slovo and his cohorts fashioned a "goverment of national unity" to jointly rule with the very people who had long been their enemies. It fell apart in a few years, but did give the Mandela government some breathing space and time to get on its feet.

Getting to know South Africans like Ruth and Joe, Johnny Makathini, Pallo Jordan, Mazisi Kunene, and Ronnie Kasrils, a fellow LSE student and now South Africa's deputy minister of defense, and so many others, sucked me deeper into the South African vortex. (Ronnie's riveting autobiography, *Armed and Dangerous*, tells of life in the military struggle and his underground experiences as the "Red Pimpernel.") But nothing had a deeper impact than going there in the summer of 1967. In America it was the summer of love. I was twenty-five years old.

GOING SOUTH

I went "out to Africa," as the English say, for a three-week holiday on a student fare. In some ways I've never come back. I'm not sure what it is about that country that exerts such a pull, but I'm not the only journalist to whom it has happened. Joe Llelyveld, now executive editor of the *New York Times*, won a Pulitzer for his book about South Africa. In it he wrote that no country he'd ever covered had the same personal impact on him.

South Africa is a special place, an eerie mix of the familiar and unfamiliar set against a landscape that is magical in its beauty. Every contrast is pointed; every contradiction, revealing. Squatter camps perch in fancy neighborhoods. Horrible racial oppression coexists with enough relaxed moments of racial interaction to make New York seem far more tense and polarized. Many white South Africans were raised by a black nanny, yet all blacks are united by a history of oppressive laws and attitudes, even when they are divided by politics or tribe.

South Africa then was firmly in the grip of its first state of emergency. There were few visible indications of black protest. As a civil rights activist, I thought that I, of all people, would be able to sniff them out if they were there. In Mississippi, at the height of the anti-segregation confrontation back in '64, white Northern college kids like me had no problem getting black people to express their feelings or talk about "the man." That had been my experience at home—but not here.

South Africa was not the American South, and apartheid was never another name for segregation. We could at least appeal to a Constitution that theoretically guaranteed everyone's rights. In South Africa, the law upheld racism and there was no constitution. Apartheid was as much a labor system as a racial one, and blatant economic exploitation was as much the problem as racial separation.

The first thing I saw when the airport bus deposited me at the Jo'burg train station was a newspaper headline: "Detroit Riot: 37 Dead." A year earlier I had worked in Detroit for Mayor Jerry Cavanagh, whose claim to fame was that he had prevented a Watts-type riot. Not this time. His luck had run out and the Motor City was in flames. And I was reading about it in, of all places, South Africa, where a police state had been established to make sure rebellions like that didn't occur. At that moment, America's racial problems seemed as bad as South Africa's. Our integrated civil rights

movement was then disintegrating in the bitterness of insurrection
and internecine racial division; South Africa's movement was on
hold, but poised to erupt again.

At first it was hard for me to meet black people. Attempts to
even make eye contact with black workers guarding white property
in Durban were unsuccessful. They stared past me and spoke to each
other in Zulu. I felt frozen out, however much I naively wanted
them to think of me as a brother, as an ally in the liberation struggle. Part of the problem was that I was white, therefore one of their
oppressors. But only part. I later realized that I had reduced the
problem to one of race, when it was far more layered and complex.
Those Zulu workers most likely didn't speak English. Many had also
been taught as children that eye contact with strangers is impolite.

I found the unextinguished flames of the South African struggle quite by accident, after I drew a bath at a small Durban beach
hotel. I started reading the local paper, noticing an announcement
that the next day a funeral would be held not far away for Chief
Albert Luthuli, president-general of the banned African National
Congress and a Nobel Peace Prize winner. He was from the generation before Mandela, for years the quiet voice of his people's aspirations, a figure of world renown. He had died mysteriously, allegedly
in a train accident in the rural area to which the government had
banished him. I was thinking about going to the funeral when I
noticed that I hadn't been watching the tub. It had overflowed, with
water spilling over into the hallway.

I jumped up, unplugged the bath and raced one floor down to
the lobby to find a mop. The Indian man behind the desk said, "No,
no. I'll send the boy up," referring to the African man sitting to his
right. I didn't see any boys. I shot back: "No, no, just give me a mop.
I made the mess. I'll clean it up."

He and the "boy" came upstairs with me, and we all dried the
small flood. I asked them to please not call me *baas*. He smiled. The
Indian guy told me that I was the first white man there who had
ever cleaned up after himself. That broke the ice. I then asked how

I could get a ride to Luthuli's funeral. At first he said it wasn't safe, then disclosed that he and a cousin were going to see their family in a nearby Indian township and that they would take me if I chipped in a few rand for gas.

Sure enough, the next day, a brilliant Sunday morning along-side the Indian Ocean, I piled into a crowded jalopy with a few other Indian passengers who were also paying for the ride. As we passed through Natal's rolling hills and vast sugar plantations, we noticed several planes up ahead, circling close to the ground. They were monitoring the funeral site. "That is the church where the funeral is taking place," I was told. "It's not safe to take you there directly."

Instead he dropped me off about three hundred yards away, on a dusty side road. "We will pick you up exactly here in one hour, sharp," I was told. "Be here because it is not safe to wait." This man seemed to have a fixation with the words "not safe."

He knew something I didn't.

As I started toward the church, camera in hand, I noticed about a hundred black people in khaki uniforms lined up for what looked like a parade, carrying black, green and gold flags. I recognized them from pictures I had seen as the flag and uniforms of the ANC. But the ANC was banned, their leader, Nelson Mandela, locked away for life on Robben Island near Cape Town, clear across the country. This wasn't supposed to be happening. Demonstrations were outlawed. I couldn't believe what I was seeing—and started taking pictures, walking with them as they marched up to and into the church.

It must have been a strange sight, that small army of chanting black militants with a skinny, long-haired white kid tagging along. (Yup, I was skinny once.) They marched right past a large army of police who had the place totally surrounded. They weren't stopped, I was told later, because much of the Western diplomatic corps, led by the Swedish ambassador, were there, along with some Western reporters. Some white policemen took pictures of us.

The place was inundated with plainclothes as well as uniformed cops. A few pointed at me as if to ask, Who is that guy and where did he come from? They probably had all the other whites accounted for. Most had been brought into this African area, with permission, under escort. I was almost surely the only who'd shown up on his own.

Inside the church, the ANC folks took up positions in front of their leader's coffin and unfurled their flag. One small, uniformed black man put his right thumb in the air in the ANC salute, keeping it there for almost the whole ceremony. I kept staring at him, awed at the strength of his defiant gesture. I learned later that some of the protesting ANC stalwarts were quietly picked up afterward.

And then the singing started, hymns that reminded me of many a hot night in Mississippi when freedom songs were the movement's first line of solidarity against the cops and the Klan. South Africa's church music and freedom hymns were even more vibrant, rich with call-and-response rhythms. The sound made you ache with its beauty. That's when I first heard "Nkosi sikelel' iAfrika" (Lord Bless Africa), then banned, now the country's national anthem, surely one of the most beautiful anthems in the world.

The speeches were electric in their intensity, including one by a young student, president of the National Union of South African Students, or NUSAS. Her name was Margaret Marshall, and she was as striking as she was eloquent. I was not prepared for someone who was so white and blond to also be so uncompromising in her denunciation of apartheid, warning the regime that its oppressive policies would not last forever. At that time in South Africa, it was dangerous to speak or write such things. Her words were received with great warmth by Luthuli's family. The late writer Alan Paton, whose *Cry, the Beloved Country* is the best-known novel of South Africa of this century, was also on hand and spoke, but Margie's remarks were more memorable. (We became friends when she moved to Boston as part of an outflow of white liberals. She later married *New York Times* columnist Anthony Lewis and today is a judge on the Supreme Judicial Court of Massachusetts.)

After spending some time in the Natal area, I moved on to Cape Town, the Mother City, a place that might have been in England if not for the beautiful Table Mountain rising behind it and the vast African townships that surrounded it. I remember visiting the Parliament buildings and watching a group of liberal whites hold a vigil. I brought them a flower or two, as a peace symbol of the hippie-yippie counterculture. Flower Power sounds out of context now, but perhaps it wasn't so stupid after all. Some of us believed in it back then.

An American friend put me up in a quiet suburban community near the beach. Her beau, a white jazz bassist, an excellent musician who played in one of the country's few interracial bands, took me on a tour of Guguletu, a nearby township. We went without the proper passes, were intercepted by the police and asked to leave. But I was there long enough to see the great gap that existed then, and exists now, between white wealth and black poverty. It remains the biggest such gap in the world.

In Johannesburg, I toured Soweto on a government tourist bus that cost about twenty-five cents and included a stop for tea at an official tourist center that would be burned to the ground years later in the Soweto uprising. The bus stopped at government-backed workshops for the disabled, took in a model crèche (nursery school), stopped at the weirdly named Uncle Tom's Hall, a community center, and toured the section of Soweto where the handful of black millionaires lived. If you could imagine a German sightseeing trip through "Auschwitzland," that's what it felt like.

I wrote about the Soweto visit anonymously for the *Village Voice*, fearing possible retaliation against people I stayed with in South Africa. Twenty-five years later, the *New York Times* carried an almost identical front page feature on the same tour, evidence of how little has changed in Soweto's conditions. When I left South Africa, I set out to meet with the ANC in exile. I stopped in Kenya on my way back to London, and to get a sense of the continent on a student budget, took the bus—hardly a popular tourist mode of travel—from Nairobi to Dar es Salaam, Tanzania. It took nearly a day of bouncing over dirt roads cutting through the savannah, with an imposing view of Mount Kilimanjaro. I was the only white on the bus, riding along with Masai tribesmen and young Africans going to school. They were startled to see me, but smiled and taught me a few words in Swahili. I learned that it was a dangerous ride after we narrowly avoided a collision, and passed a wrecked bus that had plunged into a ravine. I realized no one in my family knew where I was. I also realized how much I had to learn about the South African situation and Africa itself before I could make sense of what I was observing.

In Dar, I was welcomed into the world of the ANC and other Southern African liberation movements. I met the SWAPO leader Sam Nujoma, now president of Namibia, and went to the beach with members of the Central Committee of FRELIMO, the Mozambican guerrilla movement. I attended a lecture by Eduardo Mondlane, the U.S.-educated president of FRELIMO, who would be assassinated by the Portuguese. In those days, Dar was a low-key backwater, and I had a chance to learn about the difficulties that face real life revolutionaries—who didn't always live up to the glamorized images I had of them.

The ANC was nothing like the Vietnamese resistance, whose struggle had been sharpened by years of anticolonial warfare against the French and before them the Japanese. The countries of southern Africa, however supportive of the fight against apartheid, lacked the ability to serve as a rear base militarily as North Vietnam did. Nor was the terrain in the region conducive to guerrilla warfare.

The ANC was led by urban intellectuals—lawyers, scholars, and labor leaders, many born into rural poverty, but now deeply immersed in the values and lifestyles of cities and industrial civilization. Their foe was the South African government and white rule. The imbalance in forces was huge. Pretoria dominated the land and, with one of the most modern and technologically sophisticated military industrial complexes in the world, had the guns. The South African revolution was forced to focus less on confronting Pretoria's superior military power than on politics, specifically on isolating South Africa from its international allies.

The more I mixed with South Africans, the more I came to shed my own stereotypes and romanticized images. My respect for their movements also deepened because these were, at their core, built on traditions of struggle and democratic mobilization, and led by men and women who were totally dedicated. Thankfully, ANC leader Oliver Tambo, once Mandela's law partner, was able to keep the movement together in ways that defied all the odds. He had charisma but more than that, he had a keen organizational and strategic sense. Under his leadership, the ANC never splintered into factions, polarized racially, burned out, or gave up. This was an important achievement because South Africa was divided tribally and culturally, so each group had to subordinate its separate identities to participate in a unified movement fighting for a unified country.

The young guerrillas and organizers I spoke to told me about the pain of life in exile. It took a toll, driving some to drink and others into a pose, not a practice. The Umkhonto weSizwe (MK), the ANC's guerrilla army, was never as effective as it hoped to be. For many years, young people who fled the townships to fight the Boers were sent for training to Russia or Eastern Europe, where they were all too often given skills not suited for South Africa's terrain. Some lost touch with their country or substituted rhetoric for organizing. In its theory and publications, the ANC always struck blows against apartheid. On the ground, its external and internal problems were formidable. I noticed a clash of cultures within its ranks, where undereducated but savvy township youth mingled with London-based intellectuals well-versed in Marxist theories and international diplomacy. I remember once meeting Amilcar Cabral, leader of Guinea-Bissau's independence war and an African theoretician of the first order who was also assassinated a few years later. When I asked him about the ANC's military campaign, he snickered, "Too much London." Years later, as the leadership built its base in Lusaka, Zambia, and throughout southern Africa, that comment would prove less valid.

HOME AGAIN

After I returned to London from that first trip to the land of apartheid, I was convinced that South Africa was destined to become another Vietnam, a country in which the forces of revolution would collide with a repressive counterrevolution, aided and abetted by American intervention. As far as I could tell, that intervention was already underway, even if not yet on a military level. In those days, South Africa was still considered a bastion of Western interests and affinities. Elsewhere in Africa, the old imperial order had given way to a new one that retained its dominance through neocolonial influences, international economic institutions, and multinational corporations. The more I learned about apartheid, the more I realized that foreign capital propped it up in part because the return on investment was so high and wages were so low. An emerging market attracted trade and many foreign companies.

South African apartheid thus was not just an isolated aberration but survived through the complicity of others. You couldn't understand or combat apartheid in South Africa alone, I felt. I slowly began to see Africa as part of a world system and realize that thanks to slavery and colonial plunder, some of the West's economic overdevelopment was linked to Africa's underdevelopment. Our policies contributed to the continent's dependency, notwithstanding the rhetoric of our foreign aid agencies. Once, African slaves had been forced to help America develop its agrarian economy, which in turn fueled our industrialization. Today, our overseas assistance was primarily an exercise in self-interest, in opening new arenas to American business.

I came to think of apartheid as slavery by another name.

As a journalist I sought to use investigative reporting as a tool for exploring and explaining these relationships. I had become an investigative reporter for *Ramparts*, the San Francisco-based New Left magazine of the '60s that had helped expose covert CIA funding of student organizations. It was a complicated ruse. Phony foundations had been set up with a Byzantine "triple pass system" through which money could be funneled from one institution to another, deliberately disguising the real benefactor. In some cases the recipient group didn't know that they were being subsidized, but in many cases, they did. Usually a few key officials were in the know, "witty" in intelligence parlance. Once we learned how CIA money was being channeled—these foundations had to file IRS reports disclosing their money trail—we started to look into who got what and why.

Because I was based in London, which at that time had more direct contact with Africa than the States, I was put on the Africa beat. I investigated why some labor group in Kenya or a political magazine in South Africa was receiving CIA subsidies. Hundreds of such groups were on their payroll. What services did they perform?

Through this type of journalistic detective work, we began uncovering the existence of what we called a Free World Empire, a covertly mobilized, multilayered, cold war apparatus with a number of not so carefully disguised channels of influence, interlocking organizations and directorates, all reinforcing each other through a strategy of "cumulative impact." The Soviets operated more openly; their front groups were more obvious. Ours were shrouded in a system based on plausible deniability. We discovered that the CIA had journalists on its payroll and that it planted stories through proprietary companies and phony news agencies. Some of these stories would first run overseas and then blow back into the press at home. Americans became the target of a steady stream of anti-Communist propaganda designed to stoke our fear of the red menace and engineer assent to a bloated military and intelligence establishment.

As we learned more about these CIA networks, I realized that I needed to know more about the African countries themselves in order to make better sense of where the money was going. I had to find out more about the politicians the U.S. backed and the interests they served. In some cases, those politicians were opportunists—never bought, just rented, playing the big powers off against each other. Soon my study of the CIA network became an insufficient guide to the African situation. As my inquiries mushroomed, I started reading more African history and political economy. But I still couldn't answer many of the questions staring me in the face: Why did the Kennedy Administration back Portugal's colonialists against African freedom movements led by Agosthino Neto in Angola, Amilcar Cabral in Guinea-Bissau, or Eduardo Mondlane in Mozambique? Was it true that Nelson Mandela was in jail because of a tip to the South African police by a CIA agent? Why was the United States aligned with the likes of the dictator Mobutu in Zaire, who ran his country as if he owned it? Did we have a hand in Lumumba's assassination? Why was American civil rights leader James Farmer dispatched to Africa to challenge Malcolm X's growing influence there? What was the U.S. up to in Africa?

Small questions turned into bigger and more serious inquiries as my research began to fill file cabinets. When I returned to America in 1968, I found new friends, white and black, with similar questions. We formed the Africa Research Group (ARG) to pursue an investigation we hoped might be helpful to those opposing this nefarious web of covert political warfare, counterinsurgency and support for repressive regimes in the name of democracy.

As we began to probe American policy in Africa, we found that there were a few Africanists covering the same ground, but with a questionable and sometimes shadowy impact. It became obvious that cold war priorities had contaminated much academic research. Scores of grants were available to study what the Russians were doing in Africa and only a very few to look into what Washington was up to. Millions of dollars were invested in studying the tribes of Africa, while U.S. Africanists had become a tribe—often on the payroll of government agencies, foundations, specialized institutes and think tanks, most serving the same world view and, indirectly, the same economic interests.

In 1969, the ARG published an analysis listing these connections and naming the Africanists linked to these agencies, covertly and overtly. We called it *African Studies in America: The Extended Family*. It created quite a stir in the academic world. Our tone reflected the insurgent attitudes of the time: "The African studies industry is managed by an extended family of interconnected and incestuous 'experts' who, while living off Africa, serve a system pitted against Africa's needs.... These researchers, through well-financed jet-setting safaris, have amassed a mountain of information for filtration through the research apparatus of corporations and government agencies. There it is translated into the language of consumption or counterinsurgency or both."

We were denounced as McCarthyites of the Left for circulating our detailed docu-tract at a meeting of the African Studies Association, which was also being challenged by black students because of its virtually all-white composition. Allied with African-American students demanding more racial diversity in the field, we saw ourselves as rebuilding bridges that had collapsed when the unity of the civil rights movement splintered into nationalist rhetoric and separatist rage.

The ARG was prolific, publishing *Race to Power*, a textbook about South Africa, pamphlets, and articles that were picked up by underground papers, African magazines, and even Elijah Muhammad's Black Muslim newspaper. Over the years, that one filing cabinet in my study turned into forty or more. Soon we were operating out of a small apartment, a "secret location" identified only through a post office box. Perhaps because we had studied the CIA so closely, we were turning into an intelligence agency ourselves, turning up documents such as a Pentagon study, "Witchcraft and its implications for counterinsurgency," or the minutes of a high-level, off-the-record discussion group on intelligence practices.

The inspiration for our efforts came from one of sociologist C. Wright Mills's devotees, Martin Nicholas, who called on his colleagues to start looking up, rather than down for the causes of our problems—to study the powerful as well as the poor. We included a quote from one of his articles in our literature: "What if the machinery were reversed? What if the habits, problems, secrets and unconscious motivations of the wealthy and powerful were daily scrutinized by a thousand systematic researchers, were hourly pried into, analyzed and cross-referenced, tabulated and published in a hundred inexpensive mass circulation journals, and written so that even the fifteen-year-old high school dropout could understand it and predict the actions of his landlord, and manipulate and control him?"

This what-if scenario inspired student activists to get into radical research groups, which specialized in power structure analysis and in-depth writing about the problems of American involvement in Third World countries. The best-known work was produced by the North American Congress on Latin America (NACLA). But there was also NARMIC, a Philadelphia-based group probing the military-industrial complex; while in California, radical researchers wrote about the emerging Pacific Rim.

For a time I was fulltime with ARG, living with Africa while living in Cambridge, Massachusetts. I could survive because my then–significant other, the historian Linda Gordon, was so supportive. She was teaching at a local university and drawing a real salary. She could afford the rent. It was when I could no longer sustain myself as a fulltimer in this research and reporting effort that I started looking for work, ending up at WBCN.

As I became engaged with African issues, I was determined not to think of Africa as my own psychological or political colony. That seems to happen all too often with many area experts and missionaries, who develop a sense of ownership of a region or a country, guarding their expertise and contacts as a personal fiefdom. I never thought of myself as an African specialist, just a journalist and activist. I was mindful of the danger of turning that old "white man's burden" into a white Marxist burden; in truth, Marxism was never all that helpful to me in coming to terms with race, gender and Third World development and culture. That's why I always thought of myself more of a Groucho Marxist than any other kind.

South Africans had been speaking out to the world about their country for years, even if only a small audience paid attention initially. The country's literature and culture riveted me with a texture that went much deeper than most journalism or political tracts, in the same way that the music of our own counterculture inspired our activism in the U.S. The books of black writers like Esia Mphalele and Bloke Modisane, and white writers like Alan Paton and Nadine Gordimer, humanized the pain and pathos of the "beloved country." As did South African theater and music. What other country has produced political musicals like *Sarafina!* or playwrights like Athol Fugard and Mbegeni Ngema? Afrikaners André Brink and J. M. Coetzee, journalists Percy Qoboza, Peter Magubane and Obed Kunene and poets Dennis Brutas, Gcina Mhlope and Mazisi Kunene?

I was especially fortunate to have known the late Barney Simon, whose imaginative use of theater as a forum for uncensored expression led to his founding the Market Theater in 1976, in what was once an Indian market in downtown Johannesburg. As a cultural center, the Market became an incubator of resistance throughout the dark days of repression. A complex of stores, bars and clubs formed around it—liberated territory inside an unliberated society.

Barney was recognized worldwide for his populist approach to theater—using workshopping techniques to help ordinary people express themselves and dramatize their experiences. His methods were pioneering in part because they abandoned many of the formal aspects of the theater. Once, during my radio days in Boston, he brought tapes of a project he'd done with nurses in rural areas to teach people how to stay healthy. His actors, all unknowns, wrote songs and sketches to warn mothers against infant formulas like the ones sold by Nestlé, and encourage them to nurse their babies. I couldn't understand all the words, but the sentiments and style were fantastic. He told me his troupe inspired communities to act together. He worked with the country's top black actors—John Kani, Winston Ntshona and Zakes Mokae, among others—helping them develop their talents. He brought anti-apartheid plays like *Woza Albert!*, which Barney created with its two actors, Percy Mtwa and Mbongeni Ngema, to audiences all over the world. Humble, hostile to rhetoric of all kinds, Barney was a bridge for many between different worlds—the world of the township and the city, the world of South Africa's Jews and its gentiles, and even between America, in which part of his family lived, and South Africa. His genius for making theater matter and breaking down racial barriers earned him the respect and admiration of many within the South African freedom movement, from the leaders to the grassroots township folks he felt most comfortable with. He understood that culture often leads politics and that cultural warriors have a role to play in making change.

Many South African journalists stood out as well. People like Lewis Nkosi, Nat Nakasa, Allister Sparks Zwelakhe Sisulu, and Donald Woods. Thanks to their efforts and to the courage of many brave reporters, black and white, who fought to get the story and get it out, South Africa enjoyed more than fifteen minutes of fame on the world's media agenda. In many cases these messengers were muzzled and had to battle against a white press monopoly that sought to suppress the story. Nevertheless, South Africa was a story that could not be stopped.

COVERING THE COVERAGE

In 1976, eight years after we launched the Africa Research Group, students in Soweto staged their uprising and once more brought the brutalities of apartheid into public view. The dramatic protests and violent reaction put South Africa back on the front pages. While the press was clearly sympathetic to the protesters, they seemed unable to present their story clearly. I was asked by the editors of *More*, a media review publication, to assess the situation. I was struck by the misuse of language and the superficiality of the reporting.

Soweto was called a suburb of Johannesburg, as if the meaning of suburb, which conjures up one set of images in America, was transferable. Soweto was no more a suburb than the American Revolution was a little tea party in the colonies—it is an overcrowded township with a population that may be three times Johannesburg's. Comparisons with the American civil rights movement were made without noting that in our country, people fought to extend the protections of our Constitution to all citizens, while in South Africa there was no constitution and racism was legal. The economic underpinnings of apartheid were hardly scrutinized and the liberation movements rarely covered. The Soweto students rebelled against forced instruction in the Afrikaans language, a concern that people overseas wouldn't understand unless the strategy of separate development as a tool of enforcing white supremacy was explained. It rarely was. Instead, the emphasis was on the hot imagery of soldiers and police firing on young people waving garbage can covers. The complexities of the conflict escaped or were ignored by the media. The *New York Times*, for example, described the event as a race riot. A number of journalists in the mainstream press acknowledged to me that the public had little background information. "The press has not covered it with any sophistication," Tim Leland of the *Boston Globe* told me. Once the student uprisings were suppressed and law and order restored, the story receded.

I was among a number of journalists who tried to put South Africa in a broader context. Writing in *More,* I recommended better briefings for correspondents, more reliance on South African journalists and stringers, increased use of specialized sources instead of relying on old clips or archival footage, a team approach to coverage that would include stateside reporting on companies doing business in South Africa, and doing what Pretoria would not: recognize the liberation movements as legitimate. That was in 1977. I closed with a quote from a journalist I respected, Frances Fitzgerald, on the subject of press coverage of Vietnam: "After fifteen years of reporting the war, the news organizations appear to have learned nothing and their policies have changed rather less than Henry Kissinger's." The parallel was clear. I was thrilled when Tom Wicker cited my piece in one of his *New York Times* columns. Unfortunately, when I returned to dissecting the coverage twelve years later, I found that little had changed.

An uneasy calm prevailed in South Africa after the Soweto rebellion was put down. Thousands of students slipped out of the country into the ANC and BCM (Black Consciousness Movement), bringing fresh blood and new energy into the liberation struggle. But it was barely covered. In the press it seemed as if the struggle had gone on hiatus. But there was ferment. Black-run labor unions fought for recognition, while grassroots movements formed on the campuses and in the communities. The forces of black consciousness led by Steve Biko and others burst on the scene. From its exile base in Zambia, and in jails and prisons across South Africa, the ANC tried to hold on to its leadership.

But truth be told, the ANC had little effective control over the spontaneous insurrections that consumed the townships, where a new generation of decentralized local leaders had emerged with little training or knowledge of ANC practices. The leadership had to play catch-up or they could lose control of their own revolution.

The ANC spent fifty years pursuing nonviolence before launching an armed struggle. Many of its campaigns, including bus boycotts, predated similar tactics in the United States. In the townships, young people made their own uniforms, wore berets and carved AK-47s out of wood to show support for the ANC's military wing, the Umkhonto or MK. Many of these young lions were illiterate and uneducated, in part because of the lousy schools, in part because many young people believed in "liberation before education." Many became brutal in response to brutality suffered in occupied townships, in pitched battles, in prison torture. They were child soldiers, acting with little adult supervision; many even considered their parents sellouts for accommodating themselves to apartheid. They ferreted out informers and conducted their own terror campaigns of intimidation with marches and matches. Some were guilty of burning alive their enemies and some innocent bystanders, through the odious practice of necklacing—putting tires filled with gasoline around people's necks and setting them on fire.

That is why I lean to the belief that Winnie Mandela's infamous remark that "we will liberate this country with our matches," for which she was so roundly condemned, was partly an attempt by the only visible ANC leader inside the country—remember, the movement was banned—to win the allegiance of the militants by appropriating their militant rhetoric. It was an opportunistic and emotional attempt to co-opt them back into the fold. ANC President Tambo's call to "make the townships ungovernable" was an equally opportunistic effort to try to impose a strategy and structure on the mayhem that was most often spontaneous or local in its origins. The ANC had to make it appear as if its underground was in control even when it wasn't.

In that period, the South African government played a game of psychological warfare with the press. Horrific necklacing footage was supplied to the networks to discredit the ANC and turn world opinion against a popular rebellion. When the networks refused to air it, right-wing media lobbies like Accuracy in Media distributed the tapes, attacking the media for suppressing the truth. It was later revealed that the apartheid government had staged some of the most prominent of these ghastly incidents, using paid *agents provocateurs.*

Outside South Africa, the ANC was pursued by secret assassination squads and by military attacks by the South African security forces. There was justified and not so justified paranoia of infiltration in the organization. Pallo Jordan, whose outspoken style and militant analysis won him high jobs in the ANC, came under suspicion by ANC security officers, who detained him in May 1983, eight months after he was nearly killed by the parcel bomb that claimed Ruth First's life in Mozambique. In this environment a number of human rights abuses occurred in ANC military camps, as an embarrassed leadership later admitted. Pretoria's military aggression and campaign of destabilization against the ANC camps and the frontline states, which fed the paranoia, were virtually ignored in most of the Western press.

In 1984 and '85, it was déjà vu all over again, as South Africa's townships erupted once more. Again, platoons of foreign journalists descended. There was some graphic reporting, but it soon subsided. The "been there, done that" syndrome snapped into place. As human rights abuses increased, coverage decreased, despite the detention of more than ten thousand children and youth under the age of eighteen. Within a year, the South African government imposed the first of several legal prohibitions against aggressive media coverage. "A journalist with a poison pen," explained Home Affairs Minister Stoffel Botha, "contributes as much to the revolution as the man with a hand grenade."

Pretoria warned news organizations that there would be repercussions if they stepped over the line, but then refused to say what the line was. This shrewd and somewhat diabolical policy led to self-censorship. Eric Goldstein of the Committee to Protect Journalists said at the time, "The government has drawn a small circle, inside which lies acceptable political activity and speech. Everything outside is simply 'revolution' and 'media terrorism.'" In South Africa, the most outspoken journalists and the alternative press were targeted the most. But the American people were targeted too, only less visibly.

In August 1985, ABC, CBS, and NBC ran sixty South African stories among them. In November, the first month of the press restrictions, there were only twenty. At that time, the violence had not abated. Peter Jennings acknowledged that the restrictions had worked. Marc Kusnetz, a foreign news producer for NBC's Nightly News, who conscientiously worked to keep the story in the public eye, echoed the same theme. "Has the censorship been effective? Sure it has. Is that even a question?" I wrote a piece for *Africa Report* revealing the findings of my own non-scientific "bathroom scale test" in which I weighed the news index and abstracts on South Africa to demonstrate how coverage had been reduced.

In Russia, many Western journalists became heroes for challenging heavy-handed KGB restraints. Some were jailed; others expelled. By contrast, in South Africa, most of the foreign press pulled their punches. Only an English correspondent and a Dutch cameraman were made reporters non grata, although others were harassed and a few killed.

Back in the USA, an anti-apartheid movement was growing but had yet to reach critical mass. Organizations like Randall Robinson's Trans-Africa and Jennifer Davis's American Committee on Africa started stirring the pot for sanctions with embassy sit-ins and campus anti-apartheid protests. That movement successfully lobbied for the passage of anti-apartheid laws, the only progressive legislation to survive a veto by President Reagan, who was then up to his eyeballs in counterrevolutionary warfare in Central America. The anti-apartheid movement's multiracial character and multilevel strategy finally won bipartisan support, thanks in large part to the efforts of black congressmen such as Ron Dellums and persistent lobbying at state houses and city halls.

At that time I was working for ABC News. What attention was being paid to Africa in America soon shifted from the continent's south to the Sahel and the famine in Ethiopia that had claimed hundreds of thousands of lives. For eighteen months an African cameraman, Mohammed Amin, documented it, almost alone. He couldn't sell the story. Finally, his pictures couldn't be ignored and they brought the horror onto the world's TV screens. NBC news had them first in the U.S., but the rest of the pack soon followed. In Hollywood, Quincy Jones and Harry Belafonte responded by organizing "We Are the World," an all-star song to raise money for the victims. Artists in England did it first with "Do They Know It's Christmas," followed by Bob Geldof's "Live Aid." I was delighted when it became hip to care about Africa. Celebrities mobilized their fans and forced governments to respond. I welcomed the initiative but, journalist that I am, was distressed by the emphasis on Africa as victim, as an object for pity rather than as a player in a process of change. No one was explaining how the politics and economics of the region had contributed to a famine that was described only as a natural disaster. The rock stars who responded did better at raising consciousness than delivering aid, although USA for Africa tried hard with some success to meet needs and help African NGOs take the lead. The problem with humanitarian relief projects is that they lead to dependency on overseas benefactors who may not be interested in longer-term development needs.

FROM SUN CITY TO SOUTH AFRICA NOW

I met Little Steven, aka Miami Steve, in real life Steven Van Zandt, while producing a story about Bruce Springsteen for ABC's *20/20*. He is the Boss's best friend, a talented guitarist-singer-songwriter and then a major force in the E Street Band. Ironically, he was in South Africa at the time and only received my call on his return. The *20/20* segment was finished by then but he and I met anyway at a Broadway coffee shop. I was interested in his impressions of South Africa. He was intrigued to find out that I was so informed about the country.

Van Zandt, who had parted with Bruce at the height of Springsteen's success to go out on his own, had traveled there to research his next record. Steven writes songs the way I do stories, through an investigative process. He was interested in South Africa because he had read that the apartheid system was actually modeled after America's system of Indian reservations, an issue that was his major passion. He told me that when he was in South Africa, he was most distressed by a place called Sun City, an interracial gambling resort plunked down in the middle of an impoverished rural homeland, an obscene symbol of opulence. He was interested in writing a song about it to make parallels with the plight of native Americans. I suggested turning it into a different kind of "We Are the World," a song about change not charity, freedom not famine. He loved the idea. "Sun City" was born. (In 1997, in one of those bizarre twists of history, the man who created Sun City, Sol Kerzner, came to America to build the Mohegan Sun, an Indian gambling casino.)

Springsteen biographer Dave Marsh interviewed Steven about what happened next. "Danny really inspired the thing," Steven told him. "He said, 'It's a shame you haven't started the album yet. It would be great to get something out this year.' Finally, Schechter suggested, 'Why don't you just do a single?' "

And he did. As he was writing it, I suggested that he name the names of the artists who had played Sun City in defiance of a UN-sanctioned cultural boycott. I was probably still thinking of our exposé of conservative Africanists fifteen years earlier. Steve wasn't sure that was smart but did it anyway, asking in one of the original lyrics, "Linda Ronstadt, how could you do that?" and singling out Julio Iglesias, Queen, the O Jays, Ray Charles and Rod Stewart. We soon dropped those lyrics to avoid offending other artists who worked with those we were challenging.

He came over to my loft and played the first rough mix. It was hot: part rap, part rock—very street. The song was high-energy, danceable, a gritty New York-sounding tune, in stark contrast by its angry attitude and sound to the sweet harmonies of Hollywood's more syrupy anthem for aid to Ethiopia. It was political too, teaching with every phrase:

Relocation to Phony Homelands
Separation of Families I can't understand
Twenty-three million can't vote because they're black
We're stabbing our brothers and sisters in the back.

Simple *and* sophisticated in the way he introduced the realities of the homelands and forced relocation, Steven pinpointed the problem in human terms as separation of families and then identified the political problem accurately as the disenfranchisement of the majority. And by calling them our brothers and sisters, he makes it a universal problem that can be challenged through personal action: "I ain't gonna play Sun City."

He went further, indicting our government:

Our government tells us we're doing all we can
Constructive engagement is Ronald Reagan's plan
Meanwhile people are dying and giving up hope
This quiet diplomacy ain't nothing but a joke.

I loved the song. It was journalism you could jam to.

Steven now demanded my involvement. "You got me into this Sun City song," he told me. "You got to help me do it by encouraging other artists to participate." I was flattered and had no choice but to agree. For years in Boston radio, I saw how music could spread the news, how rock 'n' roll was often a more powerful educator than the printed or spoken word. I thought to myself, If the news isn't covering South Africa, I'll bet stars singing about South Africa will become news. I was right. I was now in the band we called Artists United Against Apartheid.

I didn't know what I was getting myself into. Over the next several months, I held down two jobs. By day, I was a network producer; by night, often into the wee hours, I was in the recording studio or on the phone begging artists to participate. Steven refused to invite his buddy Bruce Springsteen, not wanting to take advantage of their friendship. So I did it. He was too shy to call Miles Davis so I did that too. To my delight, Miles took the call personally, responding with one question: "When do you want me over there?"

Inspired by all the musical energy, I tried my hand at my own song, which actually ended up on the album. Drummer-musician Keith LeBlanc and I came up with "Revolutionary Situation," an audio-collage set to music that took its title from the words of South Africa's then-interior chief Louis Nel condemning the "revolutionary situation." Before we were through, we had Nel cheering on the revolutionary situation to a background of yapping police dogs, sounds of mayhem and revolt in the township and angry declarations by activists like Alan Boesak, Bishop Desmond Tutu and Nelson Mandela's daughter Zindzi, looped with what was at that time the most recent interview with her dad, recorded in 1961. The highly produced piece was an upgraded version of techniques I'd used at WBCN, mixing reality and beats—news you could dance to. A year later I worked with Stetsasonic, a popular rap band, on "A.F.R.I.C.A," a hip hop edutainment record aimed at informing teenagers about the wars then underway in the frontline states of southern Africa. It was one of the few rap records to be packaged with background information and a study guide. I worked on both records under my nom de media guerre, the news dissector.

I had *also* taken on the job of documenting the sessions on video and producing a behind-the-scenes documentary. I invited MTV to get involved and asked a friend, Hart Perry, to film the sessions. We wanted the public to know why we were doing the record. We asked the artists to explain their involvement in their own words. They responded with passion and prescience. "Sun City's become a symbol of a society which is very oppressive and denies basic rights to the majority of its citizens," said Jackson Browne. "In a sense, Sun City is also a symbol of that society's 'right' to entertain itself in anyway that it wants to, to basically try to buy us off and to buy off world opinion." The link between entertainment and oppression had rarely been made with such clarity.

At that point we were making the record without a record company or any money behind us. Just doing it. Steve was chipping in, while producer Arthur Baker donated studio time. Manhattan Records, under the brave leadership of Bruce Lundvall, came on board, acquiring the record, enabling us to pay some of the bills. A very committed record company lawyer, the late Rick Dutka, who brought a special sensitivity and deep commitment to the cause, rounded out our team, along with Steven's assistant, the multi-talented Zöe Yanakis.

I was surprised that many of the best-known rock 'n' rollers were so publicity shy. Most of them had publicists who staged their media appearances. They weren't used to cameras poking them in the face. Bruce Springsteen at first turned down my request for an interview.

But just as I was walking away from him dejected, he ran after me and agreed to say a few words for the documentary.

When Miles started improvising in the studio that day, Steven and Arthur insisted I not approach him with a camera. "It's *Miles*, man," Baker said. "He's erratic, idiosyncratic, explosive. Wild. Don't mess with him when he's playing." I realized that they were intimidated by his presence and his genius. They were afraid he would walk out.

"You do your thing," I told him. "I'll do mine." I barged into the booth while Davis was setting up, introduced myself and asked if we could videotape him. Through the glass I could see Steve and Arthur, heads in hands, convinced that I had blown it. Miles smiled. "Bring it on," he ordered, "bring it on." And we did, getting priceless footage in the bargain.

In all, fifty-four artists participated, many of my biggest heroes among them—Springsteen, Dylan, Miles, Jackson Browne, Nona Hendryx, Darlene Love, Bonnie Raitt, Peter Gabriel, Bono, Run-DMC and on and on. We started out to do one song and ended up with an album, with additional mixes and singles. There were 303 tracks on the single, some kind of record for a record. The job of mixing it down burned out some of the biggest names in the business. One had to be carried from the mixing board after thirty-six hours without sleep. In addition to the recordings, we produced a music video directed by Jonathan Demme with Godley and Creme, the video documentary I worked on with Hart Perry, a book, and a study guide.

At the same time, I couldn't tell ABC what I was doing on the side. They would not have approved. I knew I couldn't propose a story about Sun City either, because I had stepped over the line and become part of the story. I tried and mostly succeeded in keeping my name out of the papers and my mug out of the video. I was terrified that *20/20* would dump me if they knew what I was doing, especially if my affiliation with ABC was dragged into it, even though the network had nothing to do with the project. I worked even harder at ABC, producing more stories than many of my colleagues, so I couldn't be accused of slacking off.

"Sun City" was personally risky, but also incredibly rewarding. After five years in the networks, I came to see that independent production could be fun and fulfilling, without all the editorial restraints, layers of editorial control and pretensions of the corporate news world.

The record never achieved the financial success of "We Are the World," although Oliver Tambo and the ANC's school in Tanzania was sure happy when we gave them a big check. "Sun City" was picked as record of the year by many of the most influential music critics. But only about half of American radio stations played it, many objecting to the explicit attack on President Reagan's policy of constructive engagement. Some black stations said it was too white, while many white stations considered it too black. Such segregation still exists in radio. The song was banned in South Africa. But we raised more than a million dollars for anti-apartheid projects. It premiered at the United Nations thanks to the Special Committee Against Apartheid and such conscientious UN officers as Aracelly Santana.

The battle to make the record and the film paled before the battle to get it seen. PBS refused to air our non-profit *The Making of "Sun City"*—even though it won the International Documentary Association's top honors, in 1986—because the featured artists were also involved in making the film, and as a result, in their logic, were "self-promoting." (They didn't have the same problem with *The Making of "Raiders of the Lost Ark,"* which was made as a promotional exercise by the for-profit company that produced the blockbuster film.)

"Sun City" became an anthem of the anti-apartheid movement and its campaign for sanctions, functioning like a soundtrack for the movement. It may have helped people to understand apartheid better than the plethora of news stories and TV reports. Pop stars did what politicians wouldn't and journalists couldn't: They spoke out bravely and clearly. They took a stand. By standing up, they encouraged others to stand up with them and with the people of South Africa against a universally condemned racist system. In South Africa, our Artists United inspired musician Johnny Clegg to create a similar local organization. "Sun City" also became the catalyst for the *South Africa Now* TV series (see Chapter 8). My journalistic interests had provoked an independent musical project that, in turn, drove me back into journalism to create a news show about a story that was not being well-reported. I went around and around and was back where I started.

RUNNING WITH MANDELA

It was through *South Africa Now* that I met Nelson Mandela on the occasion of his release from prison in 1990—although at first it was on videotape, since I was not allowed into the country to join the biggest safari of journalists ever to arrive on the scene. Our work in South Africa had endeared us to the democratic movement Mandela headed. So our video team there, supplemented by Stuart Sender, a member of our New York-based staff who managed to slip into the country, got the story. Since we had been there covering Mandela's impending release every week when others weren't, our crews and personnel enjoyed unique access.

Globalvision produced a national PBS special, anchored by Charlayne Hunter-Gault, which aired in prime time that day. We featured the first post-release, on-air encounter between the ANC and the government it would soon displace. The networks were more interested in getting the jump on each other and in getting Mandela for an exclusive interview. The ANC decided to give them ten minutes apiece in the backyard of Mandela's old home in Soweto. One crew we often worked with was asked to shoot the interviews too, but for the ANC's archive. So there was Stuart, opening the gate as NBC's Tom Brokaw, CBS's Dan Rather, ABC's Ted Koppel, and others from around the world strolled in for what turned out to be similar conversations with a man who proved a master of a media that hadn't even existed in South Africa when he went to prison twenty-seven years earlier.

South Africa Now chose the veteran South African print journalist Allister Sparks for our ten minutes. Mandela knew Sparks as the former editor of the long-defunct *Rand Daily Mail* and one of the most knowledgeable white journalists in the country, while the big name TV guys were more of a blur. Sparks had never done a TV interview before but his exchange was the most newsworthy, because he knew the story best and was able to get the most of out of Mandela. In his book *Tomorrow's Another Country*, he reported on the secret history of Mandela's release from prison and the country's road to change.

Meanwhile from New York, we angled for an in-depth, hour-long interview. The ANC agreed to make Mandela available. We wanted to use the very informed Hunter-Gault, who had anchored our PBS special and was then on her way to South Africa. We approached PBS, certain that they would want such an exclusive and would promote it well—Mandela was then the biggest news story in the world. We were also sure that they would feel comfortable with Charlayne—a sixteen-year PBS veteran, the leading African-American TV journalist and an Emmy winner for a news series she'd done on apartheid.

To our surprise, the PBS brass nixed her, offering to finance the program only if Bill Moyers hosted it. Moyers is a distinguished journalist and a brilliant TV interviewer, but he will be the first to tell you, as he told me, that he was not that well-versed on South Africa. But PBS insisted that it had to be Moyers or nothing, probably because they thought that his name would clear more air time on the PBS stations than Charlayne's. What calculation. Of course it was a Mandela exclusive that would bring in the viewers.

Moyers was willing, but his schedule was overloaded, and it seemed unlikely that he could get a South African visa in time. Then the ANC told us that wouldn't be a problem because Mandela was planning to go to Lusaka, Zambia, for his first reunion with his ANC comrades in exile. Unfortunately, other logistical problems emerged. With just days to go, Moyers told us he was sorry but could not do it. PBS promptly pulled out.

I was furious and feverishly tried to think about who else to approach. The news networks were out because they had done their thing. That left the cable outlets and syndicated programs. And then I flashed on one name who would have his own reasons to want to score such a coup: Phil Donahue! As the leading afternoon talk-miester, Donahue was locked in a fierce battle with Oprah Winfrey, who had had many guests on about South Africa. I figured that if Phil could get an exclusive with Mandela and one-up Oprah in the process, he would go for it.

I was right. He jumped, and hired Globalvision to produce the interview. There were some problems. Donahue was on the road the same week Mandela was on the road. He would be in Los Angeles while the ANC was meeting in Lusaka. We would have to uplink from the Zambian TV station, which had never handled a satellite broadcast to Burbank. There were major technical problems. As it turned out, the Zambian technicians were thorough and covered every base; NBC's team in California kept forgetting the time difference and didn't realize that the sound and the video had to be routed separately. As a result, what could go wrong did.

Our technical problems were dwarfed by a major snafu on the ANC side. Mandela was due in the studio at 7 A.M., but his overzealous bodyguard would not allow the ANC's information chief to collect him. So there we were at the appointed time, with the satellite bought and paid for but no Mandela. The Donahue show had three hundred people sitting in the studio in L.A., and the program's executive producer was screaming at us over the phone. Fortunately, NBC's technical fuckups made it difficult to blame us. Finally, with a few minutes to go before we lost our satellite window, we could hear the roar of police sirens as Mandela was escorted into the studio. We put him on the line with Donahue in Los Angeles who saw him apologize profusely for being late. He asked if they could do it the next day. To the chagrin of the accountants at Donahue's company, whose costs were rapidly escalating, Phil agreed.

The next morning, Nelson Mandela was back and on time. For the first time, ordinary Americans could talk directly to the world's most famous ex-political prisoner. It was the livliest interview I had seen Mandela give. He was animated and interested in the questions. The audience was thrilled to be speaking to him. The Donahue people unfairly blamed us for all the technical problems and never worked with us again.

We did, however, work with Mandela again. We were invited to document his visit to America in June 1990, eight cities in eleven days, crisscrossing the country on a plane rented from Donald Trump with credentials that identified us as part of the ANC's delegation. You can imagine the surprise of state police and security personnel when I flashed my ANC credentials to maneuver our camera into places that were off limits to the press. I didn't feel as if I was compromising my journalistic credibility because the ANC had agreed to our condition that our film be edited independently without their guidance. At the same time, because we were not really South Africans, they sometimes "forgot" to make arrangements for our crew to travel in the motorcades. In Washington, for example, we were stranded at the airport while they all raced into town. We switched around the letters on our credentials that day to NAC— No Access Crew.

As a television producer, I was taken with how well Mandela came off on American television—appearing poised and comfortable on show after show. He almost canceled his appearance with Ted Koppel, who produced a special interview with him as part of an ABC deal with his own company. Koppel's producers had lined up a who's who of black politicians and anti-apartheid heavies, but only a few were allowed to participate. Many sat on rows of chairs on the stage, looking like they were part of the set.

Before an adoring crowd packed into an auditorium at City College of New York, Mandela seemed less than enamored of Ted's shtick. He hardly looked at his interviewer and instead played to the gallery. At one point, his comments left ABC's top newsman speechless. "Have I paralyzed you, Mr. Koppel?" he asked, and the audience roared. "He was the only one that I have ever seen who could shut Ted Koppel up," the rapper Salt of the duo Salt-n-Pepa quipped with a big smile for our film. ABC refused to even sell us a clip of that rare moment in American broadcasting.

Mandela's trip held special meaning for me. For years I had been told that no one in America cares about Africa, that South Africa was a sideshow to what was really important. That my interest in the subject showed how cut off I was from the larger culture. Tell that to the crowds that lined the streets to wave at the motorcade or packed the stadiums in city after city honoring one of the world's few authentic heroes. Tell that to the faces of black people I saw bawling along the route or to young whites who cheered a black man's triumph from the depths of their souls. Nelson Mandela and the anti-apartheid movement for a brief moment united people of goodwill all across the country. Even the editors of the *New York Post* caught the fever, headlining their edition "Amandla!"—the Zulu word for power. (Earlier, when Mandela was released from prison, when that story held world attention for nearly a week, the *Post* downgraded its coverage for much bigger news—the breakup of Ivana and Donald Trump.)

I remember the cheer that greeted Mandela at Yankee Stadium when he repeated his famous line about opposing black domination and white domination, and then when he waved his cap and shouted, "Today I am a Yankee." I felt as if my childhood idols, those Bronx bombers Babe Ruth and Lou Gehrig, were out there cheering in centerfield. When we walked into the U.S. Congress, where the president of the ANC invoked the names of our great presidents, including Washington and Lincoln, the emotion reverberated. Congressman Ron Dellums laughed with delight while giving his colleagues high fives across the aisles.

While the other press covered Mandela's visit to the White House, we went by a homeless shelter to seek a comment from Mitch Snyder, the nonviolent activist who had done so much to champion the cause of poor Americans. He spoke spontaneously and eloquently of the similarity between the conditions of disenfranchised South Africans and economically marginalized folks in our country. (I saw a sadness in his eyes when we met. It was probably his last interview because, tragically, he commited suicide a few days later.)

There was also the moment when I walked behind Harry Belafonte and Martin Luther King's son Dexter, as they led this leader of the ANC's armed struggle to the grave of the man who personified nonviolence for so many years. "Dr. King would have been sixty-one; imagine what would have happened if those two giants had met," Belafonte mused in that gravely voice of his. In his speech in Atlanta, Mandela quoted heavily from King's famous "I Have a Dream" speech. That gave me goosebumps because I was at the March on Washington in 1963 for the original address, when King turned language into music and preached with an eloquence that now belongs to the history of our country.

These parallels and points of connection separated our coverage from the mainstream media's. I followed Mandela into a Ford Motor plant in Detroit and found workers who drew parallels between their battles and South Africa's. One older white unionist told me, "He's for the little man. That's why I love him." Two black workers shouted, "This is the best thing that ever happened. That *ever* happened." In Miami, right-wing Cubans shouted anticommunist slogans while Mandela refused to back down and criticize Fidel Castro, who he said had helped the fight against apartheid while Washington turned its back. In Boston, Teddy

Kennedy spoke of his late brothers and told Winnie and her children that his family understood what it was like to grow up without fathers. In L.A., he stopped to converse with Ron Kovic, the Vietnam veteran of *Born on the Fourth of July* fame, who stared admiringly at him from his wheelchair, told Mandela who he was and that they "would win together." Mandela reached over, grabbed Kovic's hand and said "Yes, we will win together." The next day, in Oakland, Mandela surprised his handlers and us by reaching out to America's "first people, the Indians," drawing parallels about what it means to lose your land. We then sought out Native Americans who told us how his words made them cry. Ron Dellums was at his most eloquent, praising his constituents for standing up against apartheid. "Berkeley stood up," he shouted. Applause. "Oakland stood up." More applause. "San Francisco stood up." Even more. And then he looked out at the vast, multiracial crowd, urging them all to stand up. Every last person did.

Who can forget such an inspiring spectacle? It was hard for me to contain my emotion as I spoke to the many people who had been moved to act as the ANC had. We all took pride in this man's achievement, because it showed that good could triumph in a cynical time. And it was in this spirit that, over and over, Mandela spoke in terms of "we," not just "I"—in terms of a movement not just a personality. None of his entourage expected the spectacular reception he received wherever he went. Mandela's triumph in America became a triumph *for* America, reinforcing and challenging our own commitment to equality, justice and democracy. His mission was accomplished. Sanctions were secure. Money was raised. There was new momentum for change.

I decided it was time for me to go back to South Africa for an extended reporting trip. Once again, I wrote to the South African consulate seeking a visa. And they wrote back:

> *Dear Sir:*
> *Your application for a visa for the Republic of*

South Africa has reference [sic].

The Department of Home Affairs, Pretoria, has informed this office that your application has been unsuccessful.

Yours faithfully,
Vice Consul (Migration)

After that lovely word, "faithfully," there appears a chicken scratch signature that would do any Park Avenue doctor proud. Apparently, New York consular employees never gave out their names for security reasons, as I found out when I tried to reach this mysterious vice consul who handles would-be migrants like myself. When I finally reached her, she had no explanation to offer for the rejection of my visa application. "It was done at a higher level," she finally admitted.

Earlier in the year, in late January, I had received an identical letter when I had applied to go to cover Mandela's release. I joked with some ANC friends that no sooner were they unbanned than I was banned. After complaining to the State Department and being urged to reapply since the country "is changing," I received a third rebuke on September 4. If each one of these requests didn't cost $18, I would go on collecting them to wallpaper my office. I finally got into the country in November, but only to attend a conference and only for ten days. I specifically had to agree that I would do no reporting, a pledge I found difficult to uphold. Sorry, Mr. Botha.

I am sure that part of the reason for this official hostility had to do with the weekly television series I produced, *South Africa Now.* But my file in Pretoria's intelligence archive may have been extensive, though there's no way to find out. There was no Freedom of Information Act, probably because there was no freedom.

In the aftermath of Mandela's U.S. visit, I began moving away from covering South Africa exclusively. When *South Africa Now* ran out of money, we moved into human rights and other subjects. I now kept in touch with South Africa from afar.

Friends ask me, "What's Mandela really like?" The question itself echoes a curiosity manufactured in a celebrity culture where the details of the lives of the prominent and the famous consume so much media attention, in a time when every subject is reduced to personality and biography. Mandela had become an icon long before his prison release. He was the symbol of a movement, a god-like figure among his followers. Because of its understanding of Western culture, the ANC had consciously put him forth as their symbol even as their movement continued to make collective decisions in which no one individual gave the orders.

Everyone who saw him—handsome, regal and self-assured—projected onto him what they wanted him to be. For the militants, he was the man who took on the state, stood up to his jailers and survived twenty-seven years behind bars. For many, he was the loving husband of Winnie, who spent decades devoted to their storybook marriage with its long years of separation. For political leaders, he was the man to deal with, a lawyer and politician like themselves, a pragmatist who understood deal-making and compromise.

There is little space for a truly personal life when you are so constantly in the public spotlight. For years Mandela had been surrounded by prison guards; now there were security men wherever he went. He was free—but was he? Occasionally he would rebel, ducking his protectors and taking an early morning walk, once even sneaking a cab into town. His habits became a source of speculation and gossip but given his age, he knew his life was winding down, with appointments scheduled between naps and daily rituals that included making his own bed as he had for years in his cell.

Up close, he was always guarded and formal, more of a patrician than a populist. People who got closer called him a Victorian gentleman with a deeply engraved professional temperament. His poise reflected years of self-imposed discipline. After all, he was brought up in a royal family in his native Transkei and trained for leadership at an early age. His sense of duty clearly dominated all his other senses.

Mandela is not a cold man. I have seen him joke around and let his guard down. He seems to enjoy pounding the flesh and making small talk, but rarely reveals his feelings. He did a few times with me, while thinking aloud about his comrades who didn't live to see the end of apartheid. Yet as I watched him work, I had the feeling that he was playing a role, cultivating a mystique, with its success keyed to keeping people from seeing his human frailties, insecurities, arrogance, and temper. That came out years later, when he conceded political mistakes, made arbitrary decisions and went through a painful public divorce from his wife Winnie, who suffered many problems of her own. It's wonderful to know that he has found a new love after living nearly eight decades, the dynamic Graca Machel, widow of charismatic Mozambican President Samora Machel, who died in a still unsolved plane crash in 1986. (I was fortunate to have met the Machels, when I filmed him boarding the plane on which he perished a week later.)

As I watched Mandela closely, I realized that he rarely acted alone, always consulting with colleagues, more the organization man than the individualist. Many journalists missed that, although Richard Stengel, the *Time* reporter chosen to co-write his autobiography by the American publishing company that bought it for big bucks, told me he sensed a certain loneliness and also felt a distance. Mandela remained closest to his oldest comrades, who had lived through the 1940s and '50s with him and shared the Robben Island experience, lions of the struggle like Ahmed Kathrada and Walter Sisulu. I felt honored to be in his presence but never thought of myself as an intimate. His age may have something to do with it. His movement cronies called him "the old man," or referred to him by his clan name, Madiba, out of a respect for elders bred in tribal society. He has a body language and a cultural interaction that no outsider ever penetrated.

When I watched Mandela board the plane that whisked him out of the United States, I thought that was it. My moment in the same space with a world figure was over. Blessed, I was thrust back into my own less than exalted existence. My time with Mandela had come and gone.

Or so I thought.

Until I got the next call, nearly four years later. Our paths had crossed a few times in that period, once when I produced a still uncompleted film of the Dance Theater of Harlem's visit to South Africa. Now Pallo Jordan was on the line from Johannesburg. Would I come to South Africa to direct an insider film, kind of like *The War Room* of Nelson Mandela's election campaign? They wanted me to do it for worldwide distribution. Once again the ground rules were clear: I would have exclusive access and they would let me do it my way. No censorship. No politically correct guidelines.

How can you turn down an offer like that?

I'll do it, of course, was my reply, but only if Mandela personally extends the invite. I wanted to know that he was really on board. Pallo said he wasn't sure if Mandela could respond personally because he was campaigning on the road and was very busy.

Two days later, the invitation came by fax, addressed to Rory O'Connor and me at Globalvision and signed by Nelson Mandela. "While the events will be covered in the mass media," he wrote, "we believe that the inside story itself deserves coverage by independent journalists for the public worldwide and for future generations. Daily news reporting is invariably superficial, focusing only on the statements of leaders. An in-depth documentary film can bring out the story of how the people themselves, white and black, are participating in the larger process of democratization."

With the blessing of Mandela and promises of behind-the-scenes access, I thought for sure that this time some TV outlet in America would pre-buy the film and the chance to capture one of the turning points of our century.

I thought wrong.

Not one TV network responded positively to our pitch, all for virtually the same reasons: they were either going to cover it themselves and/or they had no available slots for long-form films, much less independently produced documentaries. South African Broadcasting passed also, fearing it would be perceived as too pro-ANC and thus violate election media rules.

An American newsmagazine show or two thought our story might make for a good segment, but only if we could deliver hot footage or some revelation. They all wanted the exclusive with Mandela. For them he was just one more big name to be bagged, the journalistic equivalent of big game in Africa. Few of those who got the "get" (as power bookings are called) gave much thought to what to ask him. Most of the interviews would be the same. Predictable questions in search of obvious answers.

Our task was different. We had Mandela. What we didn't have was money. And we were running out of time. Our own countdown had begun.

Strike one was no pre-sale. A second strike followed when public television in America and the philanthropic foundations with an interest in South Africa also turned us down. We had erroneously assumed that after three years of producing 156 editions of the award-winning *South Africa Now*, we might be considered qualified to take on the subject. Sorry.

After weeks of development and preproduction, we were all dressed up—with the promise of the best seats in the house to the drama marking the end of white rule in Africa—but with no means to go.

At that point, a friend in Hollywood suggested I team up with a certain documentary director, an Englishman who boasted that he would have no problem raising a million dollars to do it right, on film, with several crews. He dropped lots of names with one of those Oxford accents that inspire class envy. He personally knew financier Michael Milken; he had networks panting for his next proposal. He had credentials up the yin-yang, which I stupidly didn't check.

You guessed it: At the end of the day, our deal turned into one more Hollywood horror story, when he not only couldn't raise a million, but attempted to hijack the project and turn me into his errand boy/liaison with the ANC. When I balked, he abruptly and without a word to me pulled out of the whole project, a day before we were to start shooting. Not content with letting us proceed without him, he went behind our backs to Showtime, a pay TV cable channel that had agreed to put up modest financing (at the behest of a black executive who went out on a limb to back the project). My "partner" reportedly told them he now couldn't guarantee the quality of the project. Without checking with us, our one outlet then pulled out! (Three years later, Showtime aired an evenhanded fictionalized docudrama, *Mandela and DeKlerk*; one reviewer commented that the documentary footage was the best part of the show.)

By now, I was in South Africa, with less than one week to the election. I had one Hi-8 camera and no budget. My former network colleagues and the international news army of which they were part had already rented virtually every camera, crew, hotel room, cell phone, beeper and car to be had in Johannesburg. During my eight years at ABC news, I had learned the adage: when you care the very least, spend the very most. Now I was about to see this economy of waste in practice. At one ANC rally at Soweto's FNB stadium, almost fifty Betacams were trained on the platform. Most of the cameramen agreed that all their shooting would rate a max of twenty seconds of air time unless violence erupted. One told me that they had to follow Mandela everywhere in case he was shot, and if he was, they could only hope their cameras were running. That's called "getting the money shot."

Soon I was spending more on exasperated phone calls to New York than Nelson Mandela probably spent in twenty-seven years at the prison commissary. It looked like I was out of luck: no money, no outlet, no film.

But then a last-minute reprieve. I asked to see Anant Singh, South Africa's leading black producer, whom I had met before.

Responsible for the movie based on the play *Sarafina!*, among other anti-apartheid films, he was known for being gutsy. I wasn't sure if a documentary project would appeal because he is primarily in the motion picture business.

I told Singh the history of the project, the attitude of the TV networks, the knife in the back from the twit I had hired to direct the film. Finally, I showed him a copy of the signed invite from Nelson Mandela.

His response: "Fine, let's do it." We shook hands. That was it. No contracts, no deal memos. No long months of high-priced lawyers haggling over miles of boilerplate. Singh said he'd pay for a crew and ten days of shooting. Then we'd see what we had and where to go next. We would be partners, the first international coproduction of its kind in the new South Africa. I wasn't sure if we could do it, but there it was. Though he wasn't fully committed, I now had a dare: "Show me what you can do."

I was lucky to find a South African with faith in me, faith in his country's history, and the bucks to get the film going. Race never entered into it. Our project was now back on track—a narrower track to be sure, but at least, at this late hour, we would be able to do *something*.

That something turned into an around-the-clock shooting spree. The ANC video unit agreed to share their exclusive footage. A few friends with home video cameras, including Stuart Sender and the talented Yvette Tomlinson, volunteered to shoot on spec around the country. We were off and running, a ragtag production with a lot of heart but not much infrastructure. Anant hooked me up with Scy Productions, an efficient Jo'burg-based production company that booked a camera crew, a car, and a production manager.

My plan was to cover as many events as I could, while focusing on the behind-the-scenes process, the whys and hows, not just the who and where. Ordinary South Africans, including many blacks, knew little about the ANC in exile, its leaders or policies. The ANC had never run an election campaign before. They were not known for super-efficiency either—and that's an understatement. In contrast, DeKlerk's National Party had four decades of practice in electoral politics. They were master manipulators, and for years had pictured the ANC as terrorists and worse. They were, in 1994, aided by the global advertising firm of Saatchi and Saatchi.

Most of the Western journalists treated this white minority regime as legitimate, even though the majority had never voted for it. They believed, almost religiously, in guaranteeing equal time for the candidates, as if the oppressor and the oppressed, the white ruling elite and the black majority, had equal claim to the world's attention.

They had not explained the fall of apartheid very clearly, so that the events of April 1994 were never put in their real historical context. There were few references to the role of sanctions in squeezing the economy, to the ANC's persistence, to the years of armed struggle and revolt in the townships, to the bravery of the Cuban troops in Angola who had held off Pretoria's air force in a watershed battle in a town called Cuito Carnivale or to the complexities of the negotiation process. There were no references to the role of the UN in winning independence for neighboring Namibia or the impact of the anti-apartheid movement worldwide.

With armadas of cameras and correspondents, the networks did give television watchers a glimpse. We saw the long lines of voters. We saw threats of civil war dissolve as peace broke out. But the election was presented as elections generally are on TV, marred by a few snags to be sure but with Mandela the predictable winner. Much of this coverage was one long photo-op—smiles, sentiment and sophistry.

The voices of the people who made the change, and an analysis of how they did it, were absent.

I wanted my film to serve as an alternative and antidote to such mechanistic news thinking, without being sycophantic or propagandistic. Reality tends to escape the wide but superficial frame of most TV journalism. Like the country's gold, the truth about South Africa has to be mined by people who understand the country's nuances, as many great writers and artists have done for years. A deadline-driven, bottom-line oriented, headline-hustling mentality is usually not up to the task.

I made a point of filming the American media in action—Dan Rather interviewing an ANC official who told me afterward he doubted that the American people will learn much about South Africa judging by the questions. (The interview never aired.) I watched Peter Jennings introduce Mandela to his daughter, while outside, in the hallway of the hotel, other networks scrambled hysterically for their one-on-one with the big man. Getting journalists to share their personal feelings or even be reflective about their work in South Africa was an uphill battle. CNN's Bernard Shaw declined to go on camera with us because, he said, when he speaks, people think CNN is speaking. Come on, Bernie. Loosen up.

I wanted to look at the politics and character of the movement that had fought for over eighty years for racial justice. I wanted to show their concept of grassroots democracy, built around participation in democratic civic, community, labor, and political groups. As one labor leader explains in the film, "For us, democracy is not just about elections, it's about day-to-day accountability."

Some within the ANC were camera-shy. One campaign manager had seen *The War Room*, on Bill Clinton's campaign, and feared he couldn't compete in cleverness with that film's star, James Carville. He also liked wearing shorts to work and didn't think that would look good on camera. It was small conceits like this that blocked promised access to some key ANC meetings.

Countdown reveals the South African role played by one of President Clinton's advisors and shows how the ANC created a modern political machine utilizing the latest technology. We also reveal the claim that a computer hacker, allegedly from inside the Election Commission, attempted to tamper with the vote-counting computer. There's a great deal in the film that no one has since reported.

Countdown presents an action-packed account because I happened to be on the scene in the aftermath of a bomb blast in the center of Johannesburg. Paced with South African rhythms and with music from artists long concerned with South Africa, such as Peter Gabriel, Jackson Browne and Miles Davis, these days of change now have a soundtrack that includes songs written for the occasion.

Countdown also documents how people of all races and ethnic backgrounds worked together to ensure free and fair elections. It looks at the themes of ANC political practice—internal democracy in the form of decision-making by consensus, nonracialism, negotiations, coalition-building and a long-term view powered by a faith in the possibility of justice.

The hopes for transformation are expressed most eloquently by ordinary people, but also surface in the commentary of ANC leaders, including the late Joe Slovo, Pallo Jordan, Cyril Ramaphosa and Tokyo Sexwale. Nelson Mandela is, naturally, the central figure, sharing his analysis, commentary, and some private moments.

The real drama of the film is not expressed through individual stories but through group action. You can see it on election day when we traveled from township to township as South Africans lined up for hours to cast their ballots. At one point my camcorder wasn't focusing. And then I realized why. I was crying uncontrollably as my lens zoomed on the faces of people erupting with joy.

It was my hope that *Countdown to Freedom* could challenge those who saw it to think again about the meaning of freedom. It was a film that had to be made, and despite incredible obstacles, finally *was* made. After it was completed with narration by James Earl Jones and Alfre Woodard, our next task was to sell it. Before the election, that proved impossible because everyone was doing the election. In its aftermath, there was little interest because "it's already been done." Now we are continuing to fight to get it seen worldwide, if only to honor the century of struggle and sacrifice that climaxed with the rebirth of a nation on May 10, 1994, in Pretoria, the cradle of apartheid.

Hopefully, now that some time has passed, a more in-depth treatment will stir interest. Third World people have long claimed that the world's media is stacked against them, that the information flow only moves one way, from North to South. Yet at a time when our media seems mesmerized by the travails of one black man—O. J. Simpson—we have had a tough time finding airtime for the triumphs of another, Nelson Mandela. In America, Cinemax, a movie channel, did buy it, and in 1996 the Academy of Motion Picture Arts and Sciences chose it as one of the outstanding films of 1994 to screen in Los Angeles under its auspices. It has aired in South Africa.

While I was making the film, I ran into an old friend who was then producing specials with ABC's Peter Jennings. He was interested in what I was doing but was dismissive because "everyone knows what the outcome will be." He told me, "The real story will start after the election as the new government tries to make change." He then outlined plans to undertake a yearlong look at the transformation of South Africa.

It sounded great, and I marveled at the resources such a project would take. Here I was making a low-budget film as an independent on a budget that amounted to less than the room service bill of CNN's staff. And here ABC was, willing to commit to a year's worth of work.

The building of democracy is a complex undertaking. To show and explain it requires enough airtime to interpret events and explore the process of political change. It is precisely this type of story that the networks usually have little money or time for.

Maybe I was wrong about ABC, I thought. Maybe I should have stayed with the network.

Eight months later, I ran into him in New York. "How's it going?" I asked.

He looked perplexed.

"You know, the South Africa special?"

"Oh, that. We dropped it."

He was off to Bosnia. In TV parlance, South Africa went away. Again.

CHAPTER 10

ON THE ISLAND

When I was covering South Africa in the old days, I used to think about Nelson Mandela alone in his cell on Robben Island. There were only a few pictures of what it was like there, none of what he looked like or how he had aged. Was he aware, I wondered, of the efforts by people around the world to free him? Did he know about the marches, the songs, the giant concerts and major rallies? What was it like in that dungeon that had shut out the world for so many years?

I found out in January 1995 when I returned to South Africa to film a most moving reunion. Imagine: 1,250 former political prisoners, cadres and ANC leaders, returning to the Island not as victims but as victors. There I was, in his cell, roaming an area that had been off limits for decades. I was there to make another film for Anant Singh, along with Barbara Kopple, whom I'd I invited to collaborate on the project.

The ex-prisoners had come from every corner of the country, many now advanced in age, hobbling on crutches. Among them were many ANC leaders who owed their political growth to the years they spent behind bars with Mandela and his coterie discussing politics and planning the future. The place was nicknamed Mandela University because of the way the prisoners had turned it into a school for revolution.

You didn't have to speak any African languages, or any language at all, to understand what was being said. The camaraderie was nonverbal—men hugging, laughing, showing off their bigger bellies and balder heads. They had come through a baptism of fire together and spoke of old warders and old wounds, of how miserable life could be locked away from loved ones, about the lessons they learned about life and comradeship. There was a remarkable lack of bitterness and hatred. It was a celebration, in Walter Sisulu's words, of "great history and great achievement."

Ronnie Kasrils, now a deputy minister of defense, whom I'd met in the '60s at the London School of Economics when he was in exile and part of the ANC underground, had arranged for a huge, Russian-built ice cutter to transport the men from Cape Town harbor to the island. Uniformed members of the South African Defense Forces, defenders for years of white rule, were now transporting their former enemies. The irony was not lost on the men I spoke with.

I thought of the landing at Normandy in World War II as I watched a flotilla of small boats and helicopters ferry them from ship to shore. The boat was too large to dock there but was cutting through a kind of ice that had left the country frozen in time. A number of the men chuckled when they learned that the ship had been purchased from Russia, which had claimed for many years to support their struggle. "A war ship has become a peace ship," said one of the organizers.

Nelson Mandela was touched when a small group of children, all white, all Afrikaner, the sons and daughters of the prison guards, greeted him by singing the national anthem in an African language, while holding aloft their national flag. He was also given a present: the original warrant for his arrest. He visited his old cell and the lime quarry where he was forced to break rock with his comrades. It was dust from that quarry which damaged his tear ducts and has given him eye problems ever since. That's why he frequently wears sunglasses.

Some of the problems in the new South Africa quickly surfaced. The ex-prisoners talked about returning to communities where they had no homes or livelihoods. Many said they were better off in prison. Others complained that the white soldiers who served apartheid were receiving pensions while they had to fend for themselves.

Among the businessmen who organized the event, there were debates as well. Some thought that the island should be turned into a tourist attraction, perhaps with a casino, to generate revenue to sustain a museum or create a resort. Others, including most of the ex-prisoners, felt that was ludicrous and would desecrate a spot they wanted preserved as a symbol of resistance and of man's inhumanity. One of the businessmen compared his colleagues' discussion of the fate of the island to a group of German businessmen deciding the future of the concentration camps. (In 1997 Robben Island was opened to tourism in a limited way, but a museum is planned.)

I was moved by these scenes of reconciliation to honor the past. It gave me a sense of the power and tenacity of a movement that had survived every indignity a repressive regime could throw its way. It showed how a disciplined political organization could help people survive—and triumph. It reinforced my hope that the new South Africa could become a model for peaceful or democratic change in a chaotic world where there are so few role models of this sort. That's why we called the film *Prisoners of Hope*, a phrase used by one of the men.

Yet hope is becoming a commodity in short supply in the world's newest democracy, as the difficulties of nation building and reconstruction set in. There are challenges on every front to make good on campaign promises to deliver a better life for the country's long-deprived majority. The ANC has learned that being in power is much tougher than denouncing power.

ANC insiders are locked into debates and power struggles over the right road to the future. The socialist countries that had supported them in exile are gone. Many activists who once considered themselves socialists, now had to manage a capitalist economy, create jobs and build houses. Where was the money going to come from? The heavy hand of the past was with them too. What do you do about the people who enforced apartheid, who murdered and maimed so many people? Reconciliation can only be built on a foundation of justice.

These are the contradictions at the heart of the latest phase in the struggle—the remaking of the country.

Once in power, the ANC had to satisfy the interests of diverse and divergent constituencies. The unity that served them so well in struggle began to crack, revealing differences within the leadership. Some were and are dedicated revolutionaries, others were and are opportunists. Some fought for ideology; others were powered by racial politics, nationalism, or religious conviction. Others fought for self-interest, succumbing to the temptations of corruption, what South Africans call the gravy train. Some self-destructed or lost their way. In some cases, families fell apart while activists became bitter and disillusioned. Joe Slovo himself warned against those among his compatriots who believed that because of their sacrifices, history owed them a living. He told me that highly politicized lives are tough to sustain. Movements can degenerate into bureaucracy, personal and political compromises clash. Critics of power can all too easily become abusers of power.

The movement's most capable leaders, so adept at moving masses, now need to move institutions. It's not the same thing. The old black and white days of apartheid versus freedom have given way to the grays of tougher choices. Politics invariably requires a process of compromise, and the militants of one era may find themselves on the outside as operators and opportunists end up with prestigious government posts.

South Africa's economic problems are daunting. The country and its future are trapped by larger forces that control and influence trade and investment. Is there an alternative to dependency on World Bank formulas and foreign investment? The ANC had a Reconstruction and Development Plan (RDP), but full implementation required moving mountains of self-interest and institutional inertia. It didn't work.

In 1967, I visited the Johannesburg stock exchange and watched black men record the trades by hand—keeping track of shifts in white wealth with chalk on a blackboard. By 1994, the exchange had moved to a larger, more modern building, and this time, a few whites were itemizing trades up there too. The six major corporations that had controlled the economy, with names like Anglo-American, Sanlam, Old Mutual and Rembrandt, still did, with only a handful of blacks listing companies on the exchange or sitting as directors on companies trading there. This is finally beginning to change.

In 1967 I took a photo of the exchange. In 1994 I was back with a video crew to record Nelson Mandela's visit. Trading was suspended for half an hour while he appealed to the white power structure for help in transforming the economy. The traders watched sullenly, waiting for him to leave so that they could once again explode into their frenetic buying and selling of shares. Outside in the lobby, black employees, mostly cleaners, messengers and assistants, exploded into song while dancing the *toi toi*, the high-kicking movement dance, to celebrate his visit.

Expectations are higher than high. Many of the black cameramen I worked with on *South Africa Now* are out on their own these days, building small businesses and scrambling for a living. "We don't work for struggle wages anymore," one tells me. "We have to eat now. We have to make money." Throughout Johannesburg, an emerging black bourgeoisie is coming into its own—dressing well, moving into suburban palaces, eating at the best restaurants, driving BMWs, easily recognizable by their everpresent portable cell-phones. This black elite is being forged through its own energy and the largesse of corporations who practice affirmative action in the name of black empowerment and their own self-interest.

Many of these upwardly mobile managers and executives in training feel they deserve the lifestyle once reserved for whites only. "Isn't that what we fought for?" a longtime activist and member of this new class asked me. "Why not?" another friend remarked. "All we wanted was to have a normal society where individual initiative could prosper regardless of race." A black broadcast executive told me he felt he had to take the perks that came with his job or risk alienating his key support staff: "If it was good enough for the whites, why not me?" So he drives a Mercedes and has a member-ship in the golf club. "It is only normal," he says, confiding at the same time that he doesn't play golf.

But alas, South Africa is not yet a normal society. Not as long as the vast majority still lives in grinding poverty while a conspic-uous elite, mostly white but now sprinkled with a few black faces, lives in affluence on top of it. As the transition continues, every-one wonders whether the country's wealth can be redistributed and if it will trickle down. The South African revolution has in some ways become the establishment, not its wrecking ball, with many of the old Afrikaner and English pro-apartheid players still in place.

"The political transition resolved one set of contradictions only to replace them with another," suggests Martin Murray in *South-ern Africa Report*. "During the apartheid years, conflicts between the haves and have nots were generally regarded as political in nature, but now they are seen as disruptive and unsettling.... The political left has generally lost its sense of direction...[while the mass base of the movement and the unions] has been more or less suc-cessfully co-opted into the mainstream ANC."

When I returned to South Africa in August 1996, I listened to old ANC comrades confide that their movement had never been ready to govern, that its plans and policies were not in place. They

say that's why it has been so difficult to get a transformation underway. They did not inherit the situation they planned for, and what
they did inherit was skewed to benefit whites. During the long years
in exile, ANC planners had expected to follow a strategy of nation-
alization and socialism. But when the Soviet Union collapsed, it
became clear that a command economy could not work. Instead,
they would have to learn to master the market without totally succumbing to it.

Buffeted by the pressures of international capital, the government adopted a conservative macro-economic strategy, well to the
right of proposals suggested by the World Bank and the International Monetary Fund. The ANC was projecting modest economic
growth—a 6 percent growth rate—hardly a radical redistribution
of wealth. But they never achieved it, or even came close. Part of
the problem is beyond their control, a consequence of economic
globalization that shifted power worldwide from governments to
multi-national corporations and markets. In 1998, a small group of
financial speculators drove the price of gold down in a complicated
chain of events involving Europe's central banks. The result was
nearly 150,000 miners out of work, a devastating blow to the country's economic hopes. In 1998,

At the same time, the ANC's Reconstruction and Development
Plan had stalled, in part because of bureaucratic impediments and
inept implementation of strategies, but also because it is easier to
talk about building houses than to actually build them. It is no wonder that dissatisfaction is growing along with talk of new parties
being formed once Mandela steps aside as he plans to do when his
five-year term is up.

Most disturbing to me, during that August 1996 trip to South
Africa I made to film the visit of Tibet's Dalai Lama, was the sense
on the part of many former militants that a pro-business right wing
had become ascendant within the ANC, that pragmatic-to-a-fault
President Mandela was acting more autocratic, more like the tribal
chief he was groomed to be than the bold progressive his image-

makers project. Disillusionment with the gravy train was spreading. I had a feeling that economic development was bringing with it spiritual decline and demoralization. That was certainly a sentiment that His Holiness the Dalai Lama keyed into with his emphasis on inner peace, compassion, and nonviolence.

I was told stories about corruption in high places, hypocrisy, power tripping, and the overall erosion of the ANC's moral high ground. Too many ANC politicians were becoming like politicians everywhere—masters of compromise and apologists for inaction. Other ANC leaders quit, like Secretary General Cyril Ramaphosa, a black consciousness activist turned militant labor leader turned skillful constitutional negotiator, who announced he was leaving politics to take a high-paying job with a black-run mega business consortium.

Likewise, in May 1997, Tokyo Sexwale, a legendary ANC guerilla fighter turned premier of Hauteng (Johannesburg) asked to be relieved of his duties to pursue a career in business. The ANC justified his decision on the grounds that not all those who fought for liberation aspired to be politicians.

When I speak to ANC members who now occupy high positions in the government, the conversation takes two turns. The first deals with the positive changes that are underway, about new laws, bold programs, global initiatives and decided "progress." That's the bright side—and in comparative terms, constitutes a range of achievements of which few countries can boast. But then there is the darker side, the concerns that are shared in private, detailing frustrations with a civil service still packed with members of the old regime, and a pervasive corruption that seems to seep into every corner of life. "They have a saying, 'let's make a plan,' which is a code word for bribery, nepotism, and all sorts of self-serving dealing, often by our own ANC comrades," one prominent official who worked in the anti-apartheid movement overseas for years told me with disgust. "And the ANC does little about it; in fact, we rarely meet together anymore to exchange experiences, or even know what each other is doing." In short, a political transition has been achieved—but at a high, if often invisible, cost in terms of a weakening of principles, values, movement, and mission. Perhaps what we are seeing is just the latest evidence that power itself does corrupt.

Critics like Lawrence Mavundla of the Micro Business Chamber charged that all this black empowerment talk was enriching only about three hundred individuals through entities like the Kagiso Trust and Thebe Investments, which were controlled by the ANC, but not improving the lives of the masses. Meanwhile, in the interests of economic growth, the ANC government, which came to power through protest, passed a law regulating spontaneous protest marches, and the unions were urged to keep wage demands down. It is still unclear how much will or can change fundamentally, given the legacy of apartheid, the pressures from below, and the restraints from above. The majority of South Africans know the society can't be changed overnight or even in a few years.

This was a time when all that ordinary people talked about was crime out of control—carjackings, murder and pervasive police corruption, a time when Muslim militants burned drug dealers in the townships and the government seemed unwilling or unable to respond effectively. With violence continuing in Chief Mangosothu Gatsha Buthelezi's Natal province, South Africa was going through a painful and difficult period, even though it managed to draft a new constitution with more human rights provisions than exist in American law. It was also a period when the international climate was not exactly supportive of a just world order or a country that wants to determine its own destiny. The U.S. looks on from a distance with little by way of inspiration and only token support to offer. The Clinton administration has provided some help, but it could do so much more.

I attended an extraordinary event in the country's political history—a hearing of Bishop Tutu's Truth and Reconciliation Commission in Cape Town, at which Deputy President Thabo Mbeki, the chairman of the ANC, testified—backed by two volumes of details and documents—that the movement had committed human rights abuses in executing suspected traitors, mutineers, deserters and infiltrators in its ranks, and releasing a list of who had been abused. He admitted that almost a thousand cadres died in exile. These disclosures were praised as "unprecedented anywhere in the world" by Commission Vice Chairman Alex Boraine. The admission by the ANC and more limited disclosures by other political parties, including those who supported apartheid, included apologies to the victims, yet the ANC insisted—and most agreed—that theirs had been a just war.

Many of these revelations had been made before; I had certainly heard them years earlier and reported them on *South Africa Now*. They comprised more evidence on how wars affect the innocent, and that no one, in the end, is innocent. The ANC was at times guilty of irresponsibility and clearly got caught up in paranoia, which caused suffering to people who deserved better treatment. Its crimes were relatively minor when set against the mass killings that took place in the name of liberation in China or Russia, but they were undeniable. Revolutionaries are not exempt from moral failure and poor judgment. We all must be held accountable for our actions. In the ANC's defense, Mbeki constantly referred to the context of the times; he was right, but that can lead to rationalizing and defending the indefensible.

The testimony inspired me to reflect on my own attitudes. I thought of the aftermath of the Vietnam War, when I had criticized Joan Baez and others who spoke out against abuses in Vietnamese reeducation camps. In 1975-76, I called for more understanding of the deep scars that the war caused and explained away their brutalities as understandable in light of their suffering. I was wrong, and have since come to appreciate the nonpartisan universality of human rights. Now I am convinced one can understand political errors and be supportive of liberation struggles but must do so without moral blinders or blind allegiance.

These problems are not specific to South Africa. They were common in the U.S. as well, in movements I was part of, where immaturity, intolerance, bad leadership, sectarianism and authoritarianism undermined and divided us, turning a social force speaking to America into a subculture speaking to itself. As I reflected on South Africa, I read Garry Wills's essay in the *New York Review of Books* on Andrew Young's experience in the civil rights movement of the '60s. The piece reveals lots of in-fighting, callousness, and "dirty laundry." He writes, "We no longer see the serene picture of Gandhian saints, but flawed people up against every effort of a surrounding society to destroy them, people with few supporters (and those under constant FBI sniping, branded as Communists, anarchists or homosexuals), people often angry at each other, always depending on each other, despondent, praying, hoping that good would prevail—as it did over their dead bodies or broken lives." Multiply that by a factor of ten and you have the ANC, on the poorest and least developed continent, facing an enemy committed to hunting it down and wiping it out, using poisons, spies, military raids, and torture.

It was always clear to me that the ANC's shortcomings could not be treated as the moral equivalent of the systematic abuses linked to the system it fought. The ANC's biggest challenge in forging a democratic culture was unifying people of so many different ethnicities, backgrounds, races, and religions—illiterate farmers and cultured intellectuals, Moslems, Hindus, Christians, Jews and African religionists, young and old, women and men. In a climate charged with racial antagonism, the ANC pursued nonracialism, an attitude that was not always emotionally digestible for people scarred by a system that enforced racial inequality. It humanized its enemies and pursued a strategy of cultivating and negotiating with hostile Afrikaner adversaries. They ate with them, drank with them, even fished with them. They took the higher road. That's what always appealed to me. And still does.

Most troubling to me as a journalist and media watcher is how many of these contradictions are playing themselves out in the media. I always hoped my critique of the way Western news organizations distorted South African issues could be of use, because many of those same networks are attempting to enter, and would gladly dominate, the South African media market. Already, the South Africa media has opened itself to the rest of the world. International channels are being seen and multinational companies are buying up newspapers. CNN, MTV, the BBC, and Rupert Murdoch, among others, are already on the scene or on the way.

These companies can bring the world into South Africa, but it is a world of limited perspectives with a heavy dose of consumerism that appeals mostly to the privileged. What value will it have for the majority? South Africans, who through years of isolation and boycott were forced to operate outside the Western media orbit, will now have to find a place within it. South Africans should be warned to be wary about the promises of this new media world.

It is encouraging that some South Africans recognize the challenge. The South African Broadcasting Corporation (SABC), long a tool of white power, says it is remaking itself with a new tone and programming mission. As a judge at a UN media contest, I was impressed by a prize-winning ad submitted by the AMC agency of Johannesburg for the SABC. One would be hard pressed to find a similar one in any other country—especially mine. The ad carries a picture of five young black kids staring at a TV set:

They're Thirsting for Knowledge: (But Are the Bionic Mutant Bikers Really the Guys for the Job?)

As a public broadcaster, we're not answerable to shareholders looking for profits, but to a much more demanding body. Society.

No easy task when you consider that 40 percent of our population is under the age of nineteen.

Our first obligation is to meet the need for news and information in our eleven official languages in an unbiased and ethical manner.

But our place is also to help rebuild society. To provide all South Africans, especially the young, with a perspective and self-identity that fills them with hope and promise.

Perhaps more than anything, we can take down walls that divide communities by introducing South Africa to itself.

We can awaken a sense of awe by making the world of science, art and music accessible to everyone.

We can reveal the secrets of the universe and the beauty and wonders of our planet.

Come to think of it, we can even find a place for the Bionic Mutant Bikers.

How can we make a real contribution to your life? We'd like to hear your views on the role of a public broadcaster.

The ad gives the SABC's phone number and closes with: "You'll find we're also eager to learn."

Wouldn't it be great, I thought, if our public broadcaster in America, PBS, would adopt a similar posture? But words are one thing, programming another. I soon discovered that the SABC is caught up in a serious internal debate over how far to take its new commitment to serve the public interest and the cause of democracy.

Those challenges deserve their own chapter.

CHAPTER 11

CONTRADICTIONS, CONTRADICTIONS: THIS IS NOW

*O*n February 4, 1996, the public was to be let in on what the new SABC would look like, at a gala at the Waterkloof Air Force Base outside of Pretoria. I phoned the organizer and was told that for security reasons names of invitees had to have been handed over to the military by midnight the night before. Sorry.

A friend who worked for the SABC was equally apologetic, explaining that security would be tight and that he was only given a limited number of invites. "It is impossible," he told me.

I thought surely the deputy minister of defense would have some influence with the air force and could get me on the base. "Sorry, Danny," he replied. "I can't do it because this is an SABC function, not a military event."

I confided this disappointing news to my new chauffeur, a feisty and resourceful Afrikaner. Eddie suggested we have a go at it anyway. So that night, we did. He whisked his shiny Merc, now outfitted with a sign in Afrikaans that said On Diplomatic Service, up to Pretoria. We found the base—and much to my surprise, were waved right through by a cordon of men in uniform. We sailed through six more checkpoints even though we didn't have an invitation. Finally, we were stopped and asked for our pass. Eddie said, in his most authoritative tone, that we had forgotten it at the embassy, and that I was an ambassador.

"From the Bronx," I chimed in.

The last soldier saluted us, and we had made it. As soon as I walked into the cocktail party that preceded the event, I ran into Anton Harber, the founding editor of the *Weekly Mail and Guardian.* Fresh with the high chutzpah of our arrival, I boasted about that little act of infiltration. He then ran a tongue-in-cheek item about my caper in a column, ending by questioning the security of South Africa's air force bases.

Anyway, I was in—for an event of the type one rarely encounters outside of Las Vegas. We were ushered into a VIP seating area in a large hangar. I was sitting next to the director of marketing of England's SKY News, Rupert Murdoch's emissary. Sitting just behind us was Ed Turner, vice president of CNN. Prominent South Africans were all around us, including members of the cabinet. This was a big deal.

From its inception, the SABC had been an arm of the apartheid system and reflected its values, not only in what it broadcast but in how it was structured. South Africa didn't even get television until 1976 because apartheid's rulers wanted to suppress images from the rest of the world for as long as possible. When I first visited its huge broadcasting complex in Johannesburg in 1990, I had to pass through a group of security officers flanked by police dogs. Most of the employees I saw were white; at that time, broadcasting was strictly segregated. There were black stations and white stations, and newsrooms with special walls separating blacks and whites. There were even contingencies to seal off the black studios in the event of an uprising. The government kept the SABC under tight rein.

In writing about the SABC in *Apartheid Media* in 1986, John Phelan noted that "SABC television is both the past and the possible future of American television. It is not up to American speed in terms of video editing and remote intercutting with studio anchoring, which gives it an amateurish and nostalgic look. But it is certainly beyond the current dreams of broadcasting conglomerates in this country in concocting its own media world of images and stereotypes that make attention to the real world of events unnecessary." Today there may be a convergence underway, with the SABC slowly Americanizing, while American television in times of crisis—as during the Gulf War of 1991—apes the old-style SABC, functioning as a megaphone for the military and Washington's policy goals.

The SABC was always an enormous institution and bureaucracy—with studios galore, giant overheads and layers of executives that made it seem like an Afrikaner employment and political patronage project. Fully 36 percent of the staff was administrative. In the old days, the state president had a direct line to the news chief and virtually dictated what could and could not be covered. Censorship was the order of the day.

One example: After Stevie Wonder dedicated his Oscar for the song "I Just Called to Say I Love You" to the then-incarcerated Nelson Mandela, his records were banned in South Africa. The SABC edited out his acceptance speech when they carried a delayed broadcast of the ceremony, an entire music program was killed because it carried a Wonder video, and his records in the black music library were deliberately scratched, while ones in the white music library had stickers affixed that said AVOID.

Censoring songs was a minor preoccupation; sugarcoating reality was the priority. Unrest and human rights abuses, police brutality, and death squad activity in South Africa were not news on South African TV. Study after study offered evidence that the TV system was used to mobilize a consensus behind the government and to provide disproportionate access to the ruling party and apologists for apartheid, while shutting out the ANC and its supporters in the democratic movement.

In 1984, of eighty-five employees in the part of the news service serving blacks, all but six were white. Many of the black journalists who have come on board since came from print, not broad-casting. There is tension between them and blacks who worked for the SABC in its pro-apartheid days. One problem has been cor-ruption and payoffs at the SABC; one executive was arrested in 1995 while seeking money from programmers in exchange for air time. I'm told that most of those implicated in sleazy practices such as these were holdovers from the old regime.

Clearly, if the Mandela government was to transform South Africa, it had to transform its media. That was easier said than done. For one thing, the ANC was committed to the principles of an inde-pendent press, not just taking over the media and remaking it in its own image. Second, apartheid's legacy had left few blacks with the training and experience to run a broadcasting operation. Finally, there were concerns about how to finance the SABC; a heavy-handed takeover would drive advertisers away.

So the new government started out slowly. Zwelakhe Sisulu, son of long-time ANC leaders Walter and Albertina Sisulu and editor of the *New Nation*, an anti-apartheid weekly, was picked to head the operation. I knew Zwelakhe from his days as a Nieman fellow, and *South Africa Now* had covered his many detentions and inter-viewed him about the declining state of the free press during the anti-apartheid struggle. Running the SABC was an enormous chal-lenge, and he moved cautiously at first.

His rise to power was part of a major desegregation of the suites of media power. Another Nieman fellow, Barney Mthombothi, explained what was happening at the SABC in 1996 in *Nieman Reports*: "Its role and its culture have changed; even the faces at the top have changed. Two years ago, there was not a single black face in the upper echelon of the SABC. Today there is only one white male left.... The changes have been so dramatic that the SABC is unrecognizable from the organization of two years ago."

A black woman, Dr. Ivy Matsepe-Cassaburri, a fighter for women's rights, became chair of the corporation's board. Mean-while, a government-appointed but independent broadcasting

authority, the IBA, began developing a framework for the regulation and development of a new communications arrangement. It
ordered the SABC to divest itself of commercial radio stations and
focus more closely on public service. This would theoretically open
the market to more competition, but the SABC resisted, seeking
to hold on to three channels while the IBA wanted to cut them back
to two to make room for newcomers, i.e. black-owned businesses.

So what changes was the new SABC proposing? It had restructured and reoriented its three channels. They were imaginatively
called SABC 1, SABC 2 and SABC 3, mandated to expand the number of African languages on the air to reflect the country's eleven
official languages. That meant cutting back on the Afrikaans-language programming that had once dominated the airwaves, a decision that infuriated conservative whites and may not have been the
smartest way to promote unity or sustain revenues. The TV corporation had declared itself a public service broadcaster, roughly on
the model of England's Channel 4, but with a nation-building mission. From now on, we were told, the SABC would be a cheerleader
for the new democracy and human rights, with slogans like "Your
vision, your voice." No amount of glitz would be spared to bring
the message home.

This gala was organized so that the SABC could preview its new
programming lineup, while at the same time reassure advertisers
that there would be no compromise in its standards, production values or commercial appeal. One agency person told me over lobster
at the dinner afterward that it wouldn't work. Doug Maritz of Young
and Rubican was blunter, calling it a "complete waste of money."
In essence, the SABC would now try to be everything to everyone—
a channel that served the black poor and the white elite. I was sympathetic to these goals, but the way the proposed transformation
of the SABC was being sold showcased every contradiction in the
new South Africa. Had the new SABC sold out or sold in?

It cost them a reported 3.8 million rand (just under a million
dollars U.S.) to stage this high-tech, feel-good, patriotic rally for two

thousand VIP guests and the viewers at home. In another six months, the SABC would acknowledge that it was fifty-seven million rand in debt. It blamed this on the cost of the revamp and the fact that more and more South Africans were refusing to pay license fees. Afrikaners were the largest group that paid the fees, but many stopped to protest the cutback in Afrikaans-language programming.

The launch started with a disco-style laser light show paced by state of the art visual effects and dancers, 1,400 performers in all. One of South African Airway's jumbo jets—sporting the colors of the old regime—was wheeled into the giant hangar to serve as a staging area from which broadcast executives, invited stars and celebrities, including President Mandela, descended. Some newspaper columnist quipped that the plane was an appropriate symbol because it had two wings—a left and a right.

There was music, dancing and speechifying aplenty. Stevie Wonder sang a song, O. J. Simpson's lawyer, Johnnie Cochran, an investor in the country's now defunct Pepsi franchise, waved to the crowd, and Hollywood celebrities served as emcees along with Felicia Mabuza-Suttle, a TV talk show host known as South Africa's Oprah Winfrey. Sharon Gellman, who organized the Hollywood delegation, Artists for a Free South Africa and a longtime activist, told me that they had to change the script radically because the earlier draft was embarrassingly devoid of political content. The *Weekly Mail and Guardian* joked that the appearance of so many Hollywood stars "reveals that we are now accepted in America, the spiritual home of commercial TV. The coded message here is we are now moral and pure enough as a culture to watch soap operas, sitcoms and talk shows."

The ceremony was complete with commercial breaks, breakdancing and bizarre moments, like when a sanitized film saluting the early, all-white days of the SABC boasted how the TV company had managed to evade sanctions by covertly obtaining shows whose artists didn't want them shown in South Africa. The promo tape actually celebrated defying world opinion, yet it was being shown at an event ultimately made possible in part by the success of sanctions. Strange. Didn't anyone in authority at the SABC, I wondered, preview this presentation?

"Is this what the ANC fought and died for?" one disgusted onlooker asked.

The biggest applause of the evening was reserved for South Africa's victorious soccer, cricket and rugby teams. President Mandela, flanked by children representing South Africa's ethnic groups and led by a young tribal praise singer, was also warmly received and spoke briefly about the importance of TV as a tool of democracy and why the SABC was changing "to better reflect the reality of our lives together."

He was introduced by Minister of Broadcasting Pallo Jordan, who I'd never seen quite so dapper. Pallo was as upbeat as everyone else, celebrating what he called a "feel-good time for South Africa" in the aftermath of sports victories and the coming of rain after years of drought. "Today," he intoned, "the SABC unveils a new program, a new page in its history and hopefully a new day in South African broadcasting. This is one more step in building a democratic South Africa."

Unfortunately, he split before the endless spectacle got very far along. I am sure he would have been as distressed by its vacuousness as I was. He was even more distressed two months later when he was abruptly fired from his cabinet post by Nelson Mandela. The newspapers reported the reasons may have been his hands-off attitude toward the SABC or his hesitancy about privatizing the telecommunications industry. He was considered too outspoken in cabinet meetings, but when grassroots activists protested, he was later reappointed minister of environmental affairs and tourism.

After the politicians and Zwelhakhe spoke, a shortened version of the national anthem was sung. I was surprised that no one, Mandela included, put their fist in the air. The singing of "Nkosi sikelel' iAfrika" had always, in my experience over thirty years, been accompanied by upraised fists, as a symbol of a determination to be free and as respect for those lost in the struggle.

Was this another worrisome sign—an abandonment of the symbols of the freedom movement? The *Mail and Guardian* ticked off some of the other contradictions: "The SABC was proclaiming its commitment to local content, on which it plans to spend the bulk of its budget and over 50 percent of its screen time. So how does it mark a new commitment to South African talent? By bringing in American television stars and allowing them to take centerstage.

"And how did the SABC choose to symbolize the fact it has a new independence? By getting two members of the cabinet to proclaim it. The nation's broadcaster also wanted to demonstrate its 'new values' and commitment to public service television. How did it do that? By selling its soul to South African Airways, which seemed to get more publicity from the event than the broadcaster."

Before the long event ended, President Mandela took his leave. Murdoch's man had been telling me all night how much he wanted to meet Mandela. I told him to stick with me. Having been with the president at many functions, I had developed an instinct for his arrivals and departures. I guessed where he would leave. And sure enough, his route to the exit took him by my strategically located seat on the aisle. Our eyes locked, and he walked over.

"How are you?" he boomed, offering his hand. I seized the moment and said: "Mr. President, I want you to meet a close friend of mine from England," motioning to my right. Murdoch's man reached over, a big smile on his face. His hand was shaking. He told me he wouldn't wash for a week.

Ultimately, of course, any broadcaster has to be judged on programming not promotions. And initially there were good notices for some of the new shows. South Africa's Media Monitoring Project, the country's oldest media watch group said, "The next months will be crucial for the SABC's success.... Having promised so much, they will need to deliver or face the wrath of not just vociferous but small protest groups, but large losses in viewership and reputation." This organization noted a central problem: Changing the languages on the air doesn't necessarily change the programs. To do so may in fact alienate viewers.

The SABC claimed that the public was positive about its makeover. The country's largest black newspaper, the *Sowetan*, called the launch a big success and supported the new SABC editorially. Most opinion leaders seemed to want the new configuration to work. I wanted to be more impressed than I was. Perhaps naively, I had hoped that a country that was starting over might be able to produce progressive television that would reflect the values of the revolution and political culture that brought down apartheid.

Instead, there seemed to be a desire to clone or acquire Western broadcasting models, undoubtedly in part because it is cheaper to import than produce. As a result, the airwaves were inundated with soap operas like *Santa Barbara*, *The Young and the Restless*, and *The Bold and the Beautiful*, plus some local variants with black actors following the same old formulas.

According to *Text*, a publication of Durban's Natal University Centre for Cultural and Media Studies, black South Africans are entranced by these soaps "and are not keen to see local television productions on their screens." As one viewer put it, "South African actors are still sort of trying to learn, and we don't want to pay TV licenses and watch them trying to act on TV."

The real Oprah Winfrey had also just arrived via satellite on SABC's airwaves in syndication. Twelve hours a day of CNN International has been airing for years. In 1995, many South Africans complained to me about all the O. J. Simpson trial coverage, wondering what it had to do with them and why Americans are hooked on so much sensationalism. Unfortunately, these shows have other insidious effects: They program viewers to expect high production values in all programs and encourage producers to emulate their example. They define what "real TV" is or should be.

I can't believe that the South African audience wouldn't

respond to something different and more relevant, but such programming is rarely given a chance. Perhaps I am being unfair, expecting a country that has for years been conditioned by Hollywood hype to break the habit overnight. The SABC may not get a chance to do its own thing. Money troubles are undermining its programming mission. By early 1997, there were reports that the SABC financial crisis was so severe that it was bankrupt. It had already begun slashing its budget, and seeking a government bailout. In 1998, Zwelhakhe Sisulu stepped down, moving into a lucrative job in private industry. Meanwhile, a local consortium that includes former *South Africa Now* cameraman Rapitse Montsho won a TV license for the country's first new private station. It is partially owned by Time-Warner.

The trend toward aping American TV is also evident on South Africa's commercial pay cable outlet, MNET. I appeared as a guest on *Front Row*, MNET's version of *Entertainment Tonight*, where I was to promote my documentary *Prisoners of Hope*. Instead, the host, a beautiful, English-educated daughter of a former Inkatha official, kept asking me to be more upbeat and humorous.

"Right," I said on the air, "I have always looked at torture and abuse as funny."

She didn't get my sarcasm.

The American commercial influence is well-established at MNET, which renamed its conference room the Joan Collins Room to honor the former *Dynasty* superstar, who wrote a nice note to the staff after visiting in 1992. MNET is controlled by an Afrikaner media conglomerate, which has as its junior partners white-owned English-language newspaper monopolies. Incredibly profitable, the company has exported its technologies and cable businesses into Europe through a company called Film Net. MNET also has a direct broadcast satellite that enables it to be seen throughout Africa, reaching to Cairo, where presenters read copy drafted in Randburg. MNET has electronically colonized emerging TV markets throughout the continent. To compete, the SABC announced plans to launch a bouquet of satellite pay TV services, including an Afrikaans-language channel, although many of those plans were modified or shelved.

As I spoke with old colleagues and new friends at the SABC, I heard the same litanies and disappointments I am used to from my friends in New York. "I am being underutilized," one of South Africa's top investigative journalists told me. "They don't want investigative reporting." Another producer says she is short-staffed and that there is little support for in-depth stories.

Even the ANC has been upset. Deputy President Thabo Mbeki complained that the party that had won 63 percent of the vote and liberated the country was being given short shrift on the air. He asked for a weekly time slot so that viewers could be informed about what their government was doing and how the nation's reconstruction and development were unfolding. As if to confirm this need, an old friend who is sympathetic to the government told me, "I'm sure the government has lots of achievements but I can't name five. Can you?"

Mbeki's suggestion prompted a storm of protest from editors and journalists, including then-Minister of Broadcasting Jordan, who argued that such a move would undercut the perception of the SABC's independence and impartiality. The implication was that the government was trying to assert control over the media, again. Mbeki backed off.

Unfortunately, most free speech advocates in South Africa tend to define censorship almost exclusively in terms of government intervention, ignoring the more insidious and less transparent role played by advertisers and businesses in shaping broadcast agendas. Perhaps that is because reporters tend to have an adversarial relationship with governments and go nuts when public officials criticize them. Government abuses should be reported, of course—but so should malfeasance in the corporate sector. The former is closely monitored, the latter is not.

What do you say when Rupert Murdoch wants your TV sports

rights and may be willing to ante up $300 million, while your budgets are strained? What do you say to Channel 4 and Viacom, whose lobbyists are swarming about with attractive proposals? What do you say to black businessmen who find themselves shut out at a time when black economic empowerment is supposedly in? Does the market really have an answer that can meet the needs of the millions who have been pushed out, remain poor and are thus undesirable to advertisers? Can a TV system that only serves the market adequately market democratic ideas? Can you transform a society by relying on media institutions that reinforce the status quo?

Some South Africans are still debating these issues. I felt that one of my challenges was to bring this debate home. That's what the rest of this book is about.

PART FOUR

REMOTE CONTROL

EVERY AMERICAN is familiar with a device called the remote control. Everyone knows what that electronic channel changer does. It gives viewers a certain power over their viewing choices, or at least it appears to. It has changed the way we all watch television, enabling us to sample programming instantly, to see what's on rather read the listings, to indulge our most frenetic tastes. In some homes, there's a constant battle over who controls the remote control. Men tend to hog it; women tend to hate it. In this age of shortened attention spans, many viewers don't watch any one show—but constantly jump from image to image, creating their own electronic collages, extracting bits and pieces of visual data that can easily overwhelm the senses, fragmenting rather than unifying understanding. It is no secret that many TV shows and commercials are now being designed with that device in mind—keeping the action going at a fast enough pace to keep you from flipping, to defeat a technology that lets you shut them out. This is what's behind some of the dumbing down of program content.

News as we know it is at risk. The architects of TV programming are redesigning their newscasts to make them look and feel more like the softer morning shows with celebrity features, quickie segments, big guests and constant gimmicks, snippets of information, non-stop promos, and high story counts. "Suddenly the morning and evening approaches to news aren't so different after all," reported Frederic Biddle in the *Boston Globe* in March 1997. "Evening newscasts are cloaking themselves with the easy-to take-characteristics of their breakfast version." He quotes wunderkind producer Jeff Zucker who runs the *Today Show*. "I wanted to give people...the feeling that if they didn't like this segment, stick around and in 4 1/2 minutes there'd be another topic. It's quicker paced. There are more stories in there, more segments, and perhaps it's more lively as a result." Lively? Maybe. Informative? Rarely. It's more like a smorgasbord where you nibble on finger foods and end up hungry a half hour later.

If you don't like what you are watching, you can jump to another channel that's doing the same thing or hop to cable. Remember, the networks also own many of the cable channels—with more to come in the digital age—so that when you flip from them, you may very well be flipping to them as well.

But beyond all that, the remote control can be used as a metaphor for media analysis, raising, as it does, the idea of control itself, and suggesting that it *is* remote, at least from most of our lives. We are not always aware that we choose among the choices we are given.

Hand me the remote.

CHAPTER 12

MEDIA WORLDS IN COLLISION

"The TV business is a cruel and shallow money
trench, a long plastic hallway where thieves and
pimps run free and good men die like dogs."
—Hunter S. Thompson

"Every person who shall monopolize ... any part
of commerce ... shall be punished by fine ... or
by imprisonment ... "—Sherman Anti-Trust Law

A t the elegant Hotel Pierre, a plutocrat's palace on Fifth Avenue
just off Central Park, at $750 a pop, an elite audience gath-
ered for 1995's Big Picture Conference on the Business of Entertainment, held under the auspices of *Variety*, the bible of show
business, and Wertheim Schroder (now Schroder Wertheim)
investment bank. As one TV columnist quipped, "One well-targeted
air strike could have taken out the entire upper echelon of the most
powerful industry in America." Together, these men (and they usually are men) form a caste of mass media untouchables, who will
be seen as the robber barons of the information age, predicts *Newsday*'s Marvin Kitman, with an impact far more insidious than that
of their predecessors who won that dubious distinction.

As I mingled with this *crème de la crème*, I was driven to try and
decode how my professional life relates to this media elite that both
shapes and limits it, even as it suppresses alternative visions like the

one espoused by Globalvision and other independents like it. Despite our being a small company, we've made it our business to have access to the folks who run the business.

In the old days, when anti-trust laws were taken more seriously— e.g. when ITT's bid to buy up ABC was shot down by federal reg- ulators—there might have been more eyebrows raised by gatherings of powerful competitors. To be sure, price fixing discussions at these confabs would be unnecessary since advertising costs and pro- gramming rates tend to be similar, fixed by the marketplace. But today, as media mergers expand the conglomerates, the titans do get together in expensive and exclusive conferences that function almost like summit meetings. It is here that high-level executives outline their corporate agendas, debate their visions and try to impress the Wall Street analysts who influence the media money pumps. These gatherings celebrate, and in some instances fuel, the ongoing transformation of the media landscape. It is here that cor- porate media cultures crystallize, and sometimes collide. In panel discussions and informal conversations, a certain ideology fixing takes place. When the Communications Generals set the tone, their vast armies of employees and camp followers fall into line, unchal- lenged by critical voices or dissident perspectives.

The inside life of media-as-business deserves as much attention as the outside face of media-as-spectacle. Up close, the strategies and language of the media giants are usually at variance with the public service rhetoric spun by the hypemeisters of their well-oiled PR machines. Paradoxically, media companies project their real val- ues as much by how they operate as by what they say, or even what they produce. To give just one example, some Disney contractors were firing employees just three months short of retirement, others manufactured Pocohantas dolls in Haitian sweatshops at eleven cents an hour (according to a recent National Labor Committee report), while high-level executives pay themselves at obscenely high levels.

Under discussion at the Pierre was how the digital age is here to stay and will make a lot of people a lot of money, thanks to new technologies and the ability of some well-positioned companies to exploit them. Among the players present, represented by senior management, were Viacom, TCI, Cap Cities-ABC, NBC-GE, TBS, Comcast, Disney, Microsoft, MCA, New World and Miramax. The phone companies, aka Telcos, were also there, along with the movie studios and satellite distributors, as well as a large contingent from the cable industry. The speakers buzzed with the latest industry buzz words—orbit slots, augmented services, MMDS, platforms, branding, switched Digital, share-shifting, enjoyment opportunities.

The federal government also sent an emissary to remind these magnates, ever so discreetly, that there is still a public interest to be served in the communications sphere. This reality sandwich was delivered by Reed Hundt, then chairman of the Federal Communications Commission, who repeated over lunch, with good humor and understated authority, the unfashionable notion that in the end the airwaves do belong to the people, whether or not the media barons downing shrimp and salmon noticed or cared.

Most of those here to be briefed have become more powerful in influence and impact than any government representative, but Hundt was not intimidated. He didn't sermonize on how far we have or haven't come since President Kennedy's FCC point person, a Newt from another time, Newton Minow, described television as a "vast wasteland" 30 years earlier. Instead, he packaged his vision of the public interest in self-interest terms. While lambasting so-called laissez-faire extremists, he argued that the FCC is not the industry's enemy but in fact helps rationalize and stabilize their marketplace, saving them, in effect, from each other and themselves. He thus made the case for a strong FCC on a more-free-enterprise-than-thou basis, noting that he has been auctioning off valuable pieces of the broadcast spectrum, instead of just giving it away as had traditionally been the case. (The millions raised by the auctions went to retire the deficit, not to improve communications by, say, supplementing the PBS budget.) At the same time, he stressed that there was a government responsibility to act in the interests of those who can't act for themselves. In keeping with the times, he cleverly quoted a "great Republican," Abraham Lincoln, to hammer home the point.

So here we had Hundt, a high official in a Democratic administration, rationalizing his role in Republican terms, presenting himself as a reluctant regulator and offering his notion of public responsibility and democratic accountability with great timidity, folksy charm, and nonthreatening rhetoric. Hundt's FCC may say it exists to serve the public, but it has also barred the media from witnessing its work. According to an investigation by *Electronic Media*, 86 percent of the commission's votes were taken in secret, outside of public view.

Cable king Ted Turner also spoke, doing some good old boy bragging about the size and scale of his surging corporate portfolio, about his seven networks, movie studios, a retail store, and even a tour of CNN that brings in a million dollars a year: "And it's only a half hour long!" Turner snickered with the glee of one who knows a sucker is born at every commercial break.

Between jokes about how hard it is to sit on uncomfortable chairs all day long, and honest asides about how many of those present were really only there to inflate their stock price, he forecast that the battle over the future of telecommunications in America would soon escalate in intensity. "It will get bloody before it is all over," Turner warned, while giving no hint that he was then actively seeking to merge his company into a bigger entity, sniffing around CBS, meeting with NBC-GE, finally seducing Time Warner in a merger that has already made him richer and even more of a media powerhouse by a quantum leap. No sooner did Turner become Time Warner's vice chairman than the venomous rhetoric began to flow between him and Rupert Murdoch.

A year later, Murdoch keynoted the Big Picture conference. Introduced warmly as "*the* leader of the media industry"—from my perch in the audience, my mind jumped to North Korea, where the late Kim Il Sung was known as the "Great Leader," followed by his son, the "Dear Leader"—the formerly controversial outcast in polite media company began his speech with a Turnerism: "This business of being a buccaneer isn't as easy as it looks."

John Malone's talk was among the most eagerly awaited of the day. Malone is a shadowy figure not familiar to most Americans, yet he's one of the most powerful players in the media business. Reportedly called the "Darth Vader of cable" by Vice President Gore, Malone is president and CEO of Tele-Communications, Inc. (TCI), making him overlord of the most powerful cable television distribution system in the world. In a business known for outsized egos and irrational operators, Malone represents scientific rationality, calculated techno-wizardry, and shrewd business acumen. "John C. Malone," the *New York Times* wrote glowingly, "has been perceived by supporters and critics alike as a man with the vision to see from a mountain top—and the power, when necessary, to move the mountain."

Armed with two Ph.D.s, Malone saw the potential for cable television long before most people, and a full seven years before CNN was hatched. In 1974, he joined the board of the cable industry's association, playing a key role in cable's transformation from a reception-enhancement community antenna TV system to a national service with myriad channels that had partially replaced "free" television service with one that viewers were enticed to pay for directly.

Living in almost Howard Hughes-style seclusion on his estate in the Colorado countryside, Dr. M. is an industry loner and family man who jets home directly after his speeches. He has called himself a "billionaire flunky" to downplay his power, but his speech details TCI's evolution into a media monster with four discrete mega units, all largely self-financed and unleveraged. His programming company, Liberty Media, alone has $6 billion invested in sixty-eight different cable networks, including CNN, Discovery, Pat Robertson's Family Channel, the Home Shopping Network, and TNT.

Malone talks hardware, wires under the ground. The future, he says, is "embedded in technologies." In a talk laced with techno-babble, he projects timetables for the "deployment" of new delivery systems, once, that is, they are joined at the hip with savvy marketing, slick promotion, and good old American snakeoil salesmanship.

Malone is careful not to confuse content with conduit, focusing only on delivery systems, as if it were obvious that the range of what we will have to watch is a given, and that the values embedded in the delivery systems are neutral.

Clearly, delivery systems are in fact anything but neutral, because it is the gatekeepers at the top, people like Malone, who decide which services to offer, and which to bag.

In the Q&A that follows, no one asks him about the implications of this enormous concentration of power in one man's hands or its social consequences. Nor does anyone challenge TCI's right to continually hike cable rates, something that has infuriated consumers. It is almost as if its assumed that he has the right to rule, in the way that kings of an earlier era justified their status by invoking a divine intent.

I debate with myself whether or not to challenge Malone from the floor. I start formulating a question but am too slow off the mark. What to ask? How come we have conservative channels but no liberal ones, business channels but no labor ones? Why is the range of reporting and documentaries so narrow? I assume such questions will not get a very receptive hearing because these people honestly believe, or so they tell themselves and each other, that they are merely satisfying demand. Of course, *they* stimulate the demand they satisfy, but that's another matter.

Malone is given an ovation. When his talk ends, he is surrounded by reporters, almost all of them on the business beat. I slip into the circle and shoot from the hip, asking him about a lack of diversity in programming. He looks at me like I am a fly from another galaxy. "What lack of diversity?" he asks.

I tell him about the '90s Channel, a liberal programming service that had won time slots on a handful of TCI's cable outlets, but was at that point being dumped. '90's Channel head John Schwartz had complained that TCI would neither renew their contract nor add them to a cable tier it was setting aside for political channels.

Malone's response: "The '90s? I have never heard of it."

The channel's complaints about TCI had been reported widely, even in *Variety*. They had written to him persistently. But he claimed not to have heard of it.

"As costs come down," he assures me, "new channels will emerge—that is, if the public wants to watch them."

I ask a smirking Mr. Malone about public television. Is he worried about its demise? Again he stares past me.

"What demise? I don't think there will be one," he says with a sneer, while reminding me that his programming company has just made a multimillion dollar deal to acquire shows from the *News-Hour* production unit, one of PBS's crown jewels, long subsidized by public funds.

End of discussion. No other reporter picks up my line of questioning. It is back to financial scenarios.

A month later, a TCI programmer told a trade journal that they just couldn't find any liberal channels to carry. A week after that, TCI announced the first of its self-produced public affairs shows, called *Damn Right*, an openly and proudly conservative program. No similar liberal show was announced. The '90s Channel was finally forced off the air when it could not come up with the $250,000 monthly payment that TCI demanded as the price of carriage.

TCI's political leanings have been widely written about. The company took a 49 percent stake in the Faith and Values Channel, which was originally set up, as Vision, to be mainstream religion's answer to the right-wing Christian broadcasting channels. But along with TCI's investment came more and more fundamentalist programming. In late 1996, Faith and Values changed its name to Odyssey, dumped Hilary Maddux, the executive who had acquired *Rights & Wrongs* and brought in a new management team.

Malone would soon be criticized by none other than Brian Lamb who runs C-SPAN, a channel supported by the whole cable industry. In early 1997, Malone had kicked C-SPAN or C-SPAN 2 off of eleven cable systems and reduced its airtime in 53 others, affecting 2.5 million homes, according to a former ABC colleague Jerry Landay, who saw the decision as motivated by Malone's need for cash. "Murdoch loaned $200 million to help Malone out of his hole. With it goes a five year option to buy a 20 percent interest in Fox News." And what about Congress, which sees C-SPAN as one of the few civic resources on TV. "Members of Congress have some thinking to do," Landay commented in the *Christian Science Monitor.* "They cherish being seen on C-SPAN, but their pro-monopoly media policies helped derail it."

Malone's conservative leanings are well known. But what he's really known as is the vision man, who was supposed to make the miracle of an integrated electronic highway work. His most famous prediction was that there would be five hundred channels, accessed through digital TV set-top boxes that would also deliver telephone and Internet connections.

Only it never happened. And by the end of 1996, TCI stock was in the toilet, and the company was in retreat, retrenching and downsizing. In a New Year's interview with the *Wall Street Journal*, Malone did a mea culpa: "We were just chasing too many rabbits. The company got overly ambitious about the things it could do simultaneously."

Earlier in the year, TCI's founder and the company's biggest shareholder, Bob J. Magness, died and Malone immediately made a play to take control in a stock deal so bizarre and complex that *New York Times* business writer Geraldine Fabrikant described the financial community's reaction as incredulous: "At first the pros were left scratching their heads. One Wall Street analyst, who insisted on anonymity, said he had to read the company's release three times before he understood what was going on." The impact of the con-voluted maneuver—too complex to summarize—was that Malone ended up with even more power, and in 1998, Malone cashed in, merging TCI into AT&T in a deal valued at nearly $70 billion.

Malone's disappointing performance was matched by other media business geniuses. After Murdoch bought Ronald Perelman's unprofitable New World Communications, his share price went down by $3. Investors in Time Warner found that their shares fell 2 percent after that heavily leveraged company bought out Turner Communications. Viacom went from $47 a share in January 1996 to $36 by year's end. Opined business writer Christopher Byron on MSNBC, "For investors in those companies, there was nothing to say but 'Sorry, you'd have been better off putting your money into treasury bills.'"

To pay for all this, the public that many of these companies serve is taxed with higher entertainment expenses, including ever-esca-lating cable costs.

Interestingly, as the companies delivering the news have become part of larger entertainment-dominated companies, the programming mix has changed. Resources allocated for news and documentaries have been trimmed back, infotainment oriented syndicated shows have become more widespread.

At the same time, the one type of news that media executives can relate to—business news—receives an increasing share of the dwindling resources of news divisions. More and more time is focused on reaching a wealthy and relatively small segment of the audience. Suddenly there was CNBC, Bloomberg, and then CNN-FN—market reports for elite classes, dumbed-down news for the masses.

Is this anything other than one more example of how the media ruling class reports on itself for itself? What has disappeared is labor news. Never a well-covered subject, it soon became a nonsubject. There are no labor channels. "We have Dow Jones industrial aver-ages every night," noted radio commentator Saul Landau. "Why not a daily Dow Jones roundup on industrial accidents, which affect many more Americans?"

Malone could, of course, finance a liberal channel if he wanted to. A proposal for one has been on his desk for years. He does help create channels as well as distribute them, like the Discovery channel, on whose board he sits.

At the Big Picture conference, *Variety* distributed a special supplement, paid for by Discovery, boasting of its ten years "exploring your world." The Channel's ex-programming chief Greg Moyer explained how their documentaries consciously avoid controversy and current affairs, dwelling instead on international sightseeing, archeology and similarly safe subjects. Asked why the uprising in Tiananmen Square was not covered in a recent Discovery special on Chinese history, he responds that Tiananmen Square was merely an "outburst," not worthy of inclusion.

"It's hard to do a film about human rights abuses in Tibet," he added when queried about another China-related issue also absent from Discovery programming. A film on Tibet would be too much of a "challenge to market" (read: find sponsors for), according to Discovery's top programmer. "You can imagine," he says, "there are different ways people view issues in areas like the Middle East and Asia, and we have to be broadly sensitive to those differences" (read: we don't want to upset ruling elites). *Rights & Wrongs*, meanwhile, ran excerpts from one moving documentary on Tibet, *Satya*, by Ellen Bruno, which played at the Sundance Film Festival. PBS aired that one. In the summer of 1996, I filmed the Dalai Lama's visit to South Africa but it is unlikely to ever appear on Discovery. (A year later, the issue of Tibet would ripple over Hollywood after Disney decided to go ahead with the release of Martin Scorsese's film on the life of Tibet's Dalai Lama, risking the economic consequences of offending China. The *Los Angeles Times* later asked Scorsese how he felt about Disney justifying its support on contractual terms rather than on principle. "Do we want to make more money or stand for human rights?" he replied. "America has to be on the side of the underdog and corporations need to know that. Though I'm not a crusader we have to keep them on a straight path. Otherwise an artist won't be able to say anything for fear of stepping on so many toes." Reportedly, Universal Pictures had earlier turned the film down for fear of economic consequences on its dealings with China.)

To be fair, the Discovery Channel does run occasional issue-oriented documentaries, mostly produced in England, such as Brian Lapping's compelling look at the breakup of Yugoslavia. (Its scope also revealed, by comparison, how poorly most American TV news handled the complexities of the Balkan wars.) It aired an excellent series on the CIA and *Harlem Diaries*, but Discovery has yet to discover the UN's Universal Declaration of Human Rights, which upholds human dignity equally for all people in all lands. The channel rejected Globalvision's human rights series *Rights & Wrongs* three years running.

At the BBC, producer Nick Fraser has been the liaison with Discovery. He told Williams Rossa Cole that Discovery has gradually backed away from regularly airing Yugoslavia-type programs. "Every year they make one or two films...but they're drifting away from that. They don't like to take risks, they don't like to offend powerful pressure groups. It just causes nuisance. It causes cancellation. And it's just bad news. You have to ask whether America actually produces an adequate system of program innovation. I don't think it does." In 1997, Discovery announced a cable channel devoted exclusively to shows on animals.

Discovery is not alone in being soft on human rights. When Rupert Murdoch keynoted the next year's Big Picture conference, he only ducked one questioner, the one who asked about the state of his relationship with Communist China, where he had removed the BBC from his STAR TV satellite because of Beijing's complaints about the BBC's human rights reporting.

"No, I won't talk about that," he snapped. "I may get into trouble."

This issue may yet surface at NBC because its parent company, General Electric, has made a lucrative deal to supply power generators for a massive Chinese dam project that international environmental groups and communities in China oppose. One NBC executive told me off the record that that deal, and the network's satellite presence over China, may be why NBC news isn't aggressive in reporting on human rights in China. During the Olympics, NBC apologized to China after one of its sportscasters referred to human rights concerns. "We didn't intend to hurt their feelings," an executive explained.

"Since when does a network have to apologize for reporting the truth?" asked a trade journal.

The *Columbia Journalism Review* responded: "The answer: Ever since news departments have become smaller and smaller potatoes in an ever larger mulligan stew of corporate expansionism."

In the Big Picture world, all talk of alternatives revolves not around content but around new technologies, or new media. Interactivity is the buzzword, promising today, as cable did years ago, a cornucopia of paths to enlightenment. So far there is no consensus on quite how this brave new world will make money for the big companies, but they are gobbling it up anyway. The software-driven media industry is especially thrilled about it, because it represents a potential profit center.

One of the most fascinating participants in the Big Picture conference was Howard Stringer, the Welsh-born newsman turned CBS news chief, then CBS president, who left the world of old media for the promising frontier of the new. When he first appeared at the Big Picture conference in 1995 he had just bailed out of Black Rock. Stringer said he was "so psyched" to be away from the network world. "It's great to be free," he told the *New Yorker*. Freedom in this context usually means the freedom to make money, although Stringer actually offered a more idealistic vision, arguing that "interactivity...may be the magic that brings us together, crossing national boundaries faster than light—the social glue in the global village."

Stringer's magic was not long lasting. Phone company money and the backstage maneuverings of Creative Artists Agency's then chief Michael Ovitz got him off the ground. But then Ovitz left for Disney; and then PacTel, the telephone company that financed Stringer's Tele-TV venture, merged into SBC, another former Baby Bell. Stringer showed up at the 1996 meeting on the morning of that merger, assuring his colleagues that the new entity would stand by him, if only because they had invested at least half-a-billion dollars. By year's end, he had a rude awakening. The phone companies behind Tele-TV decided to write their losses off and pull the plug. Stringer was soon out of a job but with the traditional multimillion-dollar settlement. An executive at the company would only say about the $500 million loss, "Maybe we were too aggressive too early." In 1997, Stringer accepted a top post with Sony's U.S. operations.

One of the most articulate and self-assured of the Big Picture regulars was Michael Fuchs. In 1995, as head of HBO, he was rumored to be a possible replacement for Time Warner chief Gerald Levin. Celebrated as a *wunderkind*, Fuchs had been described in the *New York Observer* as the "tough, strong-willed, self-aggrandizing executive who has built HBO into Time Warner's most profitable division from practically nothing."

Just a month after his appearance at the Big Picture conference, his corporate duties were expanded to include overseeing the billion-dollar Time Warner music division. As he rose, he moved rapidly to consolidate control by imposing the top-down chain of command structure, so common in TV, to the music business, which is usually far more decentralized and peopled with more idiosyncratic types. As the music men began grumbling about his authoritarian reorganization, Fuchs summarily fired senior record business veteran Doug Morris, for allegedly destabilizing the company. (Destabilization is a term generally used to refer to countries—but in the media world, a company of Time Warner's size *is* in effect a country.) Fuchs played according to blood sports rules—he promised Morris in writing, via fax, that he would be promoted to an even more influential job. When Morris showed up to discuss this new post, he was handed a press release announcing his own termination. Fuchs' stated reason: he "changed his mind."

The firing was orchestrated with the support of high-priced PR specialists, although the bloodletting exercise may have been flawed by Fuchs's allegedly forgetting to invoke the proper contract language and advise Morris that he was being fired "for cause." When those two words were not uttered, Morris sued, demanding $50 million in damages, with a claim that his contract was violated. (Several other Warner music executives who had been dismissed earlier received payoffs of the same or similar extraordinary amounts.) Morris was quickly named to a senior post at competing MCA-Universal's music company, just acquired by the Canadian billionaire Edward Bronfman, the Seagrams liquor king and a longtime media dabbler.

I met Doug Morris once when we asked his company to distribute my documentary on Nelson Mandela's triumphant 1990 visit to the United States. Morris, then heading up Atlantic Records, which made millions on black music, took about thirty seconds before he agreed with enthusiasm to buy the film. He gave us enough money to complete *Mandela in America*. Part of his motivation may have been to offset flak the label was getting from an explicit, X-rated rap video by 2 Live Crew. But no matter, he cared enough to make the Mandela video possible.

In contrast, a few months earlier, just a week or two before Mandela arrived to a hero's welcome from millions of New Yorkers, Michael Fuchs's HBO turned down our proposal to make that same film for HBO. One executive actually asked me: "Does Mandela speak English?" Another complimented me on my passions, then showed me a tape exhibiting hers—the history of sex.

In late November 1995, what went around for Michael Fuchs came around. First, his press glow began to cool. The *Los Angeles Times* referred to him as sporting a "perpetual sneer and napoleonic strut." Rumors were leaked that he was after Levin's job. When he went to see his boss to clear the air, karma struck: He got the very same treatment he had dished out to Doug Morris, complete with a press release announcing his demise. Levin had earlier explained to the *New Yorker's* Ken Auletta that executives are not necessarily fired for incompetence but for other factors. "Many of these conflicts involve a CEO's comfort factor," he told him. "It's not always black and white when someone should be fired. Its judgmental. The most important thing is the feeling of a relationship."

That relationship was over, the thrill was gone. So Fuchs was suddenly dumped without warning, albeit with another reported multimillion-dollar handshake.

He showed up at the 1996 Big Picture meeting sans title or corporate affiliation. When asked if the mergers would threaten creativity, a chastened Fuchs scoffed, "This is about profits, not creativity."

Rutgers University Professor Benjamin Barber wisely put these corporate games in perspective: "A year from now the mergers and alliances will have again shifted, and some successful owners will be some other corporation's prey. The players will not have changed, however, only the line score on their current game. There will still be a great many interlocking corporate structures shifting precariously on uncertain turf."

As I watched the executives preen and posture, I realized that my big picture and theirs are at opposite ends of the spectrum. The blend of news and show business that characterizes conferences like these do not make for searching discussions. In this vaunted marketplace of ideas, the only idea is the marketplace—and how to dominate it.

I do not doubt that these executives do have a lot to teach us about how to reach people and hold their interest. Marketing and generating attention is one thing they do well. And I would like to learn their techniques. But my question remains: Is there an alternative to domination by the market and its values?

Of course there is, but it would require a sea change in think-ing. In America, the very idea of using publicly owned airwaves to broadcast in the public interest has been under attack for decades. Privatization is our ruling ideology in part because privately owned media restricts serious discussion of how it might be different. They do so less to serve abstract ideology than concrete interests, but the deeper effect is to undermine the very idea of a public interest.

"The media lens *at* which we look is also the common lens *through* which we look," wrote Barber. "In examining the meaning of public media we inevitably confront the question of the mean-ing of the public. If today democracy is in trouble in America, it is in part because public trust is in decline, public goods are increas-ingly subordinated to private interests, public citizens have become private consumers and the very idea of what it means to be a pub-lic has come under suspicion."

I am certainly not enamored of most noncommercial TV sys-tems, especially state-run systems overseas or the Washington-based public television bureaucracy in our country. Yet the BBC and Chan-nel 4 in London, for all of their many flaws, do offer one model of a successful and competitive public service enterprise, indepen-dently operated, insulated from most government intervention and with a large market share. The key point is that the very idea of "the public" and the public interest has to be fought for and preserved.

At bottom, their big picture, the one presented year after year by a cast of top executives at the Big Picture conference, isn't that big. "Most media executives operate in the valley," investment banker Ivan Lustig, the Schroder Wertheim executive in charge of the conference told me. "And here's a chance for them to hear from people who are on the mountain tops and can tell them what's on the other side of the peak." His partner in the venture, Peter Bart, editor of *Variety*, took a slightly more critical view after the 1996 meeting. "Is the Big Picture too rosy?" he asked in his weekly column, in which he regretted the conference's overem-phasis on optimism and an underappreciation of candor and plain old humanity. He chided the speakers for referring to content, without, well, content.

What he didn't say was what a parochial American picture these summits project. While panelists speak endlessly about conquering the world's markets, no one from the markets "out there" is allowed in to talk about what the inundation of American product has meant for their cultures, media businesses, or social values. (In 1997, British TV executives were invited to offer their perspective.) When media executives from more than one hundred countries gathered later in the year at the UN's World Television Forum, few American moguls showed up. Ted Turner came to give a speech, but did not stick around for much of the discussion.

On the same evening as the Big Picture conference, a very different type of get-together took place uptown on the Columbia University campus, in the World Room of the university's School of Journalism. The room is named for a great American newspaper of another era, the *World*, famous for its attacks on power and corruption. Its editor was Joseph Pulitzer, and it is in his name that the top prizes for journalism are given each year in the World Room.

This night the awards being given were considered the Alternative Pulitzers, ten plaques to ten honorees selected by Sonoma State University's Project Censored, for stories that were ignored, marginalized, or suppressed during the previous year. Each of the winning investigative journalists at the ceremony came forward to be recognized, stopping before a bronze bust of a distinguished editor, Herbert Bayard Swope, who lost Pulitzer's prized paper to merger manipulations in the second decade of the twentieth century, a time when fierce competition from irresponsible tabloids undermined the "quality" press, a scenario with parallels to our own times.

The system that celebrated itself at the Big Picture conference was described in different terms at the uptown anti-censorship soiree. Instead of the dealmakers, the reporters themselves spoke—about why their stories are important and how they were ignored.

Project Censored's annual book-length report, *Censored*, is subtitled "The news that didn't make the news."

Admission to the uptown event was just a few bucks—no catered meals, no hotel amenities. Globalvision was the only press covering the event. The folks who give out these awards have been releasing their well-researched list each year for the past twenty-one years and do get some coverage, but mostly on radio and in the alternative press. "Thus, the story about these buried stories is also buried," Mark Lowenthal, the project's associate director, told me. "The exclusion is complete."

The specific stories offered up by Project Censored are important in themselves, but so is the deeper criticism they make about a junk news culture where coverage of the O. J. Simpson case overwhelmed virtually every other story for two years. *Censored 1995* invoked Oscar Wilde's comment that "modern journalism...justifies its own existence by the great Darwinian principle of the survival of the vulgarest."

Censored led with an introduction by one of our country's best-selling commercial writers, Michael Crichton, author of *Jurassic Park* among other bestsellers: "I want to focus on another dinosaur," he writes, "one that may be on the road to extinction. I am referring to the American media. And I use the term extinction literally. To my mind, it is likely that what we now understand as the mass media will be gone within the next ten years. Vanished without a trace."

Not a prophecy that Dr. Malone will be "deploying" any time soon. The studios won't be making movies about it either. As Crichton quips, "A generation ago, Paddy Chayefsky's *Network* looked like an outrageous farce. Today *Network* looks like a documentary."

Chayefsky's real rebels were America's TV viewers, opening their windows and screaming into the streets that they were "mad as hell and not going to take it anymore." These days, most media rebels talk among themselves, at Columbia University and other campuses, and for the most part they are not heard. Only a few of their investigations are aimed at exposing media practices.

The public has a right to know how the mass media, especially TV, influence so many of our opinions, while remaining, despite its omnipresence, essentially institutionally invisible and insulated from effective challenge. It may be easier to inspect top-secret nuclear weapons plants in North Korea than have an impact on the subtle and not-so-subtle forces that control America's information flow. Yet such an inspection is needed—and hopefully the work of Project Censored and similar-minded activists can pave the way for those who will one day mount an effective challenge to the Big Picture boys.

A year later, in 1996, Project Censored moved its annual ceremony further downtown, to the Society for Ethical Culture hall, around the corner from ABC news (which sent no reporters to cover it). The relocation from a school to a church may be symbolic, suggesting that the crisis of journalism had become dire. A larger crowd showed up for the twentieth anniversary ceremony, and recognition that shifts in the media industry may pose the biggest threat to free expression. Their number one censored story of the year was the impact that the telecommunications "reform" act was having on "shutting down the marketplace of ideas." Ralph Nader and a colleague were cited for sounding the alarm about the consequences of unrestrained media concentration. Their story called the major media's lack of coverage of the issue "galling." The *Columbia Journalism Review* seconded this opinion, reporting that "virtually all the coverage of this unprecedented deluge of consolidations appeared as business news, and thus flew under the radar of most Americans."

Significantly, *Censored 1996* was introduced not by Noam Chomsky or any media critic, but by one of America's most respected media legends: Walter Cronkite. Years ago, it was said that when Cronkite dissented from the Vietnam war, public opinion followed. Today Cronkite is speaking out about the industry that turned him into an institution. "It seems to me that we have the right to demand a little courage on the part of those in the seats of power—the presidents and publishers and CEOs," he wrote in what amounted to a continuation of the book's introduction, published in the *Nation*'s special issue on the media, "a special courage to face their stockholders and impress upon them the responsibility that goes with their stewardship of our free press, the basic foundation of our democracy."

Cronkite is still hoping for change from above, but it's a start. What's needed are other forces to start mobilizing from below.

CHAPTER 13

I, RUPERT

*I*n November 1996, I watched Ted Turner rise to speak to a World Television Forum at the United Nations. He was a man on fire. One Arab delegate from the Middle East compared him to a Bible-thumping preacher (I wondered what he knew about Baptist tradition). He told media executives from all over the world that "there is a new group coming, led by that no-good SOB Rupert Murdoch. They want to control the world. They want to control the television world. We have got to do everything we can to stop them."

Months earlier, Turner had compared Murdoch to Hitler, apologized, then said it again. He called him a scumbag and vowed to squish him like a bug. When asked, in that UN forum dedicated to peacemaking, if peace between these two media giants would ever be possible, Turner shook his head, asserting that it's "a battle between good and evil."

It is rare to see media heavyweights go at each other in such a personal way. Michael Tracy, a mass media researcher at the University of Colorado, characterized Murdoch and Turner as "Masters of the Universe" who "have constructed a debate about the future of communications which...revolves entirely around the concept of the market," with two possible models: "a circus model," about the pleasures of simple entertainment, and "a civic model," which doesn't exclude entertainment but which also attempts to provide responsible broadcasting priorities. The latter becomes, according to Tracy, "more difficult by the day." But he also suggests that Murdoch and Turner have many goals in common, among them the belief in privatization, personal enrichment, and empire. Fight each other all they want, they are two sides of the same coin.

I agree, but I also think Murdoch is a special case.

The first time I met him was at the Harvard University faculty club in 1978, where he was being wooed by the Nieman Foundation in Journalism as a potential benefactor. After his post-luncheon talk, I asked him about a series of vicious and false smears that had appeared in his *New York Post* about a fellow Aussie, Wilfred Burchett, a journalist who was the first to report the atomic bombing of Hiroshima and who covered the Vietnam War from the Vietnamese side, winning awards and later a libel action against a Murdoch property. Rupert promised me publicly that he would personally investigate the matter and correct any false reporting. Two days later, when another hatchet job on Burchett appeared, I wrote to Murdoch to remind him of his promise. There was no response.

When I was at ABC News, I covered Rupert's shameful purchase and promotion of the "Hitler diaries," which were quickly unmasked as fake. It was a story that pandered to the public's endless fascination with evil and Nazis. When the scam was exposed, Murdoch's publications just reformulated their hype. Cynically, they began talking about "the furor over the führer," and the "hoax of the century," actually asking viewers in TV ads to "judge for yourself," the implication being that the diaries may have been real after all. Stories like the Hitler Diaries, whether concocted, distorted or hyped, became the signature of Murdoch-style journalism, which by the mid-'80s was successfully transplanted from print into television on his Fox Network.

Murdoch's best-known tabloid transfusion was *A Current Affair,* the tabloid news show that launched down-market TV with a flood of clones and competitors. A *Current Affair* had a Gresham's law effect on the business, with the schlock driving out the quality programs. A *Current Affair* begat *Inside Edition* and *Hard Copy*. *Entertainment Tonight* inspired *Extra!* and the E! channel, devoted to infotainment. In many cases, Australian editors and executives who had trained at Murdoch's side were brought in to run his enterprises. He once remarked that Australians make great reporters because they know nothing about journalistic ethics (a notion that my Australian colleague Kevin Sanders objects to passionately).

Soon the network shows were dumbing down their journalism and glitzing up their product in imitation of Murdoch's sleaze. The local news, long a parade of fast-paced crime victims and action stories, dumbed down even further. Some of the more slickly packaged shows aired just before or just after the network news. In survey after survey, the public indicated that they no longer always knew the distinction. Often there wasn't one. The key assist in helping the news business go down-market right along with the tabloid shows has come from Mr. Murdoch.

I was in London on the morning of the 1992 British elections. Murdoch's newspaper, the *Sun*, had been bashing the Labor Party throughout the campaign but outdid itself on election day. The *Sun*'s front page carried a picture of Labor candidate Neil Kinnock's face superimposed on a light bulb, with a headline that read: "If Kinnock wins today, will the last person to leave Britain please turn out the lights." On Page 3, which usually carries a snapshot of a topless model to attract male working class readers, there was a photo of an ugly three hundred-pound woman labeled a flab-o-gram, "the shape of things to come under a killjoy Labor government." Murdoch's crude and blatant conservative propaganda, pitched to working class prejudices, helped the Tories hold on to power. (In 1997, with the Conservative Party laggging by 20% in the polls, Murdoch decided to back Labor Party candidate Tony Blair, who went on to win. Blair had flown to Australia in 1994 and 1995 to court Murdoch and reassure him that he wasn't some fire-eating radical. "What reward is Murdoch expecting?" wondered critic Alexander Cockburn. "Blair has abandoned any rash talk about curbing news monopolies and it's thought that a Blair government would not hinder Murdoch's present bid for more broadcasting capacity in Europe.")

In 1993, Globalvision received a call from Murdoch's Fox Network. They knew about our work as investigative reporters and wanted an in-depth special, finished in a hurry—the full story of the Kennedy family and the Mob. Senator Ted Kennedy had earlier forced Murdoch to sell off his interest in the *New York Post* after buying a New York TV station. Kennedy had insisted on upholding the FCC's ban on cross-ownership of media in the same market. Murdoch was, reportedly, furious.

We got the job, but almost immediately there was a call from ex-CBS News President Van Gordon Sauter, then running Fox's fledging news division. We had already received the first check for $125,000. We had hired producers and journalists. They had even given us extra money to hire a lawyer to read their voluminous contract.

"I'm sorry, Dan, but I have been instructed to tell you to *stand down.*" His voice boomed with authority.

"Stand down? What does that mean? We just banked the check. We hired producers. We're in production. What now?"

We were told that the network had decided to postpone the air date. We were told to stop all work, stop everything, until we received further instructions. Hurry up had become hurry up and wait.

But why? Van offered no reasons, merely reminding us that he respected us and assumed we would follow his instructions in a professional manner.

We were, of course, totally freaked out. We had just done a lucrative deal and lost it with one phone call. We would have to fire the reporters we had just hired. Why?

Another New York paper, the *Daily News*, Murdoch's chief competition, helped us solve the mystery. It reported that Rupert Murdoch was now on the verge of repurchasing the New York Post. In order to do so, he needed an FCC waiver. And who still did FCC oversight? Yup, Teddy Kennedy. So a high-profile Fox documentary exposing the Kennedy family at this moment would not be smart business. And no one has ever accused Rupert of not being a smart businessman.

The *Daily News* stayed on the case. One of their reporters heard about our project. He called when he discovered it had been iced. Disclaiming all knowledge, we passed him on to Fox, whose PR spokesman insisted that our film was just being "postponed," not cancelled. He did so, emphatically! It was reassuring to read his words in print.

However, a year later, out of media view, Fox officially invoked the cancellation clause in our contract. They seemed to have lost all interest in documentaries. Incidentally, Rupert got his waiver, bought the Post and was soon back in the Kennedy bashing business. Eventually, we had to send most of the Fox money back. It sure looked good on our balance sheet, but we at least got a kill fee. Rupert's network has not called again. Van Sauter went on to run a PBS station and began giving interviews about why public broadcasting does not need government support.

In 1994, I received another call from Fox, this time from the executive producer of A *Current Affair*, John Terenzio, whom I knew from ABC. He was impressed with the way our company used Hi-8 cameras in South Africa and elsewhere. He wanted us to do some investigative stories for him.

At first that sounded bizarre. We were positioned far on the other end of the TV spectrum from A *Current Affair*. But John said he wanted to broaden the show's appeal, to do more reporting and to arm ordinary citizens with home video cameras so they could expose wrongdoing.

At our first meeting, he was popping antacids as his staff crowded into the office to watch the four P.M. satellite feed. He told me I'd like it because it featured a story, shot in Boston, about twenty-five people who died violently in Charlestown, Massachusetts, where there was so much fear that no one would talk with the police.

With a few minutes to go, one of his editors rushed in and shouted: "They have it too," referring to a promo he had just seen for one of their arch rivals, *Inside Edition* or *Hard Copy*. They were leading with the same story. There were two TVs on the table. John was chewing nervously as we watched both shows side by side.

It was amazing. Both flashed similar pictures in their flashy opens. Both announcers had alarmist voices, and both stories had identical titles: "Hell's Half Acre." The similarity didn't stop with the title. Both stories reported the same facts, featuring interviews with the same cops and the same crime expert from Northeastern University. In fact, the two stories looked almost exactly alike, even incorporating some of the same shots, shot from the same angle. Afterward, John reflected that his story was better because they shot the expert on location, not simply behind a desk like the competition. He also believed that "his" victims were more emotional. "Ours cried," one of the staffers said.

John assured us that he didn't need us to produce tabloid stories or chase Madonna. They knew how to do that. We were there to add substance. We agreed to give it a try, and for six months actually produced some strong segments for *A Current Affair*. A Globalvision producer, Brian Peter Falk, did an excellent job of coming up with compelling and journalistically valid stories on a range of investigative stories, such as boot camp-type prisons for juvenile offenders and even bizarre psycho surgery.

In the middle of our deal, the ratings came out. "The book," as they say, "was flat." Soon our affair would no longer be that current. John would be swept away in the sweeps, another victim of the ratings wars. The Aussies were put back in the saddle, to bring the show back to "basics." We were the first outside producers to go.

Within a year, after several producing teams came and went, Fox put *A Current Affair* out of its misery. The novelty had faded. The program had served its purpose in putting the Fox Network on the map, but had outlived its usefulness. Murdoch was repositioning himself—from the bad boy of broadcasting to a respected network mogul. He had bought his way into the establishment and now had to act the part.

In September 1995, I was in Washington at Jesse Jackson's Rainbow Coalition conference, talking with David Honig, an NAACP lawyer then bringing a complaint before the FCC that he claimed would bring Murdoch down. He told me that his researchers had established that Murdoch had violated U.S. legal restrictions against foreign ownership of a network property. The NAACP's concerns flowed from their argument that allowing foreign companies to buy U.S. TV stations limited opportunities for minorities. Fox, he said, was owned and controlled in Australia by Murdoch's News Corporation. He was certain that the evidence they presented would force the FCC to strip him of his network holdings.

A month later, the staff at the FCC reported that their own investigation of Murdoch's holdings had concluded that the NAACP was right: News Corp. is an Australian entity despite Murdoch having become an American citizen. Moreover, they charged, he had concealed that fact.

Murdoch, the *New York Times* reported, "was combative with reporters in insisting even if the equity was Australian, he, as an American, was in control. 'I am an American. You may not like it but you'd better learn to accept it,' he snapped." Murdoch said he was worried that a full-scale investigation would hold up his bid to build the Fox Network. Honig insisted that the law was the law, and that in sixty years, a prohibition on more than 25 percent foreign ownership had never been waived.

Hundreds of millions of dollars were in the balance. If it could be proven that Murdoch had lied, he would be in deep and costly trouble. The FCC staff was not calling for criminal prosecution, just fining him $500,000 and forcing him to divest the TV stations that he had just acquired in a billion dollar raid on CBS and NBC

In retaliation for that raid, NBC filed a star-spangled complaint of its own with the FCC on the foreign ownership issue. Murdoch's response was to offer a deal: NBC could have access to his newly acquired STAR satellite over Asia if they would drop their complaint. NBC jumped at the opportunity to broaden its international distribution, quickly withdrawing its complaint against Murdoch, in one of the fastest about-faces of the year.

With the FCC still breathing down his neck, Murdoch began a serious lobbying effort. His full court press was ultimately successful. The full Federal Communications Commission rejected the recommendations of its own staff along with the original complaint first filed by the NAACP and seconded by NBC, after Fox put itself in compliance by an adroit bookkeeping ploy. Its accountants simply moved a set of numbers from one column to another, converting a $1.3 billion investment from the Australian-based News Corp. into a "loan." The full FCC, in a decision laced with verbal gymnastics, overruled its own staff experts asserting that while there had been a "technical violation," Murdoch was contributing to the public interest by starting a fourth network that would provide more competition. (The unspoken subtext: Sure it's illegal, but so what?)

This cynical and collusive arrangement between a government agency and a company it should be regulating gave Fox a specious way around the law. In the process, the very idea of what constitutes public service and the public interest was debased. Public interest groups were infuriated by the whole charade. "It's pretty outrageous," commented onetime FCC reformer Nicholas Johnson. Gigi Sohn of the Media Access Project, a public interest watchdog group, stated the obvious: "I don't think the FCC is really willing to take on the tough issues. They just wanted to get it over with." David Honig meanwhile told me that he believes the fix was in—suggesting that the FCC staff recommendation was reversed because of threats from the Republican-dominated Congress to defund the FCC if Murdoch's application was denied.

"Our good name has been restored. We're very happy," was Murdoch's gleeful comment as he became the largest single owner of American TV stations.

Today, Rupert Murdoch runs the world's fourth largest media combine, with a $9 billion revenue flow, which he controls with a 30 percent stake. On his sixty-fifth birthday, London's *Financial Times* observed that he "has no scruples about cheapening and coarsening products if that will boost sales." Murdoch, with the help of in-house "technologists," is working to vertically integrate many branches of his empire—satellites, film, television, cable, newspapers, magazines, book publishing and an online service. For his company, and many others, this is the era of the "polymedia deal," where rights and licenses are negotiated with all ancillary possibilities taken into account, for all media, in perpetuity. To date, these high sounding synergies tend to exist more on paper than in practice and in fact Murdoch has lost millions on failed and failing news media ventures.

While Hollywood executives are famous for being bicoastal, Murdoch is tricontinental, forever hopping and media shopping between the U.S., Europe, and Asia, where his company controls 128 newspapers. His business enterprises salute their own global flag without respect for boundaries or cultures. Using a network of satellites, he has begun importing and exporting programs and personnel at will, often cross-pollinating the worst of all worlds.

Bobbing and weaving between worlds has always been Murdoch's specialty. He is a self-styled patrician who patronizes the poor. His Fox Network built its popularity with many prime-time shows aimed at urban minorities, the very people whose political hopes Murdoch's newspapers oppose and ridicule. He cleverly exploited something the other networks seem to have overlooked: that inner-city residents are among the heaviest TV viewers. With comedy shows like *In Living Color* and a bevy of black sitcoms, Fox won their allegiance, using it to build its own beachhead in broadcasting.

As many of the black producers who broke into the prime-time programming business thanks to support from Fox learned, no loyalty was intended or implied. Many of those shows were abruptly canceled after the network bought the rights to NFL football (with still more money provided by hundreds of international bankers) and reshaped its programming toward the far more numerous Joe sixpacks in the white suburbs. If Murdoch understands anything, it is that demography is destiny.

Murdoch has always worked hard at translating his economic power into political influence, then using that influence to boost his economic interests. His *New York Post*—"an unabashed shill for his Fox Network and syndicated TV shows," in the words of a former *Variety* TV editor—becomes an unapologetic and blatant Republican campaign sheet at election time, with little pretense at nonpartisanship or even conventional journalism. The traditional separation of the editorial pages and the news pages all but disappears once Murdoch picks his candidate. The paper becomes one seamless editorial section. Conservative columnists clog the op-ed page while political factors influence what goes on the cover, slanting the headlines and news stories. This is part of a larger pattern. The paper becomes a political weapon in the way his English and Australian newspapers have been for years.

In the United States, Murdoch has personally intervened in politics, lobbying Congress on his "regulatory problems," meeting with House Speaker Newt Gingrich, among some eighteen other legislators on the Hill. We only know about that encounter because of the flap involving a $4.5 million book advance given Gingrich by Harper-Collins, one of Murdoch's publishing companies. Paying large sums for books from politicians he is cultivating is apparently part of his standard operating procedure. In Britain, HarperCollins shelled out millions to Margaret Thatcher and conservative politician cum novelist Jeffrey Archer. A Murdoch-owned publishing house also paid a million to Deng "Maomao" Rong, the daughter of the late Chinese leader Deng Xiaoping. And once again, the patronage paid off. In the spring of 1995, setting all ideology aside, Murdoch, the conservative capitalist, inked a news exchange deal with the *People's Daily* in Beijing, the official organ of the Chinese Communist Party. In 1998, he ordered his HarperCollins publishing house not to release a book critical of China by Chris Patten, the former British governor-general of Hong Kong.

Publicly, Rupert Murdoch often feigns ignorance of these transactions. But here's one unnamed News Corp. exec, quoted in *Mother Jones* on his boss's legendary attention to detail: "If someone mops a floor at one of Murdoch's enterprises, Rupert knows what's in the bucket." Murdoch's personal oversight of his far-flung empire includes detailed weekly documents, once known as "The Flash," from each of his managers. Reportedly, he studies these documents every weekend, then calls key executives with questions and remonstrations.

One leaked memo some years back from Joe Rabinowitz, the news director of the Murdoch-owned TV station in Washington, to his boss, Rupert crony Les Hinton, described purging liberals from the news staff. It would be a "pleasure in coming months to replace WTTG news staff who are inept, politically correct, shallow and/or unsuitable for the job," wrote Rabinowitz. The news director promised to consult Reed Irvine and Brent Bozell, both of whom run right-wing media institutes, for guidance on the station's personnel practices.

Andrew Neil's *Full Disclosure*, about Murdoch's failed attempt to launch a conservative TV magazine show on Fox starring Neil and celebrity book editor Judith Regan, describes Murdoch as a twentieth-century Sun King. The book reveals Murdoch as obsessed with right-wing politics. "Far more right-wing than is generally thought," is how fellow conservative Neil puts it, although, he adds, Murdoch "will curb his ideology for commercial reasons."

Despite his years in the news business, Murdoch's TV journalism ventures have rarely won distinction. When Murdoch's cable channel F/X got on the air, operating out of a loft studio in Manhattan, they launched a *Nightline*-type issues program hosted by former CBS news anchor Jane Wallace. The show was canceled the day it won a Cable ACE award. "It was a soul-sucking experience," a member of the show's staff now working in network news told me. "They have no interest in journalism. They don't care about it. They can't do it. Only thirty percent of their stations even have news departments. Fox is a joke." Maybe, but who's laughing?

Shortly afterward, in June 1996, Murdoch decided that it was time for Fox affiliates to really get into news, that local news would strengthen his station's bottom line. "There is no excuse for any Fox affiliate to not be in the news business at this stage of our development," he told station managers and executives, pledging his network to supply more news programming. Seventy Fox affiliates, reaching two-thirds of U.S. households were expected to carry news by year's end. One of them, WSVN-TV in Miami, was voted the worst local news outlet in America by the Rocky Mountain Media Watch, which denounced its practice of running nonstop crime stories and dramatizing them with music. Some hotel owners in Miami beach actually canceled their cable TV service for fear that the stations newscasts made tourists fearful to leave their rooms.

This emphasis on local news was intended to tie into Murdoch's latest venture, the new jewel in his corporate crown, a twenty-four-hour Fox News Channel. This was created, he said initially, to compete against CNN, which he branded as "too liberal" (a characterization that no doubt confused ultra-right-winger Pat Buchanan, whose national audience and presidential campaign were built on nightly exposure on CNN's *Crossfire*.)

Murdoch named former Nixon, Reagan and Bush media guru Roger Ailes, who ran the CNBC business channel for NBC, as his news chief. Ailes had never worked in a newsroom, but quickly consolidated control, ousting the former CBS executive who had been in charge. The *Village Voice* uncovered a political litmus test in hiring that produced a staff for the most part certifiably Republican.

At first the experts were dubious at Murdoch's attempt to launch an all-news channel. CNN's Ed Turner scoffed at Murdoch's confessedly political motivation, telling me that it was just a ploy to win support from conservative cable operators and their hardline cable monopolist, TCI's John Malone. Then Murdoch stunned the cable industry by announcing that he would pay up to $11 per subscriber to buy his way onto cable systems, the largest amount ever offered in the history of cable. A deal with Malone quickly followed. Poof! Fox News was now in ten million homes. Soon afterward, TCI announced that it was dropping Lifetime from some of its cable systems to make room for Fox's new offering. (Lifetime is marketed as a woman's channel but is run by men and has been criticized by feminists and women's groups for its lack of pro-woman content.)

Getting on in New York, the world news and advertising hub, was key to Murdoch's plans to legitimize and expand his all-news network. In 16 weeks he carved a complete studio headquarters for Fox News into the News Corp. building on Sixth Avenue. He was soon locked in negotiations with debt-ridden Time Warner to pay as much as a record $25 per subscriber, or upward of $125 million, to be seen in New York.

Murdoch thought he had a deal, but Time Warner turned him down, choosing MSNBC instead. A political brouhaha followed, with lawsuits resulting in an initial decision affirming Time Warner's right to make its own choice. Murdoch blamed Ted Turner, placing ads denouncing cable monopolists and roasting Time Warner in the pages of the *New York Post*—which for a time even dropped TV listings for CNN. Murdoch's investment in direct satellite broadcasting may be in part an act of retaliation. ("Don't let my channels on your cable distribution system? Fine, I'll just crush cable.")

In April 1997, Murdoch was back on Capitol Hill lobbying the Senate Commerce Committee on the importance of liberalizing copyright rules to permit him to expand his SKY satellite TV operation. His plan—calculated to appeal to every broadcaster in the country—was to put every local station up on the bird so anyone could see it—regardless of where they lived. He was able to do so because of a new billion dollar deal with a company called Echostar, which has the satellites ready to go. Critics call it the "Death Star," warn of a monopoly, and pass around pins with the slogan, "Whose sky is it, anyway?" Murdoch's satellite man Preston Padden countered, "The cable guys will be calling Dr. Kevorkian," while the cable industry's spokesman Stephen Effros told Reuters, "He's going to present himself like the savior. Members of Congress will watch and applaud. But we better watch our wallets." (Murdoch's grand plan to crush cable with Echostar collapsed within days of its announcement, however, when that company reportedly refused to be bullied by Murdoch into agreeing to have one of his companies manufacture all the new set top boxes the system would need. As that deal degenerated into billion-dollar law suits, his long time loyal aide Padden quit, ending up weeks later with a top job at ABC. Murdoch finally waved the white flag, making a deal with another satellite company, PrimeStar, which is partly owned by his nemesis, Time Warner. "He's got to sue for peace with the cable guys," one financial analyst explained. Rupert finally cooled his rhetoric and agreed to play second fiddle in a deal he needed. Most likely he didn't want a repeat of the situation seven years earlier, when his overexpansion brought him to the edge of bankruptcy. At that time, if one bank in Pittsburgh had called his note, his News Corp. would have been history.)

In the end, economics won out over ideology, and in late July 1997 Time Warner agreed to provide access to Fox News in exchange for access to some of Murdoch's satellites. New York City, in turn, agreed to hand over one of five channels it controls which was devoted to educational programming, supposedly to keep 900 Fox jobs, which Murdoch had threatened to move, in the city. The result: two rival corporations win and another publically-owned channel is privatized. Power over principles one more time.

Recall that Murdoch is willing to accommodate liberals when he can make money doing it. Years ago, he owned New York's *Village Voice* without censoring it, and today Fox carries *The Simpsons*, created by the talented and sometimes subversive *Voice* contributor Matt Groening. The Fox News channel has even reached out to FAIR, the left-leaning media watch group, inviting its director, Jeff Cohen, to be a regular on a press criticism show, and in 1998, Fox signed on to produce, with *Good Will Hunting's* Matt Damon and Ben Affleck, a ten-hour miniseries based on A *People's History of the United States* by radical historian Howard Zinn.

While Fox News may want to neuter critics who claim the channel is one-sided, much of Fox Network programming remains tilted towards sensationalism. For example its May 1997 sweeps specials include the "World's Scariest Police Chases," "World's Greatest Animal Outtakes," "World's Funniest Kids Outtakes" and "Busted on the Job," footage shot secretly in the workplace. That announcement prompted the Internet columnist Matt Drudge to quip, "Can't wait for 'Busted on the Job 2' [July sweeps?], which I am sure will feature some footage of TV execs sitting around a table admitting that they ran out of ideas years ago."

Murdoch has built strategic alliances in Europe to expand his digital TV empire there, but there is a problem. Europe, unlike America, seems to still have a functioning antitrust mechanism. In June 1996, the *Wall Street Journal* reported that the EC's trustbuster Karen Van Miert pledged to review the MCI/British Telecom deal, calling on Europeans not to be soft on U.S.-led concentration and dominance: "Our main concern is to keep markets open and not allow any players to control it." But the Europeans never had a chance to intervene when British Telecom was outbid by Mississippi-based WorldCom.

As the digital age loomed, public broadcasting in England staked out a claim. "The BBC will help lead the way into the digital age with a programme-led vision," boasted Director-General John Birt in September 1996. By December, *The Guardian* reported that the BBC had already lost the race to Murdoch, leaving Murdoch "in a near monopoly position." Wrote the paper's analyst Henry Porter, "People seem simply not to grasp the implications of digital broadcasting and the speed with which Murdoch is moving to introduce it by satellite. They don't see how much power will accrue to this foreign national.... You find a mixture of trust, ignorance and defeatism that can only result in commercial triumph for Murdoch." For his own part, Murdoch has admitted that "when you are the monopoly supplier, you are inclined to dictate." (Although, even monopolists can't rig markets, and by the summer of '97, Murdoch's satellite digital domain—his SKY TV crown jewel—began to show big losses and cracks, with two top executives jumping ship.)

He recently bid $300 million to buy up sports rights in South Africa; the offer was being taken seriously by cash-starved TV executives there. The Mandela-led African National Congress later issued a statement denouncing any deal that would give Murdoch's channels exclusive access to major sports events. The House of Lords in England similarly repudiated his attempts to privatize the broadcast of leading national sports. Murdoch's strategy here is to view sports as "a battering ram and a lead offering" to further the penetration of his pay TV chain.

There are many factors behind Murdoch's financial success, but one key can be found down under, in Australia, where his family wields great influence. That country has much more elastic corporate accounting rules than the United States. According to the *Wall Street Journal*, those rules enabled him to overvalue his empire's assets and by so doing, attract large amounts of investment capital and loans from several giant international financial institutions to bankroll his heavily leveraged, debt-dependent global aspirations. "Many international operators did the same thing. Murdoch just did it better," explained Peter Chippendale and Suzanne Franks in *Dished*, a study of Murdoch's satellite TV deals in Britain. "In Murdoch's case, the lax Australian accounting rules [were] of particular use in enabling him to revalue his assets." Another book published in 1991 in England, *Murdoch: The Decline of an Empire*, noted that his borrowings "stand [in 1991] at six billion American dollars, roughly $20 for every man, woman and child in the United States, Britain and Australia."

Murdoch's expansive ambitions have always depended on large infusions of capital. At the end of 1990, 146 banks worldwide were holding Murdoch debt, with an annual interest bill in the neighborhood of $800 million. His company has careened between the edge of disaster and fat city. In December 1995, his News America Company decided to float fifty-year bonds—to ensure solvency well into the twenty-first century. But the markets weren't buying. By 1996, Murdoch was cash-rich once again, thanks to a billion-dollar equity deal with MCI and extensive backing from Citicorp, his lead banker and the financial institution that, coincidentally, led all banks in questionable currency transactions, according to the General Accounting Office. Deals like this led Ken Auletta in the *New Yorker* and on PBS's *Frontline* to label Rupert a modern-day pirate.

Since real pirates tend to find one other, it should not be surprising that Murdoch, like Ted Turner, turned for financial advice to Michael Milken, the junk bond king and ex-felon ordered by the SEC to stay away from the security business. Milken has been credited with lining up the original financing for MCI, and it was he who brought MCI and Murdoch together. When MCI sought to merge with British Telecom late in 1996 to form the telecommunications giant Concert, analysts characterized MCI's billion-dollar investment as a virtual subsidy to Murdoch. Was this a case of Milken extracting money owed him from MCI to bail Murdoch out? Whoever knows is not talking. Yet Murdoch understands one of the unwritten laws of international wheeling and dealing: Once you owe large sums of money to banks and financiers, they can't allow you to self-destruct even if your business practices are risky. That is why businesses often fail upward and are rewarded with new loans after the original ones go bust.

I wonder if anyone will ever fully investigate the perplexing financial relationship between these two giants of junk—Milken of phony money and Murdoch of phony content.

In the spring of 1994, Rupert opened Fox Studios for a National Educators awards function that Milken's Family Foundation was underwriting in lavish style. Some three thousand guests came to the reception. As I was told by an onlooker, in the ensuing days Milken was back on his "Monroe," a sophisticated machine designed to do technical calculations on bond deals that he reportedly "plays" with the skill of a musical virtuoso. He helped Murdoch structure convertible debentures that pumped more than $500 million into Revlon heir Ron Perelman's New World Communications, enabling him to raid CBS affiliates and then change their affiliation to Fox. According to the business press, Milken received a cool million for his shrewd advice. He has played a similar role in many media transactions—for companies like TCI, Turner Broadcasting, Cellular One, Viacom, etc.—in which he picked the winners, allocated the acquisition funds, chose the merger partners, and specified key market opportunities. Ted Turner considered his help in the Time-Warner merger worth $50 million. Yet, was he always operating on the up and up?

The SEC investigated Milken's activities to determine whether he profited illegally. Perhaps we will eventually learn just how involved Milken has been in shaping the new media order, as a key financial wizard behind the thrones of moguls like Murdoch, Turner, and Malone? In February 1998, Milken agreed to pay $47 million to settle a suit that charged he violated his parole by advising Murdoch. Milken was allowed to cop a plea without admitting guilt, by forking over a $42 million fee and $5 million in interest. He also agreed to finally get out of the securities business.

In May 1997, Viacom's Sumner Redstone hosted a dinner to benefit the United Jewish Appeal honoring Murdoch as Humanitarian of the Year. Henry Kissinger presented the award. ABC's Roone Arledge, MCA's Edgar Bronfman, and ex CBS boss Laurence Tisch were among the list of sponsors which, according to the *Forward*, "reads like a Who's Who of power in the news and entertainment industry." The asking price for buying the back cover of the "tribute journal" was $150,000. Media columnist Norman Solomon called the tribute an example of "how wealth and power can buy a gloss of moral legitimacy." In saluting Murdoch, the UJA praised his support for Israel over the years. One of his executives called him a "Christian Zionist." Unmentioned were reports that the Israeli police were investigating accusations of wrong-doing in at least one of his ventures there.

Media and human rights groups, some wearing Henry Kissinger masks, protested outside the ceremony, carrying signs that called Murdoch a "moneytarian." They handed out leaflets to the many media guests in black tie which charged "SHAME," but few deigned to take them. An old friend of mine from ABC was there. "I know he's a sleaze," he told me, "but I was told to come." The New York Police showed up in force, threatening arrest if the two dozen dissidents didn't move across noisy Park Avenue to a barricaded spot in which they could barely be seen and certainly not heard. They had sent press releases to every outlet in town but only the #3 wire service, UPI, showed up. Once again, Globalvision had the only camera crew on the scene. Steve Rendell of FAIR commented that not only had their rights to protest been abused, but that the protest itself was not being heard because it wasn't being covered. You can bet it wasn't news on the Fox News Channel.

Remember Marshall McLuhan's warning? "Archimedes said 'Give me a place to stand, and I will move the world.' And I say, 'Let me stand on your eyes and ears and on your other senses, and I will move the world in any pattern or rhythm that I choose.'"

Today one man, Rupert Murdoch, stands on our eyes, ears, and faces more than any other.

CHAPTER 14

THE MERGERS OF JULY
AND THE END OF JOURNALISM

Think of this chapter as being like Web sites on the
Internet—a variety of media adventures. All of these
stories deal with the set and setting of modern journalism in decline. All of them pose questions for
which there is no one right answer. All of them are
linked. Is your mouse ready?
> *Point and click.*

THE GIVEAWAY

It was the Ides of March, 1997. With apologies to Karl M., the old
specter was gone. There was a spectrum haunting America.

It was the digital spectrum—a technology that will allow the
rulers of American broadcasting to compress their electronic signals and multiply the number of channels they own. Virtually
overnight, one channel on TV can split into as many as five. In the
'60s, Che Guevara spoke of creating "One, two, three—many Viet-
nams" as a strategy for challenging American hegemony. Thirty years
later, American broadcasters speak of one, two, three—many MTVs
as a way of expanding their media/cultural power.

The digital revolution will mean enormous change, but its
importance has been ignored outside of a small circle of the

cognoscenti. "Everything will be different" due to digital television, says FCC chairman Reed Hundt. "The change is so extreme that many people have not grasped it."

I wondered why. Could it be that a change that will make everything different isn't getting much coverage? "The tragedy of it all," worried media historian Robert McChesney, "is that most Americans do not have a clue about the great giveaway of public property that is taking place at this very moment."

Broadcast companies who publicly pledge allegiance to the free market have in this instance behind the scenes put out their hands for a boondoggle of a federal subsidy, pressuring the government to turn over the digital spectrum to them, gratis. In essence, a public resource—the airwaves—was to be transferred *forever* into the same private hands that dominated the old spectrum.

Ironically, this same month the left-leaning *Mother Jones* magazine devoted its cover story to extolling responsible capitalism as *the* agency of change, while the right-leaning *Wall Street Journal* carried a front page article estimating the value of the digital spectrum at $20 to $50 billion; it reported that "the government is just days away from handing it over, free of charge—and is asking for nothing in return." The broadcasters will trade in their outdated analog channels for the digital model, but with few, if any, public service requirements tacked on. Think of it as trading in your '72 Dodge Dart for a 1997 Mercedes without it costing you a cent and having the dealer throw in any number of options at his expense to boot. The *Journal* quite correctly called this a "sweet deal" and "welfare for broadcasters." Said Hundt, "I probably should be embarrassed for asking so little in return for the people's property." Of course he should, but Hundt didn't have the power to block the deal. In May 1997, Reed Hundt announced he was stepping down from his FCC post.

April First—April Fool's Day—was the day that the Senate majority leader, Republican Trent Lott, demanded as his D (Deal)

Day in a letter to the FCC. Andrew Schwartzman, who runs the Media Access Project, a Washington, D.C.-based public interest group, told me that if the FCC didn't go along, they risked being defunded. "They won't be able to buy staples if they don't sanction this giveaway," he quipped, pointing to the enormous power of the well-funded broadcasting lobby, the National Association of Broadcasters, headed by Eddie Fritts, who went to college with Lott. As it turned out, the deal went down two days later. The industry's victory did not go unchallenged, and political wrangling over its terms is expected to continue. As the public learns the full extent of the giveaway, more protest is certain

MERGING AND PURGING

July 1995 saw spasms of merging and purging, a midsummer deal-making frenzy that brought with it a qualitative transformation of the mediasphere.

It was the hottest July on record. The heat wave and its consequences were talked about everywhere, especially after five hundred people died in Chicago of weather-related causes, sixty-eight of whom were old and unidentified and dumped in a mass grave, Third World-style.

"What's odd is not the heat," wrote environment writer Bill McKibben in the *Los Angeles Times*. "What's odd is that no one seems to be paying attention to anything but local weather forecasts and air conditioner ads." Environmentalists offered strong evidence linking the extreme weather to the greenhouse effect, but the media largely ignored that connection because the explanation is considered too complex to popularize. The anti-environmentalist lobby's credo was working: "If Dan Rather can't explain it in ten seconds, we win."

For me, the weather throughout July and the first week of August came to symbolize the seismic shifts taking place in the television industry, as two major networks changed hands, a leading newspaper closed, and billion-dollar media deals were commonplace. As it turned out, the most ominous news wasn't what was happening on television but rather what was happening *to* television.

Once upon a time—in 1984 actually—then-FCC chairman Mark Fowler made a comment that has proven as resonant as Eisenhower's military-industrial complex speech a generation earlier. Fowler said: "It is time to move away from thinking about broadcasters as trustees and time to treat them in the way almost everyone else in the society does—that is, as a business. Television is just another appliance. It's a toaster with pictures."

In early July 1995, Gannett bought Multimedia, known for the talk show talents of Phil Donahue, Sally Jessy Raphael and Rush Limbaugh, among others, for $1.7 billion, also adding ten more newspapers to its chain of eighty-two dailies that includes *USA Today*, once dubbed McPaper for its thin editorial content. The *New York Times* noted that reaction to Gannett's major media acquisition was "subdued," whereas in earlier days it would have been seen as a "threat to quality journalism or worse."

"It's a great fit," said one stock analyst. Meanwhile, in Detroit, the labor capital, a protracted strike against newspapers owned by Gannett and Knight-Ridder was being fought. The two companies spent an estimated $56 million in 1995 to break the unions. The strike was still on a year later with minimal coverage in the press, and finally was sputtering to a halt in 1997, virtually crushed by corporate power and insufficient union muscle.

The Knight-Ridder company, publishers of the *Detroit Free Press*, which had been willing to suffer a major loss in circulation revenues and prestige to show the workers who was in charge, was unmoved by criticism. In the first quarter of 1997, it made the largest single purchase of new newspapers in American history, shelling out $1.65 billion for four newspapers acquired by the Walt Disney Company in its merger with CapCities/ABC. At the time of the merger, Disney had vowed it would not sell any assets, but then changed its mind when they realized that the newspaper group could not be profitable enough to meet the company's 20% annual target.

The bombshell of July and the biggest takeover of the year came when ABC, the one network then *not* considered in play, and which itself had been merged into Cap Cities less than a decade earlier for $3.5 billion, was bought by Disney in a whopping $19 billion transaction.

"Disney's values are wonderful," wrote Tom Goldstein, dean of the Columbia Journalism School, "but they are not journalistic values. The notion of news gets pushed further and further down the corporate food chain."

Benjamin Barber, author of *Jihad vs. McWorld*, in *New Perspective Quarterly*, compared "Disneyfication" to "a very shallow but extensive flood that seeps into everything. It doesn't seem deep or disastrous at the time, but then we find that the mud is absolutely everywhere; everything is wet."

CBS got wet next.

After years of cost-cutting, the company's stock value was up but the network's morale, reputation, and ratings were down. Already extraordinarily wealthy, owner Lawrence Tisch became even more so by agreeing to sell what was once considered the Tiffany network to the Westinghouse Electric Company, a defense contractor, operator of nuclear power plants, and manufacturer of household appliances. Westinghouse thus joined its industrial counterpart and competitor General Electric as an owner of a TV Network. Westinghouse CEO Michael Jordan wrote to the CBS work force telling them how much he respected them; at around the same time, he told Wall Street analysts he hoped to cut costs by 20 percent. Many of the people who received those friendly letters began to suspect that they would soon be receiving less friendly pink slips. The CBS logo, the famous eye, went up on Jordan's headquarters wall next to the Westinghouse W. (Put them together and you get Why?)

According to the *Boston Globe*, Westinghouse's interest had "less to do with vision and television's future than its own need to rectify past mistakes and take advantage of some tax laws." It seems that the Pittsburgh-based conglomerate hoped to recoup the billions it had lost in the early '90s in bad loans. As a result of the deal, the company could carry forward a $2.94 billion tax-loss credit that could be applied against CBS earnings for ten years. In other words, it would have to pay no taxes.

The effect of the Westinghouse takeover of CBS on the news was quickly evident, especially in smaller cities. The TV network was already lean, so radio stations were targeted. The *St. Louis Journalism Review* reported the effect on the CBS-owned radio stations KMOX-AM and KLOU-FM in their hometown. "In a visit to the station in late January, Dan Mason, president of Westinghouse's radio division, made it clear that the parent company demanded a much stronger financial performance than did CBS." They wanted a 40 to 50 percent profit—not just the 22 percent the station had been making. "The directive: Double the profits.... The most immediate result was the layoff of ten fulltime staffers."

Said one on-air personality, Kevin Horrigan: "There's really no pride in working for a 'property.' This used to be a special place to work. It's not anymore. KMOX will be KDKA will be WCCO will be KCBS. These are like McDonald's restaurants. A milkshake machine that fits here will fit in Pittsburgh or San Francisco.... We're stretched too damn thin. Who wants to work for a property?" Within a year, operating profits in Westinghouse radio—strengthened by the $3.7 billion acquisition of Infinity Broadcasting—doubled, and cash flow more than tripled. San Francisco's *Mediafile* reported that Westinghouse, now with 79 stations, was projecting a billion dollars in revenue while cutting back on the size of its news departments. Bill Mann of the *San Francisco Examiner* was quoted as saying that original local coverage had shrunk. "The bottom line is that Westinghouse squeezes every dime out of its stations." This may please the shareholders, but what about the listeners?

Also in July, *New York Newsday*, widely considered the best tabloid newspaper in America, was shut down after long discussion of its future, but then with just three days notice, by Mark Willes, the CEO of the parent company, Times Mirror. Willes, a fresh import from General Mills, was quickly dubbed the "cereal killer." He claimed that the scrappy daily was just not profitable enough. Not *un*profitable—just not profitable enough!

A week later, Times Mirror slashed the reporting staff of its flagship paper, the *Los Angeles Times*, closing down widely admired special sections that covered minorities and world affairs, as well as a center that monitored public perceptions of the press. The stock price of Times Mirror, Inc. soon doubled.

Euphoria among shareholders over the rise of the stock price went hand in hand with demoralization among journalists. One *L.A. Times* star reporter, speaking anonymously, said, "People felt that it was no longer a family—it was suddenly an unpleasant place. When they announced that the news hole (an industry term for the space in the paper set aside for news and editorials as opposed to advertising) was being reduced again, nobody asked questions, there was just silence. The silence was the scariest thing of all."

Public television was not immune from the convulsions rocking the media world. One of New York City's two public television stations was sold in the name of privatization. WNYC, owned by the city, was bought by a new media duo, ITT and Dow Jones, for $207 million, nearly four times more than the original asking price. The new owners planned to turn the station—known for diverse, community-oriented, quality programs and once the home of our own series *South Africa Now*—into a superstation to be carried nationwide. So-called highbrow fare was to be replaced by twenty-four hours of sports and business news. (The station was sold again in 1997 because of internal business problems at Dow Jones to Paxon, Communications. a company known for home shopping programs.)

There was often overlap between those who were strident in their demands to destroy PBS and those who championed the interests of the most powerful commercial players. However, the efforts to "zero out" PBS funding were dropped when protests flooded Congress.

Even more ominous were other congressional telecommunications "reform" measures being debated in July, particularly the bill formally known as the Telecommunications Act of 1996. The Republican-dominated Congress worked late into the night to deregulate cable television and local telephone companies in the name of fostering competition. Critics charged that decontrol measures would lead to less competition and more consolidation, hiking consumer bills, and underserving the public interest even further.

The debate on this key measure was conducted in the early hours of the morning. "Here we are in the middle of the night considering the most sweeping rewrite of the communications legislation in the last half century," noted Ohio Congresswoman Marcy Katur. The former chair of the House Telecommunications Committee, Democrat Ed Markey of Massachusetts, said the proposed act "will make Citizen Kane look like an underachiever." After winning some compromises in the Senate version, Markey backed the final bill as did many other Democrats.

At least $11 million was spent lobbying on legislation that promised profitable returns to cable operators and the Baby Bells. "Whichever side wins," said Representative Robert A. Defazio of Oregon, "it will be done in the dark of the night because it involves real money." The *New York Times* buried these concerns at the very bottom of a story on page D-4 in the business section. The report ended with an account of Congresswoman Katur's anguished conclusion on the House floor—"I feel sorry for America tonight"—a sentiment that prompted the reporter to add, "No one took issue with her." Few TV news shows or other newspapers even reported these nocturnal events.

Newsday's TV writer, Marvin Kitman, called the legislation "the biggest giveaway of public assets in history. It makes the Teapot

Dome Scandal of 1921, the giveaway of oil reserves in Wyoming and California, seem like a tempest in a teapot." What troubled him as much as the greed of the communications czars was the lack of public debate. "Nobody sees [anything] wrong with the centralization of the information media. We have come so far around in society that any of us who object to the rape of the public airwaves...must be living in another century."

In *Wired Money*, Common Cause reported that the communications industry, including the telephone, cable, computer and entertainment companies, pumped more than $50 million into political action committees for political candidates as of 1994. The money was just about equally divided among Democratic and Republican politicians. The National Association of Broadcasters and the National Cable Television Association donated over $4 million. Common Cause also noted that South Carolina Senator Ernest Hollings received $329,411, the largest single donation from the industry in that year. He was then the point man in the Senate for the Telecoms bill.

In the year that followed, the industry increased its giving, targeting politicians more effectively, and supplementing their donations with high-priced lobbying firms. The media played along by its lack of coverage. "A somnolent press—print and particularly electronic—has failed ignominiously to report the story," concluded Neil Hickey in the *Columbia Journalism Review*. Oddly, conservatives—like Bob Dole and Senator John McCain, became the most outspoken critics, probably because of the role of the Clinton Administration in backing industry interests. William Safire, the former Nixon advisor turned *New York Times* columnist wrote, "The rip-off is on a scale vaster than dreamed of by yesteryear's robber barons. It's as if each American family is to be taxed $1,000 to enrich the stockholders of Disney, G.E., and Westinghouse." Opinions like his were noted—and ignored.

Months later, when the final measure was debated in the Senate, the telephone companies mounted a TV campaign to mobilize public support for their interests, which opposed those of the cable industry. They wanted to buy advocacy commercials on CNN, but the cable network refused to carry the ads, admitting that "the company has an interest in the bill." So much for the free marketplace of ideas. After the bill passed, there was a new round of cable price hikes. Those hikes helped end the senatorial career of South Dakota's Larry Pressler, who had quarterbacked the Telecoms bill through Congress.

As well-financed armies of lobbyists clashed, a call for more regulation came from a most unlikely corner. Barry Diller, who built the Fox Network for Rupert Murdoch and ended up running the Home Shopping Network, penned an op-ed calling on the FCC to step up its regulation to ensure that the public interest was served. "As a television executive, I know only too well the commercial pressures," he wrote, decrying a lowering of standards and calling for more regulation in the public interest. "The FCC should be instructed to set minimum guidelines for local, educational, and nonentertainment programming," he suggested. Diller blamed the FCC under Reagan for "treating televisions as if they were toasters."

WHO OWNS WHAT

A year later, in July '96, it was déjà vu all over again when Rupert Murdoch gobbled up Revlon king Ron Perelman's New World Communications, picking up ten more TV stations to become, as predicted, the largest single owner of American television outlets. A friend who has just become an employee at one of Rupert's ganglia of enterprises speaks of working in the heart of the evil empire. "And guess what?" he says with an insider's wink. "It's every bit as evil as we thought."

While his American company binged, Murdoch was busy in Europe closing a deal between his British satellite channel and Germany's Leo Kirch to conquer that continent's digital future, a deal with a projected $15 billion payoff within a decade. The July 15 headline in *Variety* summed it up: "Rupe Rewrites Rules for Global TV

Deals." Peter Bart, *Variety*'s editor, joked that Murdoch was doing so many deals at once that there must be more than one of him.

The Associated Press called me on the day of his latest station shopping spree to seek a comment. The reporter said he'd come across a ten-year-old *TV Guide* and compared the range of programming then to what's available today. "There seem to be so many more choices now," he suggested. "Isn't that good?"

"More can be less," was my retort. "More choices, fewer voices."

Benjamin Barber, my favorite expert on this issue, agrees with this assessment: "There is an appearance of diversity that is likely to be illusory in the long run. I think what we are going to see is more messengers and fewer messages."

In Washington, on the very same ninety degree day that Murdoch made his move, the Federal Trade Commission staff concluded its investigation of the $7.5 billion merger between Time Warner and Turner by giving it a green light. John Malone's TCI was dealt a few setbacks in the proposed ruling, which pushed aside a twenty-year, 15 percent sweetheart side deal buried in the fine print that looked like a payoff. The FTC also insisted that at least one other cable news channel be allowed on Time Warner systems so that CNN would not have the monopoly. But that was it. Any hopes I harbored for aggressive anti-trust intervention blocking that mega deal were dashed. That month, Time Warner's stock was at an all-time low.

Throughout the month, the business boosters in Bill Clinton's administration continued to cheer concentration in the name of competition. Their idea of media reform consisted of bullying the networks into providing three hours of children's TV and a commitment to install V-chips in TV sets, ostensibly to give parents more control over what their kids are watching, but really to give the Democrats an "accomplishment" to tout during the campaign. No one really knows what the chip will do, or even if it works. A year later, the business press reported that little of the expected competition in the industry had occurred.

Other bizarre signs flashed in the media skies. NBC's joint cable venture with Microsoft launched in July too. The amalgam, MSNBC, had intimidated its way onto many cable outlets with GE threatening cable operators that other NBC programming might be yanked if space was not made available.

A day or two earlier, NBC's former commentator-in-chief, John Chancellor, died, just shy of his sixty-ninth birthday. In his later years, Chancellor had spoken out against the greed that had begun to more openly define the broadcasting business. "When I went to work at NBC," he recalled, "it had its own symphony orchestra...its own opera company. It was wonderful. It was a big public service organization that just happened to make [money]. That's all changed. All the networks now are owned by people...demanding more profit out of the news divisions. God did not create news divisions, I think, to make profits."

No one in command in commercial television these days is talking about public service or speculating on divine intent. Quite the contrary. MSNBC announced a few days after Chancellor's passing that the outrageous radio DJ Don Imus would get his own morning slot on the new cable news channel. Shock jock Imus, hardly a newsman, worked for Infinity Broadcasting, which a few weeks earlier was bought by Westinghouse, which owns CBS, which had become the nation's largest radio broadcaster.

So as CBS effectively became a supplier to NBC, it became more obvious that all of these entities, supposedly competitors, are much more alike than they are different. When I grew up, competitors competed (when they weren't meeting surreptitiously to fix prices as in the GE scandals of the '50s). Today it seems to be all one big company, regardless of logos.

Six of the largest of these global concerns are American based; but most of these firms have fashioned equity deals and relationships with each other so that their competition for market share takes place within a self-regulated but interconnected web laced with joint ventures and strategic alliances. Here's one example of how it works. Vicaom's Chairman Sumner Redstone told *Business Week* in March 1997 that he had just received a call from Rupert Murdoch. "He suggested 'we stop being perceived as adversaries...he wants to see what we can do together.'" He then discussed his relationship with John Malone, the powerful head of TCI, the country's largest cable company. "I do not believe John Malone would cross Viacom," he says. "I just don't believe it." After meeting with Redstone, Malone reversed a decision to drop certain Viacom channels from his cable systems.

Historian Robert McChesney, who has documented these corporate relationships, compares them to mafia families who often cooperate as much as they fight with each other. This new mafia does not need kneecap-breaking hoodlums to act as enforcers. They rely on government agencies and international organzations with coercive authority, bodies like the FCC and FTC, WTO and ITO, World Bank and IMF. All promote policies designed to assist privatization, defend international copyright laws, and fund agencies that police the market against the pirating of the movies, CDs, computer software, and even the broadcast spectrum. As a cost of doing business, these companies sprinkle generous political contributions and favors to insure influence and a supportive business environment.

Ex-Federal Communications Chairman Reed Hundt himself counsels that the market needs rules, regulations, economic guidelines, and restraints lest the media warriors kill each other off. He also complains that the public is being kept in the dark about the machinations of the media compaines. Speaking to the 1997 *Big Picture* conference of bankers and media executives, Hundt noted that news about the giveaway for free of the digital TV spectrum, which will revolutionize American television, was not even being reported on television. "Television journalism," he quipped sarcastically and with contempt. "I love that term...."

Already, on the local level, media monopolies are well-established. The trend toward one newspaper towns, which has been going on for decades, has extended into radio and cable. Ben Bagdikian reports that 90 percent of some eleven thousand local cable systems already operate as monopolies in their communities. In turn, about two-thirds of them are controlled, in effect, by just two companies, TCI and Time Warner. The only hope of breaking this monopoly, in the absence of government action, is competition from direct broadcast satellite systems that can offer even more channels. Twenty million homes will have the dish-based systems by the year 2000. Murdoch hopes to become the top satellite broadcaster.

The impact this concentration has on available news and information is what I find so upsetting. The news world as I knew it is shrinking, consolidating, reconfiguring, and disappearing before my eyes. As issues become more complex, there seems to be a diminished capacity and commitment by media companies to devote ample resources to report and explain them. Was it because many large newspapers also own TV stations and stood to profit in this deregulated, blatantly pro-business environment?

While scholars were writing books about the "post journalism era," the signs of journalism's attrition were everywhere, as was the hard truth of the axiom repeated by J. Max Robins in the *Media Studies Journal*. "Understanding who owns what and who is allied with whom gives you a guide to what gets covered and why."

"They put on news and programming that does not harm their corporate interests," Ben Bagdikian told Kevin Sanders of the *War and Peace Report*. "You put out the cheapest possible product at the highest possible price." This is the bottom line's bottom line.

As this wave of media concentration mounted, one question was rarely considered: Who pays for takeovers? As some companies go deeper into debt to finance expensive acquisitions, they face more pressure to cut staff and cut corners. To pay the debt service, some companies are chopped up and divisions sold off. Staff cutbacks, work speedups, and attacks on unions follow. (Overall, 1 out of 3 job losses in general was blamed on corporate mergers, according to Department of Labor statistics.) Tighter budgets also translate into less money for investigative journalism. Programmers become more risk-averse as bottom-line pressures increase.

Programmers and news managers rarely admit that their parent companies influence program content. And it is true that when they do, their influence tends to be subtle because blatant interference in news decisions usually leaks and leads to bad publicity.

When I spoke with correspondents at 20/20, all told me that nothing has changed in the Disney era except the stationery. But that was during the initial, post-takeover period, when Disney was still consolidating its control. Wisely, Disney has maintained a hands-off policy toward the news division, but when ABC announced its "March on Drugs" in 1997, a month-long, on-air campaign to encourage parents to talk to their children about drugs, critics commented that such a high-profile, pro-family PR campaign was totally consistent with Disney marketing strategies aimed at children and their parents.

Larger worries remain and many questions are still unanswered, such as this one posed by the *Columbia Journalism Review:* "How much news will be suppressed and self-censored by news executives reluctant to invoke the wrath (or even the raised eyebrows) of their corporate overseers who don't want eager-beaver news people mucking around in the dealings of the parent company?"

The Consumer Federation of America and the Center for Media Education's detailed December 1995 report, *Economic Concentration and Diversity in the Broadcasting Media*, noted that television "as a single source of news has surpassed the total mentions of newspapers or other sources as a source of news." The authors concluded: "An increase in market power will result in less diversity and greater concentration of political control over the media.... There is sub-

stantial evidence that economic concentration and reliance on market forces results in reduced news, public interest and cultural programming."

So in the end, it's not just media workers who lose—consumers
pay more, viewers and listeners see and hear less. The world's greatest democratic experiment suffers as its public life contracts and
becomes an appendage to special interests.

Herbert Schiller puts these media trends in a larger context:
"The American economy is now hostage to a relatively small number of private companies, with interlocking connections that set the
national agenda. This power is particularly characteristic of the communication and information sector, where the national cultural-
media agenda is provided by a very small and declining number of
integrated private combines. This development has deeply eroded
free individual expression, a vital element of a democratic society."

These developments affected the quality of TV journalism well
before the current wave of media concentration. Before their merger,
CBS and Westinghouse teamed up to create a harbinger of what
was to come, a "lite news" show for midday airing called *Day &
Date*. The program, run by a former executive producer of the CBS
Evening News, quickly took a tabloid turn. A friend producing there
told me that her suggestions for more substantive stories were met
with a simple phrase: "Not for us." "Not for us" has become a
mantra for excluding journalism with substance. The public apparently took up the mantra too: The show was canceled because of
low viewership in May 1996.

In this environment, most commitment to quality and social
responsibility gives way to yet more lowest-common-denominator
programming. The shareholders' interests are put ahead of the public's. Thus, the fiscal responsibility so welcomed on Wall Street
affects what viewers see on Main Street.

In the aftermath of their victory in wresting the digital spectrum,
the broadcast lobby lashed out at "the governing elite" in such a negative manner, that Ron Aldridge, the publisher of *Electronic Media*,

a journal that usually speaks for the industry, lashed back, denouncing a speech by NAB President Fritts as "cockiness pushed to the edge of arrogance, aggresiveness that walks to the brink of insult." Aldridge wanted the industry's spokesmen to project more humility, "to stand above the fray and accept his industry's impressive victories with grace, charm, and modesty." But that was not to be. The broadcasting industry was instead gloating, daring the government or the public to talk back, and in essence revealing itself for what it is: a viewer-be-damned institution with little accountability.

After some of my views on these issues were highlighted in a column on the TV pages of *USA Today*, I was surprised to receive a call from *Reader's Digest*. They were interested in my writing a piece on local TV news practices. At first I couldn't believe that my angle of vision would be welcomed in such a traditionally conservative publication, but their interest made clear to me that media concentration is a mainstream concern.

Several months later, one of the *Digest* editors called to explain why it had taken so long for him to get back to me. "We were being downsized," he said. "Do you know of any openings for some great *Digest* editors?"

THE THREE REVERENDS

It is early 1995 and today I am a reverend for the afternoon, invited on the spur of the moment by Jesse Jackson to accompany him and Al Sharpton on a new initiative. The Rainbow Coalition Commission on Media Fairness aims to confront the networks with demands for fairer hiring of minorities.

Jesse had requested a meeting with Roger Ailes, a political operative who at the time had no previous experience running a TV network (he currently runs the Fox News Channel). Back then, he ran two NBC-owned cable channels, CNBC and America's Talking. "To the horror of his many critics," the *New York Times Magazine* noted a few weeks later, "Ailes is now directly responsible for thirty-two hours of original programming each day, more than anyone in the country. Sixty million Americans can watch his networks.... After skirmishing with the media elite for more than two decades, he's one of them."

Ailes responded by inviting Jackson to be his guest on a prime-time TV talk show that Ailes created for himself on his talk network. Every conservative wants liberals on their shows for heat, not light. A good argument, or so the theory goes, makes for good ratings. Winning the argument is never the point; winning the Nielson book is. Jackson agreed to appear.

I was supposed to meet him to discuss *Rights & Wrongs*. He was late and suggested we talk in the car. I didn't know where he was going until we arrived—Jesse and Al with me in tow—at the CNBC studios in suburban Fort Lee, New Jersey.

Ailes's producer, an old acquaintance, stops me in the hall to tell me that she will be quitting soon because working for Roger is like "working for the Gestapo.... Please tell Jesse that I can't control Roger," she implores as a warning that Roger might try to embarrass Jesse on air.

I pass this along to Jesse and Al. Sharpton is amused. Jesse grins.

Once the program starts, Jesse quickly takes control, weaving around a variety of polemical and predictable questions. He's done this all before. The unbalanced nature of the media—the reason for his visit—never comes up. I guess bashing the media is the last thing Roger wants to give Jesse a platform for, much less *his* platform.

On air, Jesse shows up the uninformed nature of the questions he's asked. With Roger so unprepared, Jesse scores a TKO. Afterward, as we elevate to Ailes' office upstairs for the meeting, Jesse remarks to Sharpton on how pathetic the on-air conversation was. He's incredulous about how little Ailes seemed to know about Haiti and the other subjects he raised.

"And that's the president of two networks.... Hot damn!" Sharpton shakes his head, laughing along.

In Ailes' office, there are pictures of George Bush and Ronald Reagan on the wall. Coffee is brewing as the four of us squeeze around a small conference table.

Ailes, 5'9" and two hundred-fifty pounds, makes himself comfortable. He stretches out across two chairs, signaling that we are on his turf. His secretary hands out pads and pens. I pocket one of each.

Ailes greets each of us.

Motioning toward Jackson and smiling deferentially, he welcomes, "Reverend Jackson."

Turning to Jesse's left, he smiles, nodding, "And Reverend Sharpton."

And then again, moving further left, bemused by his own cleverness, "Reverend? Schechter...."

Famous for his association with anti-affirmative action politicking, including the infamous 1988 Willie Horton TV ads, Ailes takes great pains to assure Jesse just how much importance he attaches to minority hiring. Earlier, in the green room, where talk show guests wait to be called, he made a joke of grabbing a young black woman, his associate producer, to show her off to his visitors. She was mortified. Sharpton and Jackson just smiled. Now he is going on about just how liberal he is on this issue. He says he raises it at every internal staff meeting. He says he has made progress hiring minorities and that he will make more.

He tells a story about a young black woman, a secretary, whom he helped became a tape editor, then bought her a car so she could commute to work from New York. "It was a used car, of course. But now she's here every day."

He projects sincerity, adding: "I am an independent guy. My image is one thing. You probably wouldn't think I care, but I do. I do."

Roger seems eager to talk about his work in furthering racial justice. He does, however, point out that CNBC, his business channel, will only hire blacks who are "pro-capitalist."

He seems to be having trouble finding them, although one minority hire has risen to become a senior producer.

He digresses about young blacks who rage about their frustrations, who make trouble. He doesn't want any militants around. "But hard workers? You bet. Kids who want to learn, who want to join the team, follow the program."

He has established his ideological parameters. "When people try to force me to do things, I stiffen up. It doesn't work with me." He's laying out a road map for how he thinks Jesse will approach him. He's saying he's a tough guy, not to be fucked with, but that he will deal. He doesn't want Jesse Jackson or, probably worse, Al Sharpton, who then lived up the road in Englewood, New Jersey, on his ass.

Suddenly he stops and asks Jesse bluntly what his agenda is.

Jesse tells Ailes that he only saw a few black faces on his brief tour through the halls. He explains how whites can be "culturally jaded," unconcerned about black realities. He calls for more minorities on the staff and on the air. Jesse knows the national picture—that the media is one of the most backward industries in America when it comes to minority hiring—but he wants more facts.

"We need information, Roger, vertical and horizontal, employment information. Right now we are doing our research. Collecting data. We think the media can do better than it's doing. But we have to know what it's doing."

Roger has visibly stiffened.

"This is not about personal racism," Jesse says in an effort to lower the mounting anxiety in the room. "It's about institutional racism." Then he adds, both to soften and at the same time strengthen the blow, that he always prefers negotiation to confrontation. "Institutional racism!" he repeats.

I am not sure if Roger gets the distinction. He asks his secretary to send for the human resources maven with the numbers. He is happy to give Jesse whatever information he wants, he says. He boasts that his talk network is up to 18 percent minority, while his aide explains that CNBC has lagged behind. But that's because Roger created the talk channel from scratch and inherited the business net. We are waiting for the data person, the bearer of the statistics.

Roger then whips out a letter that his secretary hands to him. "I think we lost him," he says soberly. None of us quite know what he's referring to. The conversation seemed to have lost its coherence. He pauses, looking pained, before passing the letter around. He explains that years earlier he took an interest in a troubled young black boy in Chicago whom he first saw on TV. He tracked him down, and helped him get out of the crime-ridden Cabrini-Green housing projects. Ailes financed his tuition at a private school. He flew to Chicago, took him out to lunch, and gave him a pep talk.

Roger discloses his private crusade flowing from a conservative philosophy that stresses individual responsibility and initiative rather than big government programs and the dependency they breed. He cares about people in the ghetto too, is the message.

But according to the letter, from a Lutheran social service agency, the subject of Roger's private welfare program is failing too. The kid quit school and is back on the streets, in trouble. Dealing drugs. Busted.

Roger is heartbroken. He tried so hard. He was now for real. The air in the room is thick with unintended irony.

Jesse offers to talk to the kid. Roger nods. Clearly, he appreciates the interest. Here is a man who has opposed all programs to help kids like these, but on an individual level tried to save one soul from ghetto hell.

Jesse seems touched. Sharpton can't believe what he's hearing.

We go around and around. Sharpton says softly that it might be really interesting if Jesse and Ailes were to find common cause. "It could work because it would be so unexpected. You could be a leader on the issue and work with the Rainbow," he suggests. Roger is silent.

We smile, knowing it will never happen.

At first all I could think of was the political differences between Jackson and Ailes. They are so clearly on different sides. But they have similarities too. Both are evangelists for their causes; both are addicted to media attention; both are political insiders and "players"; both are populist phrasemakers. There may have been a rivalry between them, but there was also respect, perhaps even a bit of fear. Jackson had the power to embarrass Ailes. Ailes had the power to dis Jackson. It was fascinating to watch the two of them dance around their differences to try to find some common ground and save face.

Roger promises to send more information. Jesse promises to stay in touch. There is catharsis in the room.

Jesse turns toward me, remembers our shared interest and mentions to Roger that he is considering picketing PBS for its treatment of Charlayne Hunter-Gault's human rights series, *Rights & Wrongs*.

Roger obviously doesn't know what he is talking about.

I see my opening and explain how NBC's SuperChannel in Europe first censored and then dropped *Rights & Wrongs*, on the grounds that we lacked European content. (A week later the European Human Rights Commission gave us a grant for having more European content than other American TV news shows. The show had aired on the channel before NBC bought it.)

Roger says he knows nothing about it. He explains that they run their shop and he runs his. He thinks they want European shows but then lets slip that his networks and NBC in America supply them with seven to eight hours of programs per day. So much for European content! I want to argue that human rights is not some American idea, but it's clear I'd be arguing with the wrong guy.

The reverends rise. The meeting is over.

Soon, Jesse, Al Sharpton and I are in the car heading back to the city. Jesse is musing on the meeting. He seems to respect Ailes, remarking that he prefers dealing with conservatives to liberals. They are tougher, he says, more committed. "Liberals are like a sock that's lost its elastic," he says. "Ailes may rave against big government, but he probably doesn't realize, just doesn't realize, that he has that network because of the government." Jesse is referring specifically to an FCC-sanctioned deal that gave each of the major networks a cable channel in exchange for cable getting the right to transmit their signals without having to pay expensive licensing fees.

Al Sharpton agrees that this meeting has to be documented: "Yeah, otherwise no one will ever believe it!"

Jesse's next stop is PBS's *Charlie Rose*, where, as I see on the tube that night, the host asks many of the same questions as Ailes, getting a more refined version—for the more upscale PBS audience—of the same answers. I wonder if Roger faxed them over. Again, media issues did not come up.

As for Jesse's Rainbow Commission on Media Fairness? I never heard about it again. It may be that Jesse needs the gaze of media attention too much to become its adversary. He's constantly on the air and has his own show on CNN. He lives in the media spotlight. How can he really take the media on, even if he knows why he should? It is a pity because he could force media reform issues on the agenda—not simply ending discrimination *in* the media, but discrimination *by* the media.

Jesse is a genius and can be very effective, but he's a motivator not a manager, a political churner more than a movement builder. His biographer, Marshall Frady, makes a similar point in his book, *Jesse*: "[He] simply tried too much, asserted himself too urgently and extravagantly to be accepted as wholly genuine by that general community.... He could wind up like a kind of apostolic flying Dutchman, forever roaming about in public life, looming imposingly from one tension after another in endless pursuit of his ultimate hour."

After the meeting with Ailes, Jesse told me he was going to initiate a media summit to bring together the best thinkers and activists on the issue. You could see his brilliant tactical mind at work, orchestrating a battle plan. He wanted me involved. "Send me a memo," he said. "Contact my key aides. Let's picket PBS. Let's keep up the momentum." For that minute, the reverend was revved.

A few weeks later, I ran into my friend who had been Roger Ailes' producer. She had left Roger's employ, as she had said she would, and could now tell me what Roger told *her* happened during our closed-door meeting.

She says he said that Jesse tried to shake him down for money. Huh?

There *was* a moment in the conversation, just as Jesse began his pitch, when Roger reached into his pocket and removed a wad of bills and just sat there fingering them. The three of us were made visibly uncomfortable by the odd gesture. Then, jokingly, Jesse reached over, making as if to grab the money, which made everyone laugh and got Roger to put away his roll real fast so that Jesse could continue with what he was saying.

I believe that on some level Ailes seriously believed what he told his then-producer. He must have thought that Jackson was there to shake him down, as absurd and untrue as that idea is. And he kept this notion in his head, believing it even though it didn't happen.

About a month later, I saw Jesse at the Rainbow Coalition's Washington conference. Reforming the media barely came up in three days of meetings. I still haven't heard from Jesse. When I called his media campaign director to find out why media reform wasn't on his agenda anymore, he told me he was trying to reach Jesse himself. "You know, Danny, that's the way Jesse is."

CORPORATE DEMOCRACY

On January 4, 1996, the company in command of one of America's principal television networks voted to go out of business—and I was there to savor the moment. It was the day the stockholders approved a $19 billion deal in which Mickey Mouse (dba the New Disney corporation) took over Capitol Cities/ABC. Incidentally, several financial analysts suggested that Disney—which had offered to buy ABC two years earlier for $11 billion—overpaid.

It was four days into a new year and four years short of a new millennium; a day of separate special shareholders' meetings for both companies, called for the same time in different corners of the same city, convened to bless a shotgun marriage posing as a corporate reorganization. Years earlier, as an ABC news producer, I had been given some company stock as a retirement benefit. Those certificates became my ticket to infiltrate this exercise in business theater. I wanted to see corporate democracy at work and personally feel the media merger experience.

ABC's coronation of commerce took place in the studio where many of the *20/20* newsmagazine shows I once worked on originated. An old set surrounded the dais, offering a graphic representation of the global ambitions of this newly merged entity with a relief map of the United States to the left, the world to the right. When the merger announcement was made, top executives defined their mission in "today Burbank, tomorrow the world" terms. "There are 250 million people in the middle class of India alone," Disney's Michael Eisner proclaimed, going on to speak of at least 150 countries that could be targeted by Disney-owned sports and children's programming. "There are many places in the world...that do not want to accept programming that has any political content. But they have no problem with sports, and they have no problem with Disney's kind of programming." Disney wanted global distribution and clearly had the means to buy it.

In Studio TV-1, Cap Cities Chairman Tom Murphy dominated an event that was also being carried live, via closed circuit and satellite, to all ABC and Disney offices. ABC CEO Bob Iger flanked him on one side, the company's general counsel, Alan Braverman, on the other. Murphy seemed uncomfortable in front of the cameras, missing his cues until he was ordered to start again in order to hit a ten A.M. satellite window. "Is it on now?" he asked twice while a floor director cued him with a loud countdown. A prerecorded announcement by one of those deep-throated, authoritative voices—what broadcasters call the voice of God—introduced him as he stood by awkwardly.

When Murphy finally took the rostrum, he reveled in a story of the company's 41-year rags-to-riches odyssey, from the early days in an Albany, New York, farmhouse that had once been a home for retired nuns, up through the consummation of the biggest deal in the history of broadcasting. At that very moment, the buyers—the Walt Disney Company—had assembled their own stockholders across town in a more upscale setting, the ballroom of the Waldorf-Astoria Hotel.

I had never been to a shareholders' meeting before and apparently neither had a lot of other people in the room. In an aside, Murphy noted that there were more people at this meeting than in all the meetings over the last four decades. "I always liked it when there weren't too many people," he confided to the amused crowd. He was soon beaming, boasting that "it doesn't get any better than this," and then closing with a "joke": "Now, as for me, I'm going to DisneyWorld." With that, amidst laughter, the hands that held the stock certificates came together. Murphy received a standing ovation for a job well done. I was probably the only one still in my seat.

Not surprisingly, the chairman's history of the company was selective and self-serving, stressing mostly how much money he made for the shareholders and how people who had bought shares in the early days were now millionaires. Three months earlier, Murphy had been on PBS's *Charlie Rose Show* talking in one breath of broadcasting as a higher calling, and then in another of his personal goal, which he said has always been winning. When pressed to explain what winning meant to him, he replied, without missing a beat: "making money. Whoever makes the most wins," he added with a smile. "That's how we keep score."

On neither occasion did he mention the seamier side of the Cap Cities story, as documented in former ABC employee Dennis Mazzocho's book, *Networks of Power: Corporate TV's Threat to Democracy*. For example, he didn't thank President Reagan's machiavellian CIA director William Casey, who became an investor and key partner in Cap Cities back in 1954. According to *his* biographer, the late Mr. Casey was known in-house as the Fixer, for shrewd IRS strategies that enabled the company to avoid paying any taxes its first six years. He was well-rewarded, with 51,000 shares of Cap Cities stock at 13¢ apiece. By the time Cap Cities swallowed ABC, it was selling for $215 a share.

Murphy, the son of a New York State Supreme Court judge, had come to Cap Cities from Madison Avenue's Kenyon Eckhardt, where he ran the Dove soap account. Nicknamed the Pope, it was Murphy who steered the company's fortunes with his retired crony Dan Burke, aka the Cardinal (honest!), a graduate of the Jell-O division of General Foods. The two proved to be effective managers. Cap Cities operated like a bottom feeder, picking up TV stations that were in financial trouble or badly managed. The company became known for ruthless downsizing and busting newspaper unions as well as for its high-level insider connections in Washington, where one of its former station managers, James Quello, a cranky conservative, became the longest-serving member on the FCC.

Cap Cities finally hit the big time by buying ABC in a multi-billion dollar acquisition, then the largest ever in broadcasting. That whole scandal-riddled saga is retold in the 1989 exposé by Huntington Williams, *Beyond Control: ABC and the Fate of the Networks*. ABC was vulnerable to a takeover because it hadn't diversified and had too many executives sucking up too much money. ABC's net income was 5.3 percent of all revenues. In contrast, Cap Cities, a quarter of its size, was keeping 15.2 percent of its net income. (ABC was not alone in its extravagances. CBS had 34 executives averaging $360,000 a year, and NBC was similarly bloated.)

Now Chairman Murphy called for the vote before any discussion was permitted. It was sort of like *Alice in Wonderland*: "first the verdict, then the trial." It turned out that ballots had not even been distributed to many in the room and so some, including myself, couldn't vote until someone made a fuss and the papers were passed out by a few embarrassed clerks. That is not to say that the vote was ever in doubt, since so many in the room stood to gain so much. The institutional investors had already voted their big blocks of stock; they were cashing out and moving on with a reported $10 billion of Disney's moolah.

Just seconds before this exercise in what passes for corporate democracy was wrapped up, an older man, John Campbell Henry, rose and insisted on asking a question. Murphy tried to quiet him but Henry, who disclosed that he owned 1,000 shares, was not intimidated. He denounced the deal, calling it "all wrong and ridiculous," saying it had been badly negotiated and was a business fiasco, perhaps because of the size of Disney's debt. He wasn't given a chance to spell out his critique. Murphy dismissed Henry with a patronizing rejoinder. In the end, a sizable 437,000 shares were voted against the merger, including my own. However, 121 million went for the Disney gold.

Only after the vote was over was the floor open to questions, which mostly turned on technical and obtuse tax issues that no one could fully answer. I raised my hand. I just had to. I was getting upset. No one but a few commentators had spoken to any of the broader issues raised by this merger or its political or cultural implications. Corporate culture may be ascendant, but what of the consequences? "In a corporate culture," *New York Times* columnist Frank Rich wrote, "original and idiosyncratic voices which by definition reach smaller markets have trouble making themselves heard." Jeff Cohen of Fairness and Accuracy in Reporting (FAIR) went even further, declaring that "more corporatization promises only more censorship." As the industry promises more choices, the critics warn of fewer voices.

Few journalists questioned what Disney control will mean for my old haunt, ABC news. The *American Journalism Review* asked whether ABC would be able to impartially cover the Disney company or its many products. Davis Thompson in *Los Angeles Magazine* referred to Disney as the company that has "done more than anyone in this century to legitimize the dumbing down of the American mind and the establishment of the child as the ideal U.S. citizen."

"Disney's reputation is that of control freaks, which is why they are good at formula pictures that my three-year-old adores," wrote Tom Rosenstiel in *Newsweek*, who wondered what would happen "when they brought Hollywood's values to the much more curious culture of news." What these critics perhaps missed was how those troublesome "Hollywood values" had *already* taken hold in the news business.

In mergers like this, the buzzword is always synergy. Yet when synergy comes in the front door, integrity tends to leave through the rear. "Synergy turns out to be a polite way of saying monopoly," opines political scientist Benjamin Barber in his book *Jihad vs. McWorld*, which argues that religious fundamentalism and global corporate capitalism are, in fact, two sides of the same coin, equally at odds with democracy. "And in the domain of information," he contends, "monopoly is a polite word for uniformity, which is a polite word for virtual censorship, not as a consequence of political choices but as a consequence of inelastic markets, imperfect competition and economies of scale."

So how do we challenge *that*, I wonder—but that's a longer range question. Right now, all I have is an opportunity to intervene in the process, however symbolically and ineffectually. My hand is still waving.

"That man in the back," Murphy barks finally, pointing to me in the very last row. I could feel the eyes of my old ABC bosses darting my way and could sense them saying, "Oh no, not him again!" The cameras focused in. I stood up nervously and said, "Years ago, the press critic Ben Bagdikian wrote that 50 giant companies control the media in America, but thanks to all these mergers there may only be six or seven by the end of the century. Are you concerned about the implications of this merger for the future of democracy?"

There was a stony silence. Murphy looked at me, took a deep breath and explained dismissively that at that very moment Disney's *über*mouse Michael Eisner was announcing that his company would not interfere with ABC news. He added that there are more news operations than ever—"the cable things," twenty-four-hour news services, including one then being planned (and later dropped) by ABC. So there is no problem. "Am I concerned?" he mused. "No, I am not concerned."

Ten months later, in October 1996, Disney physically carved a chunk out of the ABC news building, just up the street from where the meeting took place. On the corner of West 66th Street and Columbus Avenue—the location of my first 20/20 office—they fashioned a Disney retail store to sell movie-related merchandise, some of it manufactured by low-wage workers in Haiti and Burma. I was told that even as construction continued, there was an internal battle about whether ABC news and network paraphernalia would be stocked. Disney marketing purists argued that to do so would dilute their brand. ABC was finally given a few shelves to display its schlock alongside Disney's. You can buy the Regis and Kathie Lee cookbook there.

In that same month, Disney's two Michaels, chairman Michael Eisner and CEO Michael Ovitz, appeared on CNN's *Larry King Live* to deny rumors that Ovitz, who had been hired in a $100 million deal, might be leaving. Both men reassured the public—and any Wall Street analysts who might have been watching—that all was well on planet Disney. The *New York Post* headlined their account of the duo's unusual TV debut: "It's Love." *Vanity Fair* ran one of their definitive gossipy insider profiles, reporting that "Eisner and Ovitz have too much at stake to let their partnership founder." A month later, Ovitz was out after just 14 months. "I knew about 1 percent of what I needed to know," he admitted. Hollywood's legendary superagent was given a parachute package reportedly worth between $76 and $90 million (he eventually walked away with $157 million). Outraged Disney shareholders filed suit, denouncing Ovitz as having been undistinguished and unproductive at Disney and calling his severance deal "so egregiously excessive as to constitute waste and spoliation of Disney's resources." *Times* columnist A. M. Rosenthal speculated that the taxpayers would likely pick up 40 percent of the cost.

Curious about how Disney defends such practices, I slipped into *their* annual shareholders' meeting in February 1997, a year after it had acquired ABC. They say it was the largest corporate meeting in American history. What a contrast to the subdued sayonara to Cap Cities. It was a Hollywood happening staged at the Arrowhead Pond in Anaheim, the home of the company's owned-and-operated professional hockey team, the Mighty Ducks. Over 10,000 stockholders filled the arena to hear from far mightier ducks, Disney's key executives responsible for keeping their share price moving ever higher. They were treated to two and a half hours of slick speeches, promotional films, coming attractions, graphs and charts, all documenting the phenomenal growth that took the company from a value of $2 billion to $50 billion in just over a decade. Exec after exec bragged about how they dominate one market or another. Bill and Hillary Clinton even made pre-taped soundbite appearances blessing the Disney "magic." No one talked about the fact that Disney stock actually performed below the Standard and Poors average, or that there is no way to guarantee continued double-digit growth in the unpredictable entertainment industry. At one point, Joe Roth, who heads the motion picture division, offered an aside during his own bravura oration. "And this isn't just Hollywood hype," he said, but then in a moment of self-reflection, contradicted himself. "Well, I guess it is."

Also unmentioned amidst the self-congratulatory rhetoric was the report appearing in *Forbes* the same week exposing some of the company's financial magic, especially purchase-price accounting, which allows Disney to write down the value of ABC's assets in order to enhance future earnings. These tricks mask the company's real economic condition. "What happens when the accounting benefit ends?" the business magazine asked an insider at a competing studio. "We call it the cliff," he replied. "Either we come up with real earnings gains or we fall off the cliff."

There was no talk of any cliffs back at the duck pond. ABC's Bob Iger painted a rosy picture of his company's growth without dwelling on the network's poor performance. There was no mention of the disastrous ratings that had left the prime-time season down by 14 percent or any explanation for why both *World News Tonight* and

Good Morning America dropped to second, and then later third place. ABC watchers told me that the network was a mess, at war within itself and with a divided leadership. None of those issues were raised. Instead, a flu-stricken Peter Jennings was trotted out uncomfortably via satellite to preview the night's news and add a note of credibility, while the news division's most familiar faces marched by on tape as one more commodity in Disney's supermarket of product lines. (Ten days later, without any warning to the shareholders, David Westin, the president of the ABC television network, was removed, assigned to replace Roone Arledge as the head of the news division. Westin was not replaced. All ABC division heads now report directly to Iger.)

Iger revealed that ABC is bringing back *The World of Disney* as a two-hour prime-time block for Sunday nights and acquiring Disney-made children's programming for Saturday mornings. (Among the kid's shows canceled to make way for the Disney product was the highly rated *Fudge*. Cast members were told that it wasn't a good enough vehicle for selling Disney merchandise.) "By connecting media production into distribution on an unprecedented scale, a small group of investors are the new Masters of the Universe," gushed *Newsweek*. A day earlier the producers of the hit *Home Improvement* announced they were suing Disney for illegal distribution practices. The show's logo was nevertheless a part of the company's promotional parade produced for the meeting.

The merger had finally given Disney a distribution outlet where it could dump its own programming and thus recoup its TV show investments. Disney is running hard to catch up with Fox's kids network, Turner's *Cartoon Channel*, and Viacom's *Nickelodeon* in the lucrative kids' TV market. "We recognize that if we start getting kids to watch us at this age (as preschoolers), we have them for life," a Viacom executive told the *New York Times* in 1994. "That's exactly the reason we are doing it."

While pickets paraded outside the arena—one with a sign reading "It would take a Haitian 16.8 years to earn Eisner's hourly income of $9,783"—the Disney chief orchestrated the company's presentation in a darkened arena, calculated to overpower and wear down a crowd that had been expected to challenge the company's expensive patronage of Eisner's best friend Ovitz, as well as his own compensation package, which some said could reach $400 million. Discussion of the real issues was left to the end, for the lunch hour, when many of the audience members had taken their perk—a free ticket to the theme parks—and left. Many had brought their kids along to see the costumed characters who mingled among them as part of the razzle-dazzle. Mickey and friends ordinarily perform at a park that calls itself the happiest place on earth. Today, they were at their least happiest.

Eisner preempted any debate over the Ovitz matter by calling it a mistake, "not good," a risk that went wrong but had been, thanks to him, promptly corrected. So much for a mea culpa. One financial analyst praised him for "neutralizing the resistance factor," while a *New York Times* columnist snickered at the hairy leg-revealing socks he wore. The *Los Angeles Times* later produced evidence that Eisner had not acted promptly at all. In an article on lying as a "practiced art in Hollywood," the paper charged that he had, in fact, concealed his mistake for months and had even admitted as much to the *Wall Street Journal*.

With all this PR puffery in high gear, it was hard not to sense the difficulty of challenging Disney with shareholder resolutions, sincere but, sadly, symbolic rituals that must be played by corporate America's one-sided rules and in this case had no chance of success. Yet the issues on the agenda made it into the press, so the battle wasn't totally worthless. I was reminded of a poster I'd picked up back in 1968 in the streets of Paris during the student rebellion. It read: "I participate. You participate. We participate. They profit."

Resolutions to approve the cushy compensation deals sailed through, despite noisy dissent including boos and catcalls, protests rarely seen at corporate meetings. (The actual voting did not take place in the hall where a majority supported the dissidents, but was predetermined by proxies cast earlier by major stockholders and institutional investors. Major shareholders Warren Buffett and Sid Bass—two of America's richest men—were introduced by Eisner and stood to applause.) One man rose to complain that Disney's president made more than America's president, while the daughter of a former Disneyland employee movingly described how her mom had been shortchanged out of her full pension.

Shareholder resolutions to force corporate accountability on exploitative manufacturing practices overseas were overturned easily, although dissidents won about 13 percent of the vote, an unprecedented and impressive achievement. To defuse the protests against Disney-utilized sweatshops, and in response to embarrassing press disclosures, the company announced plans to require a code of conduct of its suppliers, outlawing child and forced labor. The half-measures did not satisfy the critics. A leader of the Communications Workers of America denounced Disney's union-busting tactics at ABC. Ex-employees spoke out against cuts in their benefits, while church organizations called for more corporate accountability.

The most passionate presentation was by Kent Poindexter on behalf of the Sisters of the Blessed Sacrament: "It is about the fantasies that seem to drive decision-making at Disney, decisions that result in unrealistic remuneration for a few, and an apartheid-like gulf between those executives and tens of thousands of people who actually produce the goods that Disney sells.... As one shareholder puts it: 'The lessons of Jiminy Cricket and Pinocchio have been forgotten by the board of directors.'"

At the mention of apartheid, I glanced across the floor at actor Sidney Poitier, who had just played Nelson Mandela in a TV drama then airing on Showtime, a cable movie channel that years earlier had promised funding for my documentary on Mandela, and then reneged on their commitment. Poitier, I discovered, is a member of the Disney board of directors, which, we were told, unanimously backs the Eisner regime. He stared ahead, handsome and expressionless. A review of his Mandela movie in *L.A. Weekly* that week called it "underwhelming...punctuated by documentary footage that makes the staged scenes look patently fake." It was a description that could have been used to review Disney's sell-athon.

THE VANISH AND THE VANQUISHED

In July of 1996, as I was helping to complete the production of *Rights & Wrongs*, a series of highly praised but not that widely watched human rights television programs, two transformative developments in the media industry were taking place. One occurred out of public view; the other paraded itself before an audience numbering in the billions. The first occurred at a "summer camp" on the picturesque slopes of Sun Valley, Idaho, attended by many of the most powerful media executives. The second, a month later, was the Summer Olympics in Atlanta as televised by NBC. Both offer evidence of how the TV environment was transformed during 1996, for good and, let's be clear, evil.

The summer camp is an annual closed-door, invitation-only mogul meet convened by investment banker Herb Allen, who provides a beautiful setting for informal socializing by media heavies. The talks conducted there, out of public view, inevitably seem to result in mega deal-making. A year earlier, at Herb's place, ABC and Disney decided to marry. This year, Rupert Murdoch began talks to buy New World Entertainment and become America's number one TV station owner, a development with significant cultural and political ramifications.

The 1996 session also took place during what TV critics prematurely branded the summer of disaster, a reference to the lowest level of network viewing in history. Panicked executives started calling the exodus of viewers "the vanish." Only 53 percent of TV viewers were watching the big four networks. Cable viewing was up.

Now, network viewing had been going down steadily for years, and in 1996 the nets collectively dropped to a catastrophic 20.5 rating; contrast that with 47.6 just eight years earlier. ABC's 6.3/13 share was an all-time low in prime-time TV history. The CBS *Evening News* scored a pathetic 5.4, *its* lowest ever. A week later, Dan Rather was all over the airwaves promoting his *mano a mano* documentary on Fidel Castro, which claimed that Cuba's system was in decline. But so was CBS. CBS's new owner, Westinghouse, reported quarterly earnings later in the month that showed a massive dip, thanks in part to viewer erosion. A year later, Westinghouse was still hemmorhaging millions in its TV division.

Reporting on a conversation outside ABC's offices in L.A.'s Century City, media analyst Matt Drudge captured the industry's panic for his Internet-circulated *Drudge Report*. "Where the hell are they going?" he quotes his source as asking. " 'We're down 24 percent from just two years ago and it looks like there's no end in sight. There was a time when people would watch us, not be ashamed to say they watched us.' Millions of people who once watched television have disappeared. They can't find them. It is just plain and simply a massive viewer drop-off not seen since the TV era began."

As TV viewing was dropping, one event helped bring the masses back: the heavily hyped Centennial Olympic games. NBC was able to build a huge audience for its coverage after spending over $2 billion to buy exclusive rights to televise the games. "You don't go into the Olympics on profit motivation," NBC's Bob Wright initially explained to the trade magazine *Electronic Media*, even though later the network boasted that it cleared $70 million from televising the games.

"The profit has to come from the enhancement of the network," added Mike Carson of the NBC affiliate in Boston, who explained enhancement this way: "Every Olympics I've been involved with has always been very lucrative and very rewarding in so many ways. Besides adding a lot of billing, it's a platform to showcase future programming, anchors or whatever."

Explained *Electronic Media*: "The hidden value is the captive audience of men and women a station will have for two or three weeks. The promotional value is just incomparable."

To secure its advantage, NBC announced that it would not permit competitors to even provide live TV reporting of official Olympic press conferences, thus precluding *all* real-time competitive coverage. Calling the move "a restriction on legitimate news reporting which is both unprecedented and unacceptable," five rivals jointly charged NBC with taking an "unfair and inappropriate advantage over other news organizations." NBC was nonplused, insisting that the rights to televise the sports extravaganza gave them the right to, in effect, muzzle and impose conditions on coverage by others, even when those others were reporting on official media events, not athletic contests. "It's the rights' holders advantage," a spokesperson for the Olympic Committee said. "Unfair? I don't know if it is unfair." Unfair or not, here was an unprecedented case of a network exercising a monopoly over the coverage of news—not just one news story but an entire area of coverage.

That was not NBC's only controversial programming decision. The network focused coverage on five main events, giving only perfunctory attention to most of the rest. After conducting 10,000 pre-Olympics research interviews with TV viewers, NBC consciously designed its coverage to be more appealing to women viewers, who were not known as heavy Olympics watchers. NBC's strategists borrowed from feminist narrative structure theory to create a TV reality of episodic, storytelling dramas that often required reediting of actual events and airing them on a delayed basis. Viewers were rarely told when events occurred. It is called time-shifting. The emphasis on women's sports, long given short shrift, was a plus, but overall coverage was distorted. It was a slick, cynical—and successful—attempt to target female consumers, a demographic advertisers find desirable, and boost Olympics ratings overall.

"NBC has been going where no network in the world has gone before in ignoring athletes from the rest of the world and making its profiles as sappy as possible," editorialized the *New York Times*, which criticized "dangerous decisions [to] blur reality in the name of a good story." The *Times* insisted that "the Olympic Games are still news, not a made-for-TV movie." Writers nationwide echoed the criticism. Calling NBC's game plan a flimflam, the New York *Daily News'* Bob Raissman wrote, "To watch NBC's coverage was to believe all our ancestors came over on the Mayflower. In NBC's mind our country is not a melting pot."

Americans and many viewers worldwide watched the Olympics all right, but saw only that part of the games that NBC wanted them to see, the part that would ultimately boost network profits. The network responded to critics with a simple statistic, boasting that its telecast won a 97 percent viewer approval rating. Retorted Bob Raissman, "You couldn't get a 97 percent approval of air conditioning on a 90° day." GE laughed all the way to the bank. NBC's justification—that they just gave the people what they wanted—is the one used most often to silence critics.

"I don't think we've ever talked about this in public," NBC's research director Nicholas Schiavone admitted to the *New Yorker's* David Remnick, "but the truth is we use a human-temperament approach to television, and the truth is we do it in prime time and on news too." This approach evaluates programming according to formulas including the two Rs (Is it real and relate-able?) and the three Es (Is there a mix of entertainment, education, edification?). Where that alphabet soup was missing, it was added to the recipe. Programs are tweaked and fine-tuned to conform to the desired mix and look. "News has to speak to the mind and the heart," said Schiavone. And when it doesn't, apparently it is not news.

Curiously, the ads at the Olympics—by Coca-Cola, AT&T, Reebok and other companies—featured more universal images and sentiments about global unity than the coverage itself. I wondered how Leni Riefenstahl, universally denounced for glorifying Hitler's Olympics of 1936, would have covered the games of '96? Were today's wall to wall corporate logos substitute symbols for the swastika so prominent 50 years ago?

What began a hundred years ago as an amateur event and tribute to an ideal of international brotherhood and peace, had long ago been sabotaged by packaged entertainment like the Dream Team, a squadron of multimillionaire basketball professionals, who crushed underfunded amateur opponents from countries like wartorn Angola. In the quest for higher ratings, the Olympics were turned into a salute to global capitalism and American chauvinism, demolishing in the process the goal of uniting the world's people and the ideal of showcasing human excellence. Many star athletes from other countries were ignored, by plan. When a black South African won the marathon by three seconds—a big achievement for a country that had been excluded from the competition for years because of apartheid—he was not interviewed, while several American runners were. Cuban athletes were given short shrift as were the Nigerians who triumphed in soccer. NBC presented the games as a made-for-the-USA extravaganza.

On Olympics opening night, NBC's sportscasters talked viewers through the parade of nations, joking about how little they knew about the countries and cultures taking part. They revealed how difficult it is for American commentators to abstain from cold war clichés and ethnocentric putdowns of "exotic" lands. This parochialism, at an event that had been planned and preproduced in detail for over a year, was both embarrassing and revealing.

When NBC's Bob Costas was asked about his network's nationalist biases at a talk he gave at Columbia University in March 1997, according to Marc Doussard in the *New York Press*, he said, "Every nation has its own cheerleader. Watch the Olympics in Pakistan and you see a lot of badminton." I guess if Pakistan does it, we can too. Next question.

Not mentioned as the world's athletes marched by was a just-released UN study that had made page one in the *Guardian* in England that very day. Predictably, it received scant attention in the U.S. press, and none at this global event. "The wealth of the world's 358 billionaires is greater than the combined annual incomes of countries with 45 percent of the world's population or 2.3 billion people," was the story's lead. The headline: "Gulf Grows Between Rich and Poor." Was it this growing economic gap that explains why so many smaller countries could only afford to send small teams or compete in only a few events? What is the United States' role in fueling this gap? How many of those billionaires are media moguls like Bill Gates, chairman of Microsoft and now NBC's partner, who tops the list? That was not discussed.

I watched Costas interview Tom Brokaw of NBC News on the Olympics' impact on the real world. He then introduced a montage of recycled footage from the last quarter-century of news, which seemed to have little point except to give Brokaw presence at the event and promote NBC's news division. NBC's own news ethics did not come up. By year's end, media monitors noted that reporting on the Olympics was given more airtime on NBC News in 1996 than any other story, effectively converting the news division into a promotional wing of the sports and programming divisions.

NBC's success in generating high ratings for its creative coverage will inspire other broadcasters to follow suit, so we can expect more of the same, if not worse, in the future. Reality has long since given way to a programming concept called reality-based. Perhaps the rest of the world best resign itself to being left out, even in coverage of a world event.

In the aftermath of the Olympics, NBC News began to undergo a transformation towards what the *Columbia Journalism Review* calls "you news" or "news lite," with an emphasis on "news you can use" stories and more features. Tom Brokaw says that the news has a "different woof and warp than it did twenty-five years ago. Overseas coverage has been downgraded in the makeover.

International news coverage on the American networks is down 50 percent over the last decade, according to media watcher Andrew Tyndall. The same is true in many other countries. Earlier in July, just before the Olympics got underway, the BBC announced it was cutting back support for its famed World Service, often the only source of reliable and relatively objective radio news for millions of listeners in poor countries.

The shrinking quantity is one problem, the quality another. Speaking at Harvard University—and not on ABC—Peter Jennings admitted as much. "To our peril..., we in TV [news] are obliged to get out the facts too quickly at the expense of context. They want us in Cairo on Tuesday and Calcutta on Wednesday."

As network news divisions cut back on coverage, sales divisions gear up to penetrate more world markets with entertainment-oriented programming. "Our industry has only begun to break into foreign markets, and the potential for growth is enormous," Viacom chairman Sumner Redstone bragged to an industry marketing conference a week before the Olympics. "At Viacom today, 17 percent of our revenue comes from outside the U.S. but by 2000, that statistic will grow to 40 percent."

At the same time, Rupert Murdoch (and others) gobbles up more and more media properties worldwide, branding them with his mix of conservative political values and commercial imperatives, driving out local voices and swamping native cultures. A friend who left Fox News, who had been a top news producer for Walter Cronkite in his glory days, then for years at ABC News, smirks and matter-of-factly calls Murdoch-world a right-wing conspiracy. "They make no secret about it. It's just that people don't want to believe it," he says.

My colleagues and I at Globalvision, the production company I co-founded back in 1987, had one Rupert-related chuckle during this same period after the *New York Times* business section devoted two full pages to detailing, though not investigating, Murdoch's global financial exploits, packaging their reporting with a headline: "Murdoch Banks on Global Vision." A friend called to ask if our small company had just been bought out. My response was to fax Murdoch a welcome to the ranks of us global visionaries.

It then occurred to me that the difference between his global vision and ours is partially what my life, and thus this book, is really about. I don't know for sure, but Murdoch may have actually seen the fax. Two weeks later, an expensively printed card in a red folder embossed with a gold seal arrived in our office. It was an invitation from none other than Rupert Murdoch and Roger Ailes to a cocktail party celebrating the launch of the Fox News Channel.

Fox threw up one of those Hollywood klieg lights and several tents outside the News Corp.'s building at 1211 Sixth Avenue, at 48th Street, to dazzle and accommodate the crowd, which included the likes of New York Governor George Pataki, NYC Mayor Rudy Giuliani, Barbara Walters, Connie Chung and, to my surprise, Walter Cronkite himself, who seemed to be walking around aimlessly wondering why he was there. Fox News and *Entertainment Tonight* were the only TV crews allowed in to cover it: Globalvision's crew was kept outside—alone behind police barriers. However, the term global vision was plastered all over Fox's press kit. Rupert gave a brief speech announcing the biggest launch in cable history—"a launch without a landing pad," a journalist to my left quipped.

After fleeing Mr. Murdoch's self-promotional function, which, incidentally, only served up finger food, I went to dinner at Chelsea's low-cost Bendix Diner, where I ran into a young man decidedly at the other end of the media spectrum. He's Jed Rosensweig, a video Dennis the Menace who had interned for Globalvision six years earlier. I hadn't seen him in almost as long but he had been in the papers all week because of his daring new public access TV show called *Wild Feed*, which aimed to show purloined satellite footage not intended for public consumption, including an off-camera tantrum by a Fox news personality and snide critical comments by NBC's Tom Brokaw about CBS's Dan Rather. When NBC found out about Jed's show, they immediately faxed and messengered him a legal letter warning of fines, lawsuits, and up to two years of possible jail time for contravening a federal law against retransmitting satellite feeds and messing with their property. NBC's broadcast counsel, Helene Godin, sent the letter, which read in part: "While we respect your right to expos(e) the illusions of television, we must advise you that your methods may expose you to both criminal and civil liability."

Hard to believe that anyone in the illusion business, much less NBC or its parent General Electric, one of the wealthiest corporations in America, would respect anyone's right to expose the illusions of television. I have it on good authority that Brokaw had written Rather an apology for violating the unwritten rule of etiquette that one news anchor never publicly criticizes another. He told journalist Jennifer Nix in *Salon*, an Internet magazine: "There's no doubt this was a reckless statement...but that kid effectively came into my workplace and recorded a private conversation I was having with six of my colleagues. This was the equivalent of a barstool conversation—a twenty-five-year-old piece of gossip from the days when I first arrived in Washington. This isn't news."

"The kid" was not impressed, arguing that he had simply invoked the fair use provisions of the law that guarantee limited uses of copywritten material, without credit or permission, to comment on or critique the news. "If they can expose people all the time, why can't we expose them? When we watch TV, we forget it's a business," Jed told *USA Today.* "You'd think Brokaw would be very guarded during the news, but he's just doing a job. He's just sitting there, talking."

I looked at Jed. He was just sitting there, laughing. A week later, he sent a cheeky response to an NBC executive: an invitation to coproduce a series with him for NBC "that explores this and other issues that come into play when news becomes property and corporate interests overtake journalism.... Wouldn't NBC have more credibility if it showed the tape itself?" Jed concluded: "I hope to hear from you soon. You know where I am. Your lawyers found me in 22 minutes—the amount of time it usually takes to show us the world."

O.J., OY VEY!

Los Angeles has been an epicenter of America's racial divide for at least thirty years, since the Watts riots of 1965. That uprising, and the many inner-city insurrections that followed, led to the Kerner Commission's 1970 findings that we live in two unequal Americas, one white and one black. In a hard-hitting but not widely reported annex to its report, the commission indicted the American press with what they termed a "fundamental criticism" for their failure to "analyze and report accurately on racial problems in the United States, and as a related matter, to meet the Negro's legitimate expectations in journalism."

In 1995, the O. J. Simpson murder trial was the number one news story on television. At Globalvision, we tried to ignore it, and took a "No J" pledge; *Variety* contrasted our approach to the overkill on the networks with two-column headlines, "All O. J., all the time," about the networks, and "No O. J. any of the time," about our human rights show.

O. J. had been a sports celebrity made on and promoted by television. Fans loved "the Juice." He made one of the most memorable TV ads in history, where he ran through an airport hyping rental cars. He had been an on-air commentator, best friends with NBC's Don Ohlmeyer. Media execs knew him on a first-name basis, and some golfed with him. He was even on the board of a media corporation, Infinity Broadcasting, the home of Howard Stern.

Everyone who watched the original trial came to consider themselves experts, part of a nationwide jury. It was an event everyone could consume and no one could miss, since it was broadcast in the daytime on at least three cable channels, with radio updates four times a day, and again at night, in the news recaps and on *Nightline*. O. J. Simpson and the cast of courtroom characters soon became so familiar that we all became part of the same dysfunctional family.

Never in the history of television had one event so overwhelmed all others. More air time was devoted to the trial than most other major stories *combined*.

The press emphasized racial solidarity as the only sensible explanation for why the criminal trial jury decided O. J. was not guilty. The jurors dismissed that as ridiculous and explained that it was the failures of the prosecution, not the pigment of the defendant, that convinced them. Race may have been more central to coverage of the case than to the case itself. The media was talking one language, the jurors another.

"The media has a way of treating all communities as if they are monolithic, which reinforces stereotypes," said one audience member on a *Nightline* show. "Not all blacks thought O. J. was not guilty, nor did all whites clamor for conviction."

It has been suggested that the media *needs* O. J.-type trials, not only to sustain viewer interest but because that is what today's TV newsrooms and newsmagazines are best-equipped to cover, what they, in fact, are there to cover. It is what they live for. They have addicted themselves to sensation just as they condition the audience to savor it.

Consider the sensational forerunners to O. J.—the Amy Fisher-Joey Buttafuoco case, the Menendez Brothers case, the Michael Jackson child molestation case, skater Tonya Harding's assault on her rival Nancy Kerrigan, and the trial of Lorena Bobbitt, charged with cutting off her husband's penis.

Andrew Tyndall, who monitors network coverage by counting the time allocated to each story, sees the O. J. trial speeding up a convergence between what had been considered the serious media and the more sensational tabloid press. The reason, he says, has to do more with class than race, and is a reflection of deepening class stratification. "In the last twenty years," Tyndall told Inter Press Service, "the middle class began disappearing, leaving a large gap between an elite media serving a small audience and the mass media seeking its viewers down market, directing its wares at increasingly poorer viewers. Programmers tend to assume that the audience only wants pabulum. And that's what they give them. So, there's no surprise when that's what they watch."

Was the audience so mesmerized by the case because it "has a primal need" for sensation, as Jeff Greenfield suggested on ABC, or was it because the media stoked the interest by its saturation coverage?

Institutional reasons also lay behind the decision by news management to focus on the case. Budget cutbacks for TV news had already slashed news departments, limiting serious journalism on the air. The trial was relatively cheap to cover, with no need to fly people around or go overseas. It was in Los Angeles, a network city with many crews, correspondents and a technical infrastructure, as well as a one-camera pool feed and lots of talking head analysts. All the media needed was clever packaging, so more and more money was spent on promos and hype. Suddenly the airwaves were cluttered with pseudo debates and instant analysis by lawyers. They loved the exposure; it was great for business.

Ratings rose. Profits shot up. CNN reportedly earned $70 million on top of its usual revenues in one quarter because of its O. J. coverage. The Arbitron ratings service confirmed that programs carrying and hyping the O. J. case earned higher ratings and profits. Some more than doubled their audiences. Audience researchers at ABC think that the news ratings there declined when they would not air as much coverage as their competitors.

The O. J. case made money for the media hand over fist. As the verdict neared, the networks, sensing a final major profit opportunity, jacked up their prices for commercial time to SuperBowl levels, ten times what they usually charge. The constant coverage had produced the predictable result—more Americans watched.

Despite the blatant media exploitation, the O. J. case produced a few unanticipated benefits by focusing national attention on important issues. One can hope legal penalties for crimes of domestic violence will be stiffened now that Nicole Brown's experiences are common knowledge. Certain institutional forces of society were also thrown into public view—the racism of the LAPD, the willingness of the court system to do its bidding and conversely, the reality that wealth can buy the kind of an effective defense routinely denied to most poor defendants. In some instances, the jury verdict led to honest exchanges and debates between whites and blacks about racial conflicts that have long been ignored. Debating the O. J. case became the way many people talked about race, sometimes by pretending they weren't.

Crime and race were already indelibly linked in the public mind. Media images often distort reality and reinforce racial prejudices. Almost every local news show across America showcases a parade of crime stories, often featuring black kids being arrested by white cops. But the causes of crime—poverty, lousy schools, few jobs, broken families among them—are rarely explored.

The year of O. J. was also a year of unrelenting assault on programs that serve inner-city communities. Robert Scheer of the *Los Angles Times* pointed out that the LAPD is not the only institution that operates to the detriment of black people. He linked the end of affirmative action in state jobs and cutbacks in welfare assistance, Head Start, summer job programs, and other entitlements that provide a social net to the poor, to a backlash that the case fueled. But few media outlets, if any, picked up and explored these connections within the context of their trial coverage.

As the trial wound on, Republicans in Congress were busy killing off federal funding for legal services for the poor, while in many states and cities that support had already been cut way back. Jesse Jackson, speaking about the large number of young black men who are in the custody of the legal system, called the situation a "national emergency."

Veteran journalist Richard Rovere blamed television's obsession with the O. J. case for preventing the American people from finding out what else was going on in the world. "With hundreds of reporters, hundreds of hours...what don't we know about the country and the world because a few people made decisions to cover this spectacle? We have taken a year of journalism away from the American people." He spoke on a Ted Koppel-moderated ABC *Viewpoint* program critiquing the coverage. It was followed by Ted's announcement that he would have more on the trial the next night on *Nightline*, but if you couldn't wait, *Good Morning America* would give you an early dose at the crack of dawn.

I think again of the misplaced priorities of the news business, and the final words of the Kerner Commission back in 1970. How far had we come from a critique of a press that "repeatedly, if unconsciously reflects the biases, the paternalism, the indifference of white America. This may be understandable, but it is not excusable in an institution that has the mission to inform and educate the whole of society." Could those damning words not also be applied to this whole O. J. charade? Understandable but not excusable.

By the time O. J. II finally wrapped up, the country was exhausted by a spectacle that the media had mined for all its worth. Upcutting the President's State of the Union message, the verdict in the civil trial prompted hours of sound-alike punditry, blowing off debate about the Administration's policy choices. Columnist Norman Solomon observed, "After Clinton issued his 'call to action for American education,' it was media business as usual. Not a single tough critic was on the air to point out that the most powerful institution of American education—television—is constantly promoting all kinds of destructive values for young people in order to reap maximum profits."

Yet, in more than one sense, the Simpson Trial as a made-for-TV entertainment, as *the* State of TV News, became the state of the union by other means, pointing again to the centrality of race and the ambiguities of justice in America. The trial as an industry had produced forty books by that point, with films, and fresh revelations still to come. But when it ended, little of real substance had been resolved. The most profound commentary could be found in the numbers. The ratings were way down for both events as audience logic and media logic clashed once again: "The numbers just disappeared as the night went on," an unnamed NBC producer told the Internet's *Drudge Report*, "I can't believe the verdict actually pulled in less viewers than an average Tuesday night. There must be a reason...it isn't logical." Oh yes it was. The public had moved on; the media had not.

HUMAN RIGHTS FOR A NIGHT

The Committee to Protect Journalists (CPJ) is a human rights group that monitors freedom of the press around the world and seeks to intervene when journalists are in peril. It is a decent organization built around a principle of solidarity I respect. CPJ has a million-dollar budget, a staff of many, offices that would do a small law firm proud, and one hell of a support system. Half of their money is raised at an annual black tie power dinner that I have slipped into for the last three years running.

To keep with the informality of the "we're all just journalists together" ambiance of the annual event, let's drop some names. In 1994, Tom showed up, and so did Dan and Peter, of course. Barbara appeared, along with Ted and Jane, half of *60 Minutes*, Phil Donahue, and executive producers galore from NPR and Time Warner. Rupert's minions were there in force, along with Cap City's highest honchos. Robin stopped by sans Jim, and so did Charlayne. CNN's Peter Arnett dropped in, live on tape.

The honchos showed up to honor a journalist from Hong Kong who fears for press freedom when the Chicoms from Beijing move next door in '97; a Turkish Writer who called for an end to religious fundamentalism; and a military correspondent from Sri Lanka who was terrorized after exposing army ineptitude. In a world of journalists in trouble, these three might not make the top ten list, but they are symbols of the shit governments dump on reporters doing their jobs.

While mention was made of American journalists who have been murdered, mostly while reporting overseas, the focus was on dissident foreign journalists who get killed, jailed and/or silenced every year. America's top journalists feel for them—and don their tuxes and gowns for a $500-a-head affair (mostly picked up by their employers).

I can't feel real self-righteous. While it is true I'm too cheap to rent a tux, and wear a red tie instead of a black one, it is also true that I enjoy the schmooze. Mingling with the movers, shaking hands with people from whose institutions I've fled, can be fun. Up close, it's hard to consider these people enemies because they are so warm and personable. Yet they are all key operatives in a media system I detest—but, hey, being around them reinforces my infiltrator's spirit. Why shouldn't I be here? Paid guest or not, I am one of a small circle actually doing the stories the honorees stand for, and for the most part the paying guests aren't.

This gathering of the media tribe is a feel-good function. The news anchors speak with what seems like equal composure, and equal insight. They are equally able to weave personal anecdotes into flowery journo-prose. There is some jousting. Eyebrows flutter when Peter's ex-wife, Kati Marton, preceded him to the stage; they are in the middle of a bitter divorce. A former ABC correspondent, Kati is head of the CPJ board and would eventually marry former Assistant Secretary of State Richard Holbrooke, himself once linked to Diane Sawyer. It's a small and incestuous world.

Speaker after speaker speaks of freedom of the press as a "great cause," as if journalists were an endangered species—Tom even called them that. But as one of the disenfranchised at this glittering event, it feels to me like journalism is being treated as a rare disease, and we were all there to find the cure. Most of those present, of course, understand that there is a self-interest angle in this. CPJ is like an insurance policy to be activated when you or your mates get into trouble in some godforsaken foreign land.

Not discussed is why the issues and countries that we are honoring tonight are so rarely reported on the news programs that these media power players produce. Where are the stories on repression in Turkey or the war in Sri Lanka or the dead bodies of Tajikistan? I'll bet if O. J. Simpson escaped tonight, the beepers in the room would be louder than the band. These anchors would be racing back to do special bulletins, to get their helicopters back in the air. The show must go on. That's their job.

The featured speaker in 1994 was billionaire money manager and financial speculator George Soros, who made a speech about something he really believed in—Bosnia—and why UN peacekeeping must be retooled. He was candid, admitting that he supported good causes because he could afford to. He talked about Bosnia as a warning to the world and asked this news crowd to pay more attention. Nearly a year later, his prognosis became reality. Thousands more were dead, and few media outlets were providing critical or explanatory coverage.

Soros was received with mild applause. The people at his table rose for a standing ovation as you would expect, but many tables just stared at this intrusion of reality. This was heavy stuff coming from a man who was introduced by Ted Turner as "the happy part of the night." Ted likened Soros's appearance to a kicker story at the end of a newscast, the funny coda that he said was added deliberately "to keep us from going out and killing ourselves after hearing all that bad news."

Afterward, I went up to Soros and told him he had violated the number one rule of these dinners.

He looked at me, not sure what I was going to say next.

"Yeah, you were substantive."

He laughed.

Fast forward one year to 1995. The event has been moved to the Mariott Marquis in Times Square, but the whole cast of well-heeled and finely coifed characters are back, in the same formal wear. We are soon told in a self-congratulatory manner that CPJ has become the "cutting-edge journalists' organization in America." Once again our human rights show, *Rights & Wrongs*, the only show to cover CPJ regularly, is not mentioned and our anchor, Charlayne Hunter-Gault, has not been invited to be on the program, even though she wrote the foreword to their annual report. It's par for the course. Our company has no money to donate.

A long dais extends across a stage lined with red velvet drapes, reminding me of a photo of the People's Plenary of the Chinese Communist Party. Only Walter Cronkite's picture, in Mao's place, is missing. Dan, Peter and Tom are in their appointed places. This year there is also a sprinkling of women on the stage, including Lesley Stahl and Jane Pauley, but only one black—CNN's Bernie Shaw, who is on hand to introduce Ted Turner with as many fawning adjectives as Molotov once reserved for Stalin.

Turner speaks briefly and then splits, announcing this will be his last appearance at the annual rite. He closes with a line he's used before, about his willingness to die for journalism. Tom Brokaw is less deferential, quipping that that was the second-best line he's ever heard from Ted. The first was when Ted confided that he was nineteen years old the first time he got laid; the second time was ten minutes later. That got a big laugh.

Earlier, there was an awkward moment when Ted, who has made a few billion since his appearance the previous year thanks to his merger with Time Warner, ran into *60 Minutes*'s Mike Wallace and told him, "Sorry about that cigarette thing." Wallace seemed stunned, perhaps because that very day *60 Minutes* was being bashed in both the *New York Times* and the *Washington Post* for its muzzling of its tobacco company exposé.

Next, Ted bumped into Michael Fuchs, the ex-HBO head who had just been corporately beheaded for opposing the merger. The two of them posed for pictures together, the vanquisher and his vanquished. Fuchs didn't look all too happy as he sat, sullen, head in hand, at PR man John Scanlan's table. Scanlan had been one of

Fuchs's paid image polishers in the days when he sat closer to the dais. It reminded me of the old Kremlinologists who studied photos of the Politburo at Moscow's May Day parade to determine who was in and who was a goner.

And once again, eloquence and cliché collide in the speeches. The awardees are all brave and impressive. I am moved when photographer Susan Meiselas introduces a frequently threatened Guatemalan editor as being from the "country we did not cover, the country we never saw." No mention is made of American journalists in trouble, like, say, Mumia Abu Jamal, who sits on death row in Pennsylvania.

The Guatemalan Jose Ruben Zamora Marroquin speaks words I can identify with. "You may think we are courageous but my people think we are crazy. But perhaps we are the only sane ones in a society that is mad, or is our sanity a sign of madness?... It is difficult to remember what's right when you are the only one saying it."

I also agree with Kati Marton when she notes that "a free press is not an ornament to a democracy—it's what defines a democracy" and then adds that CPJ is better known in the "nastier capitals of the world than it is in Washington D.C."

In introducing the essayist Roger Rosenblatt, Dan Rather speaks of the committee as trying to educate reporters and editors, admitting "some of us are not educable." At evening's end, after we honor *them*, including Veronica Guerin, a brave Irish crime reporter who will return home to be murdered, we are treated to a paean to one of *us*, the venerable Ben Bradlee, retired from the *Washington Post*, best remembered for his role in Watergate. One half of the Watergate whistle-blowing team, Bob Woodward, is here to praise this giant of establishment journalism, showing a clip from the Hollywood version of *All the President's Men* and reminding us what it was like back in 1973 when journalists were as Dan Rather says, more like attack dogs than lapdogs.

"Journalists take pride in their disengagement," Woodward remarks. "We are supposed to be disengaged, impartial, but dis-

engagement can keep us from responsibility and emotional risk."
He is using these words to introduce Bradlee, but what he is really
talking about is the fact that most journalists do not engage with
the issues of the day, but instead hide behind a wall of artificial
"objectivity, distant from passion."

Yes, Bob, I am shouting inside, tell it like it is! Call on them to
abandon their own callousness and jaded cynicism! Talk about the
need to expand the reach of global coverage, to put more resources
into the kind of investigative work that once helped you topple a presidency. Talk about the real threat to freedom of the press posed by
the bottom-line demands of the captains of the media monopolies.

But, no, Bob does not follow the road illumined by his own
insight, does not challenge this overpaid, self-satisfied and termi-
nally disengaged pack, who Rather intimated are "not all educable."
Is such a challenge even possible?

That question resurfaces for me a year later at the 1996 dinner,
by which time the committee has gone entirely upscale, to the Wal-
dorf Astoria. A former CPJ leader tells me she is no longer even on
the invite list: "The truth is, Danny, what was a human rights group
is now an industry organization."

The industry is once again well-represented, with business news
maven and $50,000 donor Michael Bloomberg serving as chairman
of tonight's event, with primary responsibility for raising the money.
His pitch letter, aimed at potential corporate sponsors, argues that
press freedom is not just for journalists but for "their news companies." His appeal is successful. Tonight's dinner, he boasts, will
raise $900,000, one-third more than in previous years.

Once again, the media celebs are here—anchors galore. Walter
Cronkite and the chairman of the *New York Times* are our honorees.
There are also honors for a gutsy and deserving Palestinian journalist, a brave Indian and a persistent Mexican, as well as a poignant
appeal for a Turkish editor in prison. There is also a moving musical tribute to a CPJ martyr, the late Veronica Guerin, the Irish crime

reporter struck down since last year's dinner. Thinking of Veronica (with whom I had spent some time), I wonder if I am being too hard on the CPJ. After all, they recognized her and are helping us remember her. Perhaps corporate-backed fund-raisers like this are in the end preferable to begging at the doors of foundations, though they do that too. Maybe I am just jealous of how well they stoke the money furnace. Fortunately, as my head softens under the influence of one too many brews, several CPJ staffers bring me back to my critical senses with expressions of their own disdain for the hypocrisy in the room. The feeling was that CPJ had not considered Veronica's situation of any particular concern until hers became a major media story, and that her death was now being exploited.

At least there is some awareness coming from the rostrum of the contradictions swirling all around us. Rather jokes that CPJ stands for "Classily Pretentious Journalists" or the "Club for Peter Jennings." Brokaw can't resist jabbing at Rupert Murdoch's news chief, Roger Ailes of the Fox News Channel, a company conspicuously missing from the list of CPJ's most generous patrons. Jennings has fewer jokes but more charm.

On a more relevant note, soon-to-be-ex-CPJ Chair Kati Marton surveys the crowd, asking plaintively, "Can we now—after the election and the O. J. trial—can we cover the world?" She gets slight applause. So the role of critic is left to Michael Bloomberg. He denounces the industry for practicing "cowardice and intellectual sloppiness," calls it on the mat for being "afraid to cover the stories that should be written," and accuses it of "rushing to judgment" in the case of Richard Jewell, the Atlanta security guard condemned in the media for the bombing at the Atlanta Olympics, without evidence. (NBC had just settled settled a lawsuit with Jewell for a reported $500,000.) "We can become people we are not proud of," Bloomberg warned. "We can become the cowards we condemn."

Next, dessert is served.

YIPPIES AND YUPPIES

Everyone in the media business has a mentor or role model, some-one whose media savvy got them thinking about a career in the busi-ness. One of the most influential media mavericks in my life was someone who was a subject of constant media attention for as long as he lived, and who well understood how the industry worked. His name was Abbie Hoffman.

We first met in 1966 through a transatlantic correspondence. I was a student at the London School of Economics. Abbie was in New York, running Liberty House, generating income for struggling black communities by selling goods made by southern cooperatives. A former civil rights worker like me, he was riled over SNNC's deci-sion to, in effect, kick whites out. I lectured Abbie on the impor-tance of self-determination. Our yearlong correspondence began our friendship. Some of our conversations made their way into Abbie's first book, *Revolution for the Hell of It*, and encouraged me to become one of the unpublicized founders of the Youth International Party (YIPPIE) in his East Village apartment in December 1967. (The others were Abbie, Jerry Rubin, Paul Krassner, and poet Ed Sanders.) Ours was a complicated relationship that lasted until his death, with lots of tension and many disagreements. Abbie chose to make news and I chose to cover it.

I might have been a defendant myself in the Chicago conspir-acy trial if I hadn't stayed in England that summer of '68 to protest the Soviet intervention in Prague, and so missed the summer mad-ness in the windy city. Instead I gave an American buddy in Lon-don, John Froines, a chemist on his way to Chicago, a letter to Abbie. At my request, Abbie welcomed John aboard the Yippie express. Soon, John was indicted as a co-conspirator—something about stink bombs. I was back in town by the time of the trial the following year and covered it for the alternative press. Before I became a full-time journalist, I organized a demonstration in Boston the day after the verdicts came down. The organizing principle was my idea: TDA—The Day After. Thirty thousand people showed up in Government Center. It almost turned into a riot of its own. Fortunately for me, Mayor Daley did not rule in Boston.

Now it was twenty-five years later. October 1994, the twenty-fifth anniversary of the Chicago conspiracy trial, which brought Abbie and his antics to global attention. Before O. J., it was the trial of the century. Since several of the co-defendants were going to be in town, I decide to follow them around, to PBS's *Charlie Rose* show, where they taped the show, and to a reunion that night of co-conspirators Bobby Seale, Dave Dellinger, Tom Hayden, and Lee Weiner, along with the most famous member of their team, their lawyer, the late William Kunstler. Globalvision plans to conduct interviews with these antiwar movement veterans for a documentary we hope to do on Abbie.

The trial had taken place on the twenty-third floor of the federal courthouse in Chicago (the one with the Picasso statue out front) where federal marshals strapped an uncooperative defendant, Black Panther Party Chairman Bobby Seale, into a chair and gagged him in an act of judicially approved restraint as he screamed for his constitutional rights. Abbie said that Seale's resistance was the part of the trial he remembered best, and which inspired him most.

If you remember to include Bobby as a part of the trial—his case was severed from the others—they were the Chicago 8, accused of conspiring across state lines to cause the mayhem at the Democratic Convention in Chicago in 1968. If you forget Bobby, as many historians do, they were the Chicago 7.

And here's Bobby now, forever charismatic, a nonstop speechifier whose word salad of appeals for "revolutionary, intercommunal humanism" still rouses me. I love the rhythm of his speech, but I am not sure if I fully understand its substance. Later at the reunion he'll sell us his soul food cookbook, *Barbecuing with Bobby*, and talk up his movie-in-the-making, the real story of the Panthers. He is a man with memories, but now a leader with no movement.

Abbie's only brother, Jack, is also in town, and I invite him to the Times Square offices of Globalvision to be interviewed. Jack's book about his brother, cowritten by Seven Stories Press publisher Dan Simon, is Jack's catharsis, his way of expiating the guilt he felt over his inability to prevent Abbie from killing himself. It is also his reckoning with a history he was always peripheral to—and yet connected to through blood and desire. Jack tells me that Abbie's government dossier ranks number nineteen on the list of the FBI's most requested files.

Jack tells us about Abbie's adolescence, obsessive teenage "sport fucking" armed with what Jack described as a fifteen-inch cock. Jack also disclosed one of his brother's perverse pubescent hobbies, storing a bottle of his own ejaculate in his mother's refrigerator. Between chuckles, I shifted the conversation to what was and wasn't between Abbie's neck and his flowing hair.

We talked about Abbie's media theories and, finally, the manic depression that finally sapped his energy and led to his death. It's ironic to me that the *Wall Street Journal*, never Abbie's favorite paper, recently called manic depression the CEO disease, saying that "one in three senior management types show the symptoms." The paper notes that Ted Turner has been on lithium for a decade. So was Abbie.

Some of Abbie's comrades still debate what triggered his death. Was it suicide, an accidental OD, or a CIA plot, as Dave Dellinger suspects? We'll never know. We don't have time to explore all the theories because they have to run across town to appear on PBS's *Charlie Rose*.

Charlie has moved his operation out of public television's Channel 13, which rented out its studio as an economy move, to the high-tech offices and studio of businessman turned business news entrepreneur Michael Bloomberg. His Park Avenue headquarters is a state-of-the-art electronic emporium with desks fitted out with his own audio and video terminals, appropriately called the Bloomberg. He has managed to fit more information on one terminal and TV or computer screen than anyone before or since. Capitalism is his beat, and is it ever blooming. Bloomberg's enterprise earned $200 million in 1996 and is expanding its focus beyond business news. He may yet compete with NBC and CNN. "My strategy is to build a worldwide network of serious news," he told the *New Yorker*'s Ken Auletta. He's another mogul in the making.

For many years, Wall Street firms with acres of terminals like these made deals to finance media firms. Now the distinction between the financier and the financed is disappearing. His media operation looks and feels like a Wall Street firm. He's now reporting on and for his old elite colleagues and competitors. Perhaps technology and ideology are what's merging—a trend conceived to achieve that elusive state of business nirvana called synergy.

Here these leaders of the '60s conspiracy have come. I follow with a home video camera to record this historic gathering on enemy territory. They wait in a makeshift green room, actually a supermodern lobby built around a free snack bar and coffee emporium for employees and guests. Legal lion Bill Kunstler, not one to sit around, finds some chicken soup, which he heats up in the microwave to serve Dellinger and himself.

While we wait, I ask some of the younger Bloombergers what they know about Abbie. The security guard and one production assistant never heard of him. One young man says of course he has—he's seen the movie *Forrest Gump*, which caricatures an Abbie-like agitator. "He's in *Gump*," he repeats. "The guy in *Gump*."

The makeup woman says she knows who he is too, but then asks me if he is still missing, thinking that Abbie is still on the run. I don't have the heart to tell her he's dead.

While Charlie converses with his guests about the ghosts of conspiracies past in the studio in the back, another guest comes up in the elevator. He's preceeded by Secret Service men with wires coming out of their ears. I'm reminded of a story Jesse Jackson once told me about his 1984 visit to a small black church in Texas during his presidential campaign. He was flanked by a contingent of Secret Service men assigned to guard him. An old black woman in the front pew kept nodding her head sadly. Afterward Jesse asked her what was wrong.

"Just look, Jesse," she said, "at those men with the hearing aids in their ears. Why do they assign deaf men to guard you? They jest don't treat black people right!"

These agents are here to protect President Alberto Fujimori of Peru, in town to speak at the UN. He's the other guest on Charlie's talkfest today. When I see Fujimori march in, I seize the opportunity to request an interview for our human rights series, *Rights & Wrongs*. Fujimori's human rights record is among the world's worst, so I have no compunctions about trying to sandbag him on camera.

"The president is too busy," his aides tell me. I see him sitting in a glass-enclosed conference room shooting the shit with his entourage. My hunch is that Fujimori is not here to talk about human rights.

A Secret Service agent asks me about Charlie's other guests.

"It's the Chicago conspirators and the Black Panther," I tell him. He says, "Oh, shit."

A half hour later, I accompany this conspiracy to its next destination, a public reunion organized by the Learning Alliance. I ride with Tom Hayden to PS 84 on the West Side, sometimes called "the upper left side," where he and his old cell mates have been invited to reminisce and to look forward into the future. This tribute to '60s glory is being picketed—'60s-style—by the staff of the Center for Constitutional Rights, Bill Kunstler's organization, which is experiencing hard times financially. Some of the protesters have been laid off, others fired.

"Unfair!" they shout at people who enter the hall.

"How could you?" one extremely loud protester screams at Tom. "We are only doing what you did."

Well, not exactly.

It is a great night for the oldtime religion. Tom, now a California state senator, is his usual brilliant self. "It's not over yet" is his refrain. Dave, still the activist's activist, is earnest and passionate and says Amen to Tom's words. Another co-conspirator, Lee Weiner, is as out of it today as he was then. He tells the assembled devotees that he found the trial boring.

William Moses Kunstler demonstrated that he was still the master of judicial storytelling. His best tale of Judge Julius Hoffman, who presided at the trial, concerned an envelope of primo marijuana that was delivered to the defense table by a federal marshall one morning. Fearing a drug bust setup, Kunstler advised the judge of the unexpected windfall of cannabis, asking for direction on its disposal. Judge Hoffman reportedly responded by expressing his confidence that Kunstler and company would know what to do. Attorney Bill responded by telling his honor: "It will be burned tonight."

The audience is by turns ebullient, restless, emotionally supportive of the picketers, and still tenacious in its attack on the system. I feel like I am in a church of the faithful. The crowd is graying here, balding there. Not many young people are in the house. Undoubtedly, the '60s for many of them is like the '30s were for us— a romanticized memory, not real life. Of course there are also slogans, finger pointing, and overheated rhetoric—many of the reasons there is so little left of the left. Nostalgia or neurosis?

The night's irony: the uniformed cops on hand to protect the Chicago conspiracy's right to reminisce without disruptions from militant dissidents from the Center for Constitutional Rights.

Abbie would have had a ball.

New York Newsday headlined its account: "Power to the Past." They were the only ones to cover it. They would be shut down within the year.

If Abbie had been there, the conspiracy reunion would have been on TV. He would have known how to get cameras there to cover it.

BEYOND JFK

I grew up in the *Dr. Strangelove* generation. I watched films that not only dramatized, but commented on and sometimes satirized real-life events and institutions. Over time, the distinctions between fiction and "faction" have diminished. There was the war of warring Vietnam War films, *The Ballad of the Green Berets* and *Rambo* versus *Platoon* and *Born on the Fourth of July.* I became a charter member of what one humor magazine dubbed the Vietnam War Movie Veterans Association.

Recently, there has been a spate of reality epics like *Schindler's List* and *In the Name of the Father,* whose director, Jim Sheridan, told me in an interview that he believed his film had "reached truths deeper than journalism." He was referring to scenes that dramatized a torture session and revealed the discovery of a document proving that the British government knew that the men they were prosecuting for an IRA bombing were innocent. He explained that the press was not present at either event, but that both occurred. He explained how, as a director, he could take dramatic license to show what might have happened to make those scenes real. "The news media didn't and couldn't cover them," he told me. "Who was being more honest, me for showing them, or them for suppressing them?"

Is there a truth deeper than journalism? Great writers and novelists penetrate the surfaces of personality and motivation in a way journalists rarely can. And yet there is no denying that as they visualize events, Hollywood films tend to distort them. Filmmakers are not required to stick to the facts, even when they are dramatizing facts. But what do you do when the facts in a real story are themselves in dispute, when there is little agreement about what a fact is, when different theories all have elements of plausibility?

I had stopped asking myself those questions years ago. Then, in 1991 we got a call from Warner Brothers. They were looking for producers to do a promotional video for Oliver Stone's next film, *JFK.* By the time it was completed, the project had escalated into *Beyond JFK,* a ninety-minute independent documentary feature, directed with Barbara Kopple and produced with Marc Levin, on the issues raised by *JFK.*

The assassination of President John F. Kennedy was in many ways the seminal emotional historical event of my generation. We lived through it once, and Oliver Stone wanted us to experience it again, this time to consider how and why a conspiracy might have killed the president and covered up the crime.

Over the years, the Kennedy assassination and the conspiracy-mongering that surrounded it have been a kind of sideshow to history, spawning a subculture of buffs and buffoons. Everyone had a theory. No one knew what really happened. Mainstream news organizations denigrated and ignored most of the independent researchers. Big Journalism somehow lacked the interest or will to stay with the story, as important as it was. There were reasons. Many of the theories were too speculative and complex—almost too complicated to be believable. Journalists lean towards a fuck-up theory of history, in which error is often a better explanation than calculation. They believe conspiracies require a level of coordination and calculation on a scale that would be beyond the competence of most government bureaucracies. Also, most reporters who live off of insider tips and leaks doubt that any crime could be covered up for thirty years.

Also, most of the media fell in line with the eminences on the Warren Commission. The government in the early '60s still inspired more awe than skepticism. But there were other reasons. Most news organizations don't have the resources or the inclination to mount in-depth investigations. A few tried, but gave up when a new smoking gun failed to quickly materialize.

When she was still a journalist back in 1977, Nora Ephron made that point: "This is a story that begs for hundreds of investigators, subpoena power, forensics, experts, grants of immunity.... A lot of people are dead. Some of the ones who are alive have changed their stories. The whole thing is a mess."

A mess no one seemed able to untangle either. The government failed with the Warren Commission, then failed again when the House Assassinations Committee took a second look in 1979. The press essentially stuck to its original view that Oswald acted alone and that the case was closed. A small army of citizen-investigators churned out books, articles, and pamphlets that kept the case for conspiracy alive in the popular imagination. They referred to themselves as a research community, but to the mainstream press they were still kooks.

Interestingly, in poll after poll, the majority of Americans ended up siding with the kooks, rather than the government or the press, in believing a conspiracy of some kind was behind President Kennedy's assassination.

We'll probably never know for sure.

I went down to New Orleans to film Stone in action for a few days as he worked on the film. I was amazed by the brashness and obsessiveness with which he approaches his work. He's frenetic, tyrannical, driven, egomaniacal. It was hard to have a conversation with him about the case because his knowledge is so encyclopedic and he was so confident about his conclusions. He had assembled the definitive conspiracy library on the case. He had researched all of the theories himself. He even dug up a friend of Lee Harvey Oswald to act as a technical advisor.

Stone's *JFK* hit the screen supported by a massive marketing campaign. Whether the director's presentation of the facts was true or not, it offered the general public, for the first time, a powerfully dramatized argument on an issue which up to that point had been presented without much coherence.

Big Journalism, no particular friend of coherence, went into action, unleashing its biggest debunking guns to blast away at Stone's movie as a "Hollywood happening" and a "conspiracy against reason." Many critics loved the film, even as most editorial writers and columnists hated it. TV news coverage imbibed its hostile attitude toward Stone from the *New York Times* and *Washington Post*, the establishment press organs with whom they usually march in lockstep. Television program after program denounced Stone as if he had made a documentary and violated the "fairness and balance" doctrines that allegedly govern news coverage—i.e., disclaimers, separation of invented footage and real footage, labeled dramatizations, showing both sides, and so on.

Most of these attacks seemed to miss the fact that Stone was working as a moviemaker not a TV-news producer. He always referred to *JFK*, perhaps disingenuously, as an exploration of one theory. But the journalists bent on exposing his approach never reported his own doubts and modest claims. ABC's *Nightline* blasted away at Stone and *JFK*. In setting up a *CBS Evening News* story on the movie, Dan Rather could barely conceal his enmity, asking "Is it an outright rewrite of history?" From his tone, there was no question but that he thought it was.

A Garry Trudeau cartoon portrayed Stone as JFK and the media as his assassins. This was one media crossfire that could not hide behind a grassy knoll. The media monitoring organization FAIR concluded that "the news outlets and journalists that attacked *JFK* the most vociferously were the ones with the longest records of error on the issue and defense of the lone assassin theory."

What seems obvious but is rarely acknowledged adequately is that all history—and by extension, all news—reflects someone's interpretation. Stone himself notes that "every historically based film in the history of the medium has utilized dramatic license and speculation, including documentaries." In our documentary, *Beyond JFK*, Walter Cronkite reveals that CBS news, in a documentary aired years earlier, censored a comment by Lyndon Johnson expressing his doubts about the lone assassin theory. The comment was deleted after Johnson pressured William Paley, president of CBS, with a fabricated concern about national security. For years, Cronkite had expressed belief in the Warren Report. I was surprised then he seemed to be changing his tune when I interviewed him in his office at CBS.

"Well, I hold the view that he was a lone gunman, yes. I'm not sure as to whether he was part of a conspiracy or not, however, not any longer."

Tom Wicker, then of the *New York Times*, was in Dallas when President Kennedy was shot and like Dan Rather came to national prominence on the strength of his reports. At the time, Rather reported that the president was shot from the front. He later said he had been mistaken. Both men became sharp critics of Stone. When I pressed Wicker on the issue, he confessed that he too had lost his certainty. "For a long time I felt strongly that Lee Harvey Oswald was the lone assassin," he said. "I think there's evidence that there certainly are doubts about that and I'm willing to concede those doubts. I don't know what happened."

Retired PBS anchorman Robin MacNeil was in Dallas in 1963 too, covering the president's visit for NBC. He was the only journalist traveling with Kennedy to get off the press bus after hearing shots in Dealey Plaza. Hardly a conspiracy nut, MacNeil feels that Big Journalism may not be able to handle all the possibilities. "There is a predisposition still on the part of the mainstream media to believe it all works," he told me for *Beyond JFK*, "that the system works. And it's only the crazies on the fringes who want to keep saying, no, it doesn't work, no, it doesn't work, there's a conspiracy. And the two are converging all the time because the evidence has brought them together."

So when pressed, Cronkite, MacNeil, and Wicker, leading lights of the journalistic establishment, all outspoken critics of Stone, admit to doubts. When confronted with the fact that no one agrees on the facts, honest people in the media began to take a second look and admit how little we know. As public opinion began to coalesce around the notion of opening the government's files, many of the journalists and public figures who had been dismissive of Stone began to jump on the disclosure bandwagon, which came to signify a kind of compromise with Stone's point of view. After all, what's a journalist to do when counterinterpretations of history start becoming acceptable, when the paradigm of official reality begins to slip away? That's what happened to many reporters covering the Vietnam War. They went as boosters and left as critics. Many saw through the lies and propaganda, but it took longer than it should have.

Yet such humbling events happen far too rarely to our top journalists. Most fetishize facts, clothing themselves in the pose of objectivity, projecting deep-voiced expertise on the basis of the skimpiest of details. More often than not, though, their facts, are open to question. So is their point of view—one which, above all else, takes pride in denying its own existence.

Big Journalism still hasn't explained the Kennedy assassination to anyone's satisfaction including its own. At the same time, according to Robin MacNeil, "the country has become accustomed to, conditioned to, conspiracies at the very heart, in the very breast of its own government.... Anybody would have to be a fool these days to dismiss conspiracies."

Congress passed a law leading to the declassification of hundreds of thousands of government documents relating to the Kennedy assassination. Did the press pounce on the documents to advance the story or even to prove Stone wrong? Nope.

Oliver Stone wrote about this lack of media followup in *The Nation*: "No major newspaper, magazine or television network has devoted any resources to pursuing those leads or to conducting a new investigation." He told the editors of *Cineaste*: "Our reporters are backing off stories because editors and the power of conservative media money are telling them to." To Stone, the deeper debate is to determine who has the right to comment on history. "I think many historians come at filmmakers with an attitude and with hostility. It is as though history is their territory and we don't belong.... They feel they are in possession of the facts and the truth."

"I have realized as I grow older," says the novelist Gabriel García Márquez, "that history in the end has more imagination than oneself." Longtime conspiracy proponent Norman Mailer, who in his book on Oswald argues that the alleged gunman may have done it alone after all, puts it another way; he writes that it may take "superior bullshit" to defeat "ordinary bullshit."

Stone's most debated conclusion was that Kennedy was killed when he decided to phase down the Vietnam War. When pressed about the evidence for his views, he does a neat turn, suggesting we think of the Warren Commisison as the purveyors of the offical myth, and his movie, *JFK*, as offering a countermyth. At least he admits it is not the full story. The question remains: Whose truth do you believe? Since *JFK*, the assassination debate is no longer just a quarrel among experts over wounds, bullet trajectories, or rifle capabilities. Stone brought the idea of political motive into the case and offered speculation on the "why done it," not just the "who done it." In so doing, he has pinched an exposed nerve at the center of media power. He has not proven his case, but has forced the rest of us to consider it—an impressive achievement.

Works of imagination have the power of adding nuance and texture by presenting emotional truth. I find it significant that CBS founder William Paley spent his life collecting Picassos, not old newspapers. "Guernica" still says more about war than all the instant TV specials put together. And without a fact or a footnote!

Honest journalists acknowledge that they don't have all the answers, and some admit they may have been messengers of misinformation. Stone told me he thinks most journalists have an agenda. "These are trained Doberman pinschers, these journalists. They're protecting something. They are protecting an old crime."

He may or may not be right, but director Jim Sheridan definitely had a point: There *are* truths deeper than journalism.

One footnote about the continuing saga of "JFK" and Hollywood: The late Jim Garrison's family later sued Warner Brothers with a conspiracy claim of their own, charging that they were cheated out of their share of net profits. Their lawsuit was turned into a class action against all the studios, arguing that they have conspired to fix prices and cheat armies of actors, producers, directors, and writers out of moneys due them. This case could turn into a frontal assault on deeply institutionalized, and questionable, "creative accounting" practices that turn blockbusters with high grosses into supposed financial failures. The studios say there is no such conspiracy and that net-profit deals vary. It is possible that in the end the legacy of "JFK" may not be the unraveling of a murder mystery, but an exposé and reform of corporate crime in media practices.

FOR WHOM THE BELL TOLLS

His name was Murray Kempton and he was, without debate, the dean of newspaper columnists, famous for the originality of his thinking, the artistry of his expression, and the compassion of his soul. I grew up reading his columns in the *New York Post*—and, like many others, was drawn into journalism partly because of them.

When he died on May 5, 1997, *Newsday* gave him its cover, and all the best scribes in town were quoted in his honor. The paper also editorialized subtly by showing a picture of him, suitcase in hand, being forced from the offices of *New York Newsday* on the day that paper was unceremoniously shut down by a greedy parent corporation. They noted without any sense of irony that the Los Angeles-based Times Mirror company had planned to honor Kempton—on the day after he died.

The funeral, May 8, 1997, at the Saint Ignatius Church on West End Avenue was attended by just about every prominent writer and reporter in New York. Kempton had requested a solemn service, sans eulogies. And so the mayor and the former mayor, the columnists and editors—from William Buckley to Jack Newfield to Les Payne to Liz Smith—sat quietly while the priest read the Order of the Burial of the Dead, which we all followed in the memorial pamphlet that had been passed out. But there was one unannounced ritual— the ringing of the church's bell, resonating throughout the neighborhood, not once, not twice, not even twenty-one times. It tolled seventy-nine times, one for each of Murray's seventy-nine years. You could see the media types look around, squirming, as if to ask, "Why so many rings?" "Will this ever end?" Journalists are not known for their patience.

When it was over, I overheard someone ask, "What was that about?" His colleague paused and smiled: "Don't ask for whom the bells toll. They toll for us."

Was that Murray Kempton's last column, number 11,001—a *New York Times* columnist suggested it was—beseeching his colleagues in a most soulful way, in the manner of someone who so loved jazz, to meditate on the end of news as we have known it? One of Kempton's own descriptions of the passing of a politician might just as easily be applied to his own life: "One of the last authentic heroes is fading out in the age of inauthentic ones."

Murray died in a year that also saw the loss of other great scribblers like Chicago's Mike Royko, San Francisco's Herb Caen, and ex-*New York Times* man J. Anthony Lukas. The following year we lost the great war correspondent Martha Gellhorn, and former CBS president Fred Friendly, who quit after the network refused to preempt reruns of *I Love Lucy* for Senate hearings on the Vietnam War.

Some feel that today journalism itself is in a terminal state. But, does it have to die? I don't think so.

PART FIVE

TRANSFORMING MEDIA

CHAPTER 15

WHAT WE CAN DO

*I*n this era of Mickey Mouse and Westinghouse, we cannot even talk about changing America without confronting and remaking media power.

Throughout American history, when it has become clear that media was overstepping its bounds, it has often been people on the inside who first sounded the alarm. At the turn of the last century, E.W. Scripps, the founder of the first modern newspaper chain spoke out: "The press in this country," he said, "is so thoroughly dominated by a wealthy few...that it cannot be depended upon to give the mass of the people that correct information concerning political, economical and social subjects which it is necessary that the mass of people shall have in order that they vote...in the best way to protect themselves from the brutal force and chicanery of the ruling and employing classes."

For many years, the media mixed a sense of mission with the search for profits. In his *Capitalist Fools*, writer Nick Von Hoffman notes that today "the structure of ownership and the nature of management have reduced all content to nearly identical formulas." He says that while a Ted Turner may have strong views, "you would never guess what they are from watching CNN or Turner's other properties."

As we near the end of another century, many senior level journalists have spoken out, Walter Cronkite, Bill Moyers, and the late John Chancellor among them. Reuven Frank, who I met when he headed NBC News, now says: "It is daily becoming more obvious that the biggest threat to a free press and the circulation of ideas is the steady absorption of newspapers, television and radio stations, networks, and other vehicles of information into enormous corporations that know how to turn knowledge into profit—but are not equally committed to inquiry or debate or to the First Amendment."

We live in a media culture where everything we discuss is often framed by media coverage and, then, filtered through a TV dominated popular culture. The misuse of media power, and the inattention of news organizations, should be of universal concern because when any given issue is not on television, it doesn't exist as such for most Americans. "The more things change," quips the poet Tuli Kupferberg, "the harder they are to change back."

In 1995, the Nieman Foundation of Harvard University, an organization whose fellowship program is intended to "elevate the standards of journalism," prepared a survey with pollster George Gallup of this select and selective group's attitudes toward their own field. The survey's conclusion: "de-elevation!" These masters of the media world think it's all going downhill. The findings:

+ The overall quality of the media is declining and basic principles of the journalism profession are being eroded;

+ Distinction between news and entertainment is increasingly obscured;

+ TV and radio are gaining in influence but declining in journalistic quality, while newspapers struggle to maintain quality and are losing influence;

+ Media proprietors are more concerned with profits than product quality;

+ The public is losing confidence in the media.

That's it in a nutshell: today's threat to press freedom. But to their list, I'd add a few more scandals that ought to be investigated:

+ The sham of TV ratings that all networks and advertisers live by—a system that regularly provides incomplete and skewed data used to rationalize all manner of embarrassing program decisions.

+ The power of the broadcasting industry and its lobby—and the effect of its financial contributions to politicians.

+ The collusion of regulatory agencies and the communications industries they regulate.

+ The seemingly endless ability of the media companies to borrow almost limitless sums of money to the detriment of shareholders and consumers. Linked is the question of where the money comes from. (Crooks like the late media mogul Robert Maxwell were able to dip into employee pension funds to finance their "legitimate" media empires--with impunity and without oversight.)

+ Non-existent international codes of industry behavior, public interest standards, and public affairs requirements of fairness and diversity.

+ The persistence of inequalities and discrimination against minorities in hiring and media representation. (Media managers remain 92 percent white.)

+ How certain news shows deliberately promote anxieties that encourage the consumption of certain products that just happen to be advertised on the news.

+ As celebrity news proliferates, so does the power of celebrities, through their studios, PR firms, and agents, to control their own coverage in complicity with media outlets hungry for interviews and cover poses.

But what can we do?

The first step is to build awareness. We need to move beyond criticism to consciousness raising and creative action. Enough of pointing out what is increasingly obvious. The shallowness, superficiality, and vapidity of so much jaded media has to be redefined as a political challenge, as an issue to mobilize around.

A national campaign against the presence of "Channel One," a TV news program with commercial interruptions offered to educators in exchange for satellite equipment and TV sets, has raised the issue of creeping commercialism in the schools. Other educators are introducing media literacy courses and curricula into the schools to teach critical viewing skills. A Los Angeles based Center for Media Literacy is providing schools, libraries, parents, and teachers with books, videos, and teaching units.

Media priorities have to be challenged, and become a priority of a more urgent kind on any progressive agenda. In the '60s, corporations like Dow Chemical became targets of protest and symbols of corporate greed and irresponsibility. In the '90s, many media companies deserve similar contempt. The same people who would be outraged if toxic waste was dumped on their doorstep have to be encouraged to express similar rage at no less toxic junk TV shows being dumped into their living rooms and brains.

The right to information and media pluralism has to be presented as a human rights issue. Article 19 of the UN's Universal Declaration of Human Rights, adopted by most nations in the world in 1948, speaks of it as such, linking the right to speak out with the right to take in. "Everyone has a right to freedom of opinion and expression," it reads. "[T]his right includes freedom to hold opinions without interference and to seek, receive and impart information and ideas through any media and regardless of frontiers." The International Covenant on Civil and Political Rights, another international treaty, in Article 3, mandates the protection of pluralism as well. In America, the Carnegie Commission that gave public television its mandate spoke of the need for an alternative to commercial broadcasting and a "freedom to view." Traditionally, the declarations have been used by the media industry to open up markets and block state censorship, but they can also be used to demand more access and cultural diversity from the industry.

We need a Media and Democracy Act, a legislative commitment to breaking up media monopolies, insuring access, diversity

of perspectives, universal service, free airtime for political advertising, financial support for programming that fosters democracy,
and other policies that guarantee that the people will continue to
own the airwaves.

We need to bring a global perspective to media issues as well,
and recognize that the centralized commercial institutions that we
have become so used to are also international in their reach and
rarely benign in their impact. The rest of the world is aware of the
intrusion of media-fostered intervention in their cultures.

Razali Ishmael, the Malaysian president of the UN General
Assembly, raised some of those concerns at the November 1996
World Television Forum, which was hardly reported on in the
United States: "Today's television environment enlarges choices,
creates opportunities for diversity and promotes a freer flow of information," he said. "However, such an enlargement of people's choices
would only be a false distortion of empowerment were it to be
restricted within the doctrine of consumerism, or pre-packaged by
power elites. Information technology that spans the globe can concentrate ownership, limit access, homogenize content and pit freedom of expression against certain minimum standards."

He is concerned that obsessive TV watching leads to a pervasive sense of loss, and alienation from community values. He wants
equity across the North-South divide. The countries of the north,
including its media activists, need to heed his call for more global
responsibility and international solidarity, just as countries in the
South, including Malaysia, that expect such international solidarity, need to check their tendency to censor and repress a free press.

In our country, pro-democracy media activists know they cannot just throw up their hands in the aftermath of the passage of
the Telecommunications Act. Some advocacy groups are making
themselves heard in rule-making procedures before the FCC and
at the state level at hearings conducted by public utility commissions. The Washington D.C.-based Center for Media Education has
identified a campaign to encourage disadvantaged groups to file

comments on agency dockets and make their concerns heard on issues like universal access, community access, consumer protection, broadcaster accountability, children's television, spectrum auctions, and intellectual property concerns, including fair use and public domain.

Democracy itself can only thrive when citizens are informed. The Independent Media Institute is reaching out to the public at large: "We believe that democracy is enhanced, and public debate broadened, as more voices are heard and points of view made available," they write. "In today's political and media environment we are especially concerned about increasing media concentration, and about the success of conservative and far right ideas and personalities in framing the issues relevant to us all." They and many others, including a newly organized Cultural Environment Movement, are sparking a needed political debate about the relationship between media and democracy.

It is my hope that the media reform movement can speak to growing public anxieties and disaffection and find an organizational form and focus.

Yet, even as right-wing media gadflies like Accuracy in Media (AIM) have now been challenged by progressive counterparts like Fairness and Accuracy in Reporting (FAIR), media mainstream tends to pit them off against each other with claims that attacks on the right and left only prove that they are doing their job in the center. Media companies take refuge in the middle, refusing to audit their own behavior by any other means than ratings and the bottom line. Clearly, a new force is needed to break a logjam that only celebrates the status quo.

How can that be done? And who can do it?

There are a growing number of media professionals who are willing to participate. Not everyone on the "inside" is happy. Many, perhaps most, are demoralized, especially after they've been around a few years. I have been involved in two industry initiatives that show the potential of reaching out to insiders.

One was called The New York Media Forum, an effort by a small group of journalists from a variety of outlets to organize occasional panel discussions at which colleagues could hear debates and discuss media coverage issues. Another was the effort by Concerned Media Employees to rally behind striking writers at CBS News in the late '80s. Several hundred media employees responded, for the first time, across craft and network lines—engineers and producers, correspondents and editors—all protesting CBS's treatment of its employees. Unfortunately, both of these efforts sputtered with little follow-up. More like them are needed.

A program for change needs to have at least five components.

1. It needs to build awareness of media power and irresponsibility throughout our communities. Educators, journalists, and organizers have to start talking about this issue and popularizing it.

2. It needs to be placed squarely on the agendas of all organizations representing people who are effectively excluded from media discourse, including minorities, unions, and issue-oriented organizations. Coalitions have to be forged.

3. An agenda for change is needed. Hopefully, the media charter offered below includes some useful ideas. We need to think harder and more creatively about workable and watchable alternatives to a market-dominated media system and how to create and sustain democratic public media. We need vision, ideas, and plans.

4. Leaders need to be sensitized on these issues and groomed to lead public interest campaigns for media reform.

5. Funding has to be found to finance an effective nationwide organizational and public outreach effort.

As organizing gets underway, here is some of the work a media movement might do.

1. More Monitoring. Everyone should monitor media performance. Groups like FAIR have developed manuals and lists of criteria. If teachers and their students, labor unions and their members began tracking what's on TV and radio, and how the news is being

reported, they will be able to better detect and challenge bias. One good model is the work of Rocky Mountain Media Watch, a group based in Denver that regularly tracks local TV News content. They have published a small book called *Let The World Know: Make Your Cause News* which explains how to organize seminars, train staff, and consult with non-profits.

Existing studies showing how minorities and women are misrepresented, working people excluded, and diverse perspectives suppressed need to be more widely disseminated. Charts like those that have appeared in the *Nation*, on who owns what media properties, can be especially useful. Videos on media issues like those produced by New York's Paper Tiger TV, Sut Jhally's Media Education Foundation, or Adbusters in Vancouver are very effective. A 1996 film, *The Ad and the Ego*, distributed by California Newsreel, is a powerful tool for educating audiences about the effects of advertising. Media literacy has to become part of our school curriculums and everyday life.

2. Media Accountability. Once armed with current data and well researched documentation, citizen groups will be in a better position to demand responsiveness and accountability by media corporations. When media executives meet with consumers, they do tend to get more responsive. Most are sure to resist pressure politics, but they will not be able to ignore it.

3. Legislation and Regulation. Deregulation has given media companies a free hand to do as they will, all in the name of competition. (A year after the 1996 Telecoms bill passed, government agencies admitted that the new law has not had the desired effect, leading instead, to more concentration.) Tougher anti-monopoly laws and enhanced regulation in the public interest by a revamped FCC and FTC are also in order. "And so we must begin a serious national debate," says media analyst Mark Crispin Miller, of New York University, "on anti-trust, raising crucial questions about foreign ownership, the dangers of horizontal integration, the neces-

sity of public access, the possibility of taxes both on advertising and on the use of the public spectrum and all of the other issues that this Congress has been speeding from madly in the other direction." There are anti-trust laws on the books. They need to be enforced.

Public concern has to be focused as well on reversing the give-away of the digital broadcast spectrum to broadcasters without fees or public interest obligations. "Because of increased capacity, digital television will be a powerful medium," argued the Benton Foundation, "powerful enough to do some important things for the American people. Like serving children better. Giving us political debate that really is debate. And using new interactive and on-demand features to provide the information people want and need every day. But there's no commitment from the commercial broadcast industry to serve these public needs." Can we press to expand broadcasters' public interest obligations to match the increased capacity of digital TV?

4. Public Television. There is no reason why America cannot have a publicly owned BBC or CBC-style public TV system to effectively compete with the commercial spectrum. It is time to put the public back into public television with more locally elected community boards to encourage PBS to return to its original mandate calling for alternative voices and more diverse program choices. Pressure will be needed to democratize and properly finance PBS. PBS could be funded through a tax on commercial television stations and their advertisers. There needs to be at least one channel that serves the public interest in the broadest possible way. The experience of Channel 4 in London might be a model worth examining and improving upon.

We also need to protect and strengthen public access to cable outlets and television and radio. Cable operators are now trying to drop their obligations to provide public access studios and channels because they say it violates their first amendment rights and costs too much. This is nonsense. A vital community-based media can challenge this self-serving logic. We can say to cities and to cable companies: don't mess with public access.

Outside of television, there is also a need to fight for funding for new public exhibition spaces for feature films and documentaries considered not commercial enough. Fewer and fewer theaters now show independent work, in part because the movie industry and the multi-plex theater operators have also become concentrated. As a result, fewer and fewer films, the majority studio releases, are being shown on more and more screens. Smaller independent distributors say they are being shut out.

5. Alternative Programming and Independent Media. Creating channels in and of themselves will not make for changes in the system unless new programming reflecting a non-corporate view is available. Congress already recognized discrimination against America's independent filmmakers when it created the Independent Television Service (ITVS). That agency and other media centers on the local level need to be adequately funded, with their programming guaranteed some form of distribution. Programming like that produced by Paper Tiger TV and Free Speech TV deserve support. The human rights series that I help produce at Globalvision, *Rights & Wrongs*, only survived because of ITVS backing. The weekly series ran out of money in 1998.

The calls for social responsibility in business have so far not reached the media industry. Only public awareness and pressure can move the mountain of media inertia. Happily, some of the voices associated with reform in business are moving into the media arena.

My old friend, the unflappable Anita Roddick of the Body Shop, is leading the charge. "Is the idea of a socially responsible media just pie in the sky?" she asks. "I don't think so. I know it will be complex, paradoxical, and slightly unfamiliar but censorship by ommission or indifference never works." In her inimitable style, she calls socially responsible media, "a bloody good idea." But there are many good ideas. This is one that needs to be fought for. As FAIR's Laura Flanders concludes in *Real Majority, Media Minority*, her thoughtful book on the shabby treatment of women in the media, "The right to communicate is like any other right. And like any right, it will not be given. It must be won."

THE GOOD NEWS

The good news is that a new media reform movement is in formation and I feel fortunate to be part of it. Over 700 journalists and media makers took part in the first Media & Democracy Congress held in San Francisco February 29 to March 3, 1996 and agreed to prepare a broad manifesto that would lead to the launching of a full-fledged national education campaign against media monopolies. The Congress also voted overwhelmingly to endorse an "Information Bill of Rights" for all people as part of an effort to build a more equitable, participatory, and accountable media system.

Two weeks after the San Francisco meeting, I was in St. Louis for the founding convention of the Cultural Environment Movement, an organization that brought together 200 invited delegates from over 150 organizations to form a new coalition to challenge the effects of media concentration. Here the principal actors were not just media professionals but members of religious, labor, parents' and teachers' organizations, along with students and activists.

Listen to these excerpts from their mission statement:

"Media are coalescing into an integrated cultural environment that constrains life's choices as the natural environment defines life's chances. The consequences are as diverse as they are far-reaching. For many people they mean an enrichment of local cultural horizons. But for many they also mean a narrowing of perspectives, homogenization of outlooks and limitation of alternatives.... For society this is a way of pre-empting alternatives, limiting freedom of the press to those who own it, divorcing payment from choices and denying public participation in cultural decision making....

"The Cultural Environment Movement (CEM) is concerned with such distortions of the democratic process. How can we heal the wounds of all the stories that hurt and tear us apart? How can we put culture power to liberating ends?"

Inside the networks and media institutions, it is time for media employees to speak up in defense of the values of journalism and their own integrity. In Los Angeles, a newsroom revolt at KCBS forced a news director to resign after the staff signed a collective complaint. "You are producing a cynical news product that very few of us can respect or take pride in," it read. "You mock [the viewers] continually and make us carry out your daily deceptions." Some individuals like Ross Becker, formerly an anchor at LA's KCOP, left in disgust with tabloidization and the compromises it imposes on journalistic values. "People are tired of wondering whether it's true that aliens are about to land in their back yards," he said. "They don't want to be insulted anymore.... We have had a technological revolution in this business; now we need a revolution of conscience and content."

Across the spectrum, from left to right, from the poor to the rich, new voices are taking media issues seriously. In the poorest region of Mexico, the guerrilla leader Marcos says there are three options:

"We have a choice: we can have a cynical attitude in the face of the media, to say that nothing can be done about the dollar power that creates itself in images, words, digital communication, and computer systems that invade not just with an invasion of power, but with a way of seeing that world, or how they think the world should look. We could say, well, 'that's the way it is,' and do nothing.

"Or we can simply assume incredulity; we can say that any media communication by the media monopolies is a total lie. We can ignore it and go about our lives...

"But there is a third option that is neither conformity nor skepticism, nor distrust: that is, to construct a different way—to show the world what is really happening—to have a critical world view and to become interested in the truth of what happens to the people who inhabit every corner of this world.... The problem is not only to know what is occurring in the world but to understand it and to derive lessons from it."

At the heart of the larger problem is the primacy of the market and the way market values have become dominant and unchallenged in communications worldwide. A few years ago, I was able to meet and spend some time with billionaire George Soros, who had virtually personified the triumph of market mentality.

By 1996, Soros, one of the richest men in the world, started to zero in on the erosion of democracy in America, including misguided drug policies, and xenophobic immigration practices. He began to look inward, at the larger social costs of his own fabulous personal wealth and success. "I have made a fortune on international financial markets, and yet now fear the untrammeled intensification of laissez-faire capitalism, and the spread of market values into all areas of life is endangering our open and democratic society," he wrote in the Atlantic Monthly. "The arch enemy of an open society is no longer the Communist threat but the capitalist one. It is wrong to make 'survival of the fittest' a leading principle in a civilized society." He argues that inequality is rampant because "laissez-faire ideology has effectively banished income or wealth redistribution." So far, he has not made the media his focus—but the implications are there.

In the end, the choice is ours. Which America do we want? The country with something to say or just something to sell?

Media reform is not an impossible dream. It is critical for a renewal of democracy. In my own life, I have seen what can happen when activists zero in on injustices and speak out. The demise of racial segregation in our country and apartheid in South Africa, the end of the Vietnam War and the cold war—all causes I invested energy into came to pass, in no small part because of public pressure and activism. They started as small murmurs of dissent and then turned into mighty movements for change. Some were even stimulated by books like Rachel Carson's *The Silent Spring*, Ralph Nader's *Unsafe at Any Speed*, or *The Autobiography of Malcolm X*.

After years in the media world, I know that when the public understands the issues and takes up the challenge change can happen, despite all of the media's arrogance and seductive power.

"The impulse arises to chant 'smash the TV sets, smash the TV sets,'" Todd Gitlin wrote almost twenty-five years ago. The goal, he said then, is not to replace the manipulators with new manipulators but to democratize the tools of manipulation.

Can we all, citizens and journalists alike, find some new answers that will enable us to use our mighty media resources to empower and enlighten individuals and, by so doing, change the world for the better? Fighting to democratize the media will not be an easy or quick fight, and cannot be won before the next commercial break. Eternal vigilance is still what's needed.

A DECLARATION OF MEDIA INDEPENDENCE

Two documents from historic and successful struggles for democracy have helped me frame my thinking on media independence. One was our own Declaration of Independence, the seminal statement of the American Revolution that gave the grievances of a colonized people eloquent expression. The other, from the modern era, was South Africa's Freedom Charter, adopted at a Congress of the People in 1955, a clarion call for justice that outlined a vision and the principles for a post-apartheid society. Both documents defined in their times and lands what was wrong and pointed to what needed doing.

So, with a little creative borrowing, I drafted such a document for adoption at the 1996 Congress of Media and Democracy, which appeared in the Congress's final report. I include it here with no pretensions to literary originality, as a working draft for readers to react to, revise, and, hopefully, in part or in its entirety, to put to use.

> We declare before our country and the world that the giant media combines who put profit before the public interest do not speak for us. We proclaim this

democratic media charter and pledge ourselves to work tirelessly until its goals have been achieved. We urge all Americans of good will, and people throughout the world who want to participate in a new democratic information order to join with us.

We call upon our colleagues, readers, editors, and audiences to inform themselves and the American people about the dangers posed by the concentration of media power in fewer and fewer hands. We urge that more air time and news stories be devoted to a critical examination of the relationship between media monopolies and the threat they pose to the spirit and functioning of the first amendment. We cannot have a meaningful democracy unless our media institutions provide reportage, in-depth programming and coverage that reflects a more diverse range of sources and opinions.

We urge our elected representatives to challenge excessive and concentrated media power because it poses a threat to the future of democracy.

We call for an end to all legislation that promotes censorship and corporate practices that lead to self-censorship. We need government to regulate media monopolies in the public interest and to keep our news media and new electronic information highway open and free of the undue and repressive influence of government bureaucrats, excessive corporate branding, and one-note political agendas.

We urge non-governmental groups, advocacy organizations, labor unions, community groups, and all environmental and social justice organizations to make common cause with us in fighting to create more points of access and accountability in our media system; we urge all citizens to interact more with the media in their own communities by monitoring performance, writing letters, calling talk shows, and meeting editors and radio and TV executives.

We are against techno-solutions like the V Chip—and call instead for a "D Chip," a commitment to use media to promote the values of democracy. We want more than ritualized, look-alike and think-alike coverage of elections. We want more coverage of citizen participation in civil society, political movements, non-governmental organizations, and community groups. We share the concerns of many parents with the overload of shows that glamorize violence and cheapen sex.

We demand that media institutions in our society increase the participation of minorities and women in all positions in their organizations. Our newsrooms have to stop being among the most segregated institutions in our country. Racism inside the media contributes to the toleration of racism in the culture at large. We urge news organizations to openly audit their performance in this regard and publicize the results.

We further pledge to join and support efforts to stop attacks on labor unions in our media institutions. Media workers must be guaranteed the right to collective bargaining, and to belong to unions if they so choose.

We call on media companies to reduce the growing internal gap between salaries at the top and salaries at the bottom. Fairness and equity in the media workplace is essential.

We call upon media institutions to explore the values and practices of "public journalism" so that the media can begin to better serve the needs of the people. We urge them to adopt codes of conduct that rebuild their credibility in the eyes of a cynical public which no longer trusts the media. We call upon the media to promote tolerance and equality in American life.

We call upon U.S.-based multi-national media companies who already generate more than half of their revenues outside the United States to act responsibly in trading with the nations of the world. Many already resent the dumping of American programming, however popular it may be in the short run. Other countries deserve a chance to sell as well as buy, to have their voices and concerns heard too. They have the means of production but lack the means of distribution. We oppose the growth of a new "electronic colonialism." We want more global sharing of cultures and viewpoints.

We call upon the governments of the world to respect the rights of journalists—who are in danger in many countries—and the right of the people to read and see their reports.

We call for more public funding of the arts and humanities, including documentary programming. We want America to allocate as much money proportionately to support the arts and humanities as countries like Canada, Germany, and England do. We have the money, let us find the will.

We want to put the public back into public broadcasting and create mechanisms for accountability that bring PBS back to its original mandate to provide programming not available on the commercial spectrum. We want to stop the give-away of the public airwaves and the broadcast spectrum itself. The income from spectrum sales should be set aside for public media. The corporate media sector should be taxed to help subsidize public media so that the notion of the "free marketplace of ideas" has meaning once again. Private companies can lease the airwaves, not own them.

We pledge ourselves to working cooperatively and collaboratively to help bring the media more in line with the values of democracy.

We ask all who share our goals to embrace this declaration and agree to work on behalf of its tenets so that the principles of freedom of the press, which have given America such a distinctive place among nations, will not be compromised and denied because a handful of huge companies and media moguls are in a position to dictate what our country sees, hears, reads and, ultimately, thinks.

CHAPTER 16

THE MEDIA CHANNEL

*W*hen I discovered, in early 1997, that the FCC might be willing to set aside a tiny sliver of the digital TV spectrum for noncommercial channels, an idea came to me, or rather, a fantasy: What if the media establishment I spend so much time dissecting and cajoling were finally to embrace human rights? What if I could get my hands on a slice of the digital spectrum, and funding to go with it? Armed with financial resources and airtime, I'd be in a position to launch a channel in the public interest. I'd call it the Media Channel and dedicate it to the memory of my media faves, Edward R. Murrow, I. F. Stone, George Seldes, Abbie Hoffman and Andy Kopkind. Its purpose would be to critique and challenge the other channels, monitor their performance, report on the programs they air—or refuse to air—and profile and expose the interests and conflicts of interest of their owners. The channel's goal: to wake America up from its media-conditioned stupor.

There would be no shortage of potential programming for the Media Channel. For starters, we'd present shows like *Paper Tiger* TV (carried by the Deep Dish network), which has been challenging mainstream media for years, while groups like Fairness and Accuracy in Reporting (FAIR) would be only too happy to turn its excellent radio show, *Counter-spin*, into a weekly TV roundtable. We'd show independent documentaries like *Without Fear Or Favor* or *Tell the Truth and Run*, about the towering press critic George Seldes. There are hundreds of hours of unaired documentaries on subjects ignored or trivialized by the mainstream media. There are scores of Hollywood films about the media, from *Citizen Kane* and *Network* to *Wag the Dog* and *Bulworth*. There are music videos and dramas. There are political comedians, and self-critical journalists. The material is there.

In this dream world, I'm in a TV control room splicing together reports from the field—from media watchdog groups and journalism professors, from industry conferences and tips phoned in on a hotline where media employees can blow the whistle on newsroom abuses without detection or fear of retaliation. To create even more public disclosure, perhaps we'd have our own live cameras at key editorial board meetings around town, monitoring the decision-making processes that lead to so many problems with the news. *The Media's Funniest Videos* would be a verité documentary program filmed by video flies on the wall, who manage to penetrate the inner sanctums of media corporations and record the great surrealistic encounters that occur there every day.

I'd introduce a prime-time series, *The Media Is the Monopoly*, in which media moguls would meet every week to discuss what they've bought and sold, and what it means. I'd have it set in a boardroom, with reports on earnings and layoffs, pilots and failed shows, executive shuffles and the latest hotshots. Throughout the show, the players—media titans and their investment bankers—would play a game of Monopoly on an electronic display like the one on *Wheel of Fortune*. They would play for keeps. Real deals would go down. Their game board would be shaped like a map of the world.

Instead of a commercial break I'd have *A Mogul Minute*, complete with the latest outrageous utterances from those in charge. Just as the truth is said to come from the mouths of babes, truth about media practices would explode with great force from the mouths of these moguls.

A *Mogul Minute* would be brought to you by the makers of sodium pentothal, aka truth serum. Our guests would have the option of taking the drug or being taped live in a confessional or under oath.

The Media Channel would feature sometimes satiric counter-ads produced by groups like Ad Busters, and excerpts from films like *The Ad and the Ego*, which shows the insidious impact of TV advertising.

Meet the Sponsor would be a related feature. Its subject: who sponsors what. On the pilot program, for example, we'd learn more about the anti-trust charges against the Archer Daniels Midland company ("Supermarket to the World"), which underwrites news coverage on PBS and NPR, and sponsors pundit shows on commercial channels. In its second week, *Meet the Sponsor* might examine Ford Motor founder Henry Ford's anti-Semitism and financial support for Hitler and the Nazi Party, as a commentary on NBC's unsanitized 1997 broadcast of Steven Spielberg's holocaust epic, *Schindler's List*, sponsored by Ford without commercials. Of course, our show would include in its report that Ford reversed himself later in life, issuing a pro forma apology, as well as the fact that many in the Jewish community found Ford's about-face disingenuous.

Along with counter-advertising, the Media Channel would feature bumpers and public service announcements—"edu-mercials"—in place of commercials. Great quotes about the media, set to music and with accompanying graphics, would be a highlight of our counter ads, and they would be every bit as slick as anything that's ever urged us to buy a Coke or a Chevy.

The Media Channel would also launch *Edutainment Tonight*, our version of the popular *Entertainment Tonight* with its fluffy celebrity features. Our spin would be to cover—and thus to encourage—entertainment projects that deal with real issues. Is there truth deeper than journalism? So long as the news business seems to mangle the coverage of the news, can Hollywood do any better?

The Media Channel would offer *Self-Censorship Minutes*, quick takes in which prominent journalists offer soundbites on the stories they pulled their punches on and why.

We'd also offer our own business news programming called *Who Benefits: Economics for the People.* While business news is currently aimed at elite audiences, the Media Channel's economics show would actually explain the underlying logic behind those business concepts that few people really understand, like the prime and short-term interest rates, price-earnings ratios, and why the stock market goes down when unemployment goes up. Our focus would be on the people who do the work (in the spirit of the public TV show *We Do the Work*), not just on those who score on the day's trading. We'd profile workers, their unions and communities, we would ask who benefits, who wins and loses from economic decisions. Unions would be given some airtime.

And wouldn't it be great to do a show on media literacy based on the work of popular educators such as the late Paulo Freire, a show that would seek to educate people, through their own experiences, to become conscious of and to work to change their situations. "Making Sense of the Media" (Monthly Review Press), by Brazilian educators Eleonara Castaño Ferreira and Jao Castaño Ferreira just cries out to be turned into a TV show to demystify the media. To focus attention on the content of TV news, in their educational groups, they ask people questions about newscasts like these:

+ What did you see? What were the main issues presented in the news?

+ Do you think that the news reports presented were factual? Are there other aspects of the story? Is there bias in its presentation?

+ Why did the broadcaster choose these issues and not others? Can you name other, more important issues that should be in the news and were not? Why do you think they weren't presented?

If the Media Channel did exist, would anyone watch? We may never know, although I have a hunch that if we could avoid becoming too parochial and arcane, we could create a popular, even entertaining—there, I said it—channel that could compete with the others.

I have seen critical news reports about dangerous levels of media concentration and the way journalism is being subverted to serve business interests—in Russia! But here in the U.S. I rarely see it documented or discussed on TV—the medium the masses watch. Is that healthy for a country that calls itself democratic?

The Media Channel, anyone?

(When I first imagined this I never thought it would be possible to create because of the costs involved in starting up a cable channel and the difficulties of securing distribution. But then it ocurred to me that a channel with this spirit could be launched for far less on the Internet. And now, thanks to a partnership between Globalvision and England's One World online, it will be. Watch for www.themediachannel.org, coming to your Web browser soon.)

SELECTED MEDIA REFORM GROUPS

Adbusters
1243 W. Seventh Ave.
Vancouver, BC
V6H 1B7 Canada
Phone: 604/736-9401
e-mail: adbuster@wimsey.com

Association of Independent
Video & Filmmakers
304 Hudson St.
New York, NY 10013
Phone: 212/807-1400
e-mail: Aivffuvf@aol.com

Benton Foundation
1634 Eye St. NW, Suite#832
Washington, DC 20036
Phone: 202/822-1955
e-mail: benton@benton.org

California Working Group
5867 Ocean View Drive
Oakland, CA 94618
Phone 510/547-8484
e-mail: wedothework@igc.apc.org

Center for Human Rights
Education
P.O. Box 311020
Atlanta, GA 30302
Phone: 404/344-9629

Center for Media Education
2120 L Street NW, Ste. 2200
Washington, DC 20037
Phone 202/331-7833
e-mail: cme@access.digex.net

FAIR (Fairness and Accuracy
 in Reporting)
130 W. 25th St.
New York, NY 10001
Phone: 212/633-6700
e-mail: fair@igc.apc.org

Globalvision
1600 Broadway #700
New York, NY 10019
Phone: 212/246-0202
e-mail: moreuwatch@globalvision.org

Institute for Global
Communications
18 DeBoom St.
San Francisco, CA 94107
Phone: 415/255-9035
e-mail: outreach@igc.org

Media and Democracy
Congress/Independent Media Institute
77 Federal St.
San Francisco, CA 94107
Phone: 415/284-1420
e-mail: alternet@alternet.org

Paper Tiger Television
339 Lafayette St.
New York, NY 10012
Phone: 212/420-9045

Rocky Mountain Media Watch
P.O. Box 18858
Denver, CO 80218
Phone: 303/832-7558

Libraries for the Future
121 W. 27th St. Suite 1105
New York, NY 10001
Phone: 212/352-2330

FILMOGRAPHY

Here is a partial list of my independent TV and film work through 1997. Readers interested in contacting me or ordering these films, can do so by writing me c/o Globalvision, 1600 Broadway, New York, NY 10019, or by e-mail at moreuwatch@globalvision.org. I also encourage you to visit Globalvision's Web site: www.globalvision.org/globalvision/.

INDEPENDENT FILMS

BEYOND LIFE: TIMOTHY LEARY LIVES (1998)
Director
Produced by David Silver for Mercury Records

Timothy Leary, the '60s "acid guru," famous for his "turn on, tune in, drop out" mantra, was a complex and important thinker, scientist, and philosopher. Drawing on one of Leary's last interviews, taped just before his death in 1996, this film explores his controversial career and contributions to American thinking about drugs, psychedelics, consciousness expansion, virtual reality, and death and dying. Includes interviews with Yoko Ono, Winona Ryder, Ram Dass, Allen Ginsberg, G. Gordon Liddy, the Moody Blues, Ken Kesey, Bob Guccione Jr., Paul Krassner, and many others.

SOWING SEEDS/REAPING PEACE:
THE WORLD OF SEEDS OF PEACE (1996)
Director

Turning enemies into friends and transforming hatred into healing is the mission of Seeds of Peace, a pioneering summer camp program that brings Israelis and Palestinians, Bosnians and Serbs, and inner-city Americans together to discuss and debate their fears and hopes. This film (60 minutes and 90 minutes) documents the impact of facilitated conflict resolution workshops with 150

487

teenagers—a volatile and exciting process filled with trauma, tension, and moments of mutual discovery. It is introduced by Barbra Streisand and includes comments by President Clinton, Shimon Peres, Yasser Arafat, and King Hussein.

PRISONERS OF HOPE (1995)
Co-director (with Barbara Kopple)
Produced by Anant Singh. A Videovision production.
(58 minutes)

Twelve hundred and fifty former political prisoners led by President Nelson Mandela return to South Africa's draconian Robben Island prison for a reunion and conference. The new South Africa collides with the old.

COUNTDOWN TO FREEDOM:
TEN DAYS THAT CHANGED SOUTH AFRICA (1994)
Director
Co-produced with Anant Singh and Videovision in South Africa.
(97 minutes; available in a 77-minute version for school showings)

Narrated by James Earl Jones and Alfre Woodard, the *War Room*-type insider-chronicle of Nelson Mandela's triumph in South Africa's first free elections.

SARAJEVO GROUND ZERO (1993)
Co-director (with Ademir Kenovic)
(53 minutes)

Sarajevan filmmakers chronicle the genocidal assault on their country and people. Inside the siege of Sarajevo. Winner of the Intercom International Film and Video Festival Gold Plaque and Gold Plaque of Charleston World Film Festival.

ONE WORLD NOW (1992)
Executive Producer

A half-hour TV magazine special produced for One World Now looks at the issues of the 1992 Earth Summit and examines the case for transforming and democratizing the United Nations.

THE LIVING CANVAS (1992)
Director

TV special on African-American painters hosted by Billy Dee Williams and featuring the work of Dean Mitchell and Thomas Blackshear. This program, produced for the Greenwich Workshop, aired worldwide.

BEYOND JFK: THE QUESTION OF CONSPIRACY
(Warner Home Video, 1991)
Co-director (with Barbara Kopple)

A 90-minute look at the real people, real issues, and important questions raised in Oliver Stone's film *JFK*. Features interviews with Jim Garrison, Walter Cronkite, Robin MacNeil, Marina Oswald, Kevin Costner, and others.

GIVE PEACE A CHANCE and
THE MAKING OF GIVE PEACE A CHANCE (1991)
Director

Thirty-nine popular musicians, led by Lenny Kravitz and Sean Lennon, update John Lennon's classic "Give Peace a Chance." The Globalvision "making of" documentary was shot and edited in one week to explain why some of America's best-known rock 'n' rollers wanted to stop the Gulf War before it started. (45 minutes)

MANDELA IN AMERICA (A-Vision, 1990)
Director
(90 minutes)
   The official documentary of Nelson Mandela's historic visit to the United States that toured eight cities in eleven days.

MANDELA: FREE AT LAST (1990)
Co-executive Producer (with Rory O'Connor)
   A background report on Nelson Mandela's release from prison that aired as a PBS Special on February 11, 1990, along with his complete first public speech in 27 years.

SUN CITY and *THE MAKING OF SUN CITY* (1985)
Producer (with Hart Perry and others)
   Historic program includes Little Steven's award-winning music video with 54 artists including Miles Davis, Bono, Bruce Springsteen, RunDMC, and many others, as well the documentary program explaining the reasons the artists sang against apartheid. The documentary was honored with the top award of the International Documentary Association.

STUDENT POWER (1968)
Director
(30 minutes)
   Chronicles the student uprising at the London School of Economics. Shown at the London Film Festival in 1968. In the collection of the British Film Institute.

TV SPECIALS AND SERIES

GLOBALIZATION AND HUMAN RIGHTS:
A RIGHTS & WRONGS SPECIAL
WITH CHARLAYNE HUNTER-GAULT (1998)
Co-executive Producer (with Rory O'Connor)
   A look at how economic globalization impacts on human rights
with interviews with Treasury Secretary Robert Rubin, Ralph Nader,
George Soros, Robert Mormats, Pierre Sane, Alan Nairn, Jose Ramos
Horta, Thabo Mbeki, Desmond Tutu, and others.

THE WORLD OF ELIE WIESEL (1997)
Producer
   Public television program featuring Nobel laureate Elie Wiesel's
conversations with Jesse Jackson and holocaust historian Daniel
Goldhagen.

RIGHTS & WRONGS: HUMAN RIGHTS TELEVISION
(1993-1996)
Co-executive Producer (with Rory O'Connor)
   Hosted by Charlayne Hunter-Gault. Sixty-two half-hour programs available. Each features background reports, interviews, and
cultural segments on human rights challenges all over the world.
A complete list of *Rights & Wrongs* programs is available on Globalvision's Web site.

SOUTH AFRICA NOW (1988-1991)
Executive Producer
   Globalvision produced 156 weekly editions of the Emmy-award
winning *South Africa Now* series. The one-hour compilation *Best
of South Africa Now* (1991) features highlights of the series and a
discussion of its impact.

ABOUT THE AUTHOR

DANNY SCHECHTER is a television producer and independent film-maker who also writes and speaks about media issues. He has produced and directed many TV specials and films, including *Beyond Life: Timothy Leary Lives* (1997); *Sowing Seeds/Reeping Peace: The World of Seeds of Peace* (1996); *Prisoners of Hope* (1995, co-directed by Barbara Kopple); *Countdown to Freedom: Ten Days that Changed South Africa* (1994), narrated by James Earl Jones and Alfre Woodard; *Sarajevo Ground Zero* (1993); *The Living Canvas* (1992), narrated by Billy Dee Williams; *Beyond JFK: The Question of Conspiracy* (1992, co-directed by Barbara Kopple); *Mandela in America* (1990); *Give Peace a Chance* (1991); *The Making of Sun City* (1987); and *Student Power* (1968).

Schechter is co-founder and executive producer of Globalvision, a New York-based television and film production company now in its tenth year, where he produced 156 editions of the award-winning series *South Africa Now*, co-produced *Rights & Wrongs: Human Rights Television* with Charlayne Hunter-Gault, and most recently created "The World of Elie Wiesel" (1997).

A Cornell University graduate, he received his Master's degree from the London School of Economics, and an honorary doctorate from Fitchburg College. He was a Nieman Fellow in Journalism at Harvard, where he also taught in 1969. After college, he was a full time civil rights worker and then communications director of the Northern Student Movement, worked as a community organizer in a Saul Alinsky-style War on Poverty program, and, moving from the streets to the suites, served as an assistant to the Mayor of Detroit in 1966 on a Ford Foundation grant.

Schechter's professional journalism career began in 1970, when he was named news director, principal newscaster, and "News Dissector" at WBCN-FM in Boston, where he was hailed as a radio innovator and won many industry honors, including two Major Armstrong Awards. His television producing career was launched with the syndicated *Joe Oteri Show*, which won the New England Emmy and a NATPE IRIS award in 1979. In 1980, he created and produced the nation's first live late-night entertainment-oriented TV show, *Five All Night, Live All Night* at WCVB in Boston.

Schechter left Boston to join the staff at CNN as a producer based in Atlanta. He then moved to ABC as a producer for 20/20, where during his eight years he won two National News Emmys. Schechter has reported from 47 countries and lectured at many schools and universities.

Schechter's writing has appeared in leading newspapers and magazines including the *Boston Globe, Columbia Journalism Review, Media Studies Journal, Detroit Free Press, Village Voice, Tikkun, Z*, and many others. He has a 22-year-old daughter, and lives in New York City in a large loft with an eight-thousand-album record collection, and an Apple computer that is nearly out of memory.

JACKSON BROWNE has been one of America's leading singer-song-writers since the 1970s, with many hit songs to his credit. He is also frequently outspoken on social, political, and media issues.

ROBERT W. McCHESNEY is Professor of Communication at the University of Illinois at Urbana-Champaign. He is the author of several books, including *Telecommunications, Mass Media, and Democracy* (Oxford University Press, 1993), *Corporate Media and the Threat to Democracy* (Seven Stories, 1997), and the forthcoming *Rich Media, Poor Democracy: Communication Politics in Dubious Times* (University of Illinois Press, 1999).

FEEDBACK WELCOME

You can share your comments on *The More You Watch, The Less You Know* through a special Internet site linked to Globalvision's web page. Danny Schechter also invites colleagues to share media war stories and whistle-blowing impulses about practices in their media outlets. You can join the conversation online at www.globalvision.org/globalvision/, or www.visitweb.com/moreuwatch, or you can contact Danny Schechter by e-mail at moreuwatch@globalvision.org.

INDEX

ABC (American Broadcasting Corporation): anti-environmentalist stance, 221; Capitol Cities acquisition of, 217–218, 415; conservative world view, 184–185; Disney merger, 393, 412–418, 423; Food Lion lawsuit, 209–211; *Hidden Cameras/Hard Choices*, 210–211; policy on activism of employees, 203; ratings decline, 205, 424; Roone Arledge at, 200, 216–217; South Africa coverage of, 202–203, 320; Statue of Liberty story, 227–228; stockholders meeting, 412–418; union busting by Disney, 422

ABC News: management changes, 420; ratings plunge, 419–420

Abrams, Lee, 124

Abu Jamal, Mumia, 83, 441

Accuracy in Media (AIM), 294, 466

A Current Affair, 370–371, 373–375

Ad and the Ego, The, 468

Adbusters, 468

advertising : DeBeers Mining Cartel and, 240; demographic targeting and, 221–222; elections and, 64–65, 67; Kruggerands on television, 239–240; in the media, 42, 151–152, 205; on the news, 162; using news to sell products, 463

Africa: Africa Fund and, 240; American involvement in, 269, 286–287; Congo, Cornell student march, 269; Ethiopian famine coverage, 296–297; Jesse Jackson story, 192–194; media coverage of, 54, 193, 296; WBCN coverage of, 107–108

A.F.R.I.C.A., 300

African National Congress. *See* ANC

African Studies Association all white membership, 288: *African Studies in America: the Extended Family* (ARG), 288

Africa Research Group (ARG), 287–289

Africa's Media Image, 193

Agence-France Press, 107

Agnew, Spiro T., 92, 106

Ailes, Roger: and Affirmative Action, 407; and Fox News Channel, 380, 443; and Geraldo Rivera, 188; Jesse Jackson and Al Sharpton meeting, 405–412

Aldridge, Ron, 404–405

Ali, Muhammad, 269

Allen, Herb, 423

Alterman, Eric, 253

Altheide, David, 173, 205–206, 214

Amanpour, Christiane, 61, 171–172

American Broadcasting Corporation. *See* ABC

American Committee on Africa, 296

American Media System and Its Commercial Culture (Bogart), 152

Amin, Mohammed, 296

ANC (African National Congress): Communist Party and, 273–274, 275; corruption in, 328–329; in exile, 282–283, 284; as government, 323–333; guerrilla army of, 284, 293; human rights abuses, 294, 330; Joe Slovo and, 270, 277, 319; London offices bombed, 275; non-racialism policy, 331; Oliver Tambo's leadership, 284, 294; post election, 324, 327–333; pro-business right wing, 327–328; Rupert Murdoch and, 384; SABC and, 345; 20/20's lack of interest in, 192; Stockholm-supported v. Moscow-backed, 264; strategies of, 275, 283, 293; Umkhonto or MK, 284, 293

Anderson, Jack, 127

Annan, Kofi, 61

anti-apartheid movement (American), 271–272, 296–297

anti-trust issues in media, 350, 468–469

apartheid: American anti-apartheid movement, 271–272, 296–297; American Indian model, 264; anti-apartheid strategies, 275, 293; Artists for a Free South Africa, 340; Artists United Against Apartheid, 299; Chase Manhattan Bank, 271–272; coverage in the American media, 202–203, 263–265, 291–293, 317; David Rockefeller and, 271–272; foreign investment in, 285; historical context of, 264; as international racism, 271; *Prisoners of Hope*, 321–323, 344; Southern United States comparison, 278–279; *Sun City* record and video, 299–302; United Nations Demonstration, 272

Archer, Jeffrey, 378

Archer Daniels Midland Corporation: antitrust charges 481; opinion show sponsors, 49

Arledge, Roone: ABC and, 216–217; ABC News presidency, 200; 20/20 and, 181; Av Westin resignation, 218; Disney and, 216–217; Geraldo

Rivera and, 186–187; Lee Iacocca and, 227; Marilyn Monroe story and, 227; Rupert Murdoch and, 196, 386; *South Africa Now* and, 245

Armed and Dangerous (Kasrils), 277

Artists for a Free South Africa, 340

Artists United Against Apartheid, 299

Arts and Entertainment Channel (A&E), 81

AT&T, 357

audience comprehension of news, 57–60, 88, 223

audience for serious issues, 211

Auletta, Ken: characterizes Rupert Murdoch, 385; comments on viewers as consumers, 151; on institutionalized sensationalism, 222; and numbing effect of the news, 224

Baez, Joan, 330

Bagdikian, Ben, 60, 185, 402

Baker, Arthur, 300

Baldwin, James, 260–261

Baltimore Area Youth Opportunities Unlimited (BAYOU), 91

Barber, Benjamin: on Disneyfication, 393; on diversity, 399; on invisible market system, 51; on mergers and acquisitions of media, 363; on monopoly, 417; on public media, 364

Barnes, Fred, 128

Barnett, Michael, 152–153

Bart, Peter, 364–365, 399

Barucha, Cyrus, 156–157

Bashir, Geymayel, 189

Bass, Sid, 422

BBC (British Broadcasting Corporation): and the digital age, 383; as a model for commercial media, 364; STAR TV and, 359; World Service cuts, 429

BCN. *See* WBCN

Becker, Ross, 472

Belafonte, Harry, 296, 308

Bennett, Bob, 142, 146

Bennio, Warren, 245

Benton Foundation, 469

Berliner, Alan, 186

Bernstein, Carl, 127

Bevins, Bill, 165–167

Bewkes, Jeffery, 42–43

Beyond Control: ABC and the Fate of the Networks (Huntington), 415

Beyond JFK: Barbara Koppel and, 237, 450; Marc Levin and, 450; Oliver

Stone and, 450–456; Robin Mac-Neil and, 454–455; Tom Wicker and, 453–454; Walter Cronkite and, 453, 454

Biddle, Frederic, 348

Big Picture Conference: digital age discussion, 350–351; Discovery Channel at, 358; FCC and, 351–352; Howard Stringer and, 360–361; John C. Malone and, 353–358; Michael Fuchs and, 361–363; participants of, 351; Peter Bart and, 364–365; Reed Hundt and, 351–352; Rupert Murdoch speech, 352–353; Schroder Wertheim and, 349; Ted Turner speech, 352

Biko, Steve, 293

Biography, 81

Birt, John, 383

Black Consciousness Movement, 293

Blair, Tony, 371–372

Blitzer, Wolf, 171

Bloomberg, Michael, 442, 443, 446–447

Body Shop and *Rights & Wrongs*, 256–259

Bogart, Leo, 152

Bono, 301

Boraine, Alex, 330

Bosnian War, 43, 78, 439

Boston media RMMW rating, 147

Botha, Stoffel, 295

Boutros-Ghali, Boutros, 60–61, 78

Boylan, Michael, 76

Bozell, Brent, 62, 379

Bradlee, Ben, 441

Braun, Eric, 148

Braverman, Alan, 413

Breaking the News (Fallows), 89

Brinkley, David, 49–50

British Broadcasting Corporation. *See* BBC

British Film Institute, 79

British Telecom, 383, 385

Brokaw, Tom, 70: all news channel and, 174; Committee to Protect Journalists, 440; Olympic coverage and, 428; speech impediment and, 110; on *Wild Feed*, 430–431

Bronfman, Edgar, 362, 386

Brown, Bob, 186

Browne, Jackson, 47, 204–205, 300–301, 319

Bruno, Ellen, 358

BSTV (Body Shop TV), 259

Buchanan, Pat, 175, 380

Buddy Dean Show, 91–92

Buffett, Warren, 422

bulimia story on 20/20, 224–225
Burchett, Wilfred, 127, 370
Burke, Dan, 415
Burke, David, 187
Burlingham, Bo, 101, 102, 103
Burns, Ken, 82
Burundi radio propaganda, 43
Business Channel, 254
business news, 357, 446–447
Buthelezi, Mangosothu Gatsha, 329
Byron, Christopher, 357

Cable News Network. *See* CNN
cable television: deregulation of, 396;
    documentaries and, 84–85; Fox
    News Channel and, 381; John C.
    Malone and, 353–358; monopolies
    of, 402; MSNBC and, 400; public
    access of, 469–470; rate hikes, 354,
    357, 398; in South Africa, 344–345;
    Tele-Communications, Inc. (TCI),
    353; Telecommunications Reform
    Act of 1996, 396–398
Cabral, Amilcar, 284, 287
Caen, Herb, 458
Caldwell, Christopher, 74
Camus, Albert, 72–73
Cannon, Lou, 71
Caper, Jane, 155–161
Capitalist Fools (Von Hoffman), 461–462
Capitol Cities: buys ABC, 217–218, 415;
    union busting and, 415; William
    Casey investment in, 414–415;
    Capitol Cities/ABC, Disney
    takeover, 393
Capitol Cities/ABC, takeover by Disney,
    412–423
Carlson, Margaret, 49, 67–68
Carnegie Commission mandate for pub-
    lic television, 246–247, 464
Carson, Mike, 424
Cascio, Michael, 84–85
Casey, William, investment in Capitol
    Cities, 414–415
Castro, Fidel, 274, 308
Cavanagh, Jerry, 278
CBS (Columbia Broadcasting Corpora-
    tion), 153: *Eye on People*, 173;
    Westinghouse Electric Company
    and, 393–394; Westinghouse
    media empire, 400
CBS Evening News ratings plunge, 424
Cellular One and Michael Milken, 386
Censored, 366
censorship: by corporate owners, 403,
    416; and the Declaration of Media
    Independence, 475; in news, 53,

182, 208, 365–368, 403; Project
    Censored awards, 365–368; in
    South Africa, 238, 295; in televi-
    sion, 53, 182; at WBCN, 106
Center for Media Education, 403–404,
    465–466
Center for Media Literacy, 464
Central Intelligence Agency. *See* CIA
Chancellor, John, 400, 462
Channel One, 209, 464
Charles, Ray, 298
Charlie Rose Show, 414, 445, 446–448
Chase Manhattan Bank, 271–272
Chayefsky, Paddy, 366
Chiapas, 44–45
Chicago Conspiracy Trial, 444–445,
    447–449
Chideya, Farei, 57
China: influence on American media,
    359–360; reporting on, 358–359;
    Rupert Murdoch and, 359,
    378–379; Universal Pictures fear
    of, 359
Chippendale, Peter, 384
Chomsky, Noam, 51–52, 53–55, 107, 205
CIA (Central Intelligence Agency):
    African networks, 287–288; anti-
    Communist propaganda, 286;
    Freedom of Information Act,
    114–115; Free World Empire and,
    286; funding of student organiza-
    tions, 285–286; infiltration of
    media, 127; in Iraq, 58; journalists
    on payroll of, 115; Mobutu Sese
    Seko and, 269; Nelson Mandela
    and, 287; Patrice Lumumba and,
    269, 287; Radio Hanoi, 111;
    Schechter's file, 115–116; South
    Africa, in, 285–288; William Casey
    and Capitol Cities investment,
    414–415
Cinemax, 320
Citicorp and Rupert Murdoch, 385
Citizen Election Project, 70
Civil Liberties Union Lawsuit, 115
Civil War, The and PBS, 82
Clegg, Johnny, 303
Clinton, Bill: Bob Dole and, 67–68, 70;
    campaign donations, 64; Disney
    stockholder meeting and, 419; at
    Oxford, 272; the press and, 62–63
Cloud, Stan, 70
CNN (Cable News Network): Caper,
    Jane and, 156–161; CNN Center,
    158; conservative bias, 175; early
    days, 155–160; expansion of, 160;
    Freeman Reports, 161; conspiracy

theory show, 170; reviews of, 163; Ted Turner and, 164–168; Globalvision meeting with Ted Turner, 175–176; John C. Malone and, 159; Liberty Media and, 353; *Newsstand,* 175; ratings, 174; Reese Schonfeld and, 158, 163, 170, 171; sarin gas story, 175; Securities and Exchange Commission, 166–169; Telecommunications Reform Act and, 398; Time Magazine and, 175; Time Warner merger, 352; United Nations and, 172; William Colby as conference speaker, 176

Cochran, Johnnie, 340

Cockburn, Alexander, 66, 72, 372

Coetzee, Dirk, 276

Cohen, Bernie, 178–179

Cohen, Jeff, 383, 416

Cohen, Richard, 53, 202

Cohn-Bendit, Danny, 272

Colby, William, 114–115, 176

Cole, Williams, 79

Columbia Graduate School of Journalism, 75

Committee to Protect Journalists (CPJ), 437–443

Common Cause, 397

Communist Party in South Africa, 273–274, 275

Competitive Media Reporting, 65

Concerned Media Employees, 467

Congress of Media and Democracy, 474

Consumer Federation of America, 403–404

Contra-Flow in Global News (Thussu), 58

Contras, 204

convention coverage, 65–67

Copper, Sam, 103

corporate culture in the media, 416

corporate friendly programming at PBS, 254

corporate mergers. *See* individual companies

Costas, Bob, 427, 428

Countdown to Freedom: Academy of Motion Picture Arts and Sciences, 320; Alfre Woodard and, 319; American media in action and, 318; Anant Singh and, 315–316; ANC leadership interviews, 319; Cinemax and, 320; James Earl Jones and, 319; Mandela invitation to make, 313; SABC and, 314; Stuart Sender and, 316; Yvette Tomlinson and, 316

Counterspin, 480

Couric, Katie, 157

Crichton, Michael, 366

Croatian television propaganda, 43

Cronkite, Walter: in *Beyond JFK,* 453, 454; memoirs, 77–78; newsmen and politics, 50; news pioneer, 74–75; speaks out on media, 462

C-SPAN, 356

Cultural Environment Movement, 466, 471

cultural imperialism, 234–235, 365, 477

Cumings, Bruce, 58

cynicism in the media, 89

Dalai Lama, 327–328, 358

Damn Right, 355

Davis, Jennifer, 296

Davis, Miles, 299, 301, 319

Day & Date, 404

D-Chip, 476

D (Deal) Day letter, 390–391

Dean, Buddy, 91–92

DeBeers advertising on Nightline, 240

Debray, Regis, 234–235

Declaration of Media Independence, 474–478

Defazio, Robert A., 396

DeKlerk, F.W., 277, 317

Dellinger, Dave, 445, 446

Dellums, Ron: American anti-apartheid movement, 296; Nelson Mandela and, 308, 309; PBS protest, 249

Demme, Jonathan, 260, 301

democracy and television, 62–71

demographic targeting, 221, 252

Deng "Maomao" Rong, 378

Deutsch, Robert, 88

Didion, Joan, 73

digital television and Rupert Murdoch, 383, 398–399

digital television giveaway. *See* Telecommunications Reform Act of 1996

Diller, Barry, 398

direct broadcast satellite systems, 402

Discovery Channel, 353, 358–359

Dished (Chippendale and Franks), 384

Disney (Walt Disney Company): ABC News and, 216–217; cancels *Fudge* on ABC, 420; Capitol Cities/ABC takeover, 393, 412–423; Haitian sweatshops and, 250, 350; *Home Improvement* suit, 420; influence at ABC, 403, 420; Knight-Ridder and newspapers, 392–393; Martin Scorsese and, 358–359; Michael Ovitz's sever-

ance, 418–419, 421–422; restructuring, 41; retail store in New
York, 418; stockholders meeting,
418–423; unethical firing practices, 350; union busting at ABC,
422
dissidents and media, 46, 48
Dobra, Klee, 119
documentaries: and cable, 81, 84–85; distribution of, 84; in England, 79;
fundraising for, 83; and HBO, 83;
and major studios, 85; and optioning books, 82; and PBS, 81–82; as
tabloid features, 83
Dole, Bob, 67–68, 70, 397
Donahue, Phil, 305–306
Donaldson, Sam, 200
"Do They Know It's Christmas," 296
Douglas, Susan, 211
Dowd, Maureen, 67
Dow Jones buys WNYC, 395
Downs, Hugh: *20/20* and, 181–182, 215;
Marilyn Monroe/Kennedy story
and, 187; Middle East story and,
190; Victor Neufeld and, 219
Drudge, Matt, 424
Duggan, Ervin, 248–251, 254
dumbing down of the news, 88: audience
research and, 215; Disney and,
416; local news and, 148; newscast
design and, 347–348; tabloid jour-
nalism and, 370–371
Dutka, Rick, 300
Dyer, C.C., 188
Dylan, Bob, 301

Echostar, 382
*Economic Concentration and Diversity in
the Broadcasting Media,* 403–404
Edison, Thomas, 205
Edwards, David, 54
Effros, Stephen, 382
Eisner, Michael, 413, 417, 418, 421
elections: and advertising, 64–65, 67:
coverage of, 67–71, 476: coverage
of conventions, 65–67
El Salvador story on *20/20,* 191–192
Engelman, Ralph, 247
environmental issues in media, 221, 391
Ephron, Nora, 127, 451
Erwin, Diana Griego, 59
Ethiopian famine, 296–297
ethnic cleansing coverage in media, 43
Evans, Harold, 42
Every Secret Thing (Slovo), 274
Eye on People, 173
Eyes of the Storm, 252

Fabrikant, Geraldine, 356
FAIR (Fairness and Accuracy in Report-
ing): on Disney merger with ABC,
416; Fox News channel and, 383;
John Stossel and, 220; Media
Reform and, 466; Rupert Murdoch
protest, 387; Victor Neufeld and,
219
Faith and Values Channel, 246, 355–356
Falk, Brian Peter, 374
Fallows, James, 64, 89
Faludi, Susan, 62
FANLAN. *See Five All Night, Live All
Night*
Farmer, James, 287
FBI (Federal Bureau of Investigation):
Bill Zimmerman and, 117; Bob
Smith (agent), 118; Schechter
Investigation, 114, 116, 117;
WBCN and, 113–114
FCC (Federal Communications Com-
mission): at Big Picture Confer-
ence, 351–352; and digital
television, 391; fines Howard
Stern, 122; and Rupert Murdoch
investigation, 375–377; secret vot-
ing, 352; Trent Lott threat to,
390–391; WBCN and, 99;
WHDH-TV scandal, 140
Fenton, David, 180
Ferreira, Eleonara Castaño, 482
Ferreira, Jao Castaño, 482
Fiferling, Joe, 186
Film Net, 344
Filner, Bob, 249
First, Ruth: Ann Scott and, 275–276;
assassination of, 276; Communist
Party and, 273–274; Joe Slovo and,
273–274; in London, 273–276;
Oginga Odinga and, 275
Fitzgerald, Frances, 292
Five All Night, Live All Night (FANLAN),
141–146
Flanders, Laura, 470–471
focus groups, 215
Fonda, Jane, 110, 176, 225
Food Lion, 209–211
*Four Arguments for the Elimination of
Television* (Mander), 48
Fowler, Mark, 392
Fox Network, 377, 383
Fox News Channel: Committee to Pro-
tect Journalists and, 443; conserva-
tive bias, 380–381, 429; FAIR and,
383; launch party, 430; New York
Market and, 381, 382; origins of,

173; Roger Ailes and, 380; Time
Warner and, 381
Frady, Marshall, 411
Frank, Reuven, 462
Franken, Al, 64
Frank N. Magid Associates, 148
Franks, Suzanne, 384
Fraser, Nick, 359
Freed, Barry. *See* Hoffman, Abbie
Freedom Forum, 90
Freeing the Media, 44
Freeman, Sandi, 155–157, 161–162,
163–168, 171
Freeman Reports: producing, 155–158,
161–164; reviews of, 163; Ted
Turner interview, 164–168
Free Speech TV, 470
Free World Empire, 286
Freire, Paulo, 482
FRELIMO, 283
Friendly, Fred, 458
Fritts, Eddie, 391, 405
Froines, John, 444
From Hollywood to Hanoi, 112
Frontline, 82, 237, 250
Fruchter, Norm, 79
FTC investigation of Time Warner and
Turner, 399
Fuchs, Michael: Big Picture Conference
and, 361; fired by Gerald Levin,
363; fires Doug Morris, 361–362;
Ted Turner and, 440–441; Time
Warner music and, 361–362
Fujimori, Alberto, 448
Full Disclosure (Neil), 379
Fussell, Paul, 60

Gabor, Zsa Zsa, 76
Gabriel, Peter, 301, 319
Gannett, 392
Gans, Curtis, 70
Garafalo, Reebee, 121
Garrison, Jim, 456
Gast, Leon, 86
Gelbart, Larry, 42
Geldof, Bob, 296
Geller, Alfred, 156
Gellhorn, Martha, 458
Gellman, Sharon, 340
General Electric (GE): and China, 360;
and MSNBC, 400; opinion show
sponsor, 49
General Motors (GM), 82
Gergen, David, 63
Geymayel, Bashir, 189
Gingrich, Newt, 378
Ginsberg, Allen, 127

Gitlin, Todd, 474
Give Peace A Chance, 115, 235
Glasscock, Duane. *See* Laquidara,
Charles
Globalvision. *See also Countdown to
Freedom; Mandela in America;
South Africa Now; Beyond JFK*,
237, 450–456; clients of, 259–260;
A Current Affair, 373–375; *Eyes of
the Storm*, 252; Fox Network and,
372; *Give Peace a Chance* and,
115, 235; Haiti and, 259; Kennedy
family and the mob story,
372–373; management style, 256;
meeting with Ted Turner,
175–176; origins of, 231–232;
Rockefeller Foundation and, 260;
Sarajevo Ground Zero, 237; Sun-
dance Film Festival and, 260;
United Nations Award, 78; ups
and downs, 260
Godin, Helene, 430–431
Godley and Creme, 301
Goldstein, Tom, 393
Gooding, Richard, 75–76
Goodman, Fred, 109, 121
Goodman, Walter, 65
Gordon, Linda, 289
Gordon, Vicki, 143–144, 146, 221
Gould, Stanhope, 190
government: media and, 200; pro-
monopoly media policies, 356;
television and, 47
Granath, Herb, 205
Grant, Angeleynn, 142
Grant, Jane, 79
Greenberg, Stan, 69
Greenfield, Jeff, 54, 434
Grossman, Larry, 53
Guardian Angels, 178–179
Guerin, Veronica, 441, 442–443
Gulf War: censorship of, 208; coverage
of, 44; *Eyes of the Storm* and, 252;
Give Peace a Chance, 115, 235;
television coverage of, 56
Gunter, Barrie, 88
Gunther, Marc, 184, 216, 217

Hackfield, Taylor, 86
Hacks (Wren), 74
Hadges, Tommy, 103
Hampton, Henry, 84, 250
Hanoi Hannah, 110–111
Harber, Anton, 336
Harris, Kevin, 238
Harvard Crimson, 130–132
Hastings, T. Mitchell, 99–100

Hayden, Tom, 445, 448
HBO (Home Box Office), 83, 362
Heimlich Henry, 143
Hendryx, Nona, 301
Henry, John Campbell, 416
Hepburn, Katharine, 221
Herald Traveler Company, 140
Herbert, Bob, 248
Herman, Ed, 54
Hertzgaard, Mark, 64
Hess, Stephen, 44
Hewitt, Don: hidden cameras, 210; and
    60 Minutes, 181; political bias, 50;
    show biz *vs.* news biz, 222
Hickey, Neil, 44, 397
Hidden Agendas (Pilger), 175
hidden cameras, 210
Hightower, Jim, 71
Hinton, Les, 379
Hoffman, Abbie: "birthday party," 260;
    Chicago Conspiracy Trial and, 445;
    Freeman Reports guest, 163; *20/20*
    guest, 178; *Joe Oteri Show* guest,
    138; Liberty House and, 444;
    manic depression and, 446; on the
    '60s, 124, 125; WBCN guest, 104;
    YIPPIES and, 444
Hoffman, Jack, 445–446
Hoffman, Julius, 449
Hollings, Ernest, 397
Holmes Norton, Eleanor, 250
homogenization of media, 57, 173, 207,
    209, 471
Honeywell Inc., 106–107
Honig, David, 375–377
Horowitz, David, 239, 253
Horrigan, Kevin, 394
Houser, Cheryll Miller, 84
House That Roone Built, The (Gunther),
    184, 216
Hoynes, William, 247
human rights: Discovery Channel and,
    359; General Electric (GE) and,
    360; issues in the media, 464; PBS
    and, 248–249; programming,
    243–244; Rupert Murdoch and,
    359
Human Sexual Response, 144–145
Hume, Ellen, 211
Hundt, Reed, 351–352, 390, 401
Hunter-Gault, Charlayne: Committee to
    Protect Journalists and, 440; Nel-
    son Mandela interview, 303–304;
    NPR Correspondent, 252; *Rights
    & Wrongs*; anchor, 244–245; PBS
    battle, 249–250
Hussein, Saddam, 57–58

Iacocca, Lee, 225–228
*If You Don't Like the News, Go Out and
    Make Some of Your Own* (Nisker),
    123
Iger, Bob, 413, 419–420
Iglesias, Julio, 298
Imus, Don, 63–64, 400
Independent Feature Film Market
    (IFFM), 80
independent media, 470
Independent Television Service (ITVS),
    253, 470
Indiana University survey, 207
Infinity Broadcasting: buys WBCN, 119;
    cuts news at WBCN, 121; O.J.
    Simpson board member, 432; and
    Westinghouse, 122, 400
Information Wars, 47
Independent Media Institute, 466, 486
international news, coverage of, 43–44,
    60–61, 101–102, 107–108, 110, 429
*International News and Foreign Corre-
    spondents* (Hess), 44
Iraq, 57–58
Irvine, Reed, 379
Ishmael, Razali, 465
ITT buys WNYC, 395

Jackson, Jesse: in Africa, 192–194; on
    black youth in custody, 435; PBS
    protest, 249; Roger Ailes meeting
    with, 405–412; and Secret Service,
    447–448
Jackson, J.J., 103
Japan trip with Nieman Fellowship,
    127–130
Jarriel, Tom, 186, 190, 226
Jarvik, Lawrence, 253
Jarvis, Sharon, 221
Jennings, Peter, 438: Nelson Mandela
    interview, 318; *Peter Jennings
    Reports*, 223; on quality of the
    news, 429; Roone Arledge and,
    216; on South African press ban,
    295; Statue of Liberty host, 227
Jewell, Richard, 443
JFK (the movie), 452–456
Jhally, Sut, 468
Joe Oteri Show, The, 138–139
Johnson, Nicholas, 376
Johnson, Tom, 175
Jones, Quincy, 296
Jordan, Michael, 393
Jordan, Pallo: and *Countdown to Freedom*,
    313, 319; in exile, 272, 277, 294;
    fired from post, 341; at SABC gala,
    341; and Thabo Mbeki, 345

Jose Ruben Zamora Marroquin, 441
journalists: as celebrities, 90, 463; as
    fourth branch of government, 89;
    job satisfaction, 207; numbing of,
    208, 224; objectivity and, 206,
    441–442; in peril, 437–438; public
    trust of, 90
Junk Science, 220
Jurkowitz, Mark, 68

Kalb, Marvin, 132, 174
Kaplan, Rick, 175
Karmazin, Mel, 122
Kasrils, Ronnie, 277, 322
Kathrada, Ahmed, 312
Katur, Marcy, 396
Katz, Jon, 59, 78
KCBS, 472
KCET, 239
Kees, Beverly, 90
Keifo, 143
Kempton, Murray, 72, 457–458
Kendrick, Abby, 119
Kennedy, Dan, 254
Kennedy, Joe, 88
Kennedy, John F., assassination and theo-
    ries, 450–456
Kennedy, Ted, 308–309, 372–373
Kerner Commission, 436
Kerzner, Sol, 298
King, Dexter, 308
King, Larry, 171
Kinnock, Neil, 371
Kirby, Bill, 241–242
Kirch, Leo, 398
Kissinger, David, 131
Kissinger, Henry: diplomatic language
    and, 108; Nieman Gala speech,
    130–133; Nobel Peace Prize, 118;
    Rupert Murdoch and, 386–387
Kitman, Marvin, 243, 251, 255, 349, 396
Klein, Joe, 73–74
Klite, Paul, 42, 65
Kluge, John, 140
Knight-Ridder, 392–393
Konner, Joan, 75
Kopkind, Andrew, 72, 74, 110, 120, 479
Koppel, Ted: apartheid and, 240; Good-
    ing, Richard and, 76; Gore Vidal's
    comment on, 184; Mandela, Nel-
    son and, 306–307; O.J. Simpson
    and, 436; Republican convention
    and, 66; Statue of Liberty coverage
    and, 228
Kopple, Barbara, 84, 237, 321, 450
Kovic, Ron, 309
Krassner, Paul, 77, 444

Kravitz, Lenny, 235
Kruggerands protests, 239–240
KSAN, 123
Kunene, Mazisi, 277, 290
Kunstler, William, 445, 447, 449
Kurds, 58
Kusnetz, Marc, 295
Kuwait, 58

labor, coverage of, 183–184, 253, 357
labor unions in the media, 476
Lamb, Brian, 356
Landau, Saul, 357–358
Landay, Jerry, 148, 356
Lantos, Tom, 249
Lapping, Brian, 359
Laquidara, Charles, 103, 106, 108, 123
Larry King Live, 175
Lasch, Christopher, 60
Lavender Hour, 110
Lawson, Jennifer, 250
Lear, Norman, 249
LeBlanc, Keith, 299
Ledbetter, Jim, 203
Le Duc Tho, 118
Lee, Martin, 200
Lee, Spike, 86
Leland, Tim, 292
Lennon, John, 115, 235
Lennon, Sean, 115, 235
Leno, Jay, 59, 142–143
Leonard, John, 40, 248, 251
*Let the World Know: Make Your Cause
    News* (RMMW), 468
Levin, Gerald, 361, 363
Levin, Marc, 450
Lewis, Anthony, 130, 281
Liberty House, 444
Liberty Media, 353
Liebling, A.J., 72
Lifton, Robert J., 208
Lights, Camera, War (Neuman), 44
Litter, Kitty, 144
Live Aid, 296
Llelyveld, Joe, 277–278
Loach, Ken, 252
Lock Up, 110
London School of Economics, 78–79,
    272
Los Angeles Times cuts news, 395
Lott, Trent, 390–391
Love, Darlene, 301
Lovett, Joe, 186
Lowenthal, Mark, 366
Lukas, J. Anthony, 458
Lumumba, Patrice, 269
Lundvall, Bruce, 300

Lustig, Ivan, 364
Luthuli, Albert, 279–281
Lydon, Christopher, 136

Mabuza-Suttle, Felicia, 340
MacArthur, John R., 208
MacArthur Foundation, 241
Machel, Graca, 312
Machel, Samora, 312
MacNeil, Robin, 454
Macy, John, 247
Maddux, Hilary, 355
Madonna, 50
Magid, Frank, N., 148
Magness, Bob J., 356
Mahoney, Yule, 116–117
Mailer, Norman, 77, 455
Makathini, Johnny, 277
Making of Sun City, 300–301, 302
Malan, Magnus, 239
Malcolm X, 287
Malone, John C.: cable and, 353–354;
    CNN and, 159; C-SPAN and, 356;
    Federal Trade Commission and,
    399; Liberty Media and, 353; *New-
    shour* and, 355; '90s Channel and,
    354–355; Rupert Murdoch and,
    356, 381; Tele-Communications,
    Inc. (TCI), 354–357, 399; Viacom
    and, 401
Mandala, Mark, 151–152
Mandela, Nelson. *See also Countdown to
    Freedom*; *Mandela in America*; *Pris-
    oners of Hope*: CIA and, 287; Fidel
    Castro and, 308; Grace Machel
    and, 312; Joe Slovo funeral, 277;
    Native Americans and, 309; net-
    work interviews with, 303–304;
    personality of, 311–312; Phil Don-
    ahue and, 305–306; release from
    prison, 303; SABC gala, 340, 341;
    treason trial, 273; visit to stock
    exchange, 325
Mandela, Winnie, 294, 309, 312
Mandela and DeKlerk, 315
Mandela in America: American cities vis-
    ited, 307–309; Dexter King and,
    308; Doug Morris and, 362; Harry
    Belafonte and, 308; MacArthur
    Foundation and, 241–242; produc-
    ing of, 306–309; Ron Dellums and,
    309; Ron Kovic and, 309; U.S.
    Congress and, 308; William Kirby
    and, 241–242
Mander, Jerry, 48
Mann, Bill, 394
Mansion on the Hill (Goodman), 109, 121

Marist Institute, 68
Maritz, Doug, 339
Market Theater, 290–291
Markey, Ed, 396
Marsh, Dave, 298
Marshall, Margaret, 281
Martin, John, 75
Marton, Kati, 438, 441, 443
Mason, Dan, 394
Matsepe-Cassaburri, Ivy, 338
Mavundla, Lawrence, 329
Maynard, Bob, 127
Maysles, Al, 86
Mazzocho, Dennis, 414–415
Mbeki, Thabo, 329–330, 345
McCain, John, 397
McChesney, Robert, 56, 390, 401
McKibben, Bill, 391
McLuhan, Marshall, 46, 387
Media Access Project, 376, 391
Media and Human Rights, 60
Media Channel proposal, 479–483
Media & Democracy Congress, 471
Media Education Foundation, 468
media moguls conference. *See* Big Pic-
    ture Conference
media moguls summer camp, 423
media monitoring groups, 467–468
Media Research Center, 62
Media Virus (Rushkoff), 46
Media Worlds in the Post Journalism Era
    (Altheide and Snow), 205–206
Meiselas, Susan, 441
mergers and acquisitions. *See also* indi-
    vidual companies: anti-trust issues
    and, 468–469; corruption in, 401;
    coverage of in media, 401; impact
    on media, 52, 394–395, 402–405,
    416–418, 475; media war and, 41
Merrit, Mark, 66–67
Microsoft, 41, 173, 400
Miliband, Ralph, 272–273
Milken, Michael, 385–386
Miller, Mark Crispin, 52, 468–469
Mills, C. Wright, 288
Minow, Newton, 351
Mitchell, Pat, 81
Mitroff, Ian, 245
MNET, 344
Mobutu Sese Seko, 287
Mondlane, Eduardo, 283, 287
monitoring the media, 467–468
Monroe, Marilyn 187, 227
Montsho, Rapitse, 344
Moore, Jonathan, 127
Moore, Michael, 82
Morgan, Michael, 56

Morris, Dick, 76, 94
Morris, Doug, 361–362
Moses, Judith, 186
Moyer, Greg, 358
Moyers, Bill, 84, 304–305, 462
MSNBC, 173, 400
Mthombothi, Barney, 338
Multimedia sold to Gannet, 392
Murdoch, Bill, 109
Murdoch, Rupert. *See also* Fox Network;
    Fox News Channel: Barbara Wal-
    ters and, 194–197; Bernie Stone
    and, 194–197; Big Picture Confer-
    ence, 352–353; China and, 359,
    378–379; Chris Patten and, 379;
    Citicorp and, 385; Congress and,
    378, 381–382; conservative politics
    of, 379, 380–381, 429; debt,
    384–385; Deng "Maomao" Rong
    and, 378–379; direct broadcast
    satellite systems and, 402; Echostar
    and, 381–382; European market
    and, 383–384; FCC (Federal Com-
    munications Commission) and,
    372–373, 375–377; Hitler diaries
    and, 370; Howard Stern and, 123;
    Jeffrey Archer and, 378; John C.
    Malone and, 356, 381; Margaret
    Thatcher and, 378; MCI and, 385;
    media empire, 377; Michael Milken
    and, 385–386; as modern day
    pirate, 385; NAACP and, 375–376;
    Newt Gingrich and, 378; New
    World Communications and, 398;
    New York Post and, 196, 372–373,
    378; PrimeStar and, 382; protest
    against, 387; Roone Arledge and,
    196, 386; SKY satellite and,
    381–382; South African sports
    rights, 384; STAR satellite, 376;
    Ted Kennedy and, 372–373; Ted
    Turner and, 369, 381; Time Warner
    and, 381, 382; Tony Blair and,
    371–372; unions, breaking of, 196;
    United Jewish Appeal tribute and,
    386–387; *Village Voice* ownership,
    382; Wilfred Burchett and, 370
Murdoch: The Decline of an Empire, 384
Murphy, Tom, 413–415
Murray, Martin, 326
Murrow, Edward R., 78, 151, 479

NAACP (National Association for the
    Advancement of Colored People),
    375–376
NACLA (North American Congress on
    Latin America), 289

Nader, Ralph, 68, 367
NARMIC, 289
National Association of Broadcasters
    (NAB), 391, 405
National Endowment for the Arts, 83
National Institute for Mental Health, 48
National Security Agency files, 115
national security and the news, 208
National Union of South African Stu-
    dents (NUSAS), 281
NBC Europe and *Rights & Wrongs*, 410
NBC (National Broadcasting Corpora-
    tion), 153: and CBS programs,
    400; and GE's China connection,
    360; and GE's threat to cable over
    MSNBC, 400; Microsoft venture,
    173, 400; Olympic Games cover-
    age, 424–428; and Richard Jewell,
    443; and Rupert Murdoch deal,
    376; and *Wild Feed*, 430–431
Negroponte, Michel, 80
Neil, Andrew, 379
Nel, Louis, 299
Nelson, Jack, 90
Neto, Agosthino, 287
*Networks of Power: Corporate TVs Threat
    to Democracy* (Mazzocho),
    414–415
Neufeld, Victor, 218–219, 221
Neuman, Johanna, 44
Newfield, Jack, 237
news: audience comprehension of, 58,
    88, 209, 223–225; audience for
    serious issues, 211; business news,
    357, 446–447; censorship, in, 53,
    182, 208, 365–368, 403; commer-
    cial pressures on, 61, 217, 360,
    402–403; conservative policy fram-
    ing of, 466; control, 200; credibility
    of, 210; definition of, 88–89; dissi-
    dents and, 46, 48; "dumbing
    down" of, 88, 148, 215, 348, 371;
    elections, role in, 67–71; as enter-
    tainment, 222, 223, 228; fiction *vs.*
    reality, 48; homogenization of, 57,
    173, 209; human-temperament
    approach, 426; John Chancellor
    on, 400
    local: "dumbing down" of, 371; Frank
    N. Magrid, 148; Rocky Mountain
    Media Watch (RMMW) survey,
    65; viewership, 148; mergers and
    acquisitions, impact on, 394–395,
    402–405, 416–418, 475; as profit
    centers, 400; "Promos," 214; pub-
    lic television and, 253–254; rat-
    ings, 56–57, 424; at WBCN,

101–113; youth audience for, 56–57, 209
news channels, 173
news coverage of: Africa, 54, 193, 296–297; China, 358, 360; crime and race, 432, 435; digital television giveaway, 390–401; environmental issues, 391; ethnic cleansing, 43; Gulf War, 44, 56, 57–58, 208; international news, 60–61, 74, 110, 243–244, 429, 439; *JFK* (the movie), 452–453; labor, 252, 357, 392; the masses and, 44–45, 253; media, 41, 390–391, 401; O.J. Simpson trial, 433–437; sensational news stories, 433; South Africa, 202–203, 263–265, 291–293, 317; Tibet, 358; Vietnam, 102, 107–108
newsmagazines, 177–178: credibility and, 210; formats for, 213–215
Newsstand, 175
Newswatch (Westin), 213
New World Communications, 357, 386, 398
New York Media Forum, 467
New York Times, 226–227, 265
Nexis, 201
Nicholas, Martin, 288–289
Nieman Fellowship: at Harvard, 71, 126–133; Japan trip, 126; Kissinger speech, 130–131
Nieman Foundation survey, 462–463
Nietzsche, Friedrich, 208
Nightline: "America Held Hostage," 184; DeBeers Mining Cartel and, 240; O.J. Simpson and, 433, 436; Republican convention, 66
'90s Channel, 354–355
Nisker, Scoop, 123
Nitz, Michael, 221
Nixon 49, America 1, 108
North, Oliver, 185
North American Congress on Latin America (NACLA), 289
Northern Student Movement (NSM), 92
North Korea radio propaganda, 45
North Vietnam. *See* Vietnam
Nujoma, Sam, 283

O'Brian, Dave, 100
O'Connor, Rory. *See* Globalvision
Odinga, Oginga, 275
Odyssey, 355
O Jays, 298
Olatunji, 268, 272
Old Mole, The, 77

Olympic Games, NBC coverage of, 424–428
117 Days (First), 273
$100 Million Dollar Lunch, 140
Ono, Yoko, 115
opinion shows, 49
Oppenheimer, Harry, 192
Ortega, Daniel, 204–205
Oteri, Joe, 137–139
Ovitz, Michael, 361, 418, 421

PacTel and Tele-TV, 361
Padden, Preston, 382
Palestinian Liberation Organization, 189–190
Pants, Nancy, 144
Paper Tiger TV, 468, 470, 479
Parry, Jim, 103
Parton, Dolly, 218
Paton, Alan, 281, 290
Patten, Chris, 379
Paxon, Communications buys WNYC, 395
PBS: Behind the Screen (Horowitz), 253
PBS (Public Broadcasting Service): alternative mission compromised, 252; Business Channel, 254; Carnegie Commission mandate, 246–247, 464; commercialization of, 254–255; conservative bias, 244, 247, 253, 254; corporate friendly programming, 254; demographic targeting and, 252; documentaries and, 81–82; entrepreneurial culture of, 255; funding cuts protest, 395–396; Gulf War and, 252; human rights programming, 247, 248–251, 258; international news coverage and, 244; *The Making of Sun City* and, 302; Nelson Mandela release interview, 303, 304–305; *Newshour*, 355; *Reader's Digest* and, 254
Rights & Wrongs: arguments against, 250; rejection of, 243–244, 248
South Africa Now, 242–243; *Sun City*, 302; Williams Companies and, 254; women and minorities and, 249
Peifer, Alice, 186
Pennebaker, D.A., 83
Perelman, Ron, 386, 398
Perlmutter, Alvin, 247–248
Perry, Al, 103
Perry, Hart, 236–237, 238–239, 300
Persian Gulf War. *See* Gulf War
Peter Jennings Reports, 223

Pew Research Center for the People and the Press, 209
Phelan, John, 336–337
Phillips, Barbara, 224
Phillips, Bill, 90
Phillips, Stone, 186
Pilger, John, 175
Poindexter, Kent, 422
Poitier, Sidney, 422–423
Ponsonby, Arthur, 107
Porter, Henry, 383–384
Potter, Dennis, 195–198
POV, 250
Powell, Colin, 66
Press, The (Liebling), 72
Pressler, Larry, 398
Price, Ray, 127
Primary Colors (Klein), 73
PrimeStar, 382
Prime Time Live, 209–210
Prisoners of Hope, 321–323, 344
processed news, 206
Progressive America, 62
Progressive Caucus, 68–69
Project Censored, 182
Project Censored awards, 365–368
promos for news, 214
propaganda in the foreign media, 43, 45
propaganda model, 54
Public Broadcasting System. *See* PBS
public exhibition spaces, 470
Public Radio and Television in America (Engelman), 247
public television. *See* PBS
public television reform, 469, 478
Pyle, Barbara, 172

Queen, 298
Quello, James, 415

Rabinowitz, Joe, 379
Race to Power (ARG), 288
racism in the media, 127, 265, 433, 435–436, 463, 476
Radice, Frank, 214
Radio and Television Correspondents Association, 63
Radio Hanoi, 111
Rainbow Coalition Commission on Media Fairness, 405–412
Raissman, Bob, 426
Raitt, Bonnie, 301
Ramaphosa, Cyril, 319, 328
Rather, Dan, 89, 208, 318, 441, 453
reality-based television, 428
Real Majority, Media Minority (Flanders), 470–471

Real Paper, The, 117, 119
Reasoner, Harry, 182
Redford, Robert, 85, 222
Redstone, Sumner, 386, 401, 429
reform of media, 54–56, 461–474
Regan, Judith, 123, 379
Rendell, Steve, 387
Republican convention, 65–67
Republic of South Africa. *See* South Africa
repurposing, 81, 173
Revolutionary Situation, 299–300
Revolution for the Hell of it (Hoffman), 444
Rich, Frank, 416
Riepen, Ray, 103, 107
Rights & Wrongs, 243–255: Alvin Perlmutter and, 247–248; American Program Service, 251; Anita Roddick, 256–259; Body Shop and, 256–259; cable and, 246; Charlayne Hunter-Gault, 244–245, 249–250; Committee to Protect Journalists and, 440; Congressional protests to PBS, 249; Discovery Channel and, 359; distribution and, 245; Faith and Values Channel, 246, 345–345; funding of, 248, 260; Independent Television Service (ITVS), 253, 470; Lawrence Jarvik comments, 253; *Media and Human Rights*, 60; NBC Europe and, 410; PBS and, 243, 246–251, 248, 255; Rockefeller Foundation and, 260; Roone Arledge and, 245; Tibet story, 358; WNET and, 251; Rivera, Geraldo, 181, 186–191
Rivers, Jerry. *See* Rivera, Geraldo
Rivonia arrests, 275
Robben Island, 272, 321–323
Roberts, Cokie, 66
Robins, J. Max, 52–53, 237, 402
Robinson, Randall, 296
Rockefeller, David, 271–272
Rockefeller Foundation, 260
Rocky Mountain Media Watch (RMMW), 468: Boston ratings, 147; local news survey, 65; Pavlov index of WHDH, 147; WSVN-TV rating, 380
Roddick, Anita, 256–259, 470
Roddick, Gordon, 257–259
Roger and Me, 82
Rogers, Will, 68
Ronstadt, Linda, 298
Rose, Charlie, 414, 445, 446–448
Roseanne, 39–40

Rosen, Jay, 206
Rosenstiel, Tom, 170–171, 416–417
Rosensweig, Jed, 430
Rosenthal, A.M., 76, 418
Roth, Joe, 419
Rovere, Richard, 435–436
Royko, Mike, 458
Rubin, Jerry, 444
Rubin, Ken, 269
Run-DMZ, 301
Rushkoff, Douglas, 46
Rush Limbaugh is a Big Fat Idiot
    (Franken), 64
Russell, 142–143, 144
Rwanda radio propaganda, 43

Saatchi and Saatchi, 317
SABC (South African Broadcasting Cor-
    poration): Afrikaans programming,
    339–340, 344–345; ANC and, 337,
    338, 345; as arm of apartheid,
    336–337; censorship at, 337; CNN
    and, 343; corruption at, 338;
    Countdown to Freedom and, 314;
    financial crisis, 344; gala, 335–342;
    Independent Broadcasting Author-
    ity (IBA) and, 339; Ivy Matsepe-
    Cassaburri and, 338; Pallo Jordan
    and, 341, 345; *Prisoners of Hope*
    promotion, 344; programming,
    343–344; restructuring of, 339;
    Rupert Murdoch and, 345–346;
    segregation at, 336, 337–338;
    South Africa Media Monitoring
    Project and, 342; South African
    Airways and, 342; Stevie Wonder
    and, 337, 340; Thabo Mbeki and,
    345; Zwelakhe Sisulu and, 338,
    341, 344
Safire, William, 397
Safro, Nola, 186
Salhany, Lucie, 138–139
Salisbury, Harrison, 48
Sanders, Bernie, 69
Sanders, Ed, 444
Santana, Aracelly, 302
Sarajevo Ground Zero, 237
Sartori, Maxanne, 103
Sauter, Van Gordon, 372
SBC and PacTel, 361
Scagliotti, John, 110
Scanlan, John, 440–441
Schechter, Sarah Debs, 125
Scheer, Robert, 435
Scher, Lynn, 186
Schiavone, Nicholas, 426
Schiffrin, Andre, 93

Schiller, Herbert, 152, 404
Schlow, Steve, 141
Schonfeld, Reese, 158, 163, 170, 171
Schreiner, Olive, 276
Schwartz, John, 355
Schwartzman, Andrew, 391
Scorsese, Martin, 358
Scott, Ann, 275
Scripps, E.W., 461
SDS (Students for a Democratic Soci-
    ety), 102, 271
Seale, Bobby, 445
Second Front (MacArthur), 208
Segal, Ronald, 274
segregation in media, 91–92, 127, 265,
    476
Seldes, George, 72, 206, 479, 480
Selling Free Enterprise (Wolf), 209
Sender, Stuart, 303–304, 316
sensational news stories, 433
Sexwale, Tokyo, 319, 328
Shapiro, Mark, 220
Sharon, Ariel, 190
Sharpeville massacre, 269, 272
Sharpton, Al, 405–412
Shaw, Bernard, 318, 440
Sheridan, Jim, 450, 456
Showtime, 315
Siegel, Matt, 141, 146
Siegenthaler, Robert, 203
Simon, Barney, 274, 290–291
Simon, Dan, 446
Simon, Paul, 89
Simpson, O.J.: benefits of, 434–435;
    impact on real news, 435–436;
    Infinity Broadcasting and, 432;
    jurors *vs.* media, 433; *Nightline*
    and, 432, 433, 436; ratings, 434,
    436–437
Singh, Anant, 315–316, 321
Sisulu, Albertina, 338
Sisulu, Walter, 312, 322, 338
Sisulu, Zwelakhe: resigns from SABC,
    344; at SABC gala, 341; SABC
    leadership, 338
60 Minutes: hidden cameras, 210; history
    of, 180–181; ratings, 222; substan-
    tive programing of, 61–62; time
    slot, 218
SKY satellite TV, 381–382
Sliwa, Curtis, 178–179, 180
Slovo, Gillian, 274
Slovo, Joe: ANC leadership, 319; ANC
    militants and, 277; Communist
    Party and, 273–274; funeral of,
    276–277; on post election strug-
    gles, 324; Ruth First and, 273–274;

speech to East German Community Party, 270; treason trial, 273
Slovo, Shawn, 273
Smith, Mike, 226
Snow, Robert, 173, 205–206, 214
Snyder, Mitch, 308
Social Venture Network, 257
Sohn, Gigi, 376
Solomon, Norman, 67, 200, 387, 436
Solmon, Paul, 135–136
Sommer, Mark, 255
Soros, George, 439, 473
South Africa. *See also* apartheid; *Countdown to Freedom*: American media coverage of, 202–203, 263–265, 291–293, 317; artists and literary figures, 290; author's 1967 trip, 278–284; ban on media coverage, 238, 295; Black Consciousness Movement, 293; cable television in, 344–345; CIA influence in, 287–288; Clinton administration and, 329; Communist Party arrests, 275; Dalai Lama visit, 327, 358; economic problems, 325–327; foreign capital investments in, 285; journalists, 291; music of, 268; National Union of South African Students (NUSAS), 281; Russian influence in, 274, 286; Security Forces, assassination squads, 294; Southern United States comparison, 278–279; Soweto, 282, 291–293; stock exchange, 325; Sun City, 297–298; Sun City scab performers, 298; theater in, 290–291; transition issues, 323–333; Truth and Reconciliation Commission, 329–330; 20/20 coverage, 192–194; visa for author, 309–310
South African Airways, 340, 342
South African Broadcasting Corporation. *See* SABC
South African Communist Party: ANC connection, 274; Joe Slovo leadership, 270; Rivonia arrests, 275
South Africa Now. See also Mandela in America: Africa Fund, The and, 240; Dirk Coetzee interview, 276; distribution of, 242–243; financing, 240–242; Hart Perry and, 238; KCET and, 239; Kevin Harris and, 238; Nelson Mandela release interview, 303–306; news ban in South Africa and, 238; Roone Arledge and, 245
Soweto, 282, 291–293

Sparks, Allister, 304
Springsteen, Bruce, 236, 300–301
Stack, Jonathan, 81
STAR TV and BBC, 359
Statue of Liberty story, 225–228
Stengel, Richard, 312
Stern, Howard, 121–123
Stetsasonic, 300
Stewart, Rod, 298
Stoddard, Brandon, 218
Stoia, Judy, 136
Stone, Bernie, 194–198
Stone, I.F., 72, 127, 479
Stone, Oliver: *Beyond JFK*, 237, 450–456; characatured by Garry Trudeau, 453; and *JFK* (the movie), 452–453; PBS protest, 249
Stossel, John, 219–221
Stringer, Howard, 360–361
student movements worldwide, 270
Student Power, 79
Subcommandante Marcos, 44–45, 472–473
Sunbeam Broadcasting buys Channel 7, 147
Sun City record and video: artists involved with, 299–301; banned in South Africa, 302; *Making of Sun City*, 300–301, 302; Manhattan Records, 300; money raised, 302; PBS and, 302; radio play and, 302; *Revolutionary Situation*, 299; Steven Van Zandt, 297–298, 299, 300, 301
Sundance Film Festival, 85, 260, 358
Sverak, Jan, 86
SWAPO, 283

tabloid television, 87–89, 223, 370–371
Talk of the Town, 218
Tambo, Oliver, 284, 294
TBS (Turner Broadcasting System), 160
Tele-Communications, Inc. (TCI). *See also* Malone, John C.: Bob J. Magness and, 356; cable monopolies, 402; conservative politics of, 355; *Damn Right*, 355; Faith and Values Channel, 355–356; Liberty Media and, 353; Michael Milken and, 386; rate hikes and, 354; AT&T merger, 357
Telecommunications Reform Act of 1996: advocacy groups and, 465–466; Barry Diller and, 398; Bob Dole and, 397; CNN and, 398; Ernest Hollings and, 397; industry gloats over victory, 404–405; lobby-

ing efforts for, 396–397; media coverage of, 367, 390, 396, 401; National Association of Broadcasters (NAB), 391, 405; public service, impact on, 390; Reed Hundt and, 390; reversing the giveaway, 469; Robert A. Defazio and, 396; Trent Lott threatens FCC over, 390–391; value of, 390; William Safire on, 397
Tele-TV, 361
television: advertising and, 42; conservative bias, 49; coverage of Ethiopia, 296–297; coverage of Gulf War, 44, 56, 208; democracy and, 62–71; government and, 47, 200, 356; negative impact of, 46–47; profits in, 42; public opinion of, 59; ratings sham, 463; time slot programming, 218
Television, Mythinformation and Social Control, 90
Terenzio, John, 373
Thatcher, Margaret, 378
Thompson, Davis, 416
Thomson, Jim, 131
Thussu, Daya Kishan, 58
Tiana, 112–113
Tibet, 358–359
Time magazine and CNN, 175
Times Mirror, 395
Time Warner: cable monopolies, 402; CNN and, 352; Doug Morris and, 361–362; Fox News Channel and, 381, 382; Michael Fuchs and, 361–362; Ted Turner and, 399; Turner Communications buy out, 357, 399
Tisch, Lawrence, 386, 393
TNT and Liberty Media, 353
Tomlinson, Yvette, 316
Tracy, Michael, 369–370
Trans-Africa, 296
Trilateral Commission, 170
Trudeau, Garry, 453
Truth and Reconciliation Commission, 329–330
Turner, Ed, 174, 336, 381
Turner, Ted: attitude toward the news, 162, 211–212; Big Picture Conference speech, 352; canine anchor, 162; CNN and, 155–164; Committee to Protect Journalists, 437, 439, 440–441; *Freeman Reports* and, 155, 164–169; Globalvision, 175–176; on lithium, 446; *60 Minutes* Interview, 164; Phil Donahue

interview, 169; Reese Schonfeld and, 171; Rupert Murdoch and, 369, 381; Time Warner and, 399; Turner Broadcasting System and, 160; United Nations and, 172
Turner, Tina, 268
Turner Broadcasting System, 160, 386
Turning Point, 194
Tutu, Desmond, 329
TV Free America, 92
TV News Off Camera (Zousmer), 212
20/20: Abbie Hoffman and, 180; advertising and, 222; apartheid story, 192; Arab stereotype show, 190–191; Av Westin and, 177, 178, 182–184; baby lift story, 183; Barbara Walters and, 182, 191, 201; bulimia story, 224–225; demographic targeting, 221; Disney influence on, 403; early days of, 181; editorial process, 183–184, 191; El Salvador story, 191–192; FAIR and, 219; focus groups and, 215; formulas for, 214; Geraldo Rivera and, 181, 186–189, 215; Guardian Angels story, 178–179; Hugh Downs, 181–182; Iran-Contra story, 185; Jesse Jackson story, 192–194; John Stossel and, 219–221; *Junk Science*, 220; labor stories, 183–184; Marilyn Monroe/Kennedy's story, 187; Middle East story, 189–191; Nicaragua story, 185; origins of, 181–182; serious issue stories, 186; South Africa story, 192; Statue of Liberty story, 225–228; time slot, 221
Tyndall, Andres, 433
Tyndall Report, 67

Umkhonto, 284, 293
union activity, media coverage of, 392
United Electrical Workers (UE) at WBCN, 108–109
United Nations and CNN, 172
United Nations Award, 78
USA for Africa, 297
Utley, Garrick, 61

Valenti, Jack, 234
Van Miert, Karen, 383
Van Zandt, Steven, 297–298, 299, 300, 301
V-Chip, 399, 476
Viacom: and Michael Milken, 386; restructuring, 41, 357; and TCI, 401
Vidal, Gore, 184–185

Vietnam, 110–113: anti-war sentiment, 51, 108, 271; author's visit, 113; baby lift story, 183; coverage of, 51; *From Hollywood to Hanoi,* 112–113; language issue, 107–108; WBCN coverage of, 102, 107–108, 111–113

Viewers, as consumers, 151–152, 205

Von Hoffman, Nick, 461–462

Wald, Dick, 177

Walker, T.J., 62

Wallace, Jane, 245, 380

Wallace, Mike, 440

Walters, Barbara: Bernie Stone and, 194–198; Katharine Hepburn interview, 221; Rupert Murdoch interview, 194–198; speech idiosyncrasies and, 110; Statue of Liberty coverage, 227–228; 20/20 and, 182, 191, 201; Victor Neufeld and, 218–219

Warfield, Nelson, 67

Warner Brothers, 456

Waters, John, 92

Waxman, Henry, 249

WBCN: Arbitron incident, 106; censorship at, 106; FBI encounters with, 114, 116–118; FCC and, 99, 101; hotline, 103–104; Howard Stern and, 121–122; Infinity Broadcasting, purchase of, 119; Infinity cuts news, 121; international news coverage, 110–111; New England Patriots and, 122; *Nixon 49, America 1,* 108; origins of, 99–101; strike, 119–120; twenty-fifth Anniversary, 121; unionization of, 108–109, 120; Vietnam coverage, 102, 107–108, 111–113; women's demonstration, 118–119

WCVB, 139–146

Weapons of Mass Distraction (Gelbart), 42

"We Are the World," 296

Weather Underground Organization, 102

Weiner, Lee, 445, 448–449

Wenner, Jann, 127

Wenner, Kate, 186

Westin, Av: editorial process, 223; formulas for television, 213–214, 217;

Jesse Jackson story and, 192–193; Roone Arledge and, 218; 20/20 and, 177, 178, 182–184, 190, 192

Westin, David, 216–217, 420

Westinghouse, 393–394, 400, 424

we-we phenomenon, 200

WGBH/Channel 2, 135–137

WHDH-TV: FCC scandal, 140; Rocky Mountain Media Watch (RMMW) rating, 147; Sunbeam Broadcasting acquisition of, 147

When We Were Kings, 86, 269

Wicker, Tom, 292–293, 453–454

Wiesel, Elie, 253

Wild Feed, 430–431

Will, George, 70, 185

Willes, Mark, 395

Williams, Huntington, 415

Williams, Raymond, 46

Williams Companies and PBS, 254

Wills, Garry, 331

Wilonsky, Robin, 122

Winer, Norm, 103

Without Fear or Favor, 53

WLVI-TV Channel 56, 138

WNET and *Rights & Wrongs,* 251

WNYC, sale of, 395

Wolf, Elizabeth Fones, 209

Wolfe, Tom, 54

Wolpe, Howard, 265

Wonder, Stevie, 337, 340

Woodward, Bob, 73, 441–442

WorldCom, 383

World Television Forum, 60–61, 465

Wren, Christopher, 74

Wright, Bob, 424

WSVN-TV, RMMW rating, 380

Yanakis, Zöe, 300

YIPPIES (Youth International Party), 444

Young, Andrew, 331

Zaire massacre, lack of coverage of, 54

Zapatistas, 44–45

Ziem, Grace, 220

Zimmerman, Bill, 117

Zinn, Howard, 141–142, 383

Zoglin, Richard, 162

Zousmer, Steve, 212

Zucker, Jeff, 348

Zwick, Ed, 80